D1169879

13th BOY ①

SANGEUN LEE

Translation: JiEun Park
English Adaptation: Natalie Baan

Lettering: Terri Delgado

13th Boy, Vol. 1 © 2004 SangEun Lee. All rights reserved. First published in Korea in 2004 by Haksan Publishing Co., Ltd. English translation rights in U.S.A., Canada, UK, and Republic of Ireland arranged with Haksan Publishing Co., Ltd.

English translation © 2009 Hachette Book Group, Inc.

Yen Press
Hachette Book Group
237 Park Avenue, New York, NY 10017

Visit our Web sites at www.HachetteBookGroup.com and www.YenPress.com.

Yen Press is an imprint of Hachette Book Group, Inc.
The Yen Press name and logo are trademarks of Hachette Book Group, Inc.

First Yen Press Edition: June 2009

ISBN: 978-0-7595-2994-6

10 9 8 7 6 5 4 3 2 1

BVG

Printed in the United States of America

13th Boy Translation Notes

Page 12
Boong-au-bbang: Korean carp-shaped bread.

Page 49
KAIST: Korea Advanced Institute of Science and Technology.

Page 92
10,000 won: A rough conversion rate is 1,000 won to one USD.

Duk-bok-gi, Kim-bab: Seasoned rice cake fried with Korean hot pepper sauce, and Korean sushi. A favorite snack of teenagers in Korea.

Page 140
Deadly Love: Parody of a real Korean drama in which Jun-Sang is the main character.

Jeju Island: one of the scenic islands located off the southern coast of South Korea.

Page 142
The actors listed here are parodies of real popular actors: Eun-Ha Sim, Dong-Gun Jang, and Yong-Jun Bae.

All of the lines from the drama are parodies of well-known lines in which key words like "love" and "sin" have been replaced with "fate."

Page 168
Han River: The river that flows through Seoul, South Korea.

Page 178
Bun-Dang: A city near Seoul in South Korea.

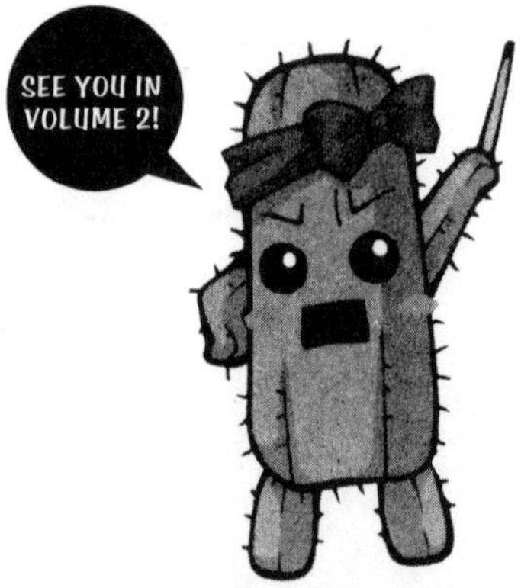
SEE YOU IN VOLUME 2!

13th BOY♥ CONTENTS

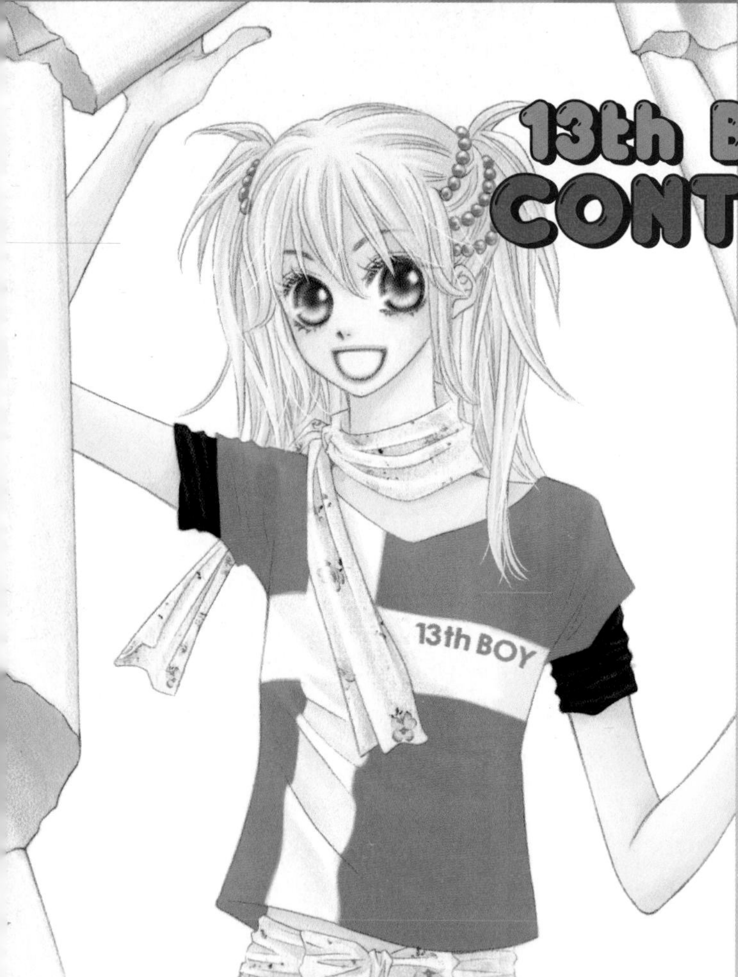
13th BOY

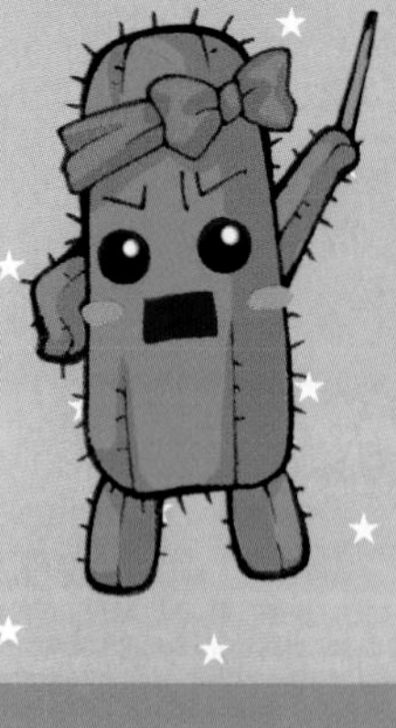

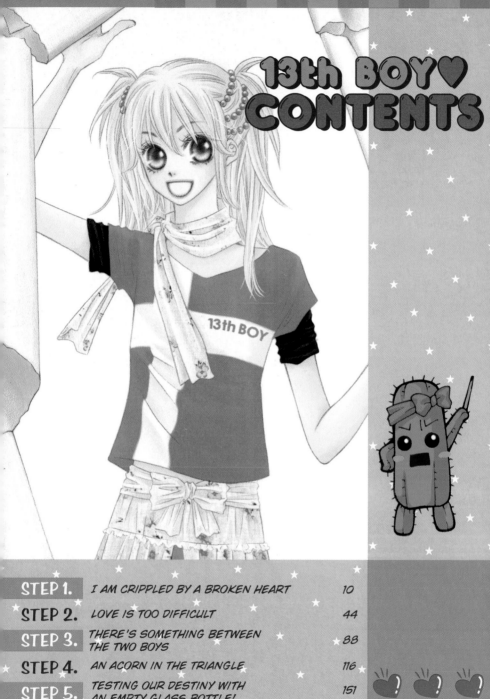

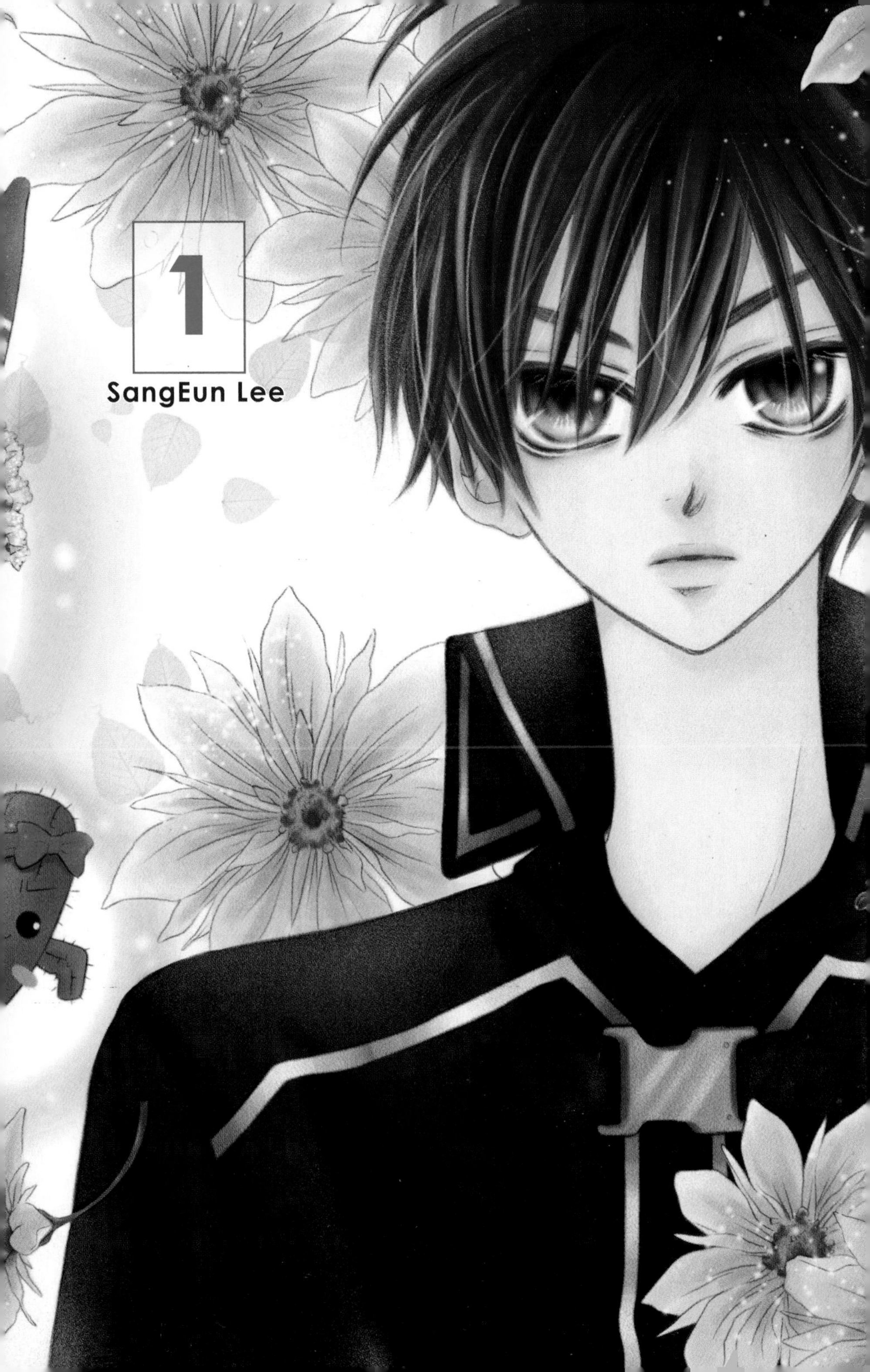
1
SangEun Lee

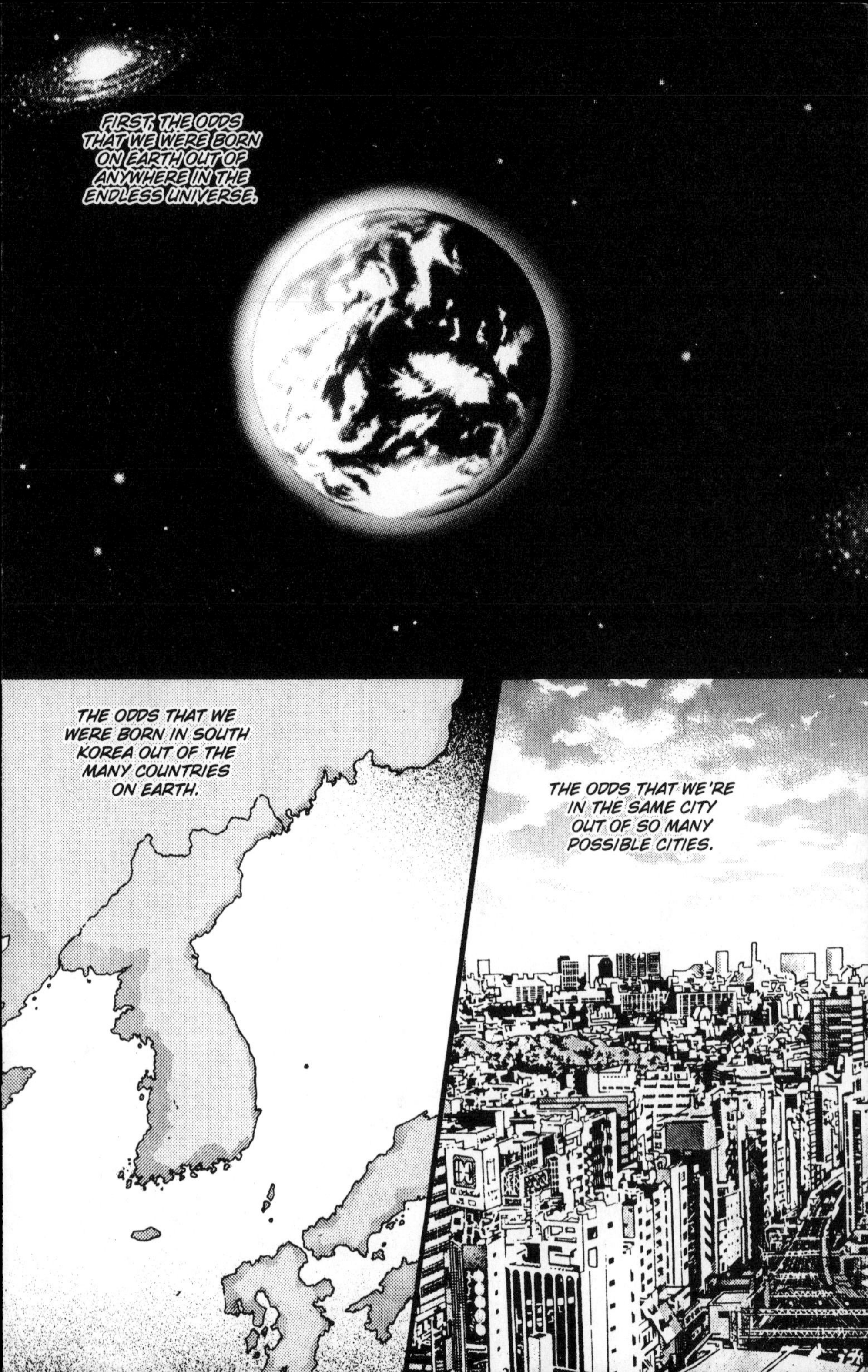
FIRST, THE ODDS THAT WE WERE BORN ON EARTH OUT OF ANYWHERE IN THE ENDLESS UNIVERSE.
THE ODDS THAT WE WERE BORN IN SOUTH KOREA OUT OF THE MANY COUNTRIES ON EARTH.
THE ODDS THAT WE'RE IN THE SAME CITY OUT OF SO MANY POSSIBLE CITIES.

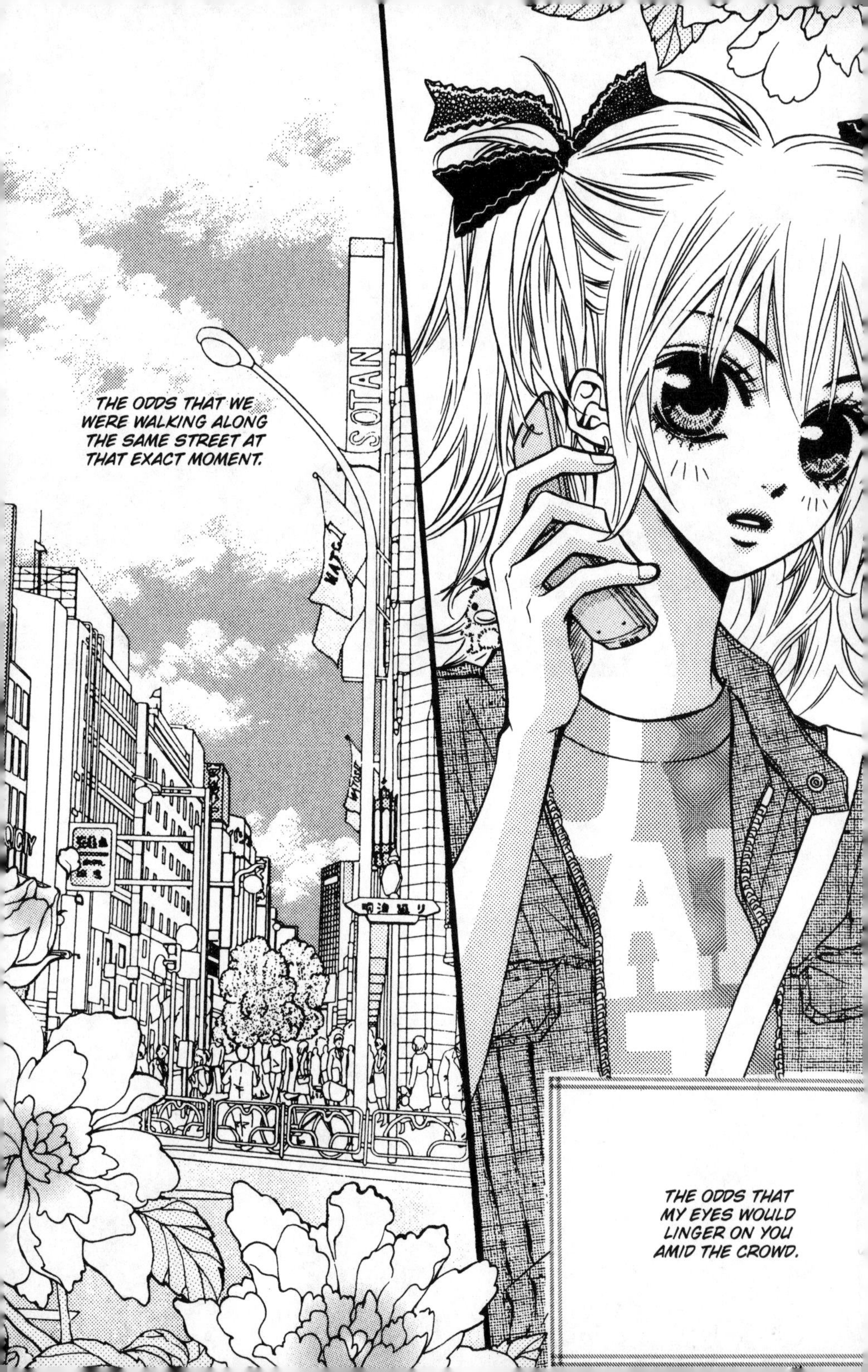
THE ODDS THAT WE WERE WALKING ALONG THE SAME STREET AT THAT EXACT MOMENT.
SOTAN
THE ODDS THAT MY EYES WOULD LINGER ON YOU AMID THE CROWD.

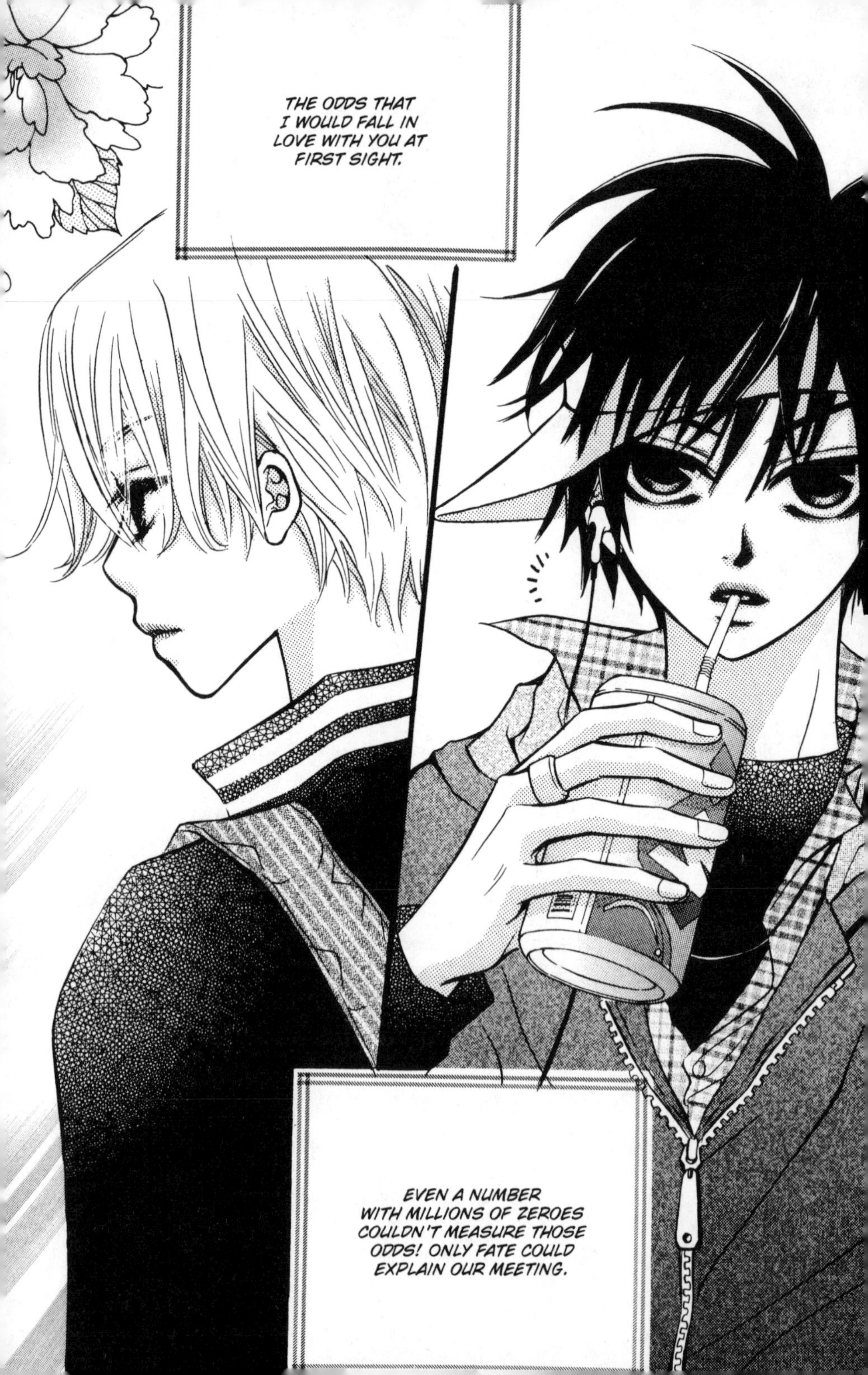
THE ODDS THAT I WOULD FALL IN LOVE WITH YOU AT FIRST SIGHT.
EVEN A NUMBER WITH MILLIONS OF ZEROES COULDN'T MEASURE THOSE ODDS! ONLY FATE COULD EXPLAIN OUR MEETING.

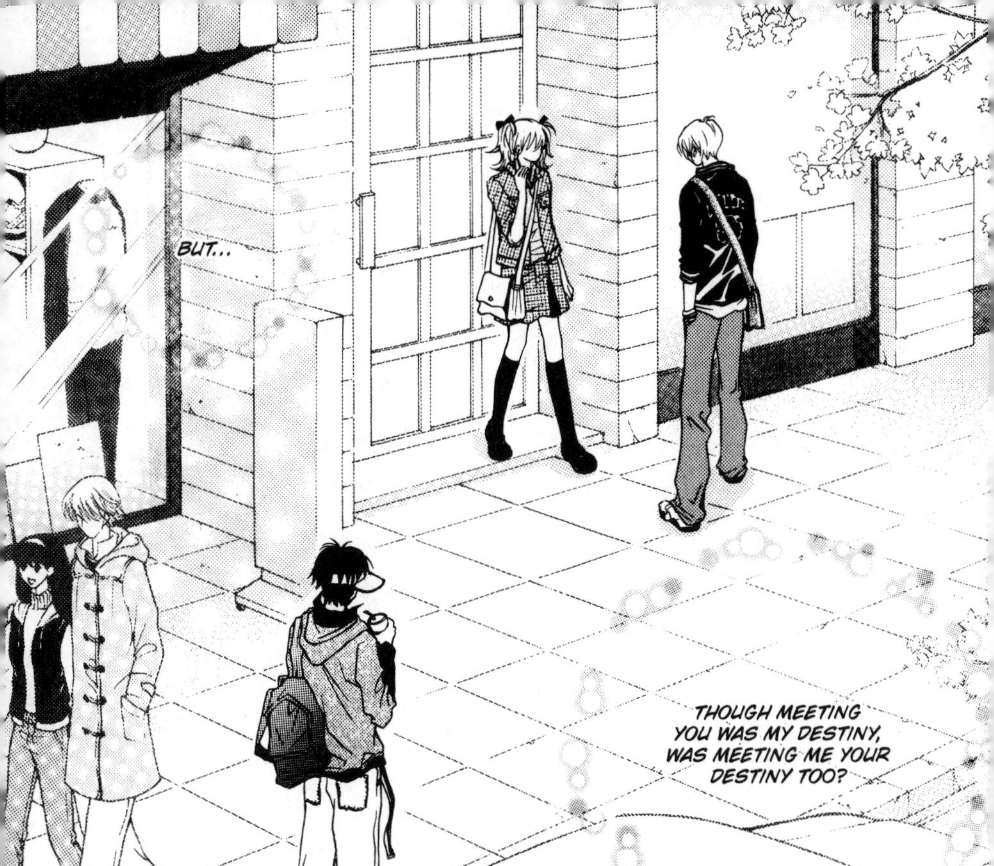
BUT...
THOUGH MEETING YOU WAS MY DESTINY, WAS MEETING ME YOUR DESTINY TOO?
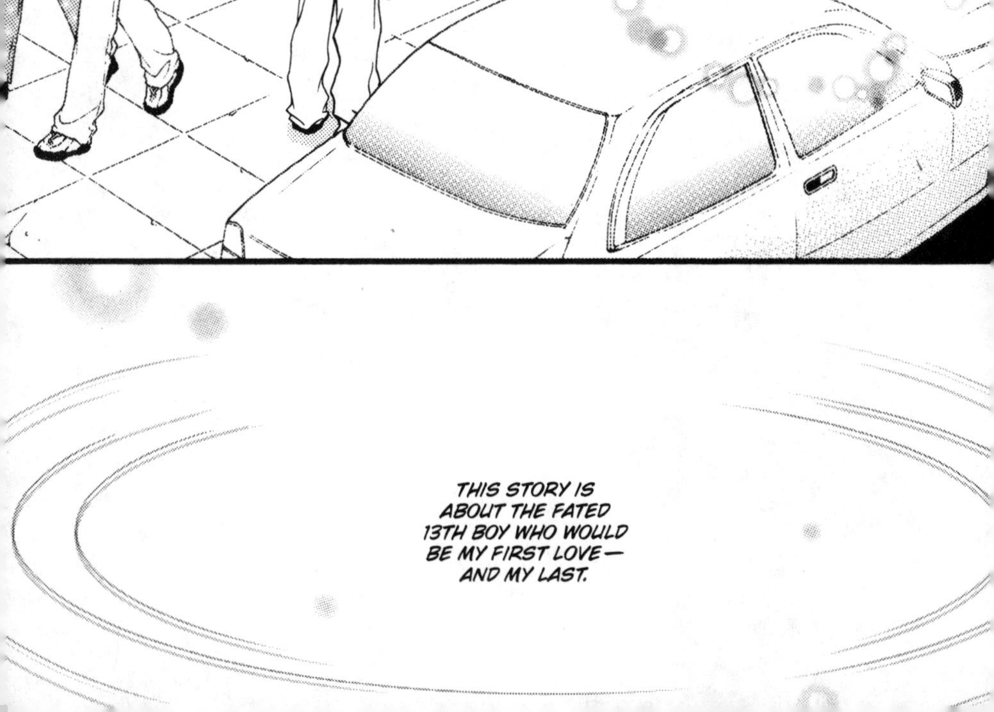
THIS STORY IS ABOUT THE FATED 13TH BOY WHO WOULD BE MY FIRST LOVE— AND MY LAST.

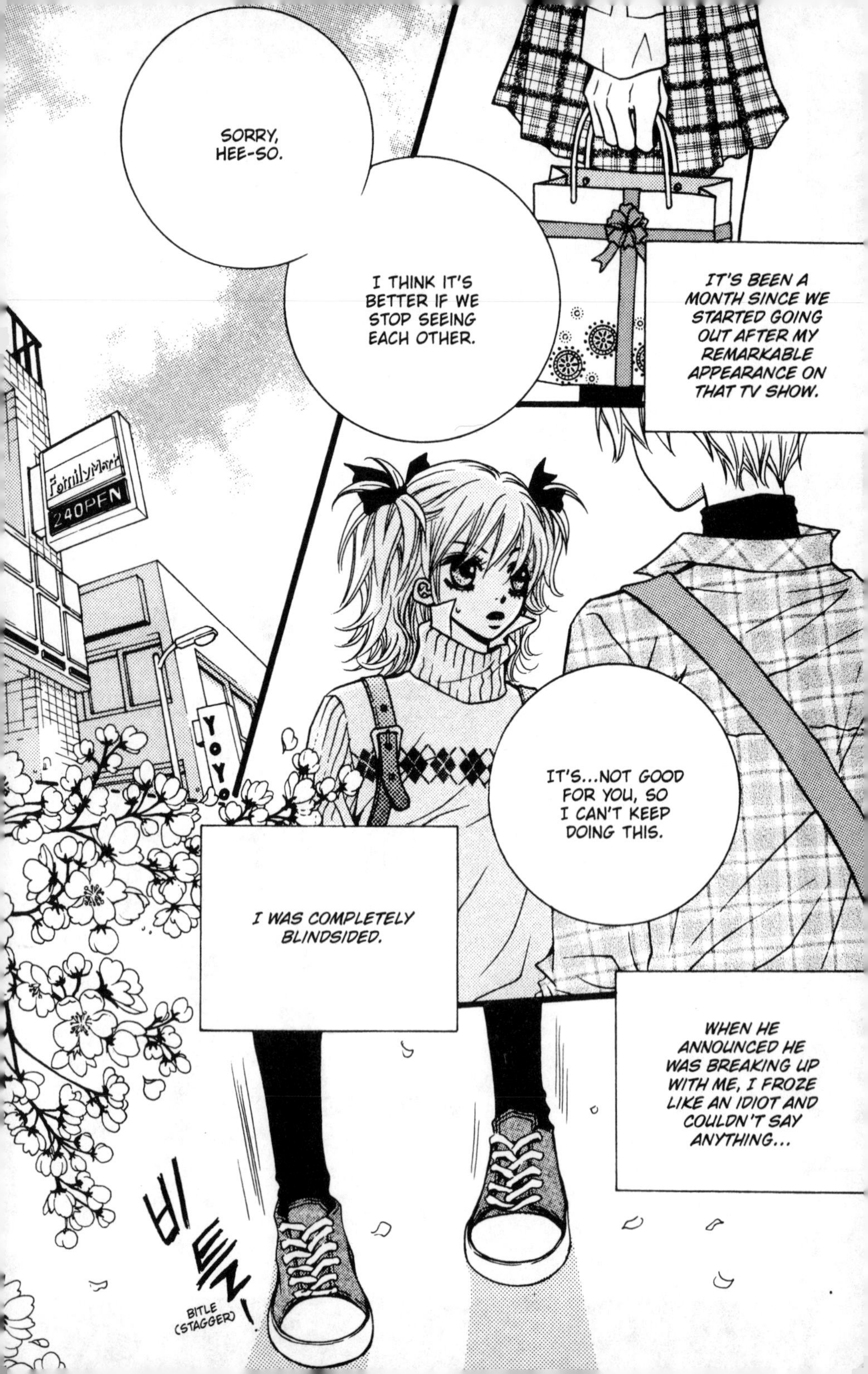
SORRY, HEE-SO.
I THINK IT'S BETTER IF WE STOP SEEING EACH OTHER.
IT'S BEEN A MONTH SINCE WE STARTED GOING OUT AFTER MY REMARKABLE APPEARANCE ON THAT TV SHOW.
IT'S...NOT GOOD FOR YOU, SO I CAN'T KEEP DOING THIS.
I WAS COMPLETELY BLINDSIDED.
WHEN HE ANNOUNCED HE WAS BREAKING UP WITH ME, I FROZE LIKE AN IDIOT AND COULDN'T SAY ANYTHING...
BITLE (STAGGER)

STEP 1. I AM CRIPPLED BY A BROKEN HEART.

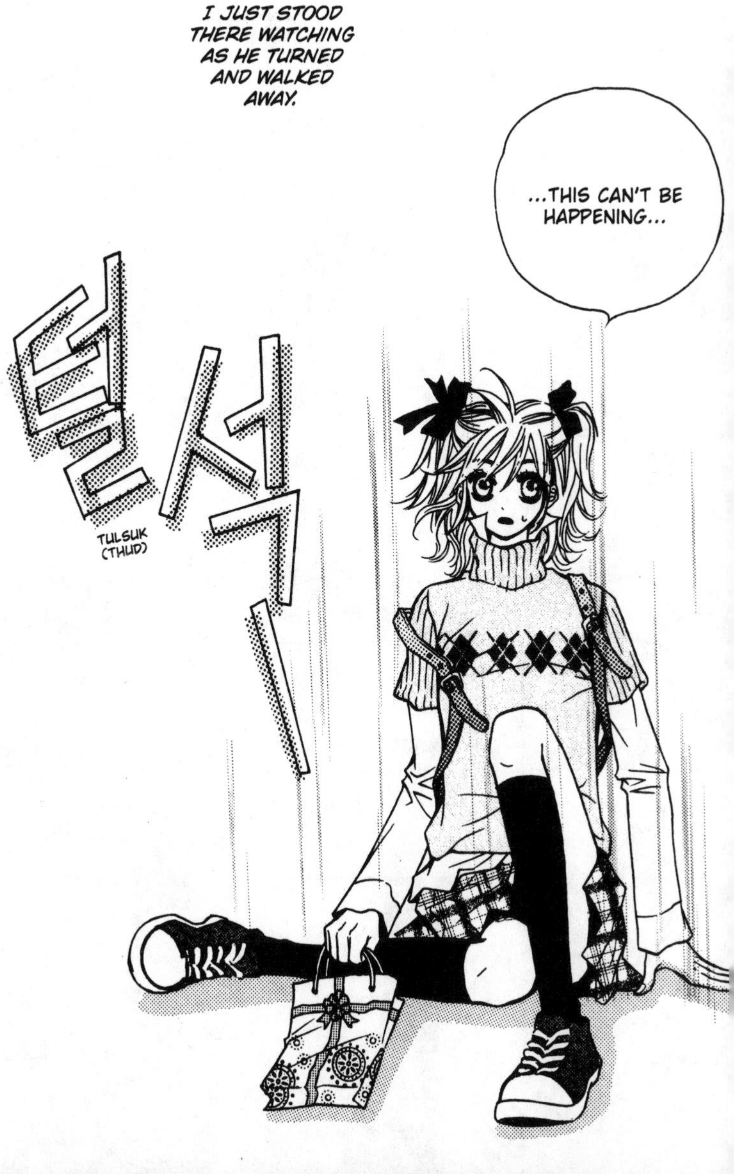
I JUST STOOD THERE WATCHING AS HE TURNED AND WALKED AWAY.
...THIS CAN'T BE HAPPENING...
털썩
TULSUK (THUD)

SFX: HUNGEL (HUMM)
HUNGEL

BOONG-AU-BBANG, PLEASE.

IT'S SO NOISY AND PATHETIC...

SHE'S BEEN AT IT FOR OVER AN HOUR NOW. WHAT COULD POSSIBLY HAVE MADE HER CRY LIKE THAT?

SSK?T

......

WHO?

OVER THERE. THAT GIRL BEHIND YOU.

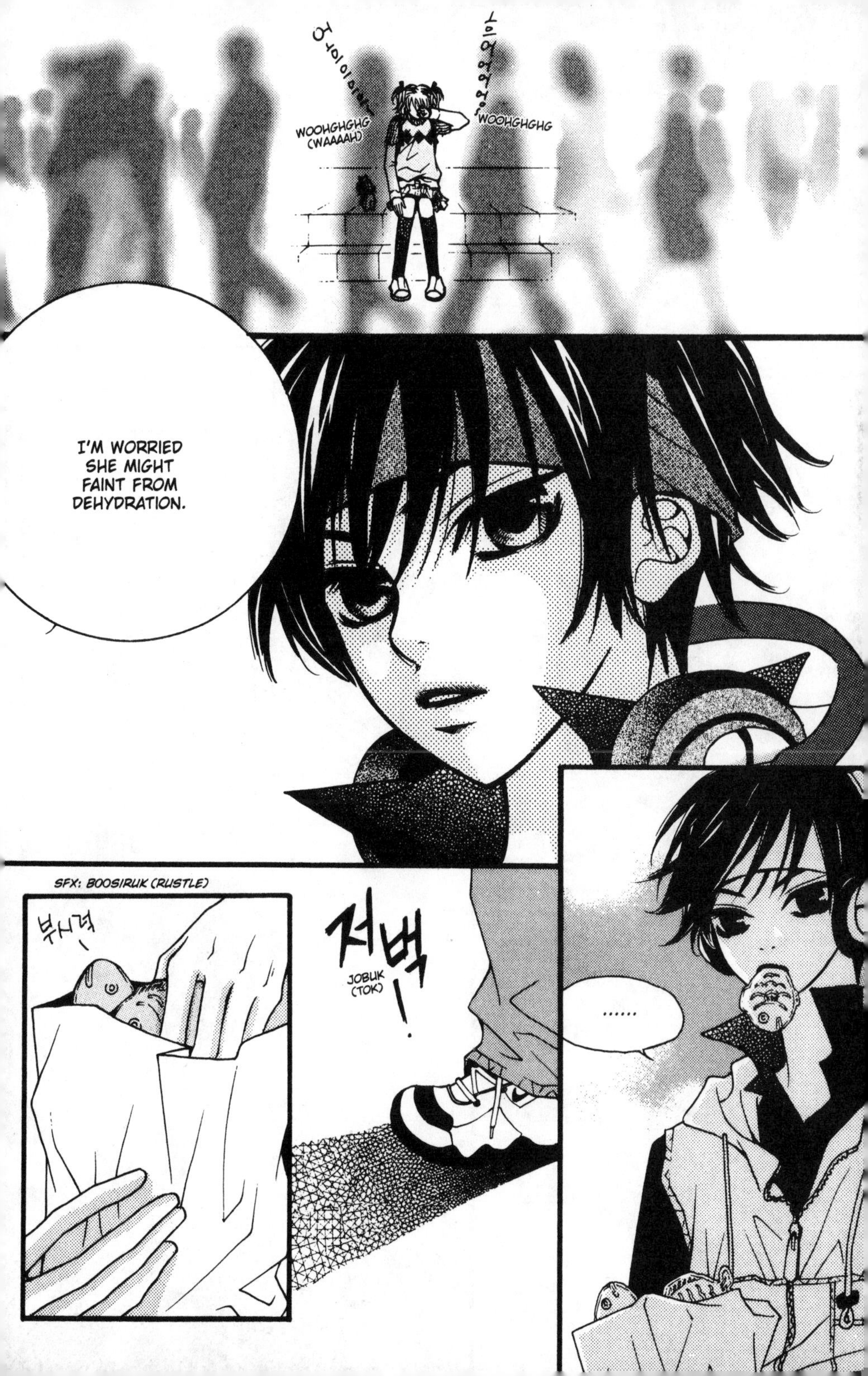
WOOHGHGHG
(WAAAAAH)
WOOHGHGHG
I'M WORRIED SHE MIGHT FAINT FROM DEHYDRATION.
SFX: BOOSIRUK (RUSTLE)
부시럭
저벅
JOBUK (TOK)
......

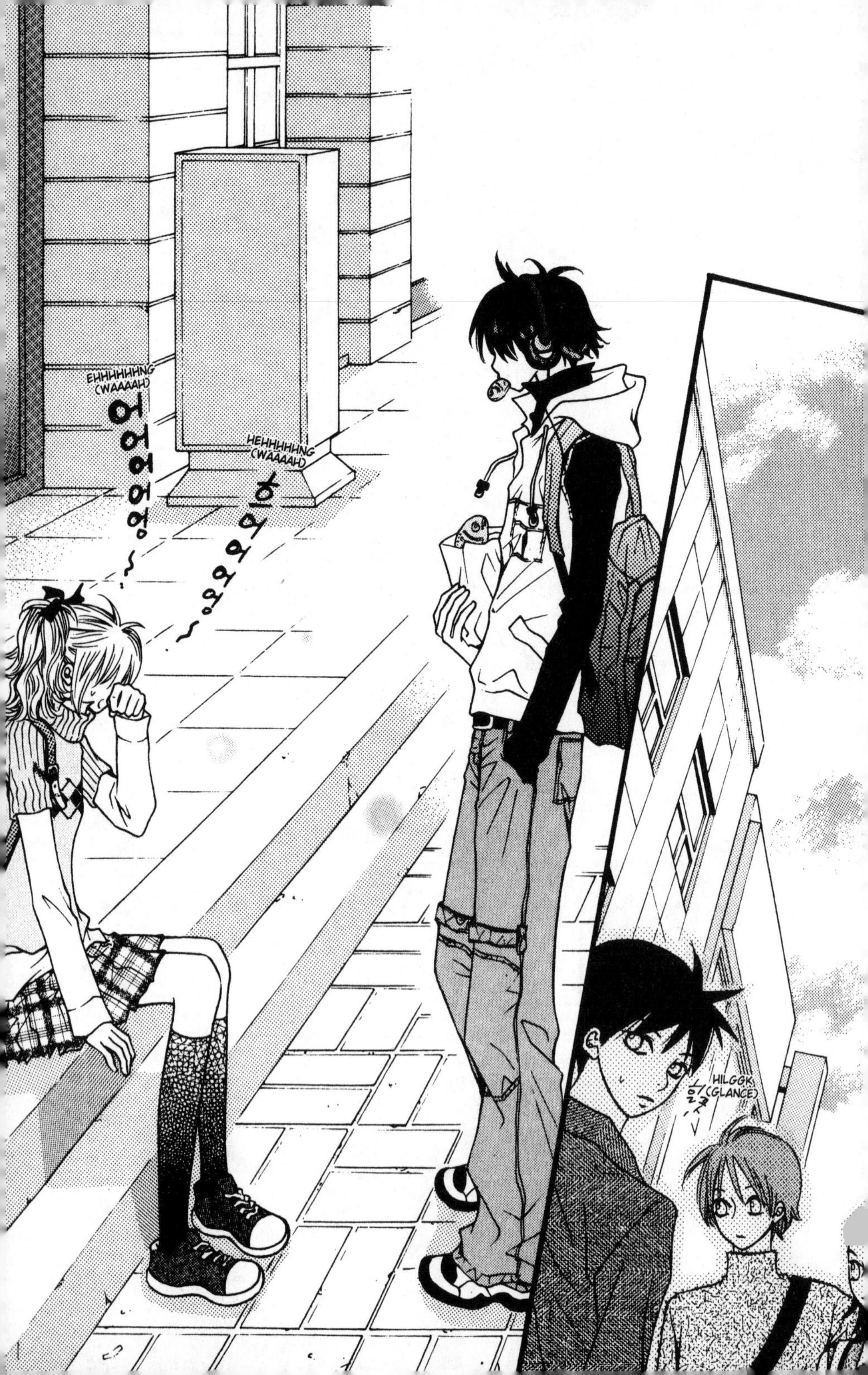
EHHHHHHNG (WAAAAH)
어어어어엉~
HEHHHHHNG (WAAAAH)
흐어어어엉~
HILGGK (GLANCE)
힐끗

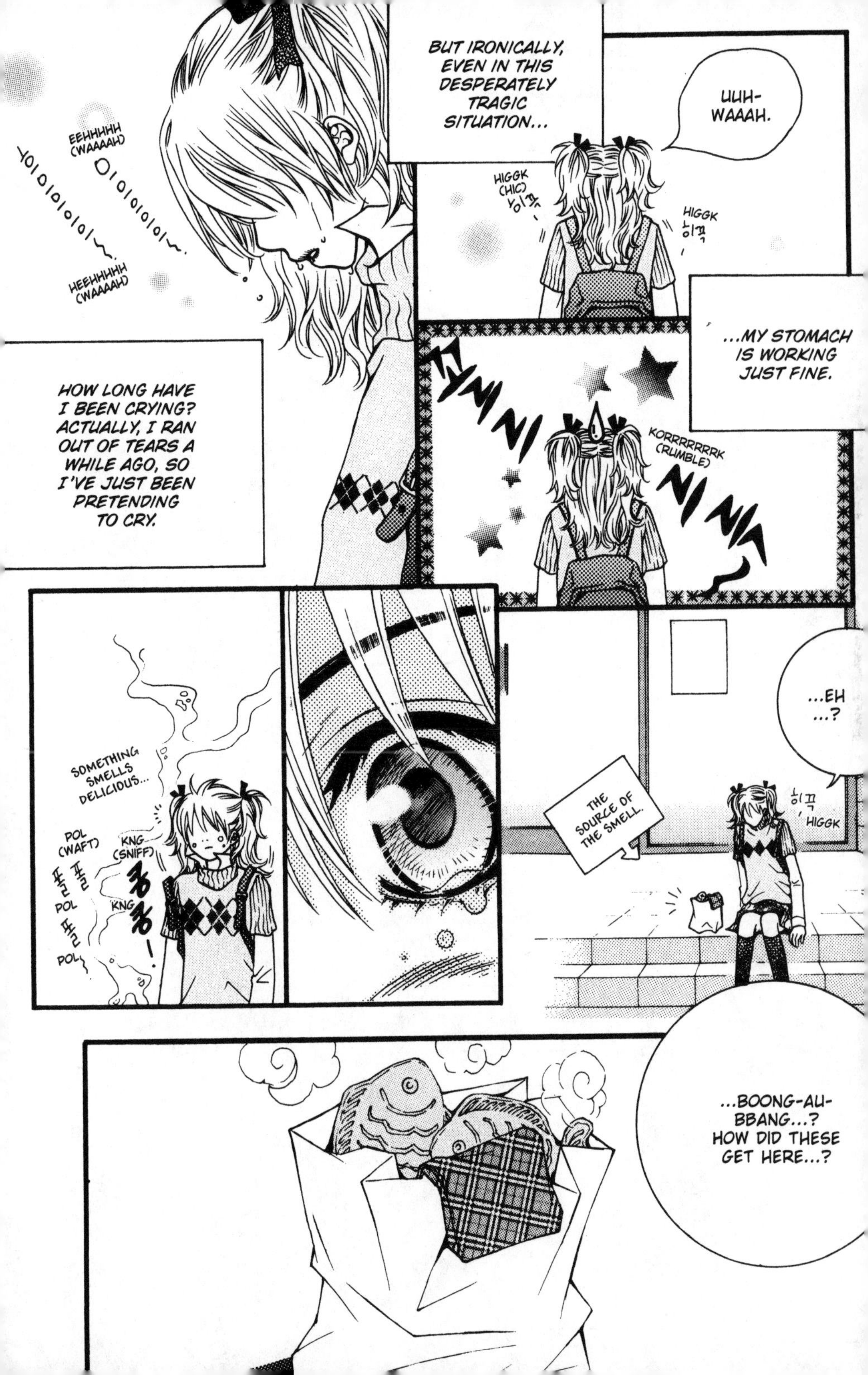
EEHHHHH (WAAAAH)
HEEHHHHH (WAAAAH)
HOW LONG HAVE I BEEN CRYING? ACTUALLY, I RAN OUT OF TEARS A WHILE AGO, SO I'VE JUST BEEN PRETENDING TO CRY.
BUT IRONICALLY, EVEN IN THIS DESPERATELY TRAGIC SITUATION...
UUH-WAAAH.
HIGGK (HIC) 히끅
HIGGK 히끅
...MY STOMACH IS WORKING JUST FINE.
KORRRRRRRK (RUMBLE)
SOMETHING SMELLS DELICIOUS...
POL (WAFT)
KNG (SNIFF)
POL
KNG
POL
...EH ...?
THE SOURCE OF THE SMELL.
히끅 HIGGK
...BOONG-AU-BBANG...? HOW DID THESE GET HERE...?

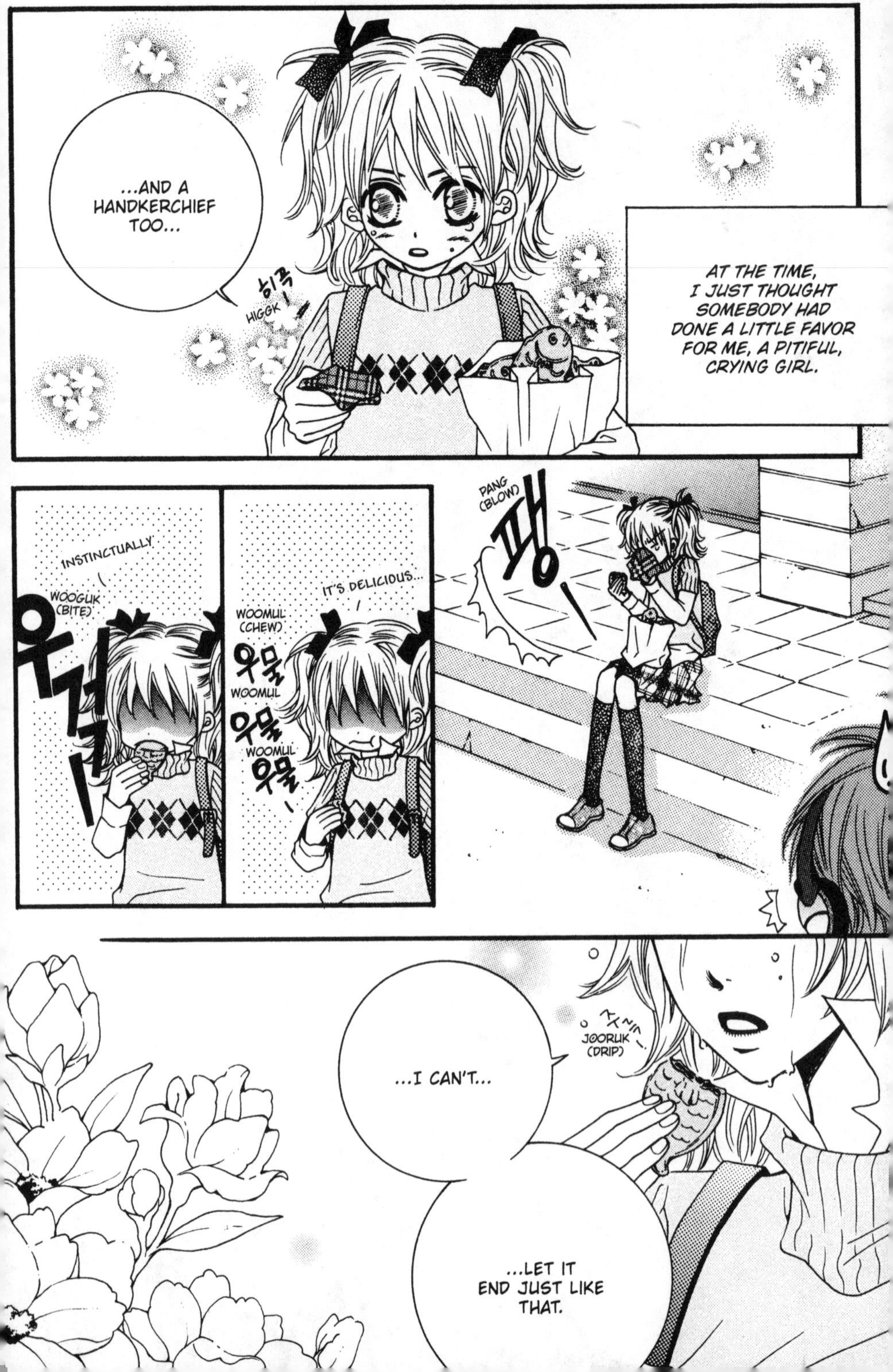
...AND A HANDKERCHIEF TOO...
히끅
HIGGK
AT THE TIME, I JUST THOUGHT SOMEBODY HAD DONE A LITTLE FAVOR FOR ME, A PITIFUL, CRYING GIRL.
INSTINCTUALLY
WOOGUK (BITE)
IT'S DELICIOUS...
WOOMUL (CHEW)
우물
WOOMUL
우물
WOOMUL
우물
PANG (BLOW)
팽
JOORUK (DRIP)
...I CAN'T...
...LET IT END JUST LIKE THAT.

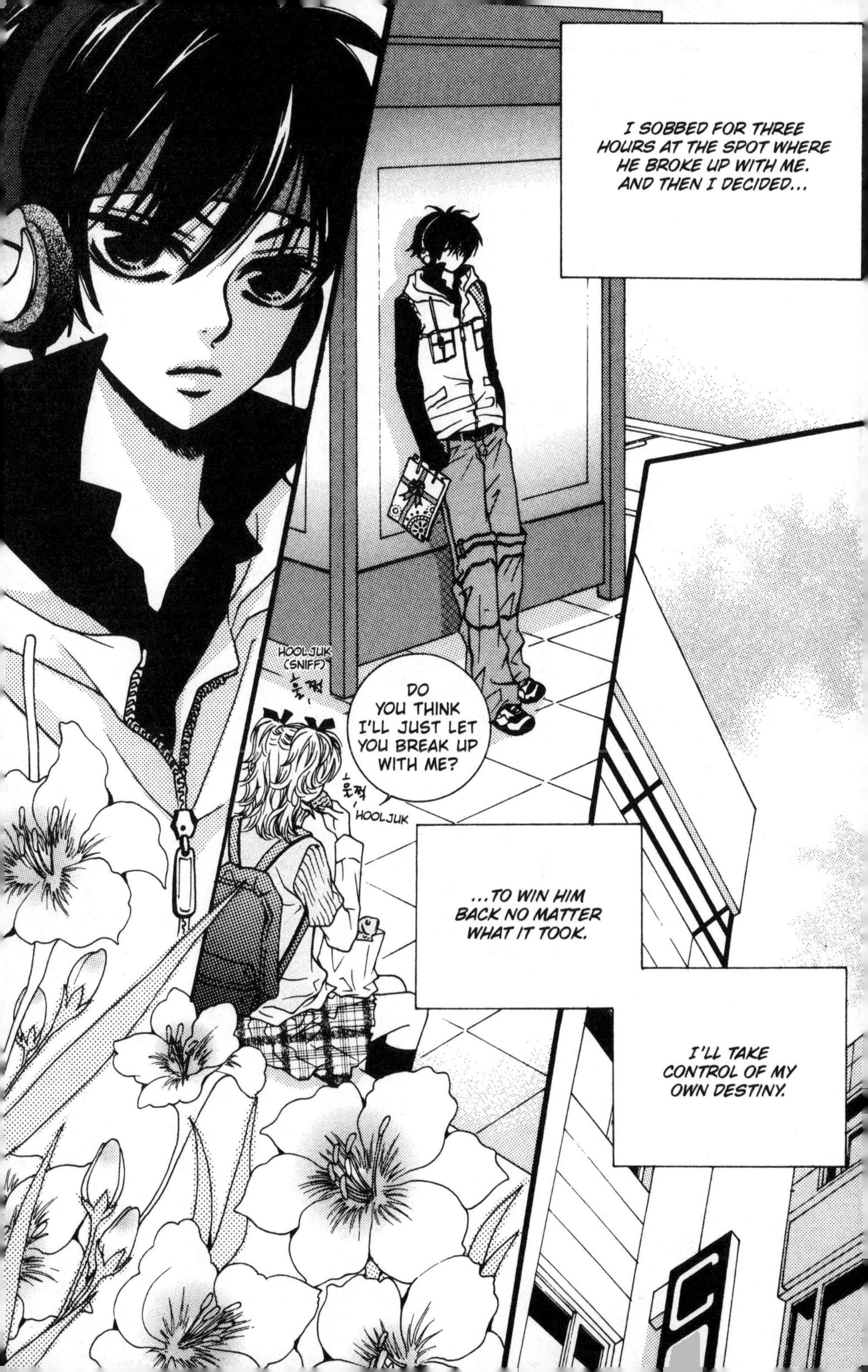
I SOBBED FOR THREE HOURS AT THE SPOT WHERE HE BROKE UP WITH ME. AND THEN I DECIDED...
HOOLJUK (SNIFF)
DO YOU THINK I'LL JUST LET YOU BREAK UP WITH ME?
HOOLJUK
...TO WIN HIM BACK NO MATTER WHAT IT TOOK.
I'LL TAKE CONTROL OF MY OWN DESTINY.

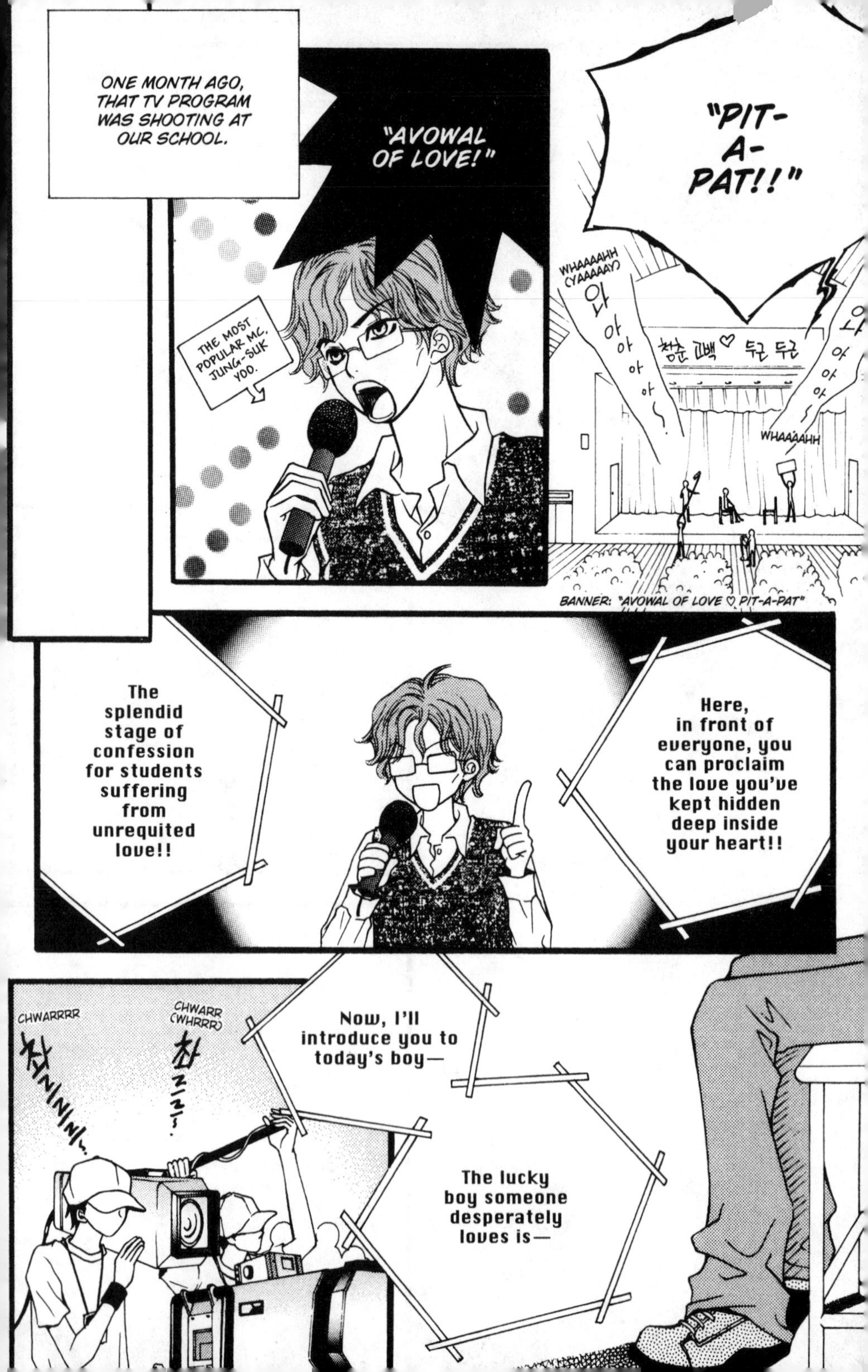

ONE MONTH AGO, THAT TV PROGRAM WAS SHOOTING AT OUR SCHOOL.
"AVOWAL OF LOVE!"
THE MOST POPULAR MC, JUNG-SUK YOO.
"PIT-A-PAT!!"
WHAAAAHH (YAAAAAY)
와아아아아
청춘 고백♡ 두근 두근
와아아아
WHAAAAHH
BANNER: "AVOWAL OF LOVE ♡ PIT-A-PAT"
The splendid stage of confession for students suffering from unrequited love!!
Here, in front of everyone, you can proclaim the love you've kept hidden deep inside your heart!!
CHWARRRR
CHWARR (WHRRR)
Now, I'll introduce you to today's boy—
The lucky boy someone desperately loves is—

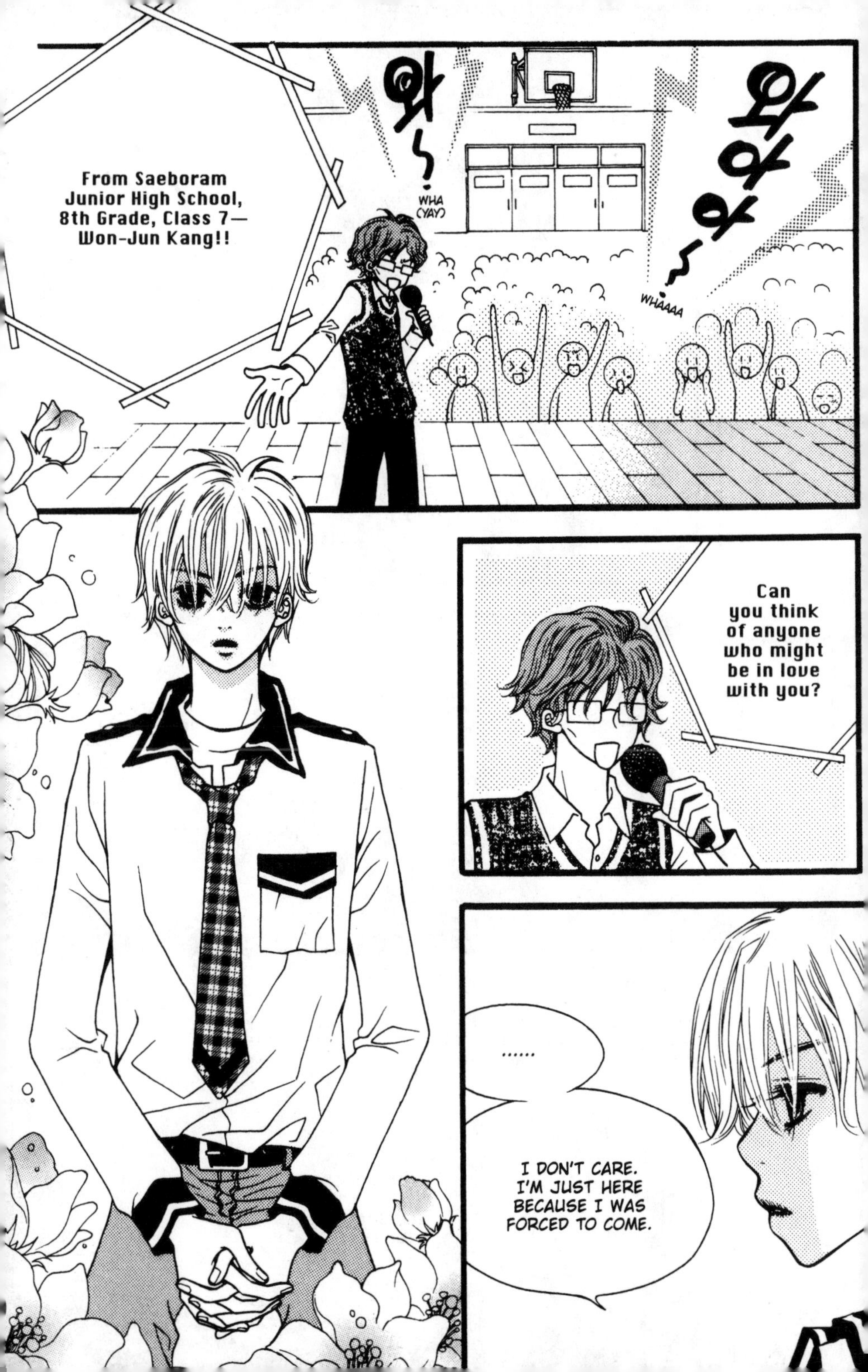
From Saeboram Junior High School, 8th Grade, Class 7— Won-Jun Kang!!
와~
WHA (YAY)
와아아~
WHAAAA
Can you think of anyone who might be in love with you?
......
I DON'T CARE. I'M JUST HERE BECAUSE I WAS FORCED TO COME.

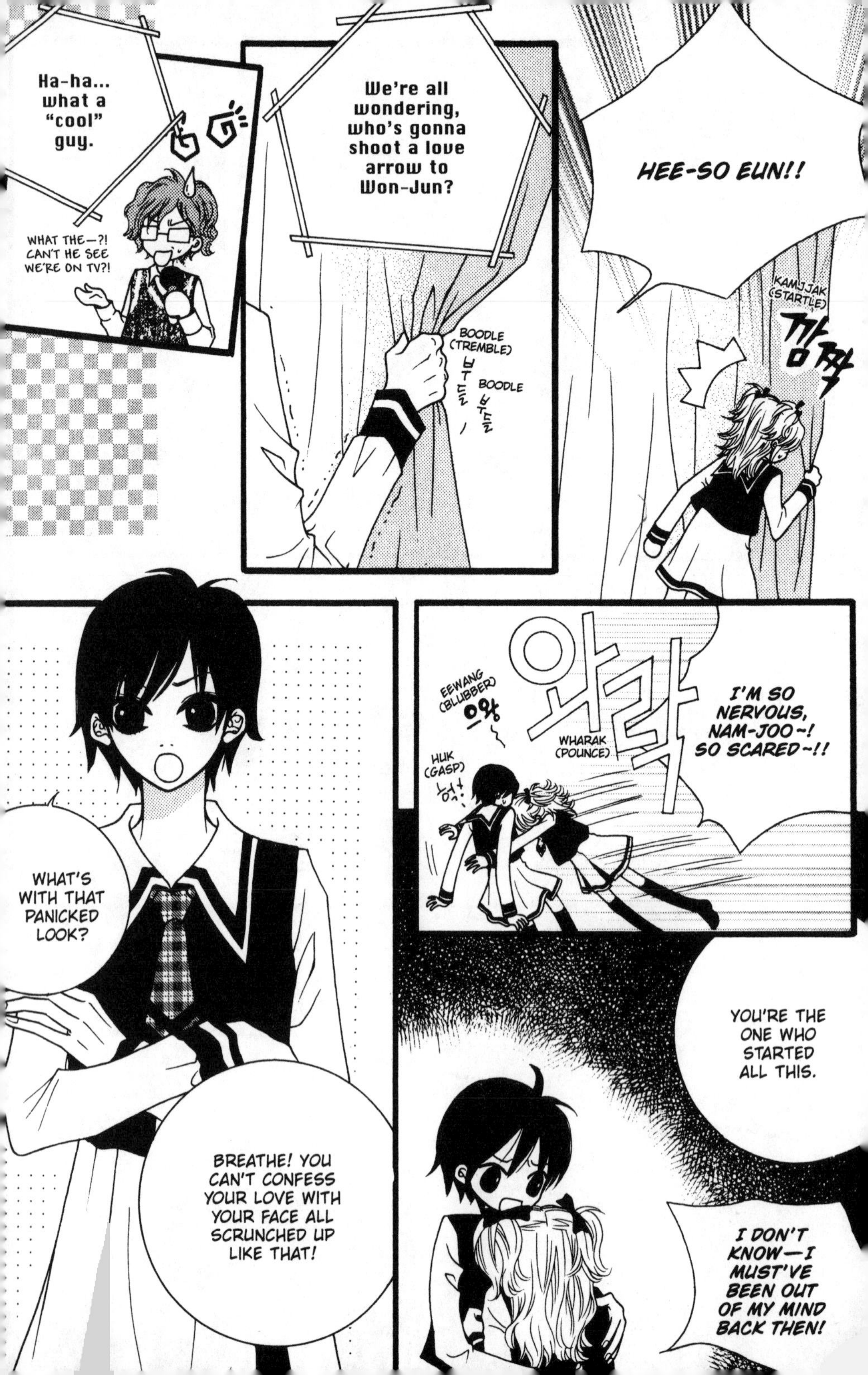
Ha-ha... what a "cool" guy.
WHAT THE—?! CAN'T HE SEE WE'RE ON TV?!
We're all wondering, who's gonna shoot a love arrow to Won-Jun?
BOODLE (TREMBLE)
부들
BOODLE
부들
HEE-SO EUN!!
KAMJJAK (STARTLE)
깜짝
WHAT'S WITH THAT PANICKED LOOK?
BREATHE! YOU CAN'T CONFESS YOUR LOVE WITH YOUR FACE ALL SCRUNCHED UP LIKE THAT!
와락
EEWANG (BLUBBER)
으앙
WHARAK (POUNCE)
HUK (GASP)
헉
I'M SO NERVOUS, NAM-JOO~! SO SCARED~!!
YOU'RE THE ONE WHO STARTED ALL THIS.
I DON'T KNOW—I MUST'VE BEEN OUT OF MY MIND BACK THEN!

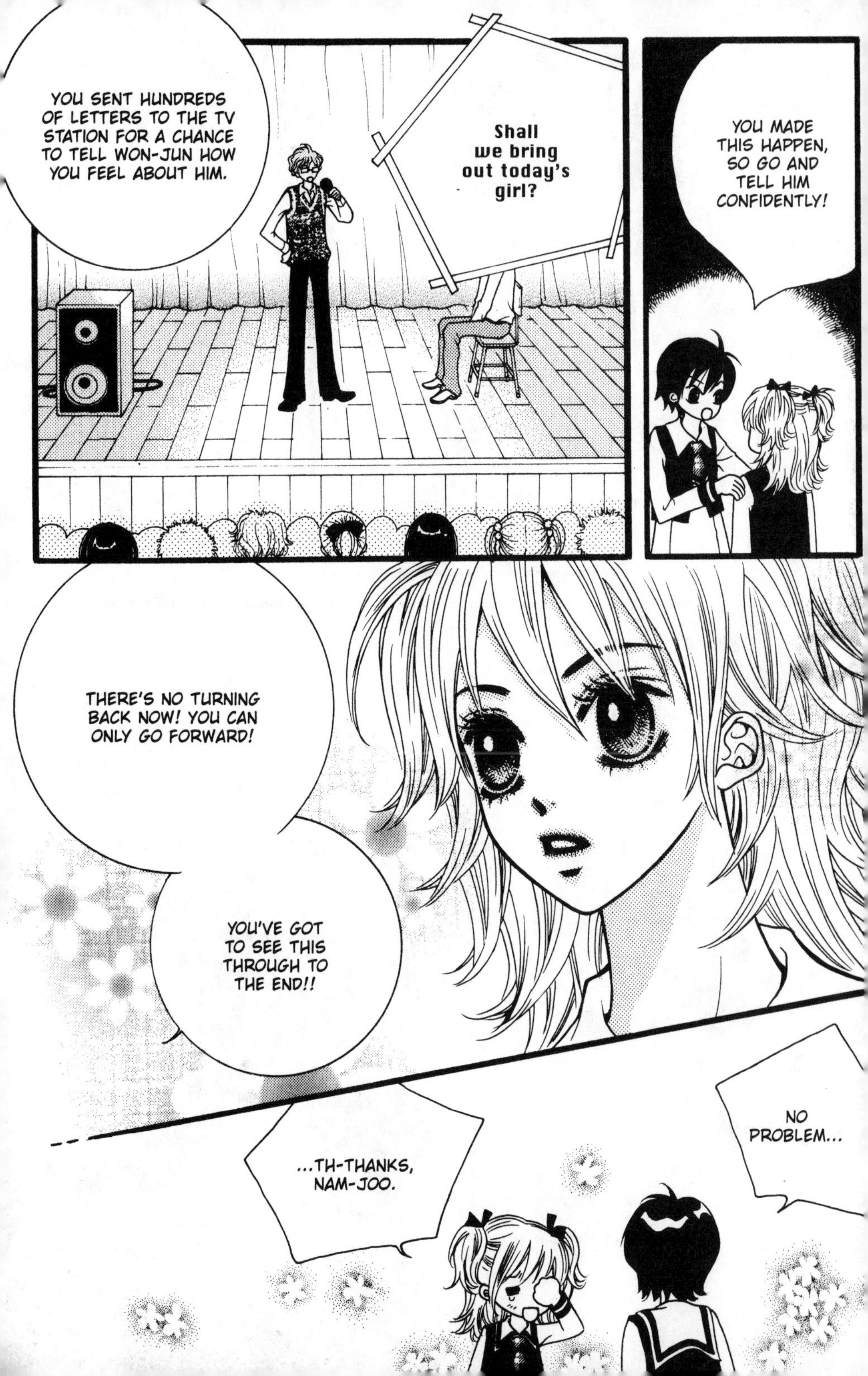
YOU SENT HUNDREDS OF LETTERS TO THE TV STATION FOR A CHANCE TO TELL WON-JUN HOW YOU FEEL ABOUT HIM.
Shall we bring out today's girl?
YOU MADE THIS HAPPEN, SO GO AND TELL HIM CONFIDENTLY!
THERE'S NO TURNING BACK NOW! YOU CAN ONLY GO FORWARD!
YOU'VE GOT TO SEE THIS THROUGH TO THE END!!
...TH-THANKS, NAM-JOO.
NO PROBLEM...

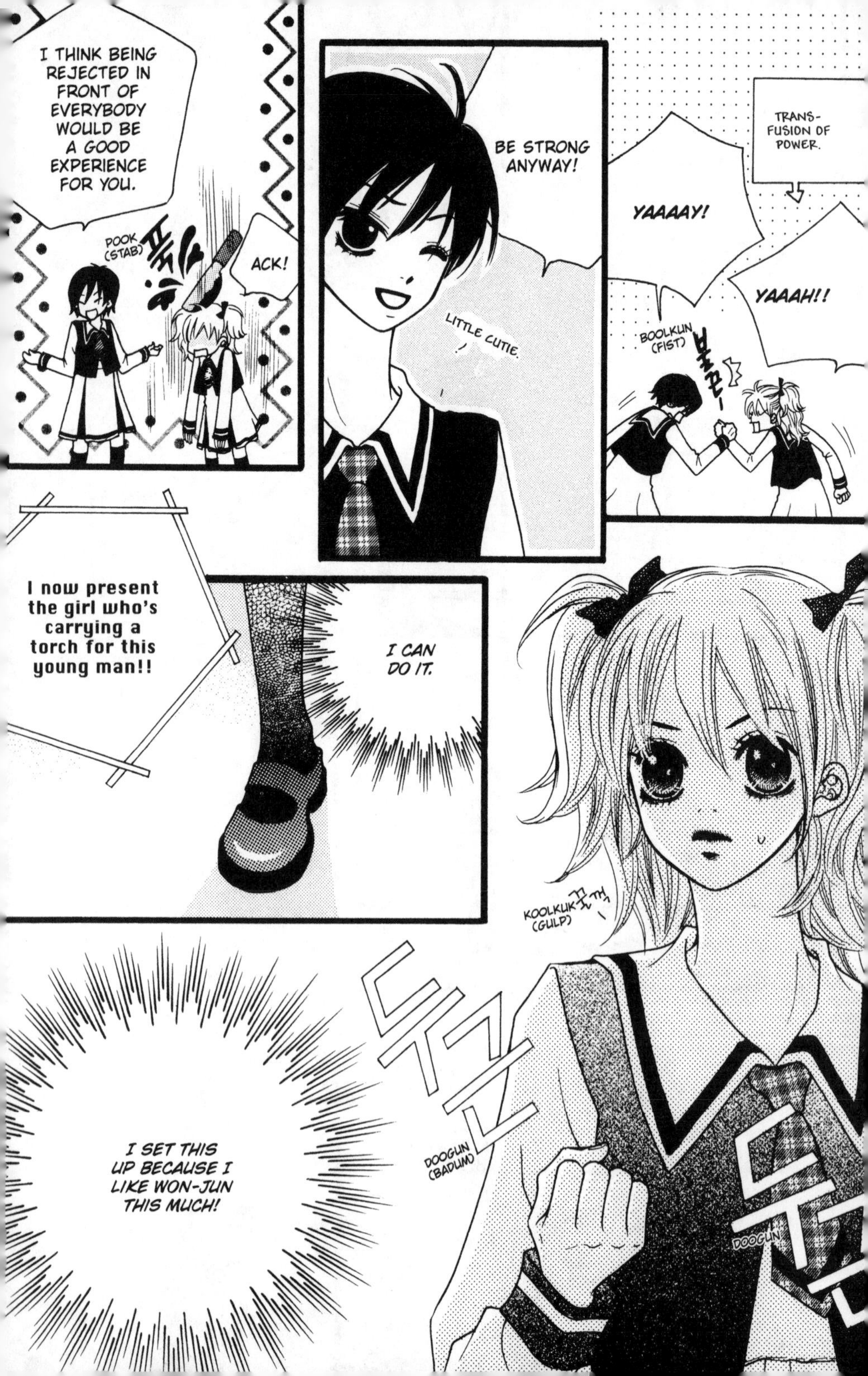
I THINK BEING REJECTED IN FRONT OF EVERYBODY WOULD BE A GOOD EXPERIENCE FOR YOU.
POOK (STAB)
ACK!
BE STRONG ANYWAY!
LITTLE CUTIE.
TRANS-FUSION OF POWER.
YAAAAY!
YAAAH!!
BOOLKUN (FIST)
I now present the girl who's carrying a torch for this young man!!
I CAN DO IT.
KOOLKUK (GULP)
I SET THIS UP BECAUSE I LIKE WON-JUN THIS MUCH!
DOOGUN (BADUM)
DOOGUN

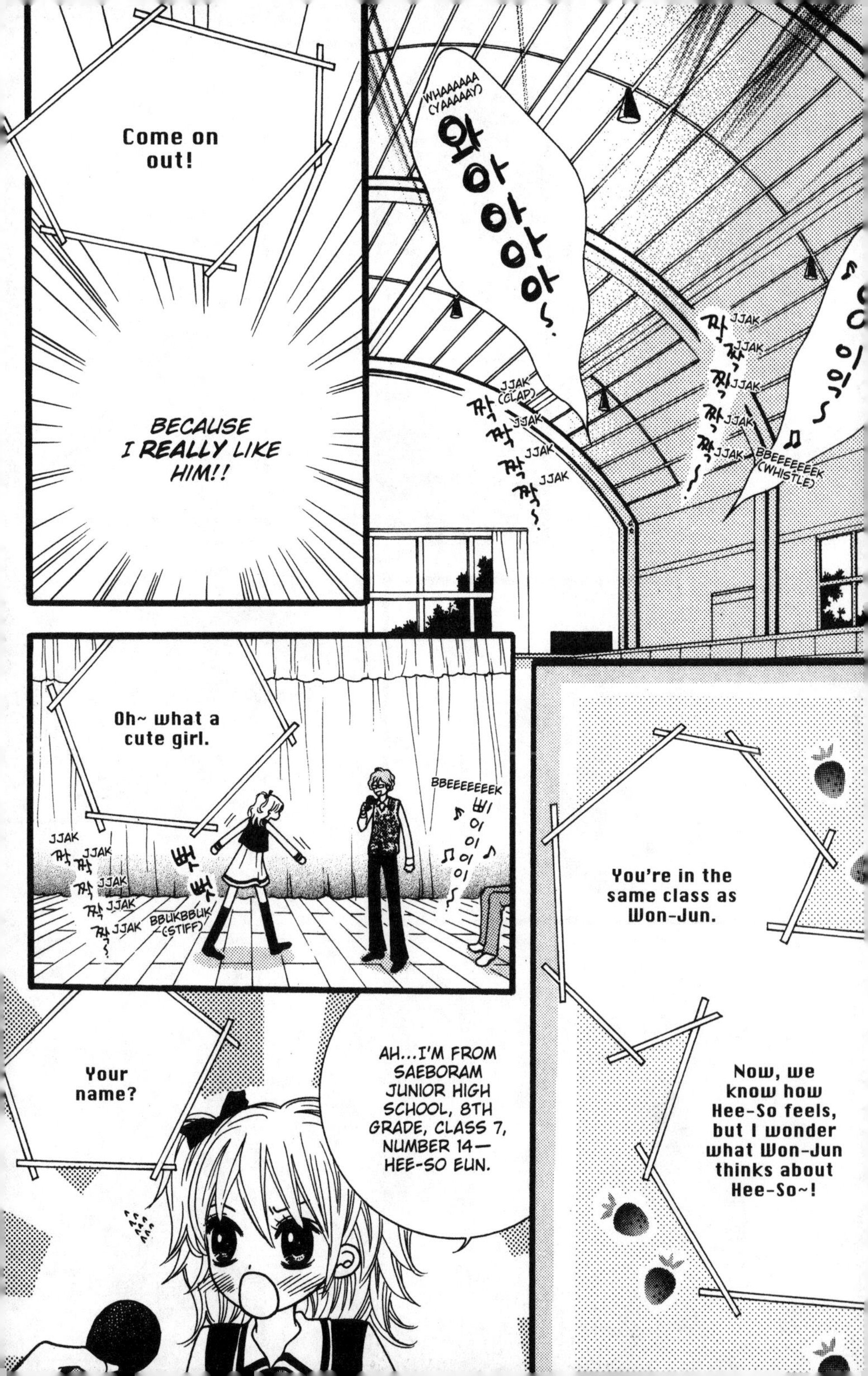
Come on out!
BECAUSE I **REALLY** LIKE HIM!!
WHAAAAAA (YAAAAAY)
와아아아아~
JJAK (CLAP) JJAK JJAK JJAK
짝짝짝짝~
JJAK JJAK JJAK JJAK JJAK
짝짝짝짝짝~
BBEEEEEEEK (WHISTLE)
Oh~ what a cute girl.
JJAK JJAK JJAK JJAK JJAK
짝짝짝짝짝~
뻣뻣
BBUKBBUK (STIFF)
BBEEEEEEEK
삐이이이이~
You're in the same class as Won-Jun.
Your name?
AH...I'M FROM SAEBORAM JUNIOR HIGH SCHOOL, 8TH GRADE, CLASS 7, NUMBER 14—HEE-SO EUN.
Now, we know how Hee-So feels, but I wonder what Won-Jun thinks about Hee-So~!

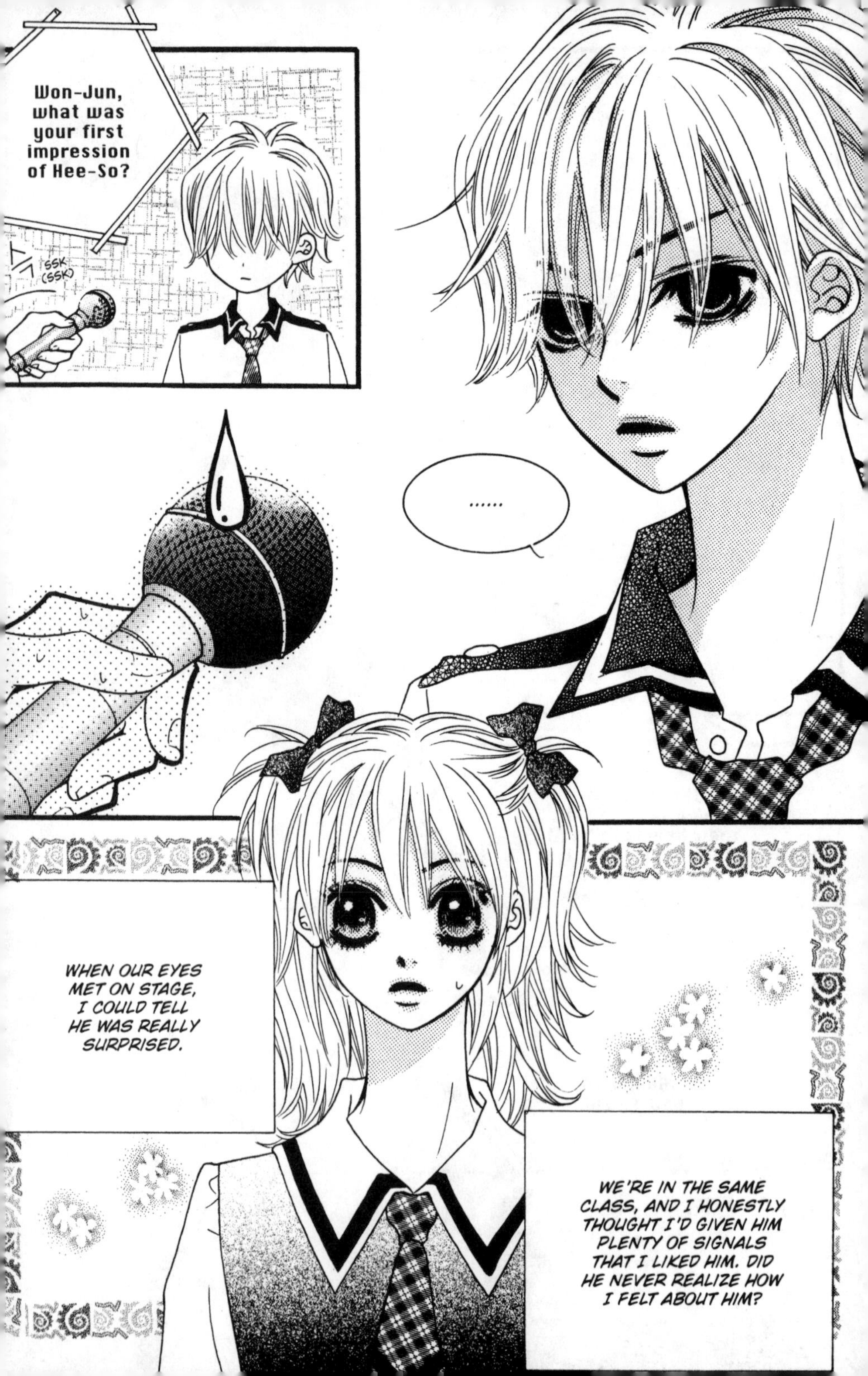
Won-Jun, what was your first impression of Hee-So?
SSK (SSK)
......
WHEN OUR EYES MET ON STAGE, I COULD TELL HE WAS REALLY SURPRISED.
WE'RE IN THE SAME CLASS, AND I HONESTLY THOUGHT I'D GIVEN HIM PLENTY OF SIGNALS THAT I LIKED HIM. DID HE NEVER REALIZE HOW I FELT ABOUT HIM?

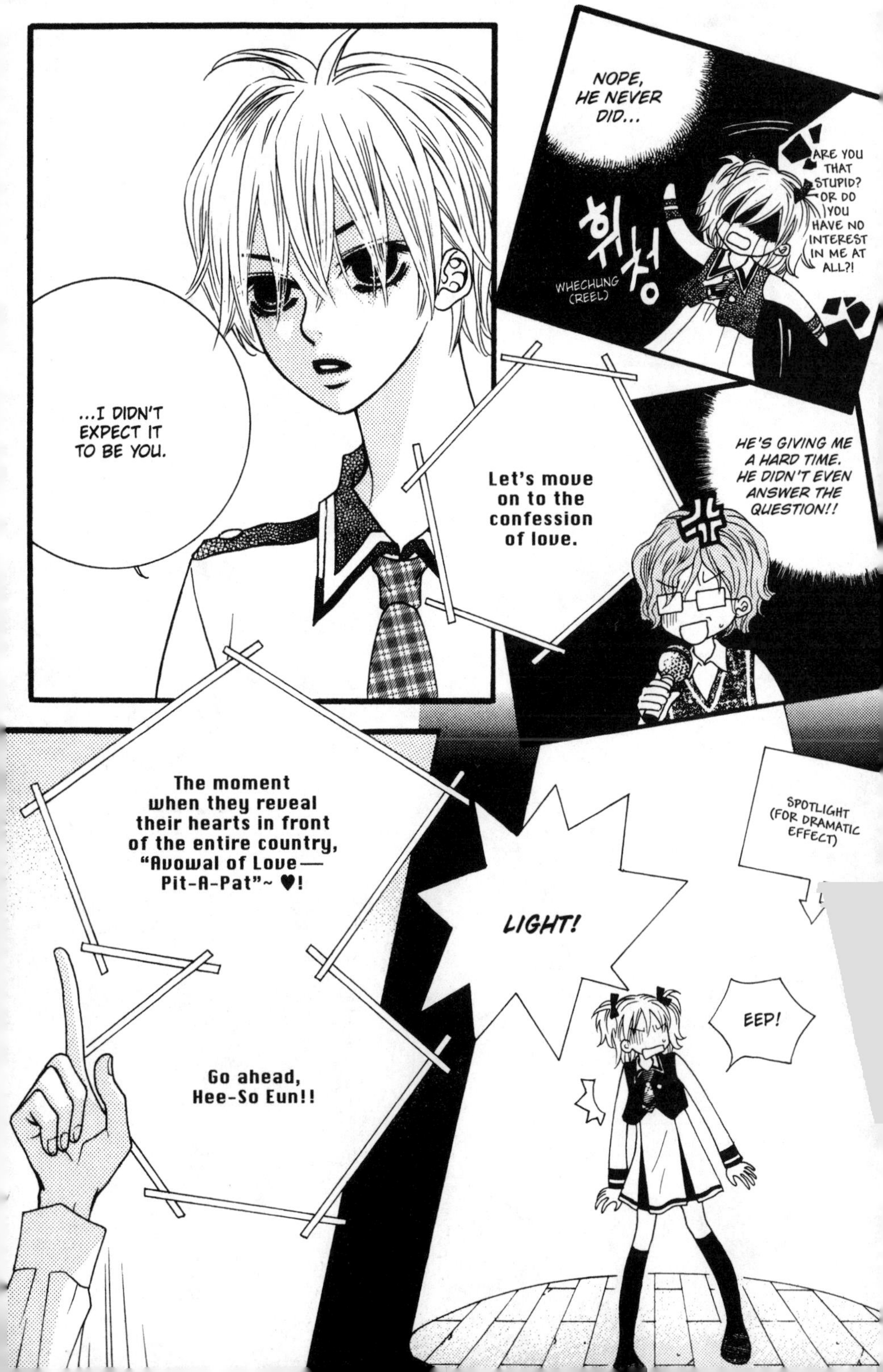
...I DIDN'T EXPECT IT TO BE YOU.
NOPE, HE NEVER DID...
휘청
WHECHUNG (REEL)
ARE YOU THAT STUPID? OR DO YOU HAVE NO INTEREST IN ME AT ALL?!
Let's move on to the confession of love.
HE'S GIVING ME A HARD TIME. HE DIDN'T EVEN ANSWER THE QUESTION!!
The moment when they reveal their hearts in front of the entire country, "Avowal of Love— Pit-A-Pat"~ ♥!
Go ahead, Hee-So Eun!!
LIGHT!
SPOTLIGHT (FOR DRAMATIC EFFECT)
EEP!

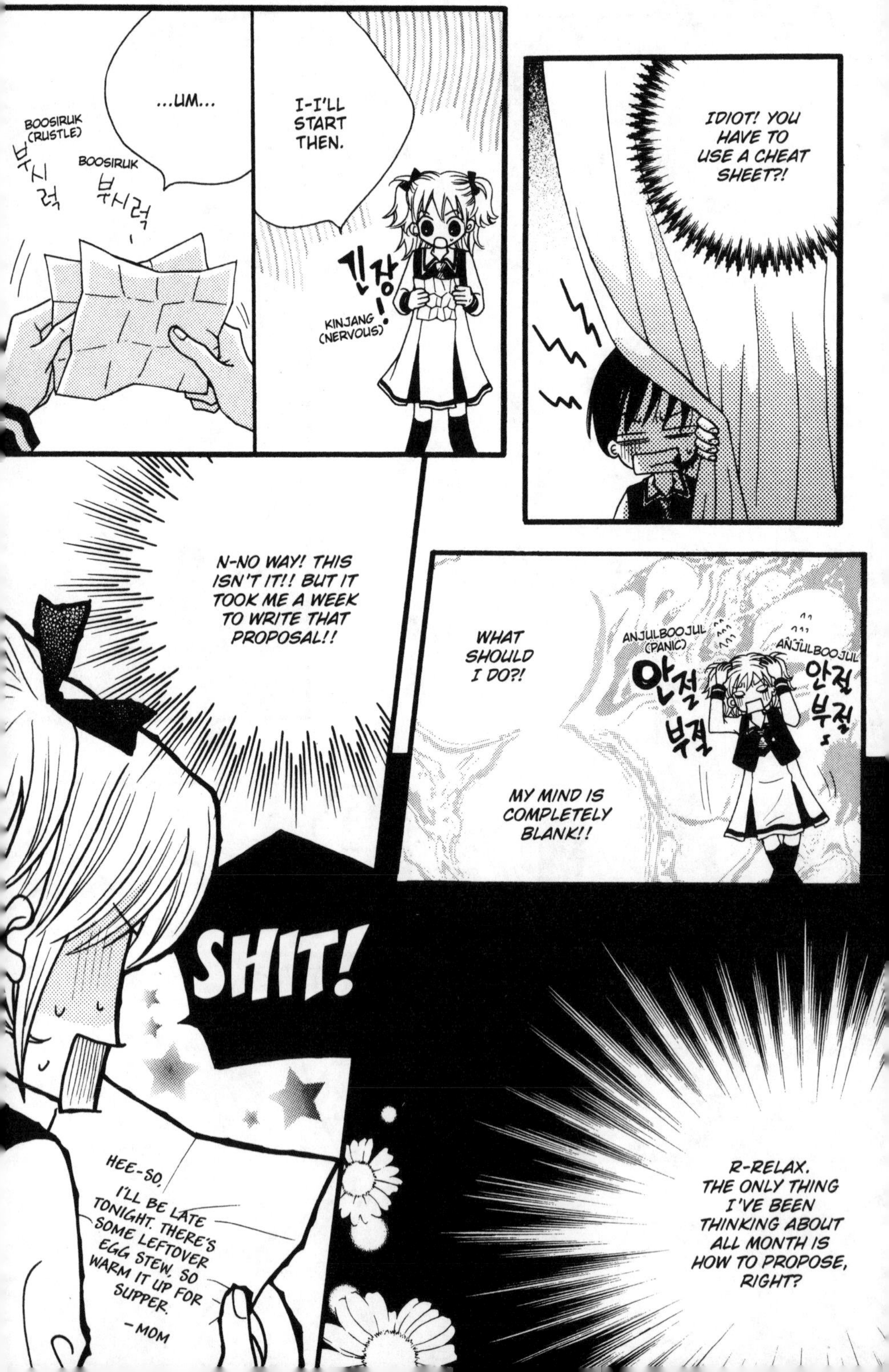
BOOSIRUK (RUSTLE)
부시럭
BOOSIRUK
부시럭
...UM...
I-I'LL START THEN.
긴장!
KINJANG (NERVOUS)
IDIOT! YOU HAVE TO USE A CHEAT SHEET?!
N-NO WAY! THIS ISN'T IT!! BUT IT TOOK ME A WEEK TO WRITE THAT PROPOSAL!!
SHIT!
WHAT SHOULD I DO?!
ANJULBOOJUL (PANIC)
안절부절
ANJULBOOJUL
안절부절
MY MIND IS COMPLETELY BLANK!!
HEE-SO,
I'LL BE LATE TONIGHT. THERE'S SOME LEFTOVER EGG STEW, SO WARM IT UP FOR SUPPER.
–MOM
R-RELAX. THE ONLY THING I'VE BEEN THINKING ABOUT ALL MONTH IS HOW TO PROPOSE, RIGHT?

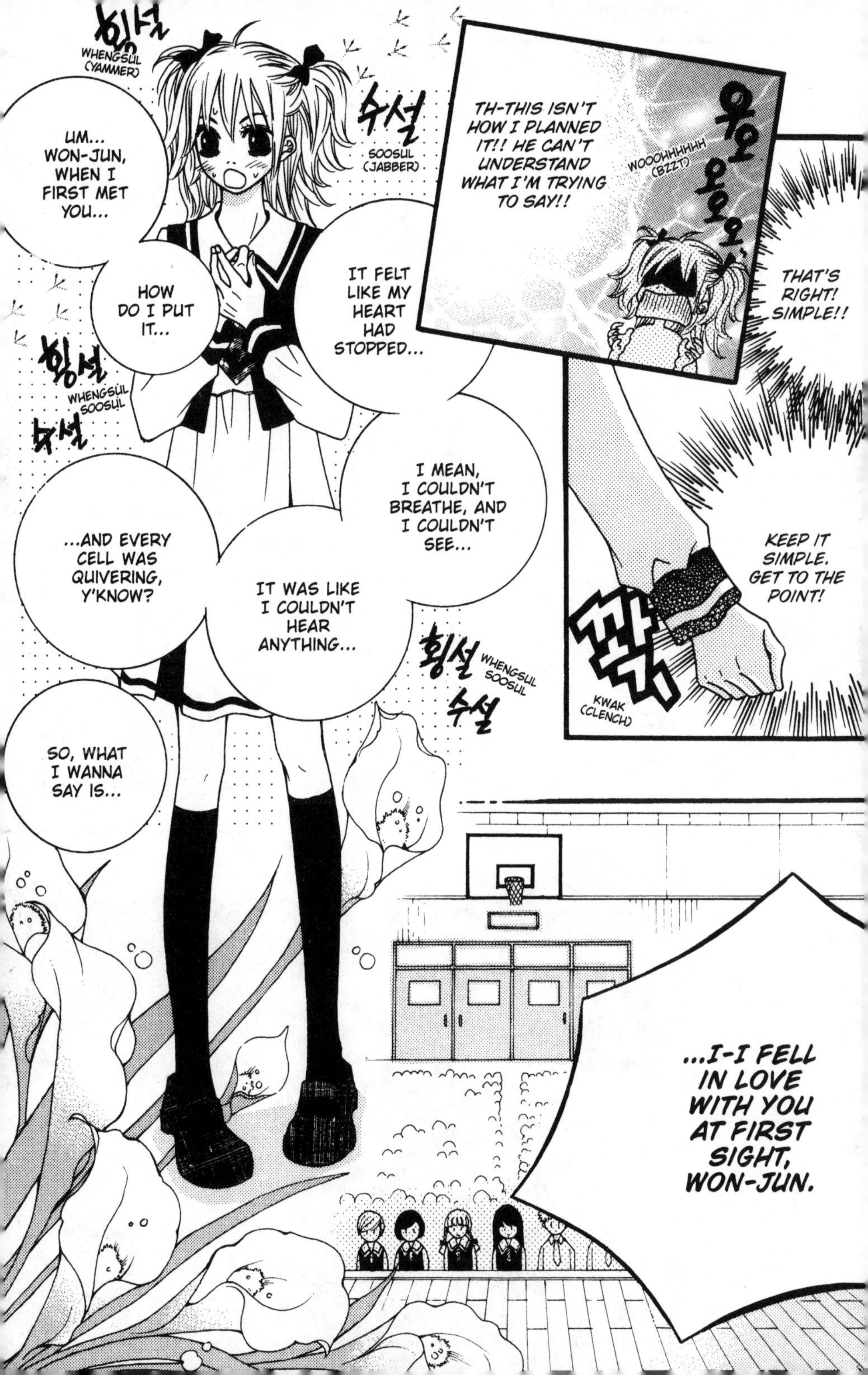

횡설
WHENGSUL (YAMMER)
UM... WON-JUN, WHEN I FIRST MET YOU...
수설
SOOSUL (JABBER)
HOW DO I PUT IT...
IT FELT LIKE MY HEART HAD STOPPED...
횡설
WHENGSUL SOOSUL
수설
I MEAN, I COULDN'T BREATHE, AND I COULDN'T SEE...
IT WAS LIKE I COULDN'T HEAR ANYTHING...
...AND EVERY CELL WAS QUIVERING, Y'KNOW?
횡설
WHENGSUL SOOSUL
수설
SO, WHAT I WANNA SAY IS...
TH-THIS ISN'T HOW I PLANNED IT!! HE CAN'T UNDERSTAND WHAT I'M TRYING TO SAY!!
우오오오오
WOOOHHHHHH (BZZT)
THAT'S RIGHT! SIMPLE!!
KEEP IT SIMPLE. GET TO THE POINT!
꽉
KWAK (CLENCH)
...I-I FELL IN LOVE WITH YOU AT FIRST SIGHT, WON-JUN.

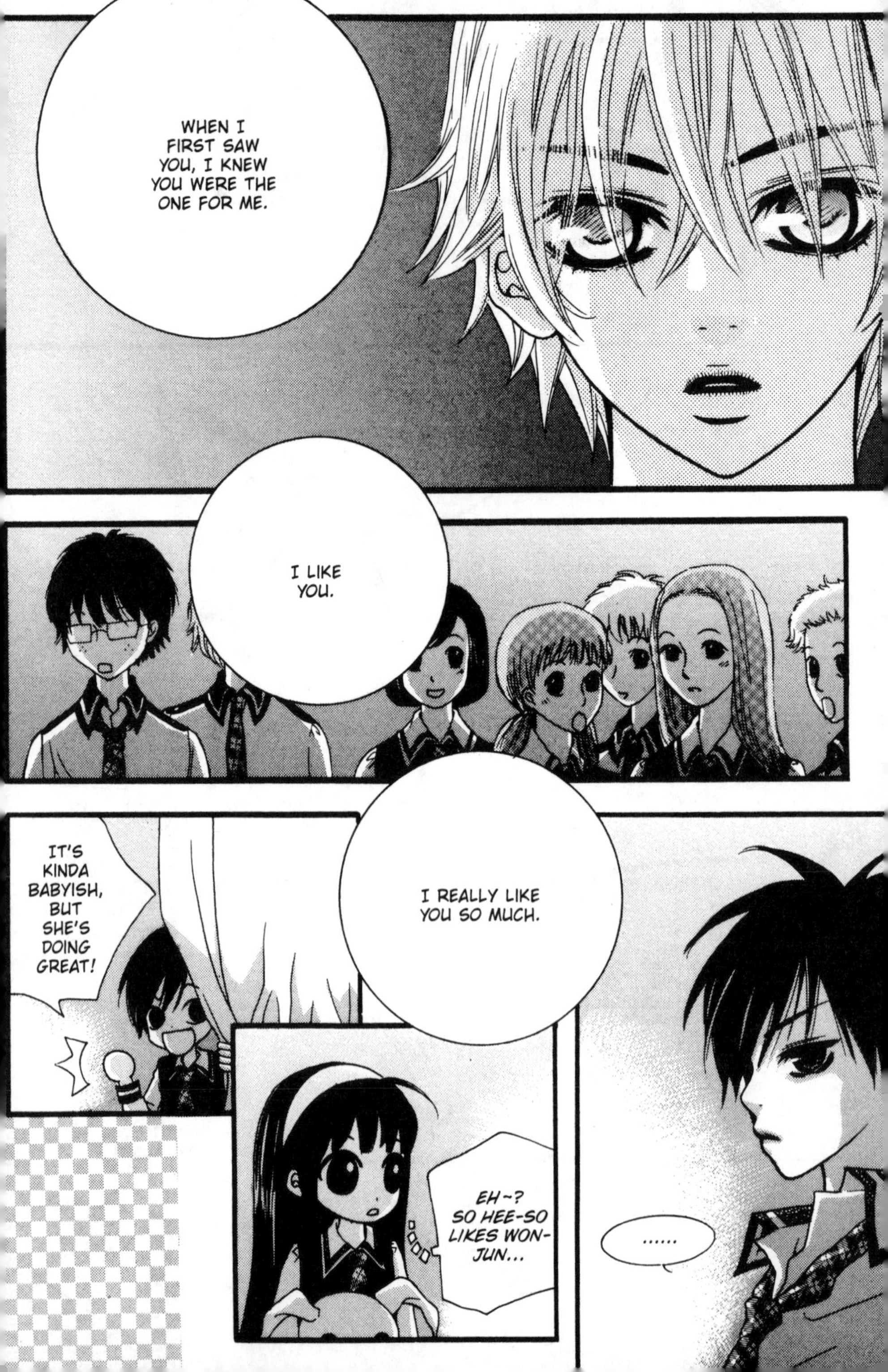
WHEN I FIRST SAW YOU, I KNEW YOU WERE THE ONE FOR ME.
I LIKE YOU.
IT'S KINDA BABYISH, BUT SHE'S DOING GREAT!
I REALLY LIKE YOU SO MUCH.
EH~? SO HEE-SO LIKES WON-JUN...
......

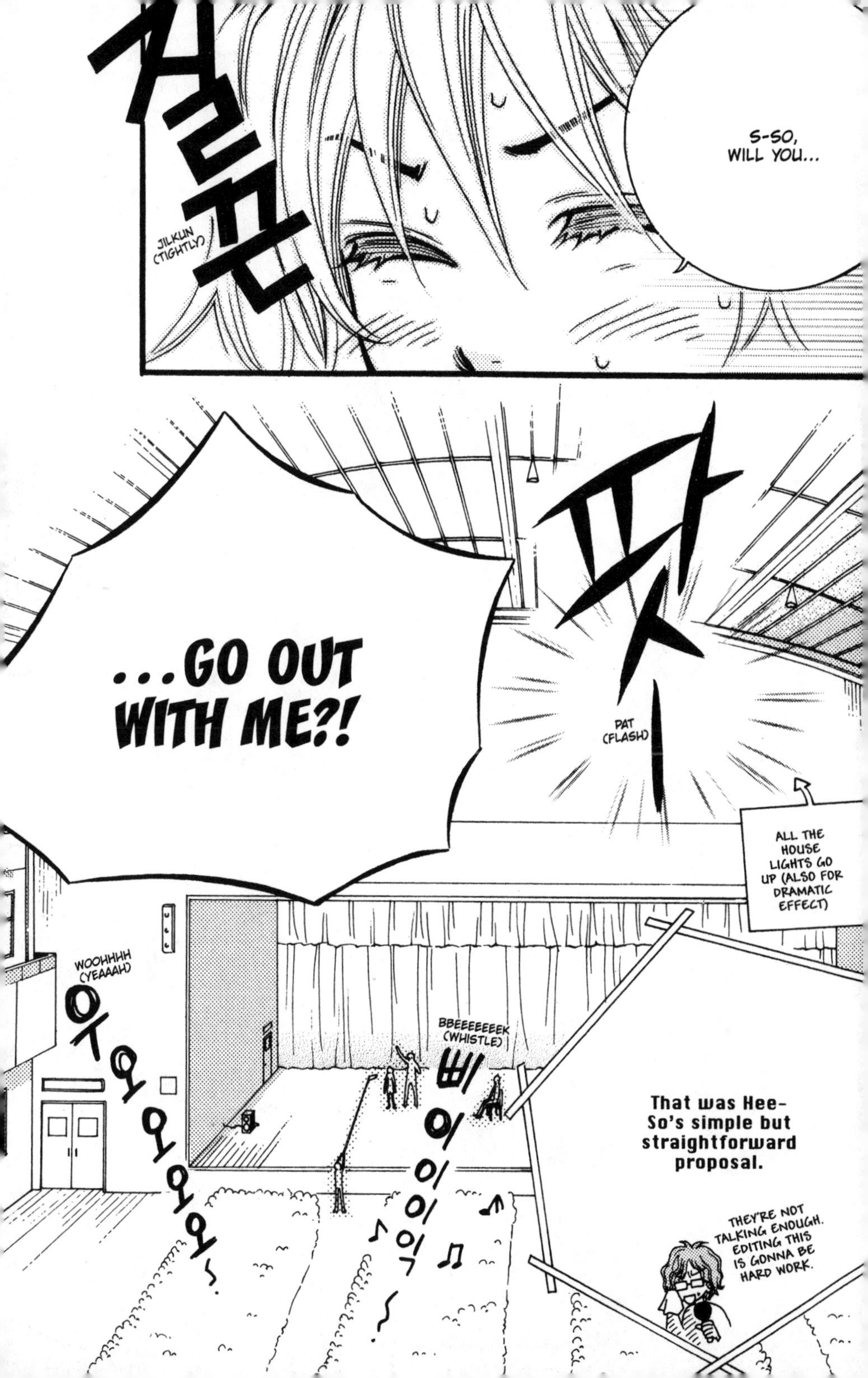
질끈
JILKUN (TIGHTLY)
S-SO, WILL YOU...
...GO OUT WITH ME?!
팟
PAT (FLASH)
ALL THE HOUSE LIGHTS GO UP (ALSO FOR DRAMATIC EFFECT)
WOOHHHH (YEAAAH)
BBEEEEEEEK (WHISTLE)
That was Hee-So's simple but straightforward proposal.
THEY'RE NOT TALKING ENOUGH. EDITING THIS IS GONNA BE HARD WORK.

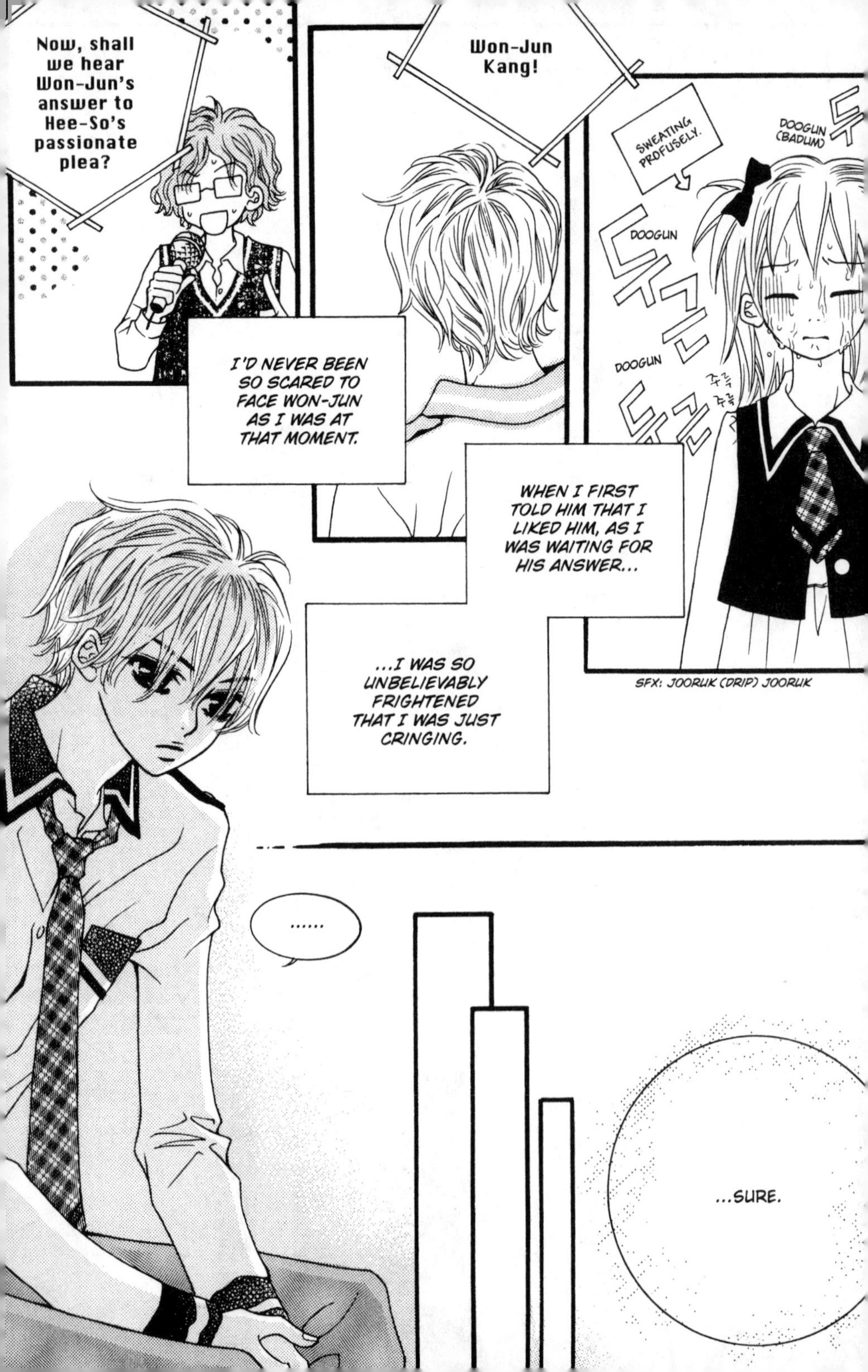
Now, shall we hear Won-Jun's answer to Hee-So's passionate plea?
Won-Jun Kang!
I'D NEVER BEEN SO SCARED TO FACE WON-JUN AS I WAS AT THAT MOMENT.
SWEATING PROFUSELY.
DOOGUN (BADUM)
DOOGUN
DOOGUN
SFX: JOORUK (DRIP) JOORUK
WHEN I FIRST TOLD HIM THAT I LIKED HIM, AS I WAS WAITING FOR HIS ANSWER...
...I WAS SO UNBELIEVABLY FRIGHTENED THAT I WAS JUST CRINGING.
......
...SURE.

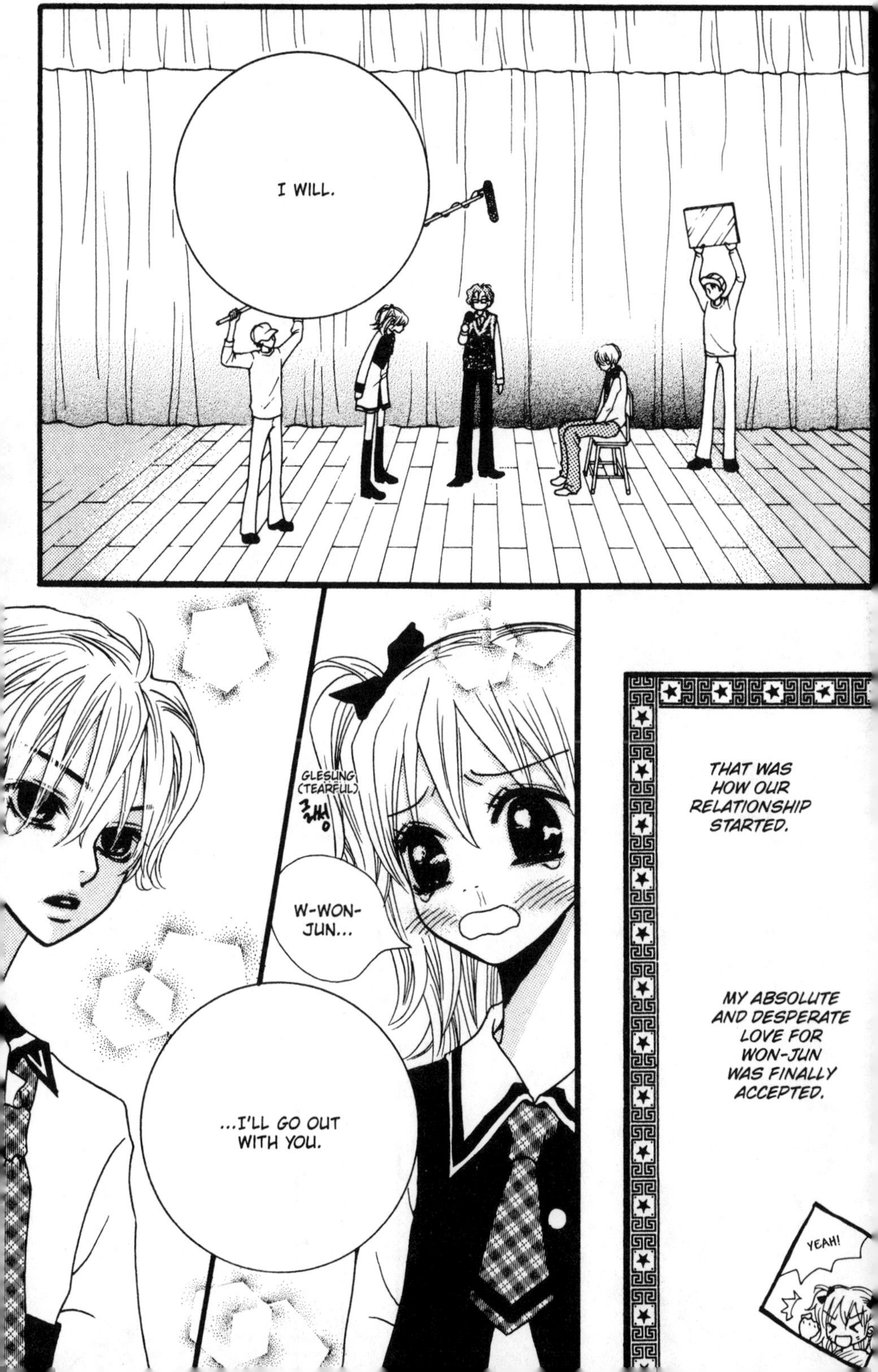
I WILL.
GLESUNG (TEARFUL)
글썽
W-WON-JUN...
...I'LL GO OUT WITH YOU.
THAT WAS HOW OUR RELATIONSHIP STARTED.
MY ABSOLUTE AND DESPERATE LOVE FOR WON-JUN WAS FINALLY ACCEPTED.
YEAH!

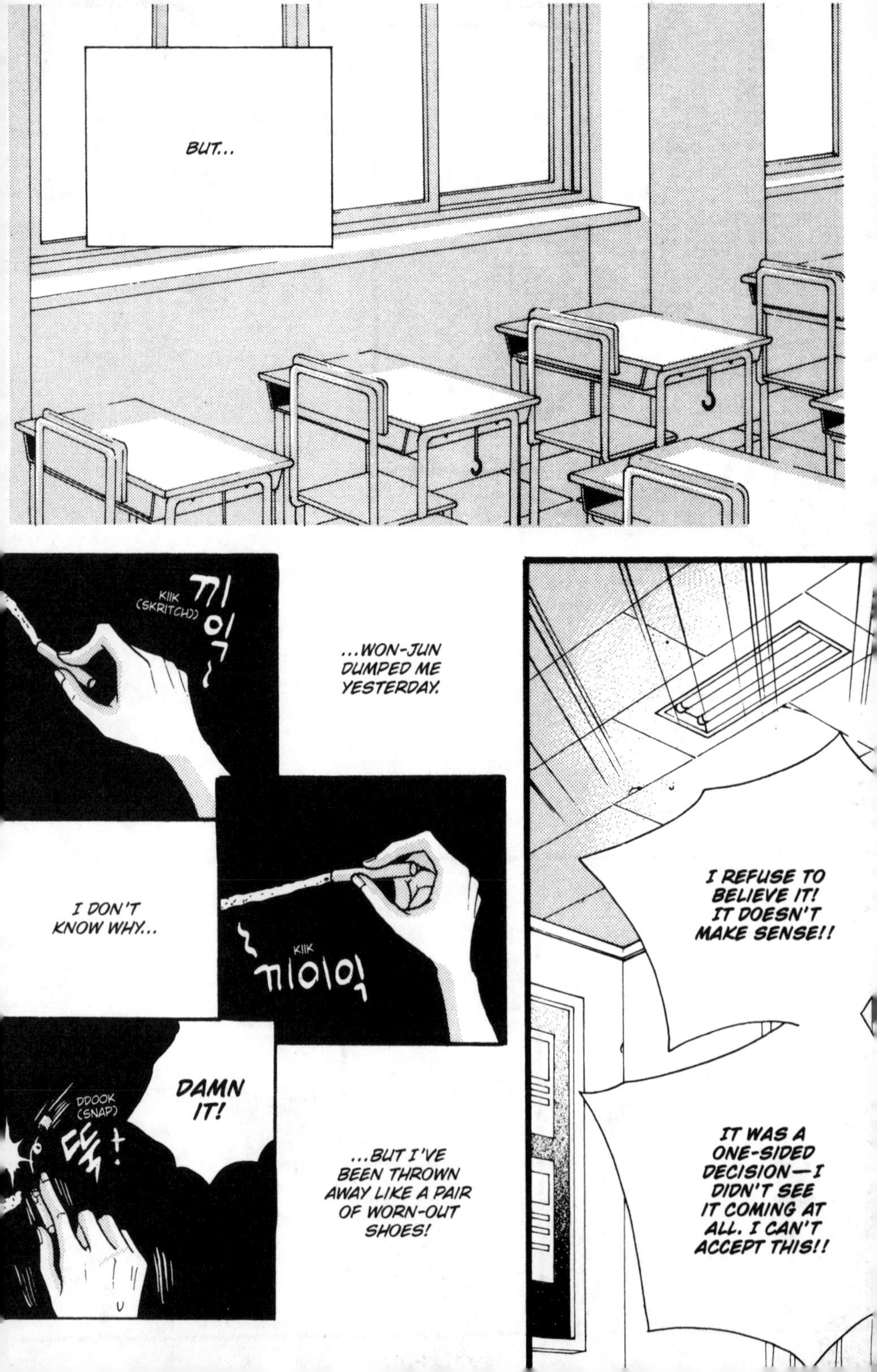
BUT...
KIIK (SKRITCH)
끼익~
...WON-JUN DUMPED ME YESTERDAY.
I DON'T KNOW WHY...
KIIK
~끼이이익
DDOOK (SNAP)
뚝!
DAMN IT!
...BUT I'VE BEEN THROWN AWAY LIKE A PAIR OF WORN-OUT SHOES!
I REFUSE TO BELIEVE IT! IT DOESN'T MAKE SENSE!!
IT WAS A ONE-SIDED DECISION—I DIDN'T SEE IT COMING AT ALL. I CAN'T ACCEPT THIS!!

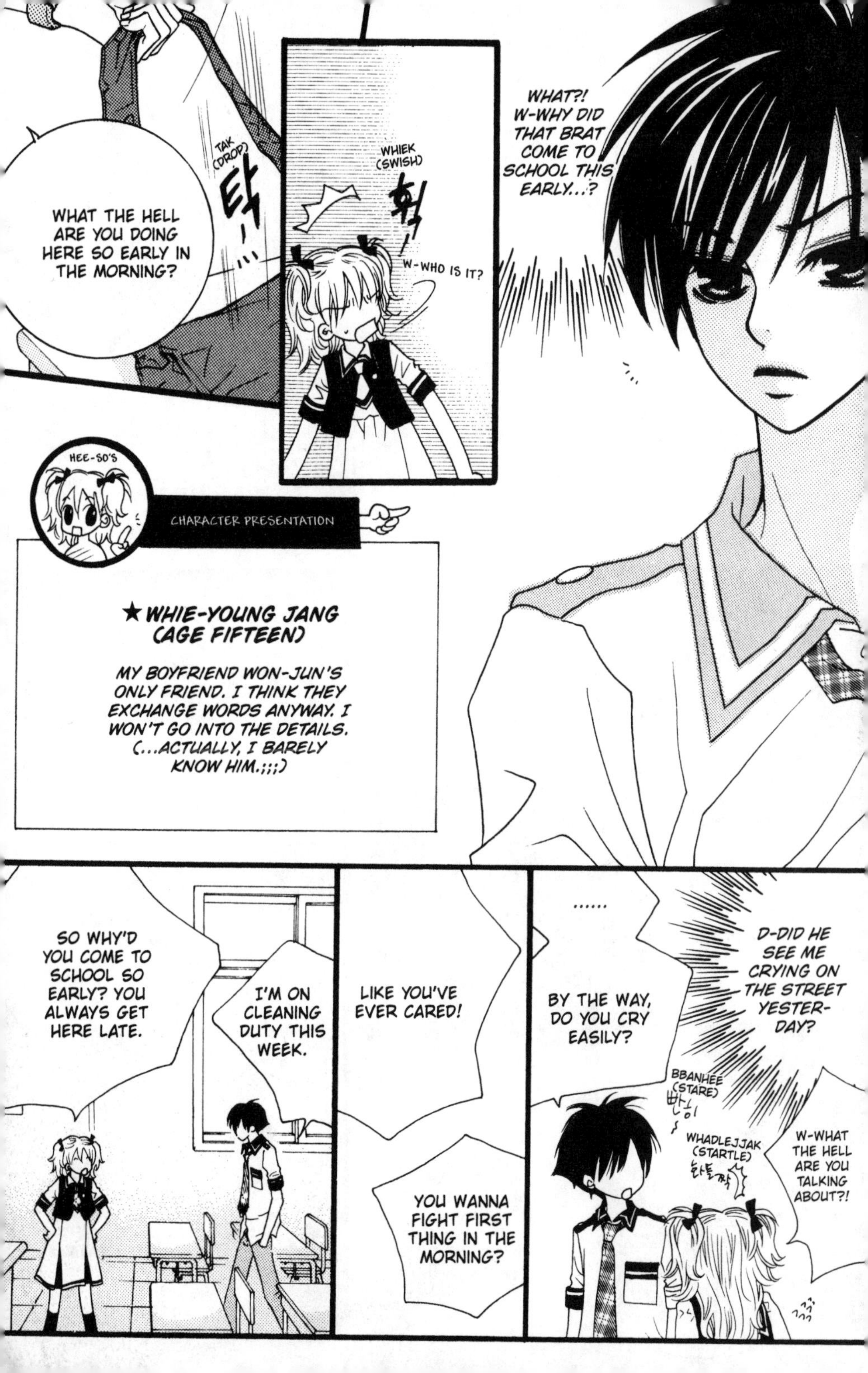

WHAT THE HELL ARE YOU DOING HERE SO EARLY IN THE MORNING?
TAK (DROP)
탁
WHIEK (SWISH)
휙
W-WHO IS IT?
HEE-SO'S
CHARACTER PRESENTATION
★WHIE-YOUNG JANG (AGE FIFTEEN)
MY BOYFRIEND WON-JUN'S ONLY FRIEND. I THINK THEY EXCHANGE WORDS ANYWAY. I WON'T GO INTO THE DETAILS. (...ACTUALLY, I BARELY KNOW HIM.;;;)
WHAT?! W-WHY DID THAT BRAT COME TO SCHOOL THIS EARLY...?
SO WHY'D YOU COME TO SCHOOL SO EARLY? YOU ALWAYS GET HERE LATE.
I'M ON CLEANING DUTY THIS WEEK.
LIKE YOU'VE EVER CARED!
YOU WANNA FIGHT FIRST THING IN THE MORNING?
......
BY THE WAY, DO YOU CRY EASILY?
D-DID HE SEE ME CRYING ON THE STREET YESTER-DAY?
BBANHEE (STARE)
빤히
WHADLEJJAK (STARTLE)
화들짝
W-WHAT THE HELL ARE YOU TALKING ABOUT?!

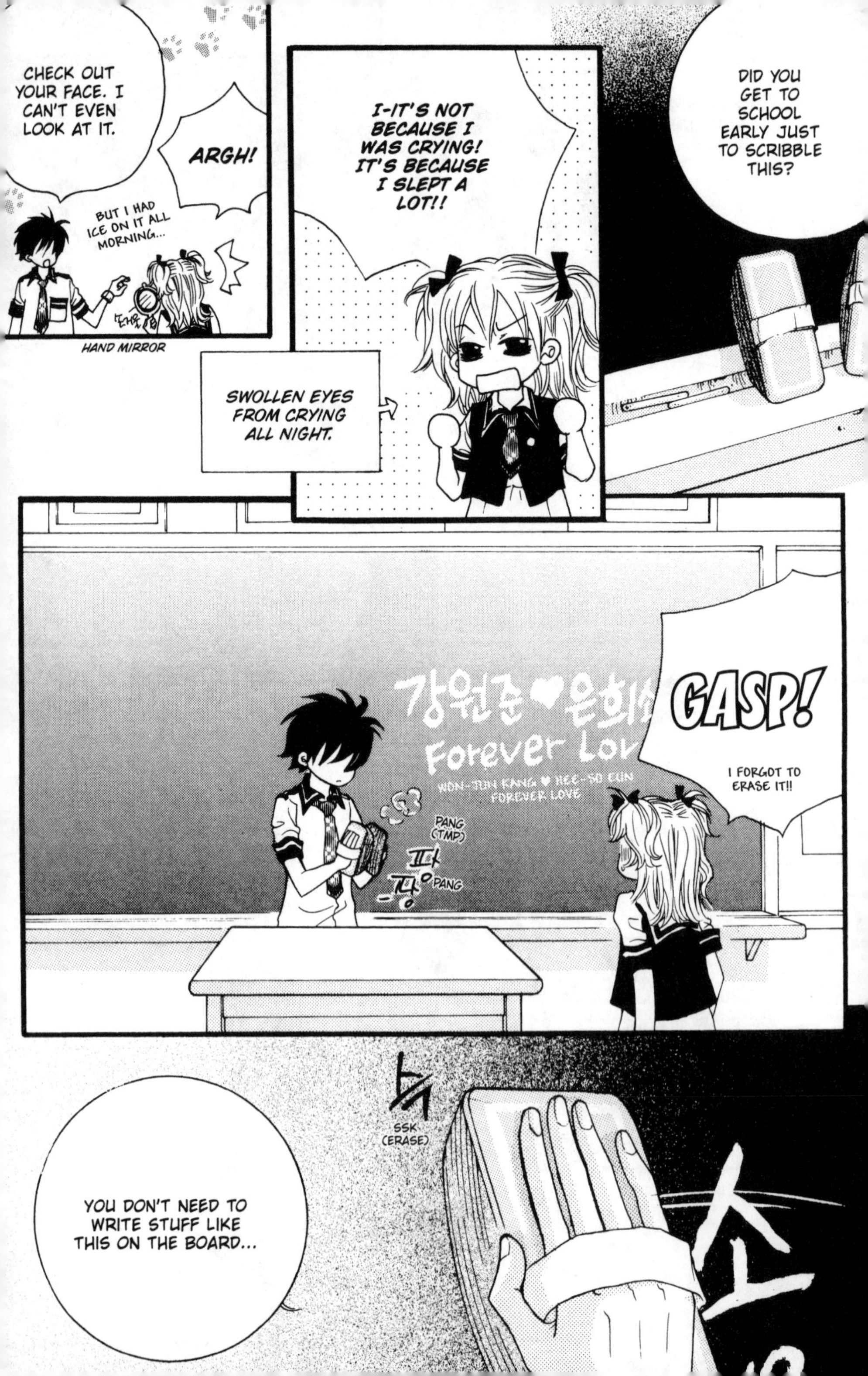
CHECK OUT YOUR FACE. I CAN'T EVEN LOOK AT IT.
ARGH!
BUT I HAD ICE ON IT ALL MORNING...
HAND MIRROR
I-IT'S NOT BECAUSE I WAS CRYING! IT'S BECAUSE I SLEPT A LOT!!
SWOLLEN EYES FROM CRYING ALL NIGHT.
DID YOU GET TO SCHOOL EARLY JUST TO SCRIBBLE THIS?
WON-JUN KANG ♥ HEE-SO EUN FOREVER LOVE
PANG (TMP)
PANG
GASP!
I FORGOT TO ERASE IT!!
SSK (ERASE)
YOU DON'T NEED TO WRITE STUFF LIKE THIS ON THE BOARD...

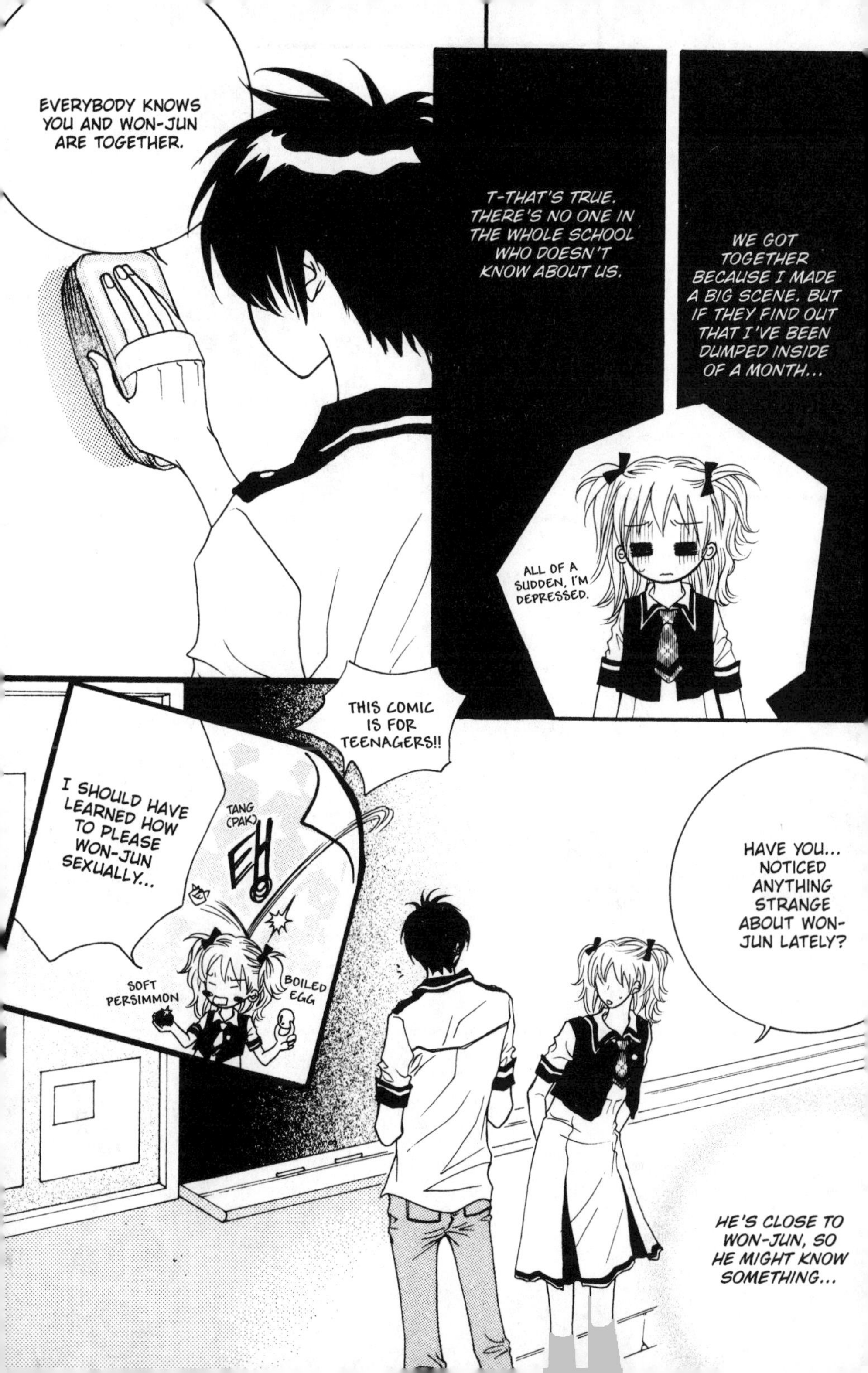
EVERYBODY KNOWS YOU AND WON-JUN ARE TOGETHER.
T-THAT'S TRUE. THERE'S NO ONE IN THE WHOLE SCHOOL WHO DOESN'T KNOW ABOUT US.
WE GOT TOGETHER BECAUSE I MADE A BIG SCENE. BUT IF THEY FIND OUT THAT I'VE BEEN DUMPED INSIDE OF A MONTH...
ALL OF A SUDDEN, I'M DEPRESSED.
I SHOULD HAVE LEARNED HOW TO PLEASE WON-JUN SEXUALLY...
TANG (PAK)
SOFT PERSIMMON
BOILED EGG
THIS COMIC IS FOR TEENAGERS!!
HAVE YOU... NOTICED ANYTHING STRANGE ABOUT WON-JUN LATELY?
HE'S CLOSE TO WON-JUN, SO HE MIGHT KNOW SOMETHING...

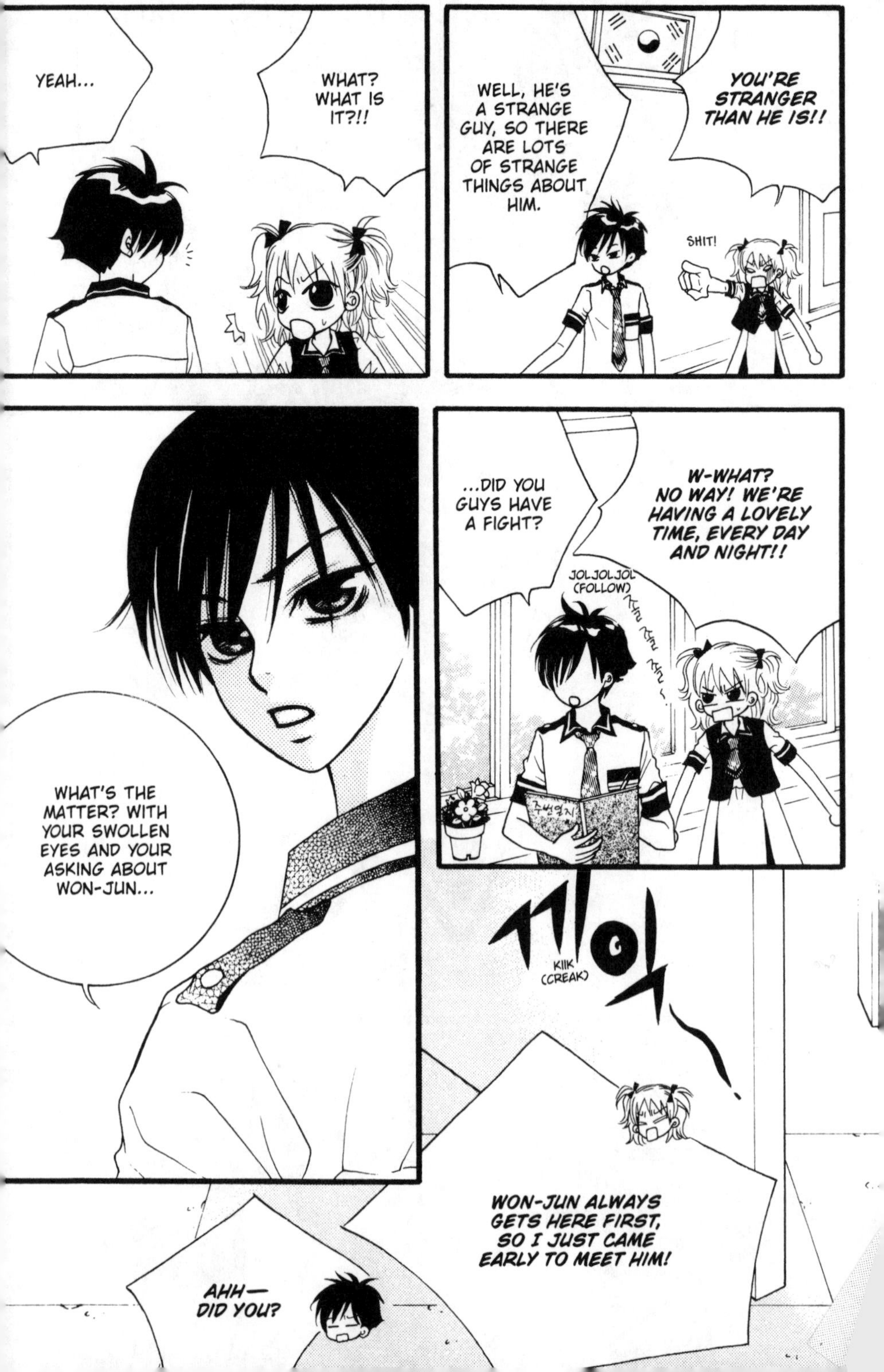
YEAH...
WHAT? WHAT IS IT?!!
WELL, HE'S A STRANGE GUY, SO THERE ARE LOTS OF STRANGE THINGS ABOUT HIM.
YOU'RE STRANGER THAN HE IS!!
SHIT!
WHAT'S THE MATTER? WITH YOUR SWOLLEN EYES AND YOUR ASKING ABOUT WON-JUN...
...DID YOU GUYS HAVE A FIGHT?
W-WHAT? NO WAY! WE'RE HAVING A LOVELY TIME, EVERY DAY AND NIGHT!!
JOLJOLJOL (FOLLOW)
주번일지
KIIK (CREAK)
WON-JUN ALWAYS GETS HERE FIRST, SO I JUST CAME EARLY TO MEET HIM!
AHH— DID YOU?

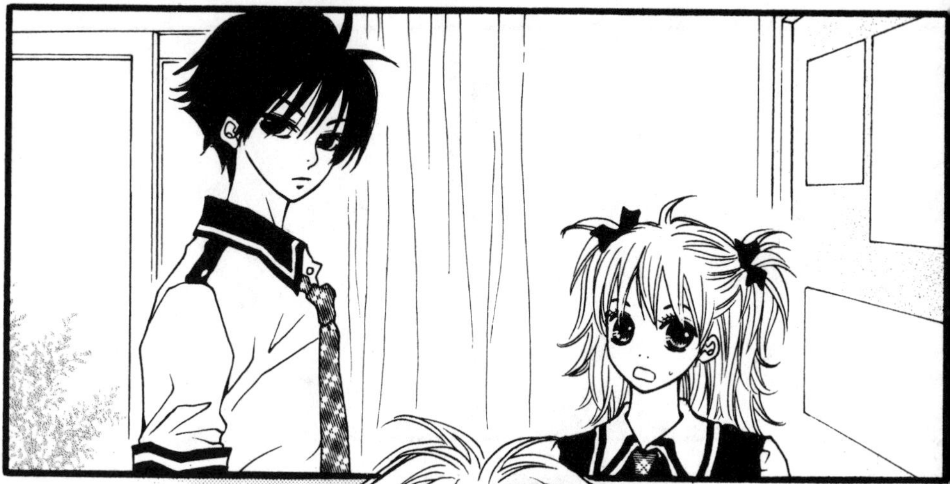
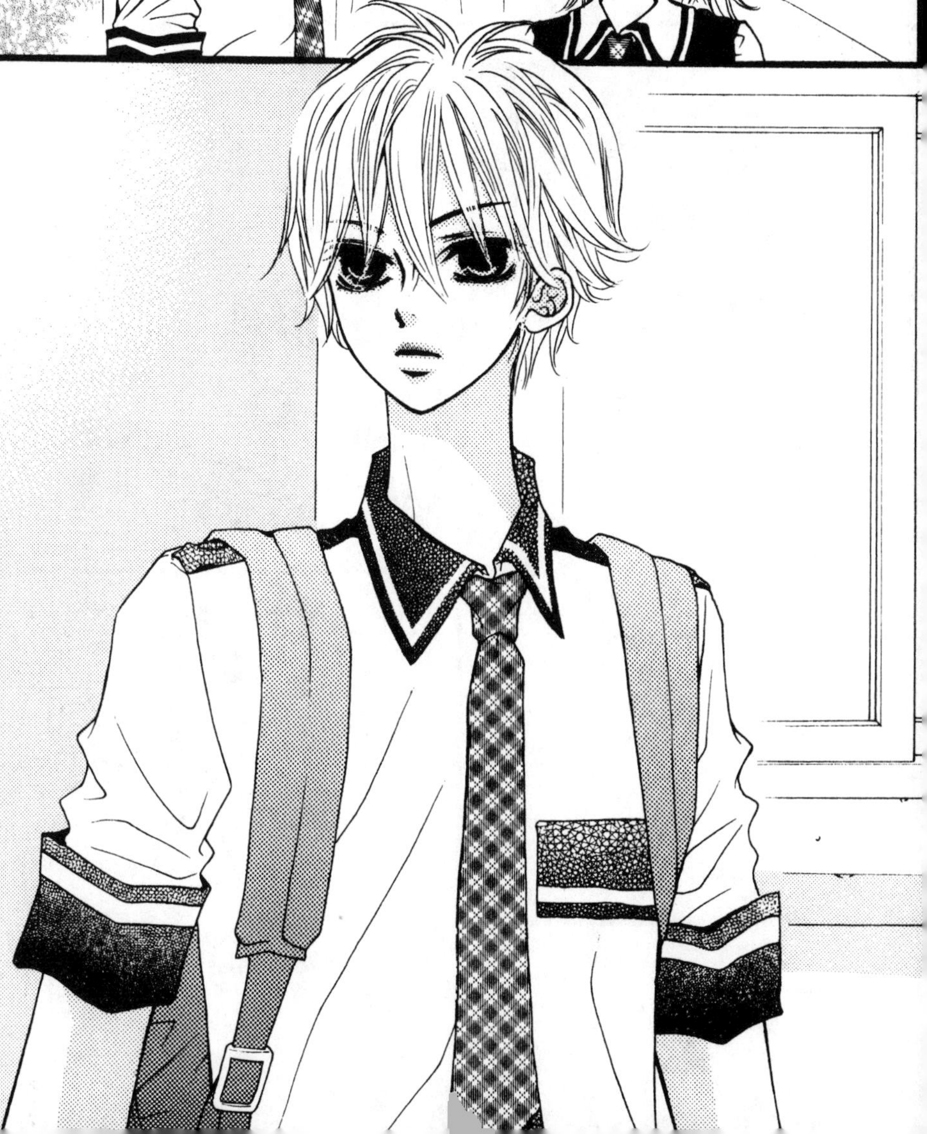

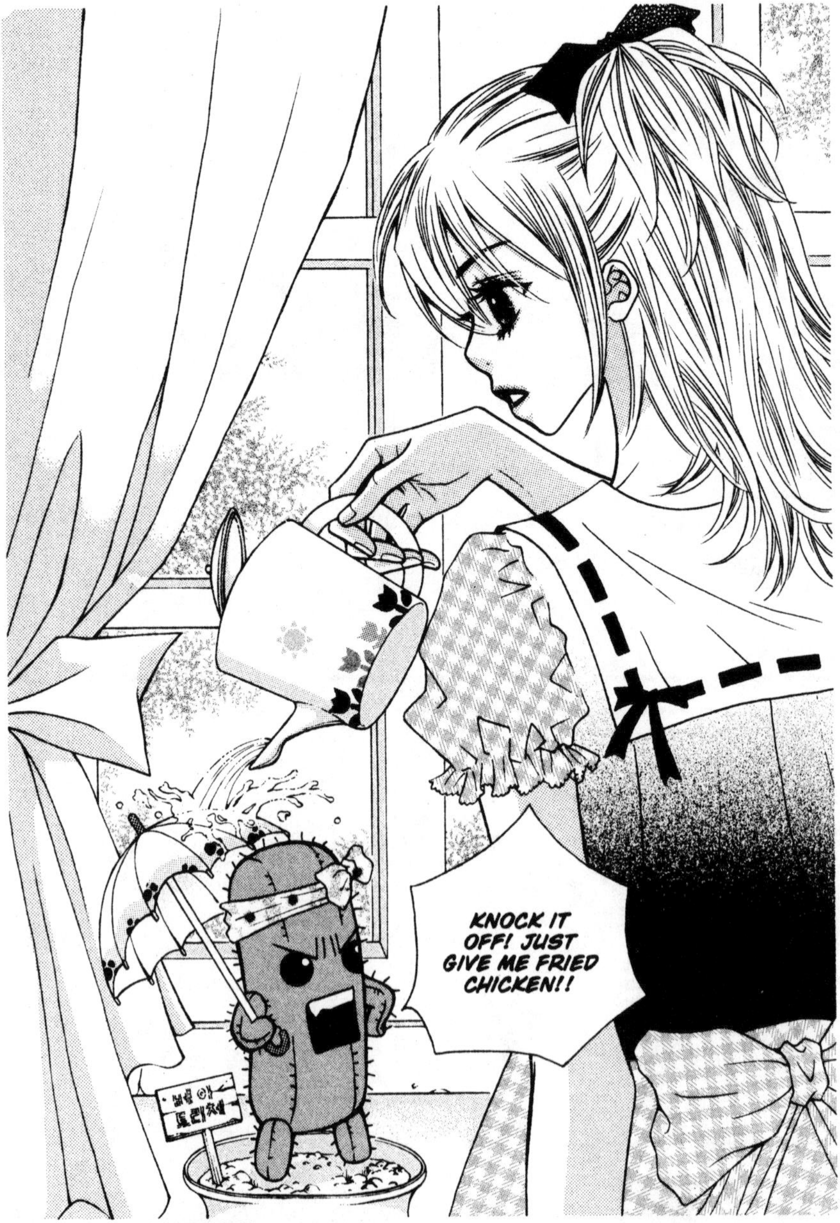
KNOCK IT OFF! JUST GIVE ME FRIED CHICKEN!!

SIGN: BEATRICE

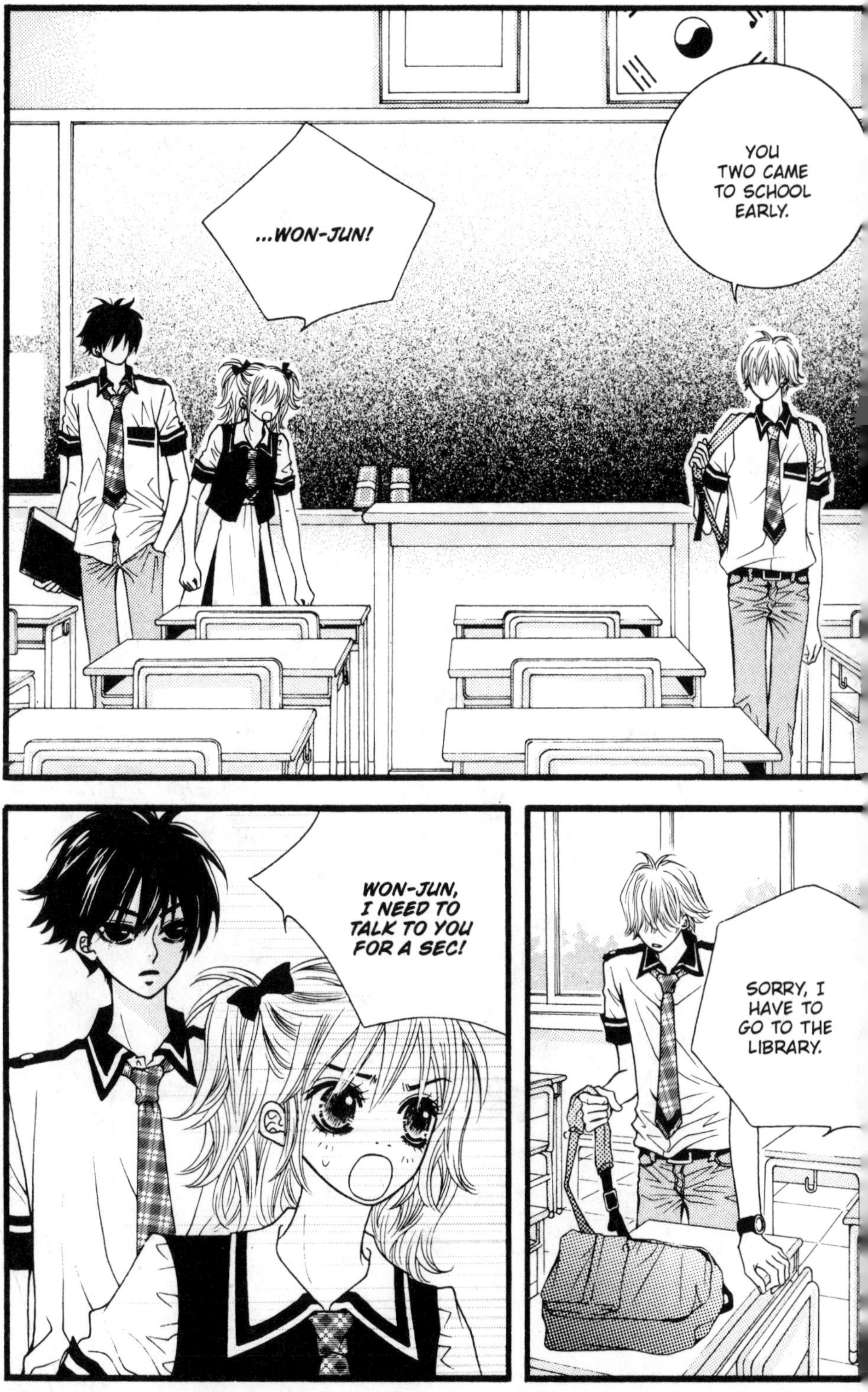
...WON-JUN!
YOU TWO CAME TO SCHOOL EARLY.
WON-JUN, I NEED TO TALK TO YOU FOR A SEC!
SORRY, I HAVE TO GO TO THE LIBRARY.

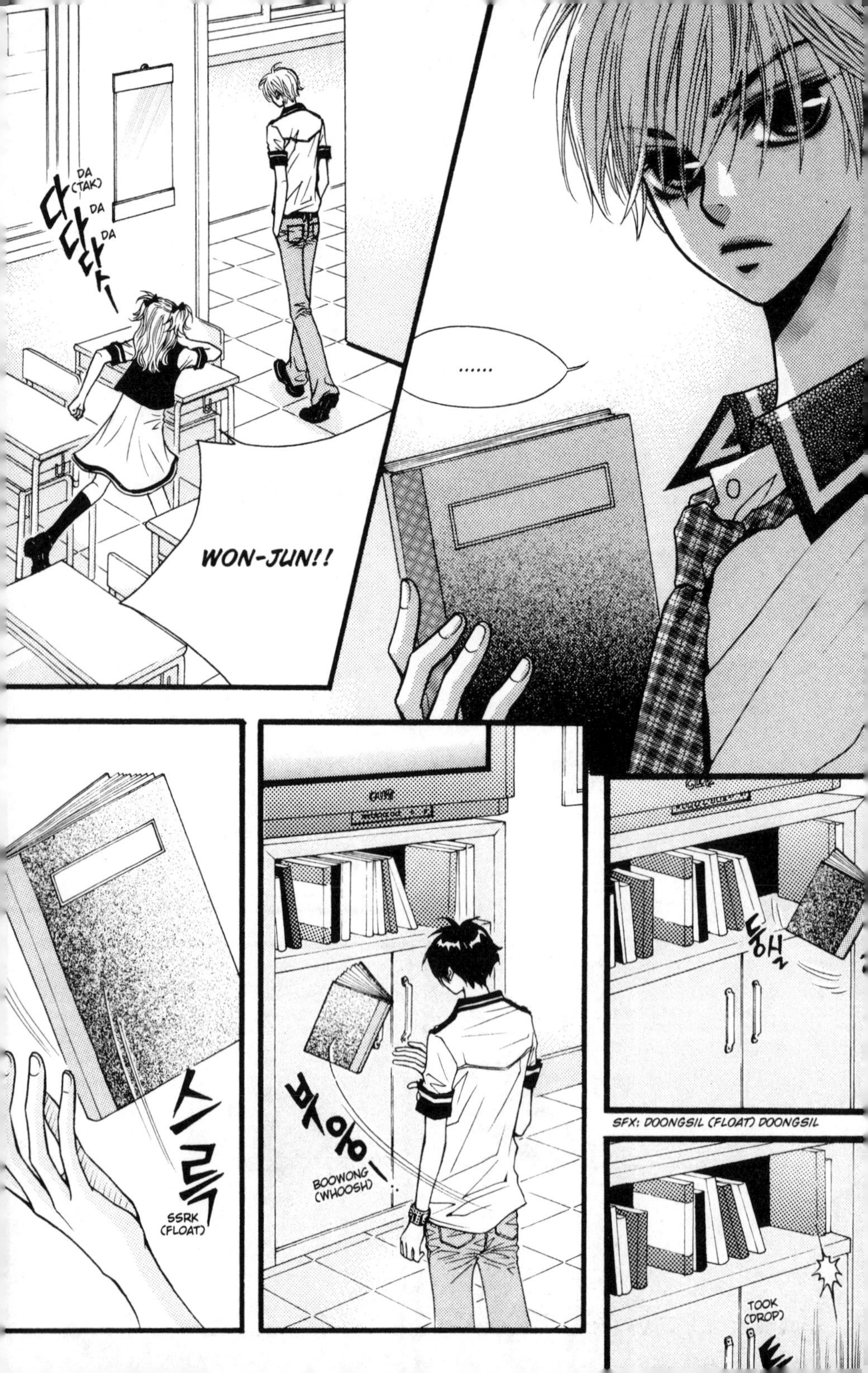
DA (TAK) DA DA
WON-JUN!!
......
SSRK (FLOAT)
BOOWONG (WHOOSH)
SFX: DOONGSIL (FLOAT) DOONGSIL
TOOK (DROP)

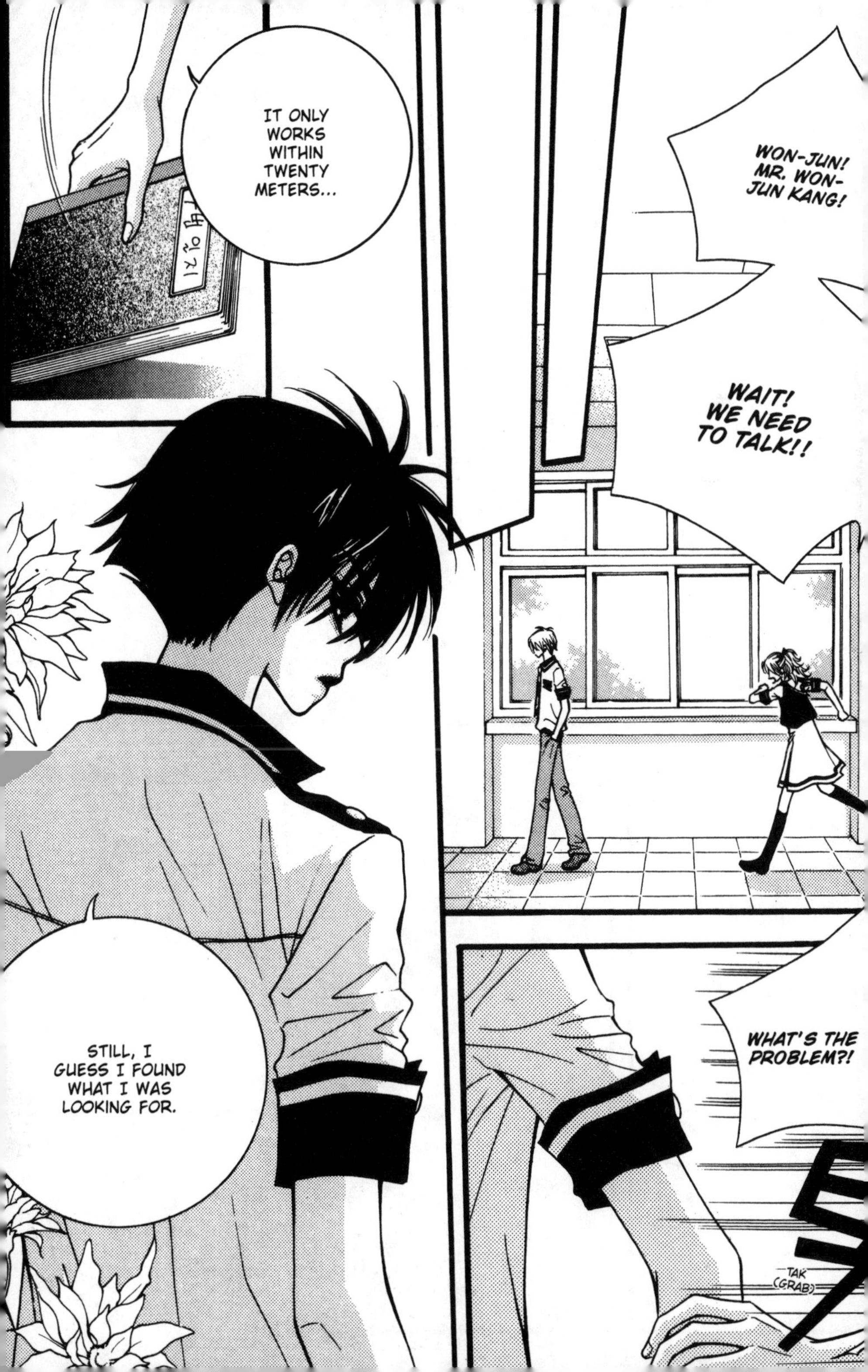
IT ONLY WORKS WITHIN TWENTY METERS...
WON-JUN! MR. WON-JUN KANG!
WAIT! WE NEED TO TALK!!
STILL, I GUESS I FOUND WHAT I WAS LOOKING FOR.
WHAT'S THE PROBLEM?!
TAK (GRAB)

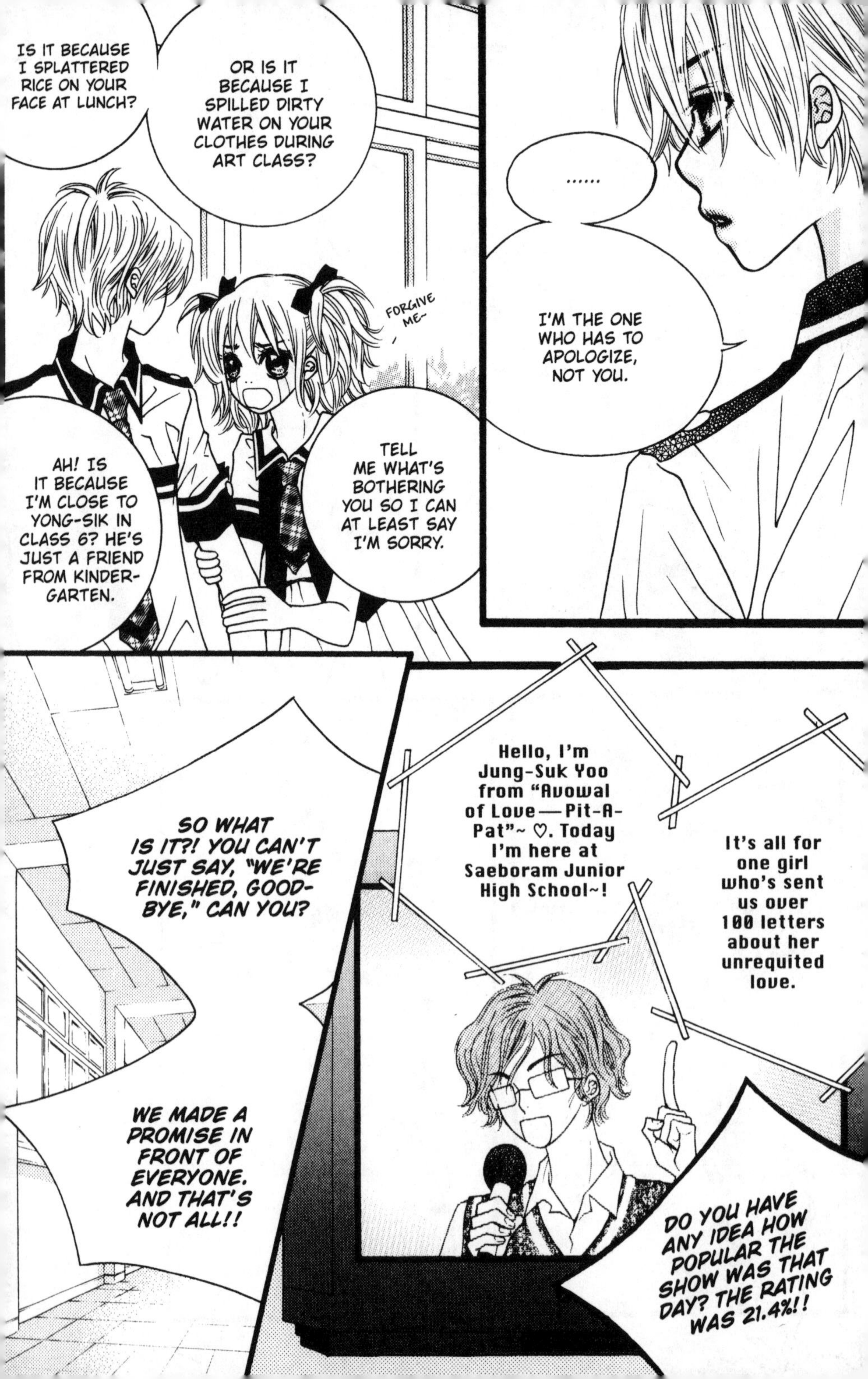
IS IT BECAUSE I SPLATTERED RICE ON YOUR FACE AT LUNCH?
OR IS IT BECAUSE I SPILLED DIRTY WATER ON YOUR CLOTHES DURING ART CLASS?
FORGIVE ME-
AH! IS IT BECAUSE I'M CLOSE TO YONG-SIK IN CLASS 6? HE'S JUST A FRIEND FROM KINDER-GARTEN.
TELL ME WHAT'S BOTHERING YOU SO I CAN AT LEAST SAY I'M SORRY.
......
I'M THE ONE WHO HAS TO APOLOGIZE, NOT YOU.
SO WHAT IS IT?! YOU CAN'T JUST SAY, "WE'RE FINISHED, GOOD-BYE," CAN YOU?
WE MADE A PROMISE IN FRONT OF EVERYONE. AND THAT'S NOT ALL!!
Hello, I'm Jung-Suk Yoo from "Avowal of Love—Pit-A-Pat"~ ♡. Today I'm here at Saeboram Junior High School~!
It's all for one girl who's sent us over 100 letters about her unrequited love.
DO YOU HAVE ANY IDEA HOW POPULAR THE SHOW WAS THAT DAY? THE RATING WAS 21.4%!!

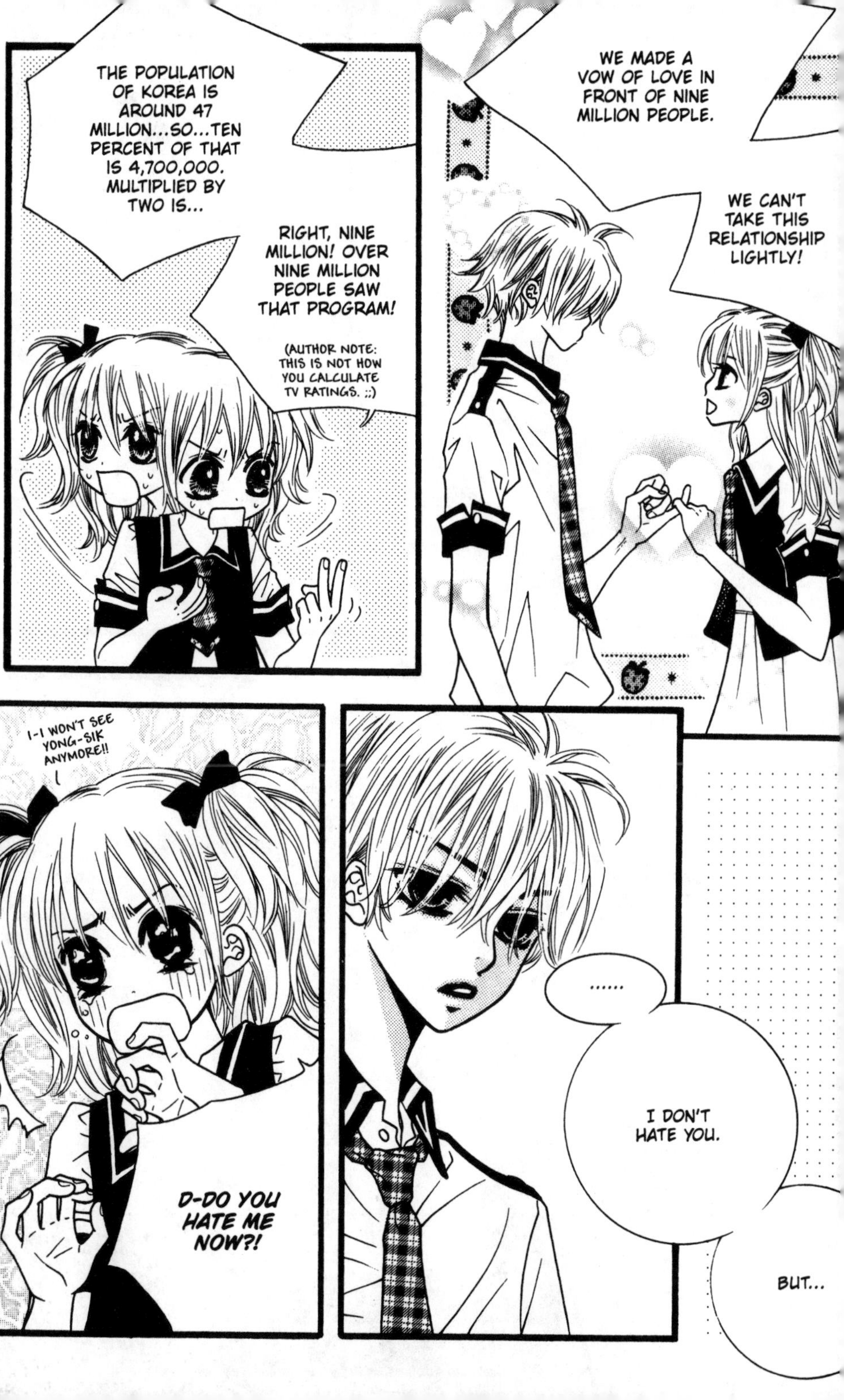
THE POPULATION OF KOREA IS AROUND 47 MILLION...SO...TEN PERCENT OF THAT IS 4,700,000. MULTIPLIED BY TWO IS...
RIGHT, NINE MILLION! OVER NINE MILLION PEOPLE SAW THAT PROGRAM!
(AUTHOR NOTE: THIS IS NOT HOW YOU CALCULATE TV RATINGS. ;;)
WE MADE A VOW OF LOVE IN FRONT OF NINE MILLION PEOPLE.
WE CAN'T TAKE THIS RELATIONSHIP LIGHTLY!
I-I WON'T SEE YONG-SIK ANYMORE!!
D-DO YOU HATE ME NOW?!
......
I DON'T HATE YOU.
BUT...

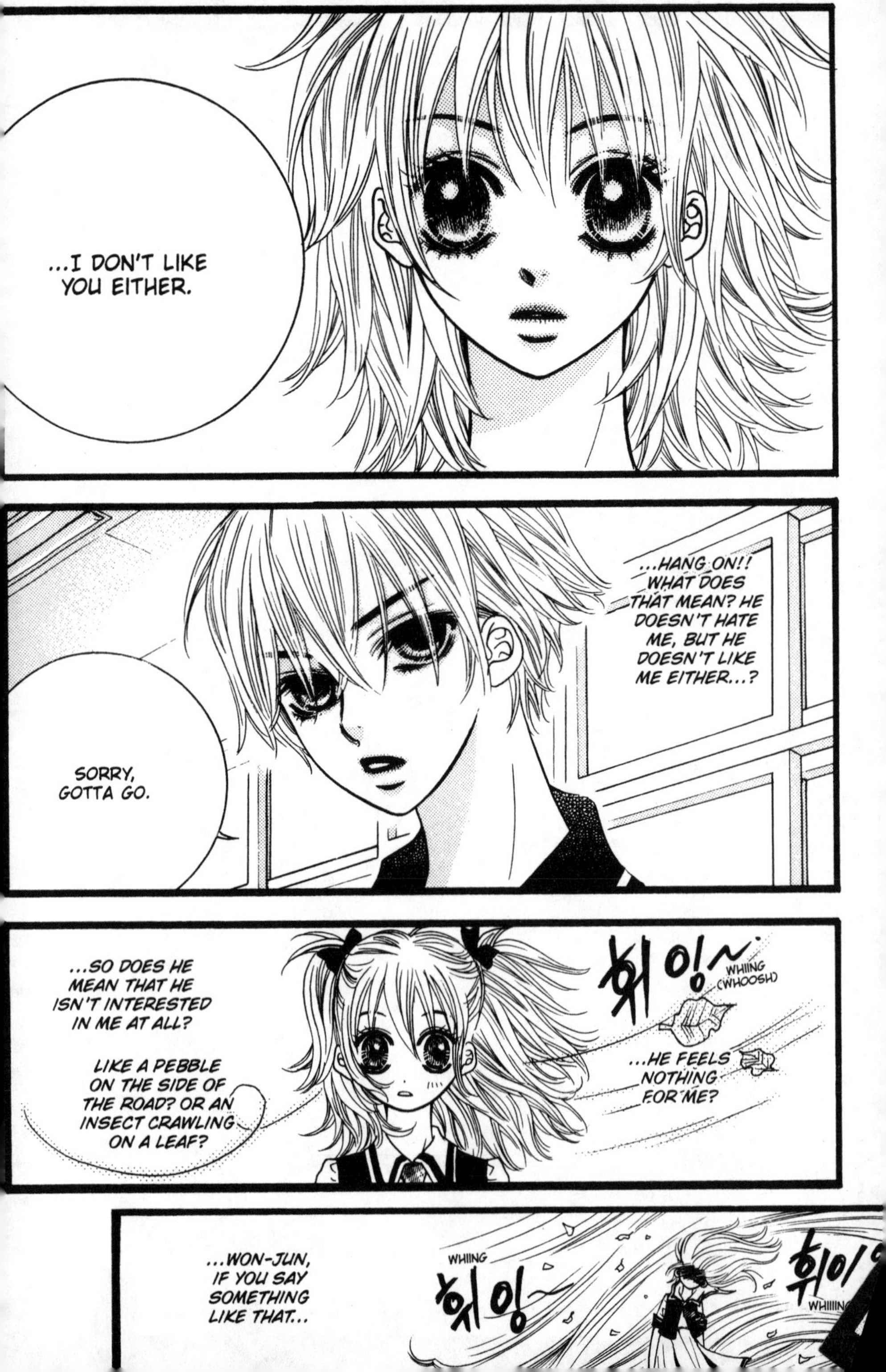
...I DON'T LIKE YOU EITHER.
SORRY, GOTTA GO.
...HANG ON!! WHAT DOES THAT MEAN? HE DOESN'T HATE ME, BUT HE DOESN'T LIKE ME EITHER...?
...SO DOES HE MEAN THAT HE ISN'T INTERESTED IN ME AT ALL?
LIKE A PEBBLE ON THE SIDE OF THE ROAD? OR AN INSECT CRAWLING ON A LEAF?
휘잉~
WHIING (WHOOSH)
...HE FEELS NOTHING FOR ME?
...WON-JUN, IF YOU SAY SOMETHING LIKE THAT...
WHIING
휘잉~

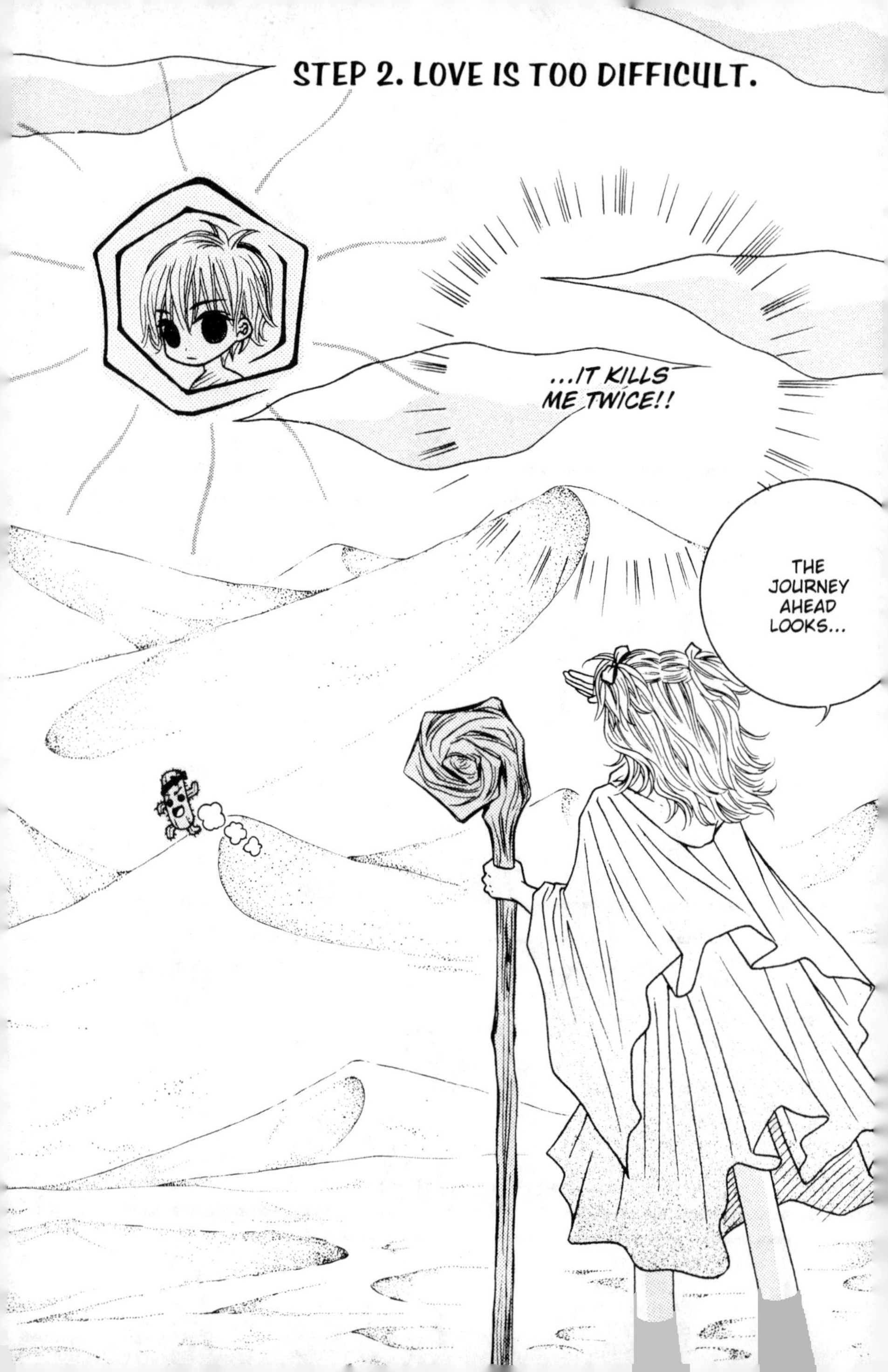
STEP 2. LOVE IS TOO DIFFICULT.
...IT KILLS ME TWICE!!
THE JOURNEY AHEAD LOOKS...

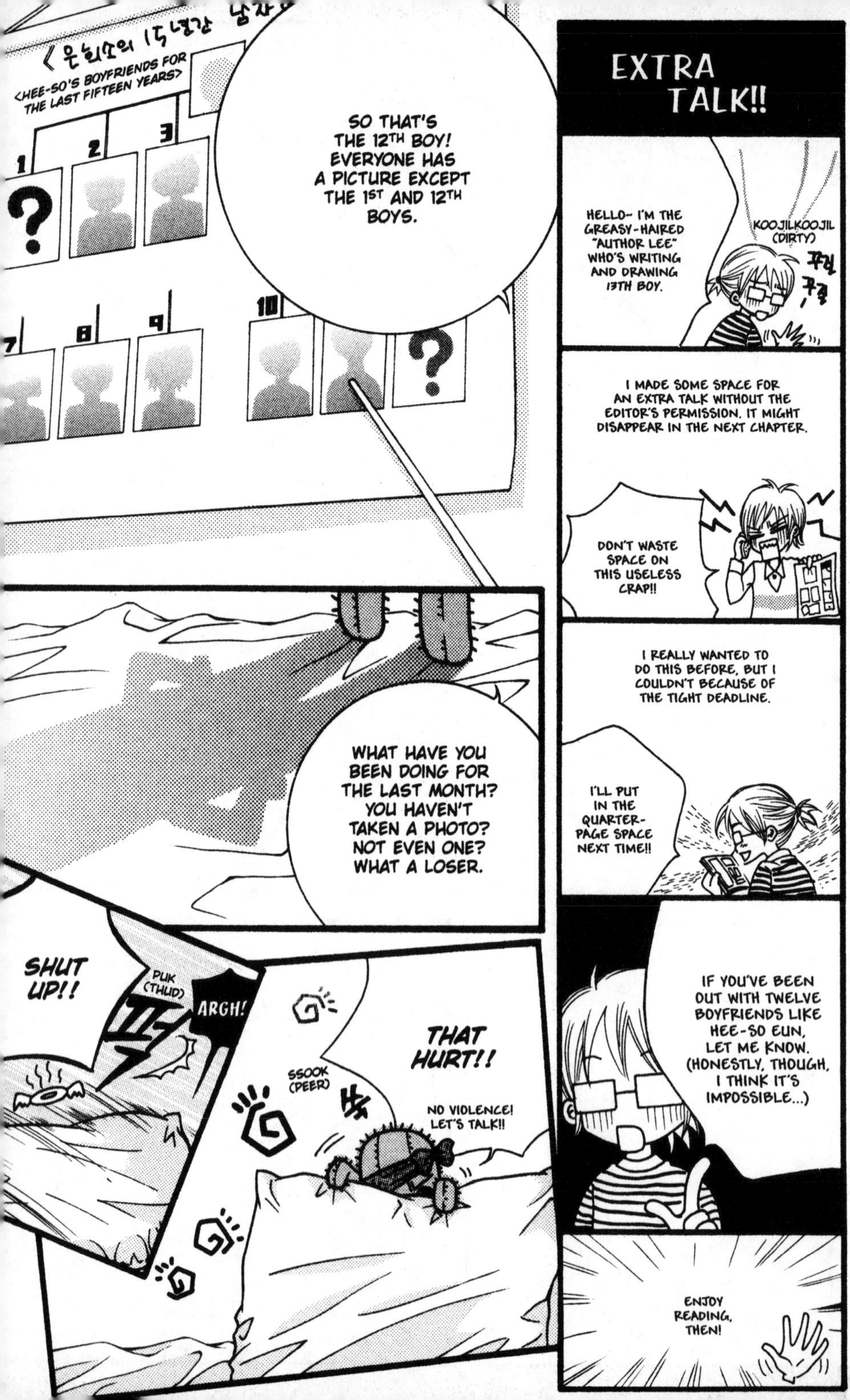

《은희소의 15년간 남자
<HEE-SO'S BOYFRIENDS FOR THE LAST FIFTEEN YEARS>
1
2
3
?
7
8
9
10
?
SO THAT'S THE 12TH BOY! EVERYONE HAS A PICTURE EXCEPT THE 1ST AND 12TH BOYS.
WHAT HAVE YOU BEEN DOING FOR THE LAST MONTH? YOU HAVEN'T TAKEN A PHOTO? NOT EVEN ONE? WHAT A LOSER.
SHUT UP!!
PUK (THUD)
ARGH!
THAT HURT!!
SSOOK (PEER)
NO VIOLENCE! LET'S TALK!!
EXTRA TALK!!
HELLO~ I'M THE GREASY-HAIRED "AUTHOR LEE" WHO'S WRITING AND DRAWING 13TH BOY.
KOOJILKOOJIL (DIRTY)
꾸질 꾸질
I MADE SOME SPACE FOR AN EXTRA TALK WITHOUT THE EDITOR'S PERMISSION. IT MIGHT DISAPPEAR IN THE NEXT CHAPTER.
DON'T WASTE SPACE ON THIS USELESS CRAP!!
I REALLY WANTED TO DO THIS BEFORE, BUT I COULDN'T BECAUSE OF THE TIGHT DEADLINE.
I'LL PUT IN THE QUARTER-PAGE SPACE NEXT TIME!!
IF YOU'VE BEEN OUT WITH TWELVE BOYFRIENDS LIKE HEE-SO EUN, LET ME KNOW. (HONESTLY, THOUGH, I THINK IT'S IMPOSSIBLE...)
ENJOY READING, THEN!

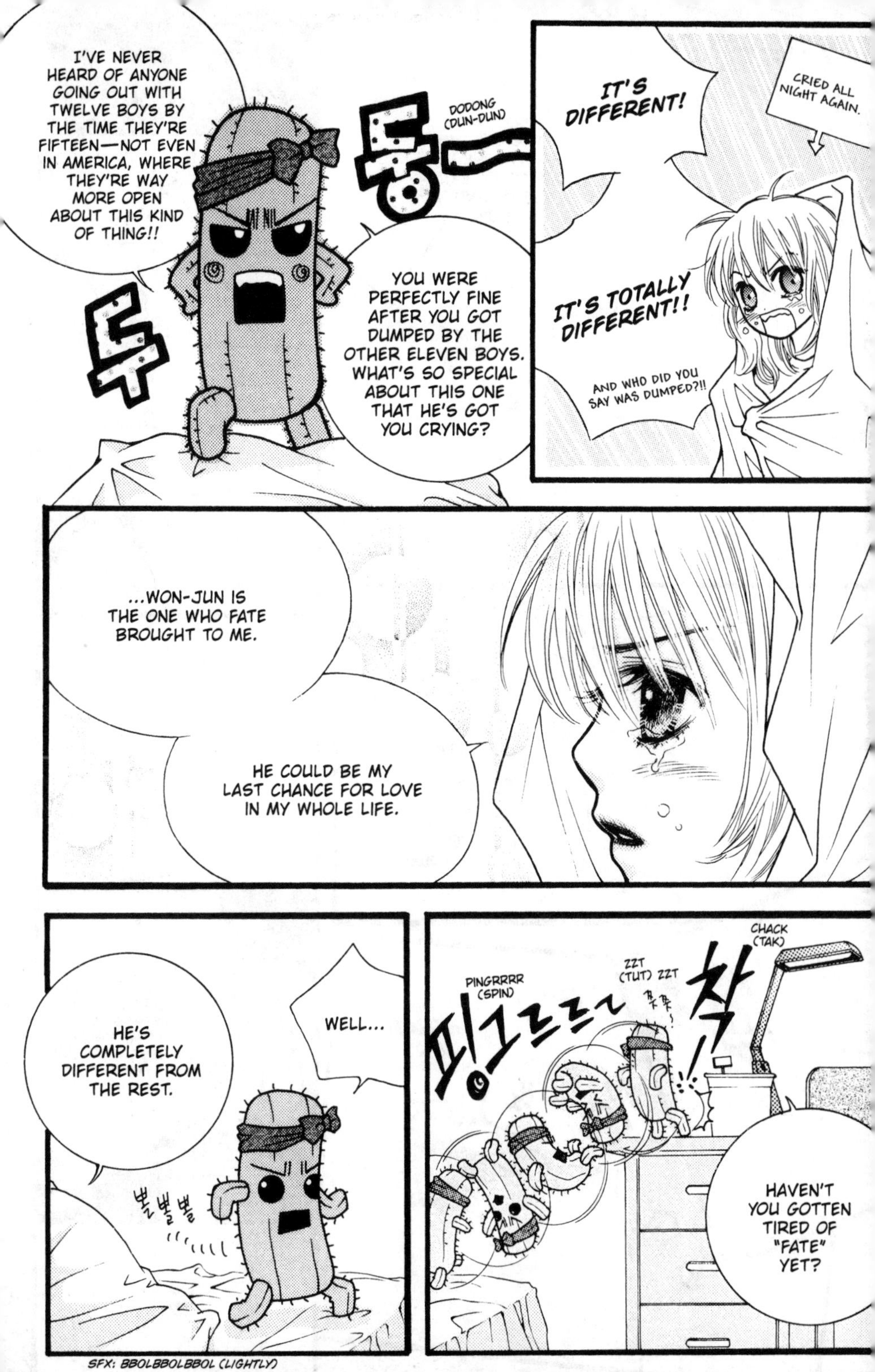
I'VE NEVER HEARD OF ANYONE GOING OUT WITH TWELVE BOYS BY THE TIME THEY'RE FIFTEEN—NOT EVEN IN AMERICA, WHERE THEY'RE WAY MORE OPEN ABOUT THIS KIND OF THING!!
DODONG (DUN-DUN)
YOU WERE PERFECTLY FINE AFTER YOU GOT DUMPED BY THE OTHER ELEVEN BOYS. WHAT'S SO SPECIAL ABOUT THIS ONE THAT HE'S GOT YOU CRYING?
CRIED ALL NIGHT AGAIN.
IT'S DIFFERENT!
IT'S TOTALLY DIFFERENT!!
AND WHO DID YOU SAY WAS DUMPED?!!
...WON-JUN IS THE ONE WHO FATE BROUGHT TO ME.
HE COULD BE MY LAST CHANCE FOR LOVE IN MY WHOLE LIFE.
HE'S COMPLETELY DIFFERENT FROM THE REST.
WELL...
뽈뽈뽈
PINGRRRR (SPIN)
ZZT (TUT) ZZT
CHACK (TAK)
HAVEN'T YOU GOTTEN TIRED OF "FATE" YET?
SFX: BBOLBBOLBBOL (LIGHTLY)

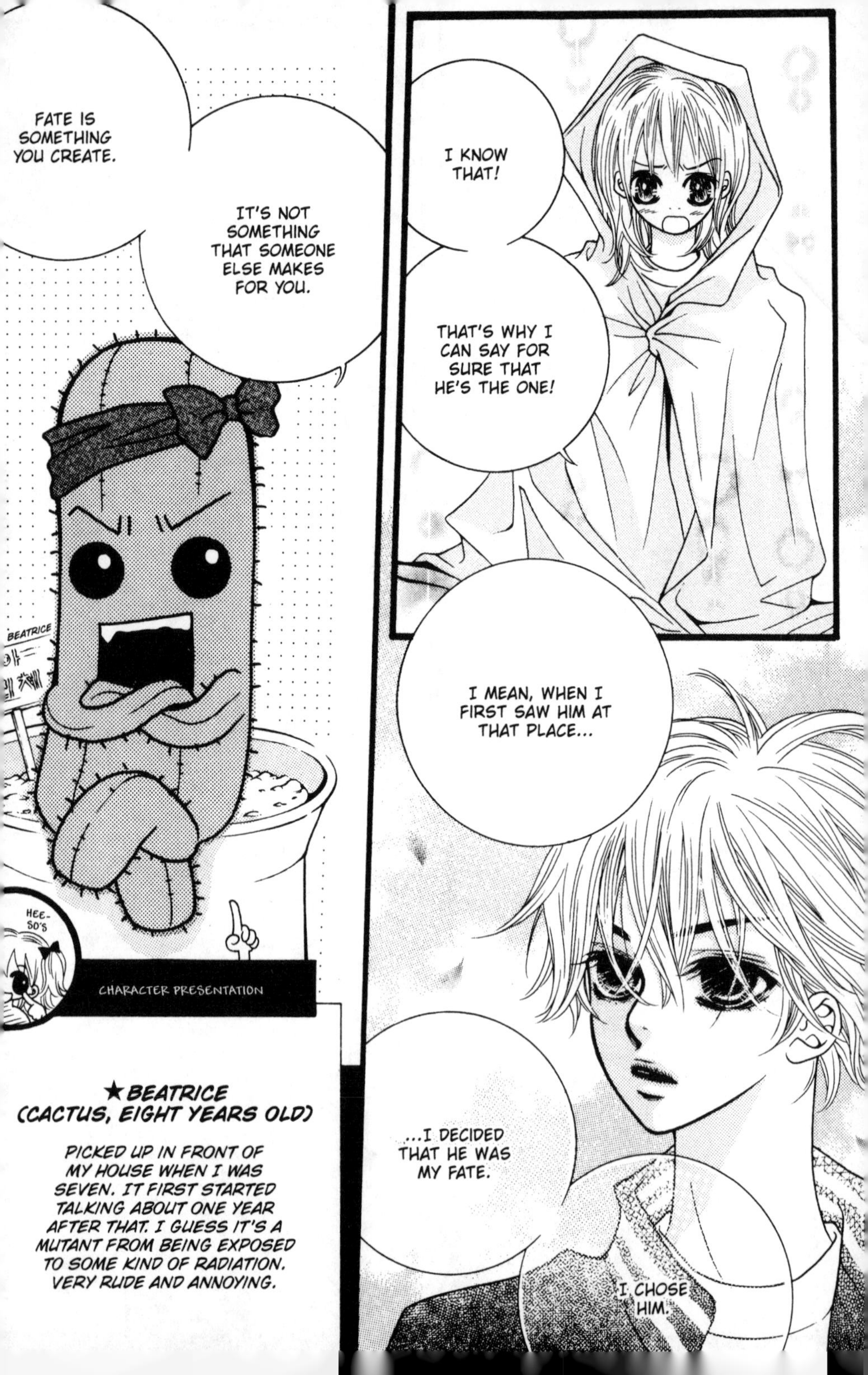
FATE IS SOMETHING YOU CREATE.
IT'S NOT SOMETHING THAT SOMEONE ELSE MAKES FOR YOU.
BEATRICE
HEE-SO'S
CHARACTER PRESENTATION
★BEATRICE (CACTUS, EIGHT YEARS OLD)
PICKED UP IN FRONT OF MY HOUSE WHEN I WAS SEVEN. IT FIRST STARTED TALKING ABOUT ONE YEAR AFTER THAT. I GUESS IT'S A MUTANT FROM BEING EXPOSED TO SOME KIND OF RADIATION. VERY RUDE AND ANNOYING.
I KNOW THAT!
THAT'S WHY I CAN SAY FOR SURE THAT HE'S THE ONE!
I MEAN, WHEN I FIRST SAW HIM AT THAT PLACE...
...I DECIDED THAT HE WAS MY FATE.
I CHOSE HIM.

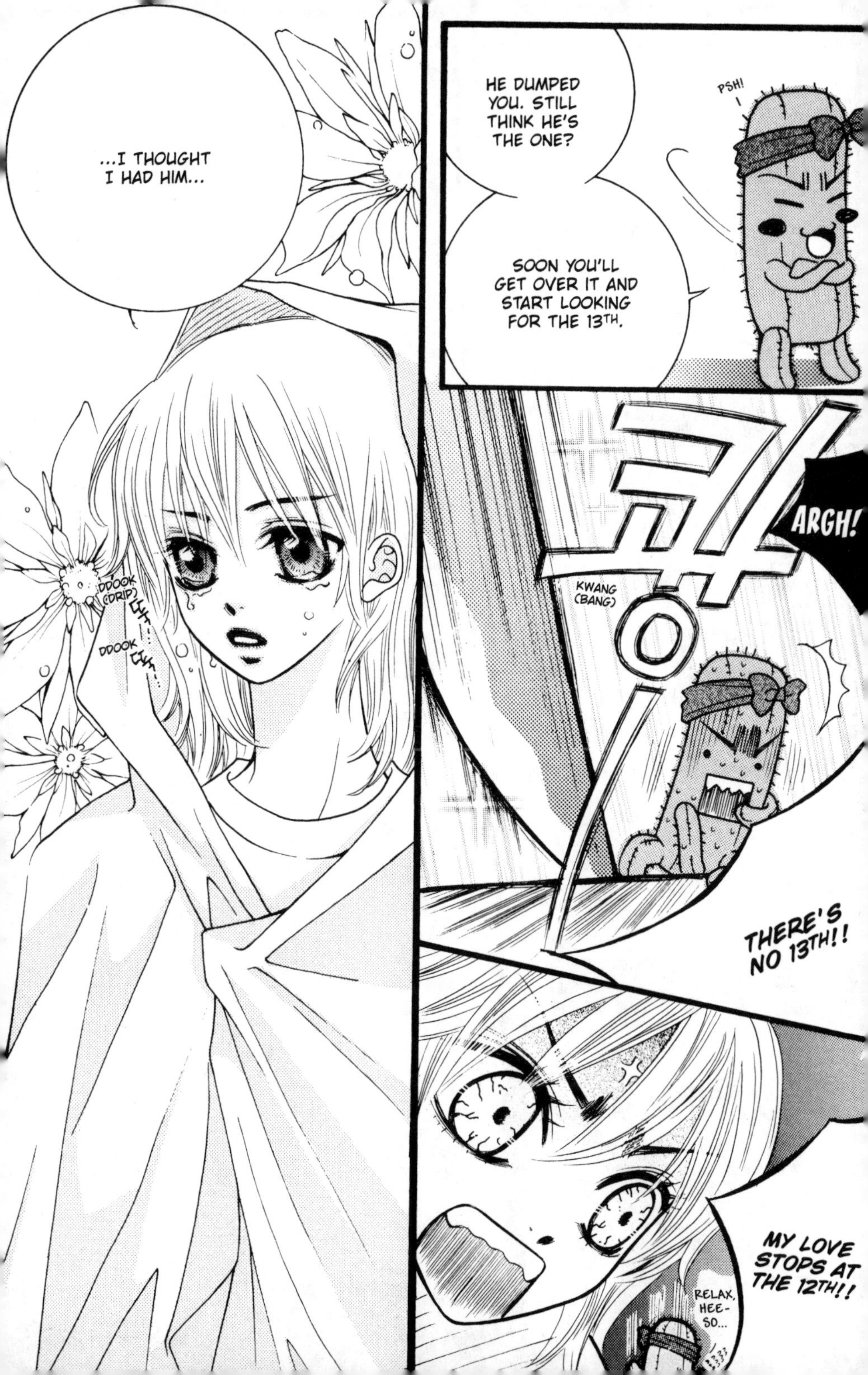

...I THOUGHT I HAD HIM...
DDOOK (DRIP)
DDOOK
HE DUMPED YOU. STILL THINK HE'S THE ONE?
PSH!
SOON YOU'LL GET OVER IT AND START LOOKING FOR THE 13TH.
KWANG (BANG)
ARGH!
THERE'S NO 13TH!!
MY LOVE STOPS AT THE 12TH!!
RELAX, HEE-SO...

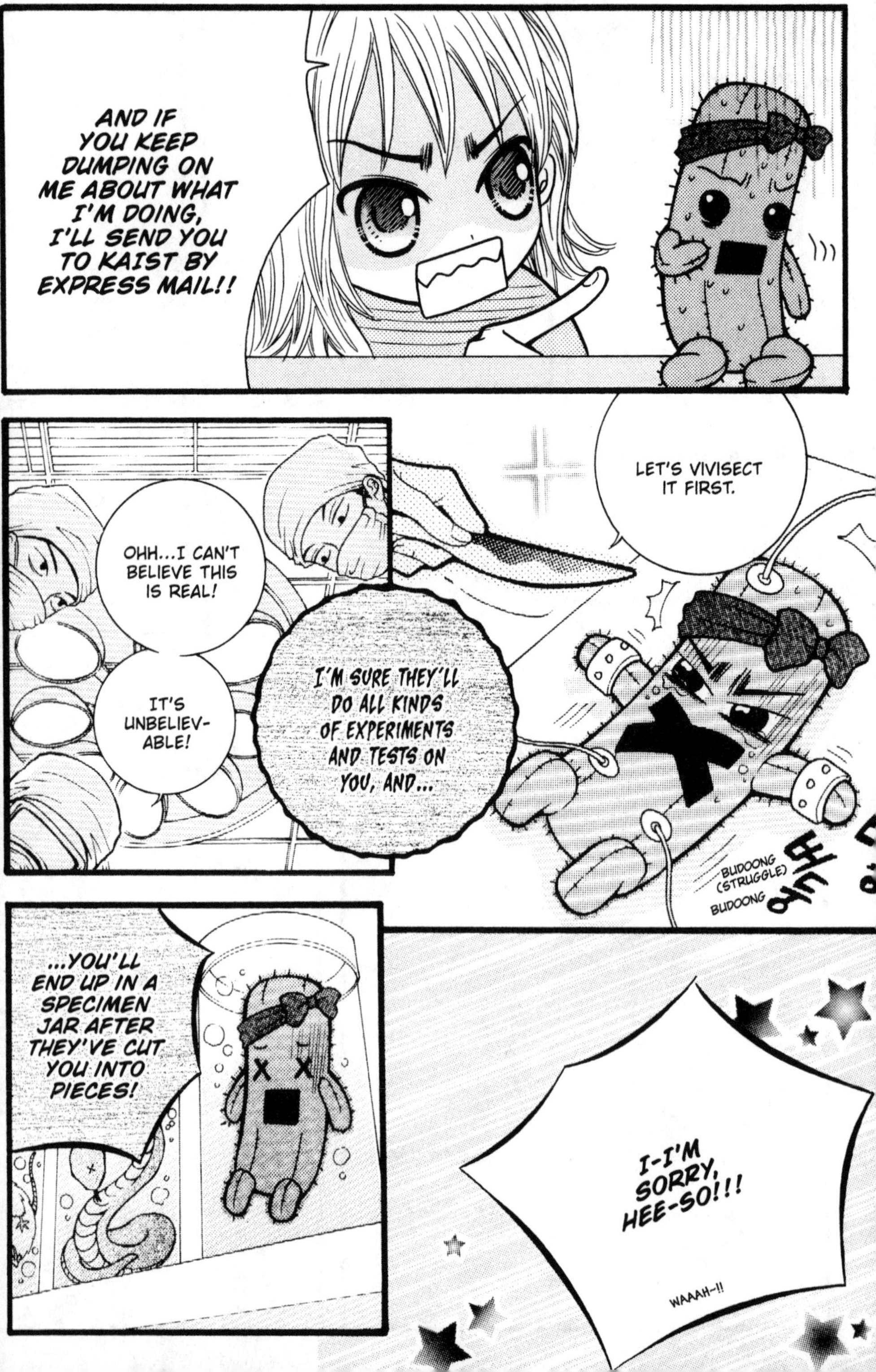
AND IF YOU KEEP DUMPING ON ME ABOUT WHAT I'M DOING, I'LL SEND YOU TO KAIST BY EXPRESS MAIL!!
OHH...I CAN'T BELIEVE THIS IS REAL!
IT'S UNBELIEV-ABLE!
I'M SURE THEY'LL DO ALL KINDS OF EXPERIMENTS AND TESTS ON YOU, AND...
LET'S VIVISECT IT FIRST.
BUDOONG (STRUGGLE) BUDOONG
...YOU'LL END UP IN A SPECIMEN JAR AFTER THEY'VE CUT YOU INTO PIECES!
I-I'M SORRY, HEE-SO!!!
WAAAH-!!

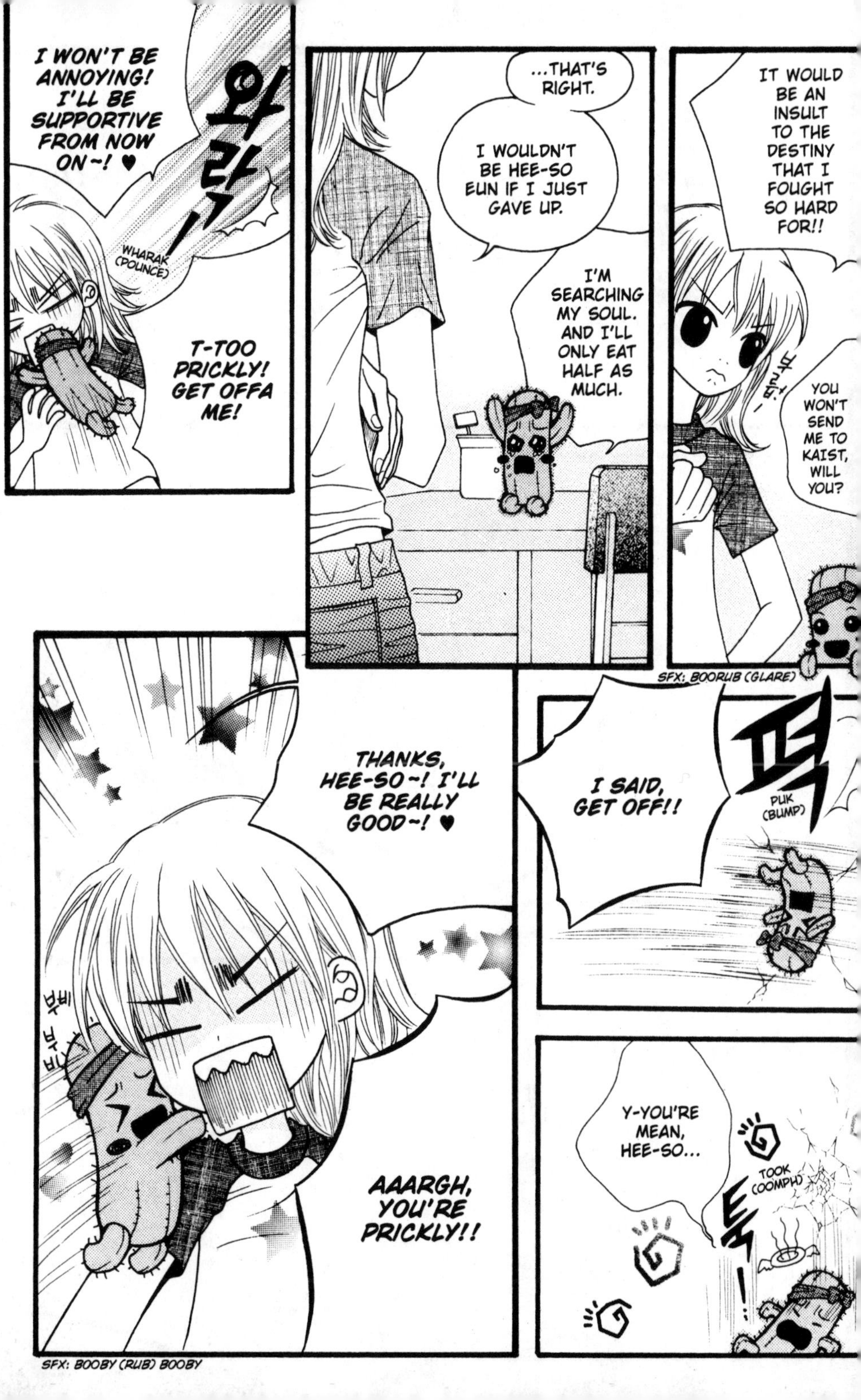
I WON'T BE ANNOYING! I'LL BE SUPPORTIVE FROM NOW ON~! ♥
와락
WHARAK (POUNCE)
T-TOO PRICKLY! GET OFFA ME!
...THAT'S RIGHT.
I WOULDN'T BE HEE-SO EUN IF I JUST GAVE UP.
I'M SEARCHING MY SOUL. AND I'LL ONLY EAT HALF AS MUCH.
IT WOULD BE AN INSULT TO THE DESTINY THAT I FOUGHT SO HARD FOR!!
YOU WON'T SEND ME TO KAIST, WILL YOU?
SFX: BOORUB (GLARE)
THANKS, HEE-SO~! I'LL BE REALLY GOOD~! ♥
AAARGH, YOU'RE PRICKLY!!
SFX: BOOBY (RUB) BOOBY
퍽
PUK (BUMP)
I SAID, GET OFF!!
Y-YOU'RE MEAN, HEE-SO...
TOOK (OOMPH)

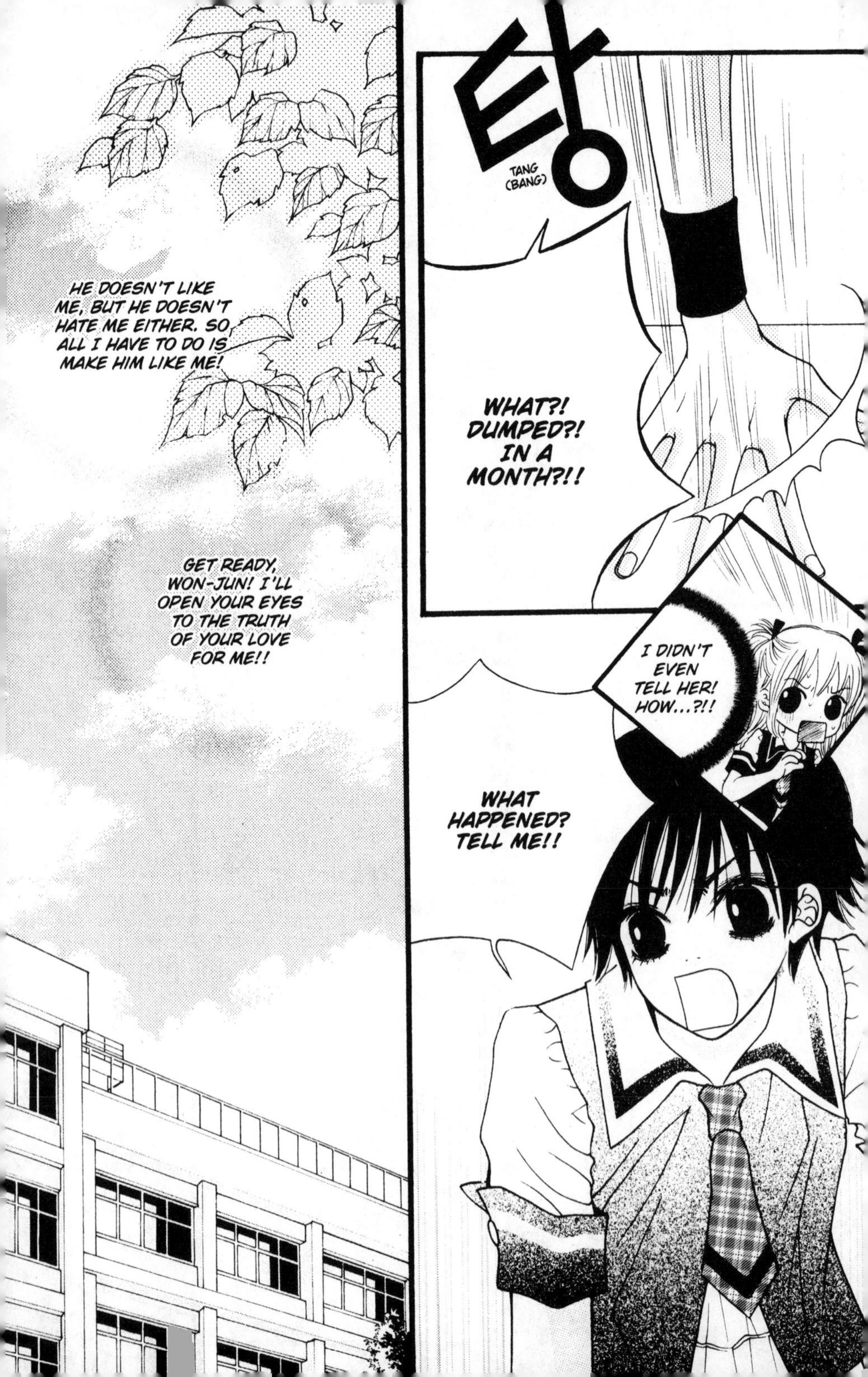

HE DOESN'T LIKE ME, BUT HE DOESN'T HATE ME EITHER. SO, ALL I HAVE TO DO IS MAKE HIM LIKE ME!
GET READY, WON-JUN! I'LL OPEN YOUR EYES TO THE TRUTH OF YOUR LOVE FOR ME!!
탕
TANG (BANG)
WHAT?! DUMPED?! IN A MONTH?!!
I DIDN'T EVEN TELL HER! HOW...?!!
WHAT HAPPENED? TELL ME!!

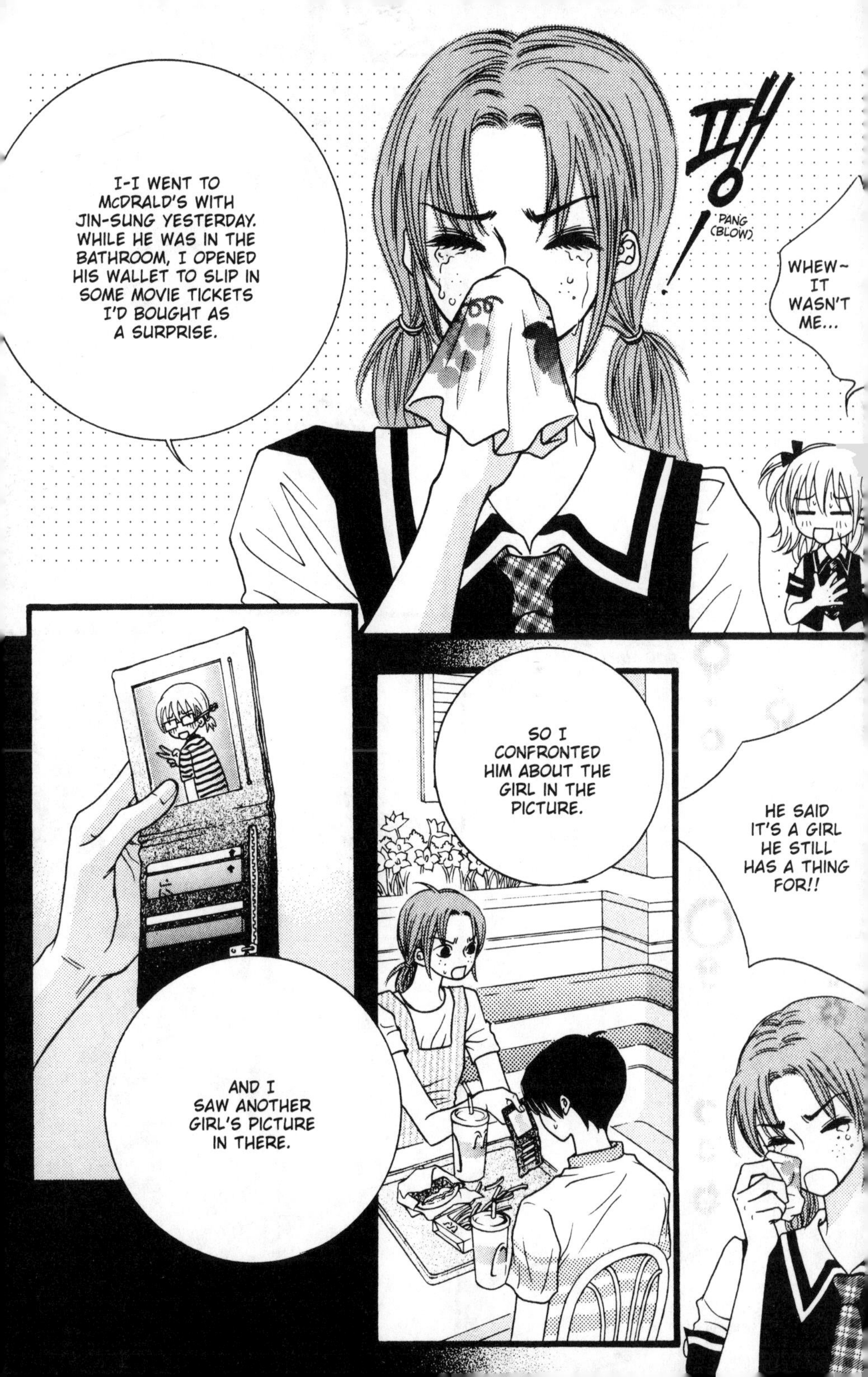
I-I WENT TO McDRALD'S WITH JIN-SUNG YESTERDAY. WHILE HE WAS IN THE BATHROOM, I OPENED HIS WALLET TO SLIP IN SOME MOVIE TICKETS I'D BOUGHT AS A SURPRISE.
팽!
PANG (BLOW)
WHEW~ IT WASN'T ME...
AND I SAW ANOTHER GIRL'S PICTURE IN THERE.
SO I CONFRONTED HIM ABOUT THE GIRL IN THE PICTURE.
HE SAID IT'S A GIRL HE STILL HAS A THING FOR!!

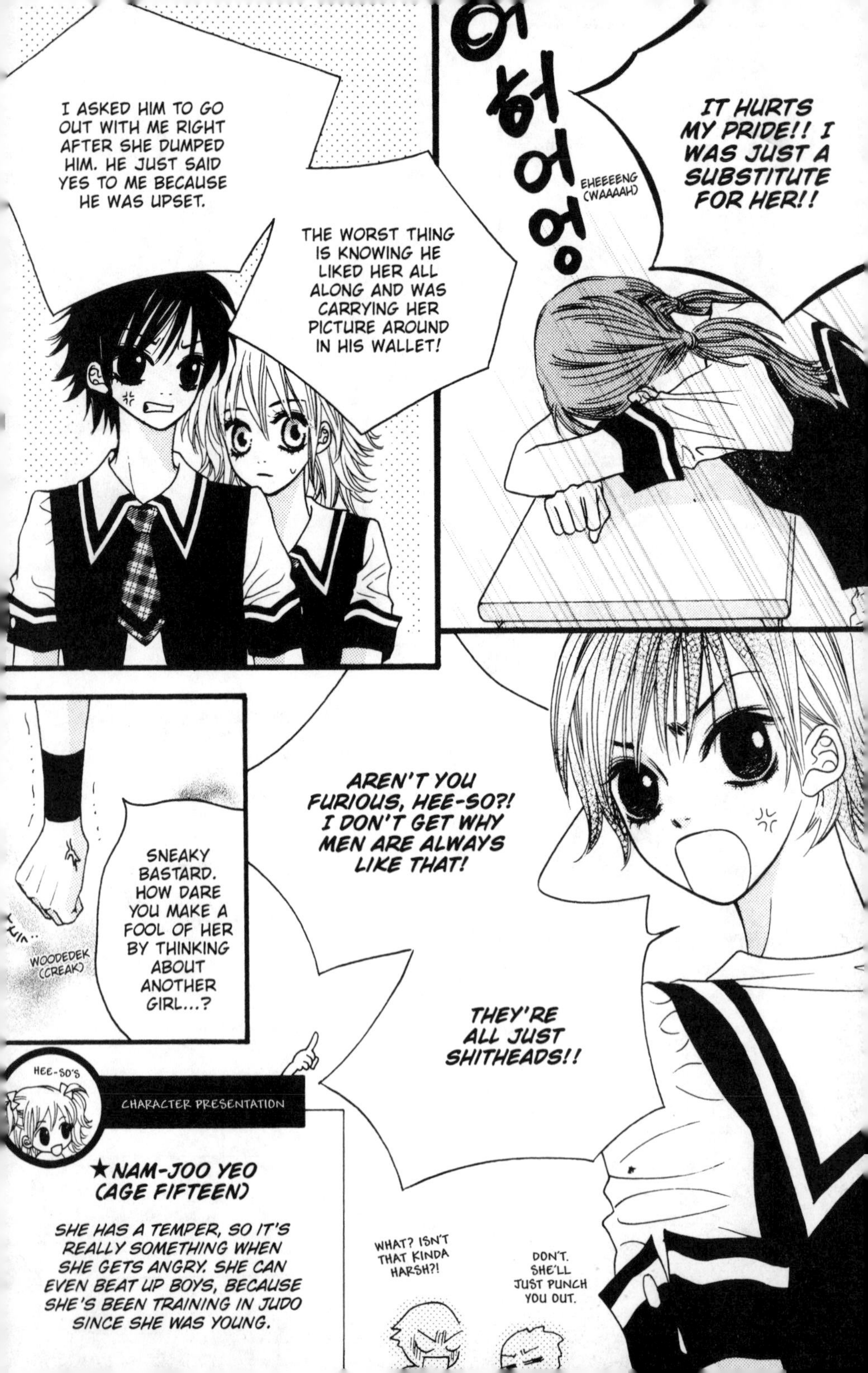

I ASKED HIM TO GO OUT WITH ME RIGHT AFTER SHE DUMPED HIM. HE JUST SAID YES TO ME BECAUSE HE WAS UPSET.
THE WORST THING IS KNOWING HE LIKED HER ALL ALONG AND WAS CARRYING HER PICTURE AROUND IN HIS WALLET!
어허어엉
EHEEEENG (WAAAAH)
IT HURTS MY PRIDE!! I WAS JUST A SUBSTITUTE FOR HER!!
SNEAKY BASTARD. HOW DARE YOU MAKE A FOOL OF HER BY THINKING ABOUT ANOTHER GIRL...?
WOODEDEK (CREAK)
AREN'T YOU FURIOUS, HEE-SO?! I DON'T GET WHY MEN ARE ALWAYS LIKE THAT!
THEY'RE ALL JUST SHITHEADS!!
HEE-SO'S
CHARACTER PRESENTATION
★NAM-JOO YEO (AGE FIFTEEN)
SHE HAS A TEMPER, SO IT'S REALLY SOMETHING WHEN SHE GETS ANGRY. SHE CAN EVEN BEAT UP BOYS, BECAUSE SHE'S BEEN TRAINING IN JUDO SINCE SHE WAS YOUNG.
WHAT? ISN'T THAT KINDA HARSH?!
DON'T. SHE'LL JUST PUNCH YOU OUT.

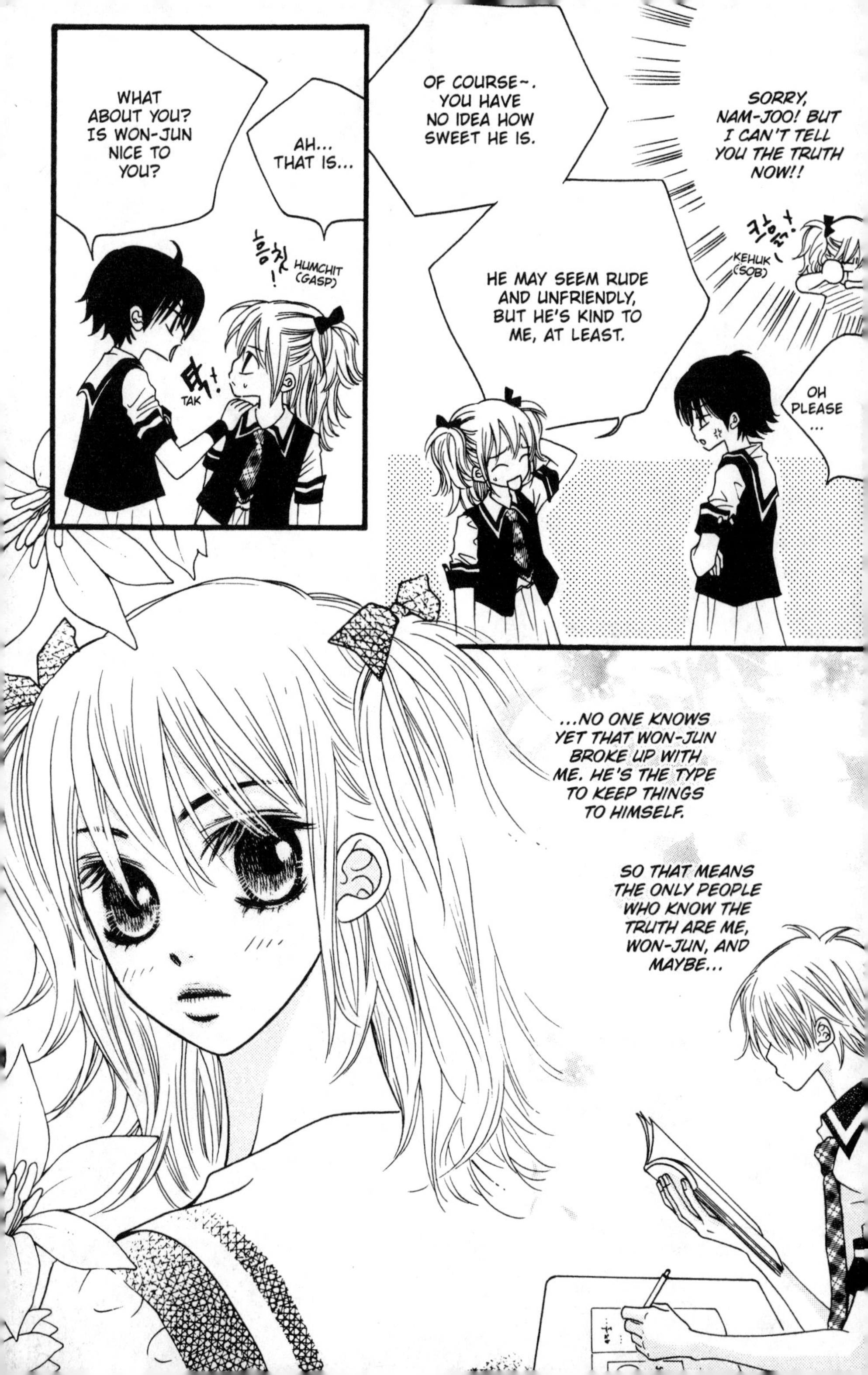
WHAT ABOUT YOU? IS WON-JUN NICE TO YOU?
AH... THAT IS...
흠칫!
HUMCHIT (GASP)
탁!
TAK
OF COURSE~. YOU HAVE NO IDEA HOW SWEET HE IS.
HE MAY SEEM RUDE AND UNFRIENDLY, BUT HE'S KIND TO ME, AT LEAST.
OH PLEASE ...
SORRY, NAM-JOO! BUT I CAN'T TELL YOU THE TRUTH NOW!!
KEHUK (SOB)
...NO ONE KNOWS YET THAT WON-JUN BROKE UP WITH ME. HE'S THE TYPE TO KEEP THINGS TO HIMSELF.
SO THAT MEANS THE ONLY PEOPLE WHO KNOW THE TRUTH ARE ME, WON-JUN, AND MAYBE...

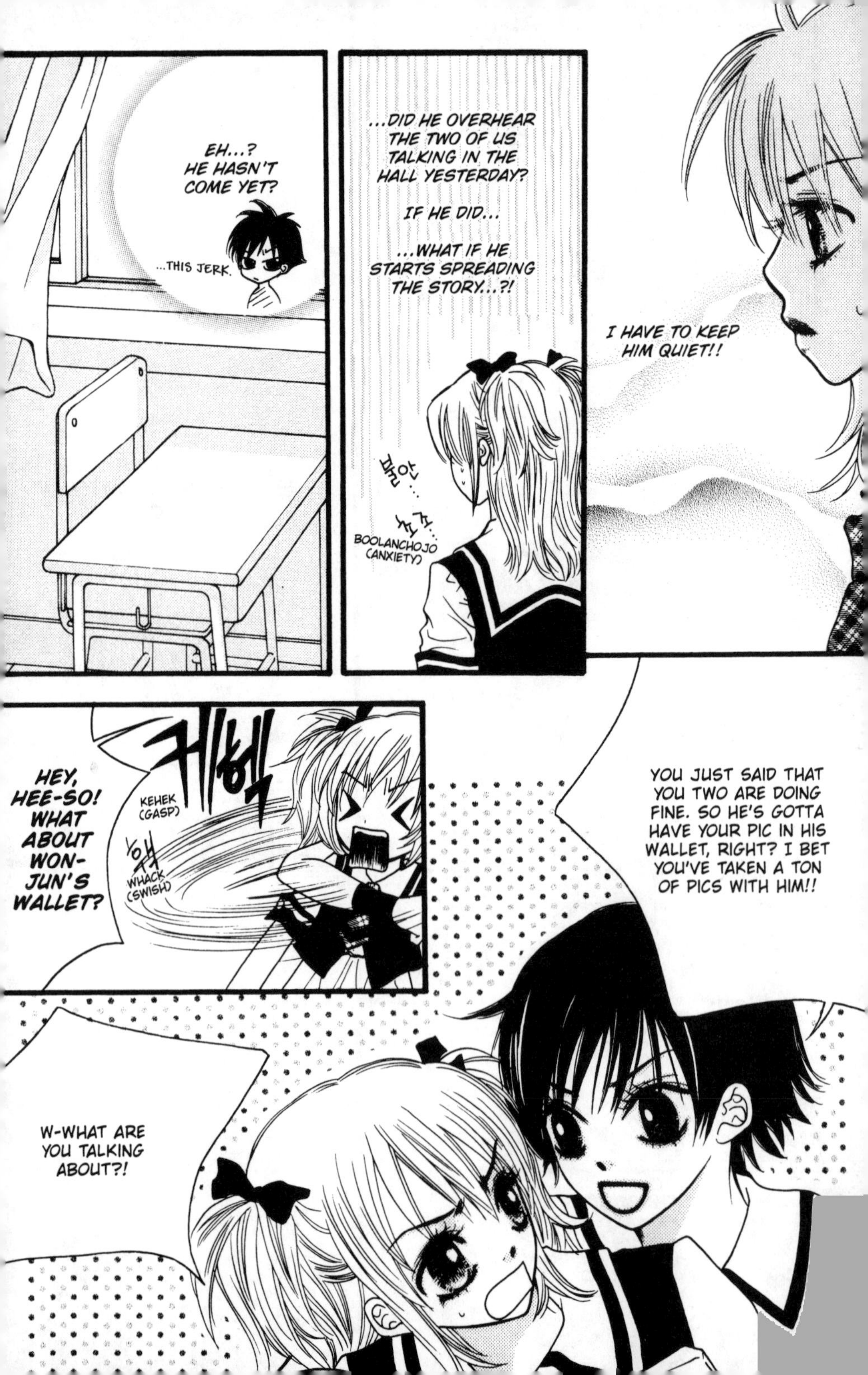
EH...? HE HASN'T COME YET?
...THIS JERK.
...DID HE OVERHEAR THE TWO OF US TALKING IN THE HALL YESTERDAY?
IF HE DID...
...WHAT IF HE STARTS SPREADING THE STORY...?!
BOOLANCHOJO (ANXIETY)
I HAVE TO KEEP HIM QUIET!!
HEY, HEE-SO! WHAT ABOUT WON-JUN'S WALLET?
케헥
KEHEK (GASP)
휙
WHACK (SWISH)
YOU JUST SAID THAT YOU TWO ARE DOING FINE. SO HE'S GOTTA HAVE YOUR PIC IN HIS WALLET, RIGHT? I BET YOU'VE TAKEN A TON OF PICS WITH HIM!!
W-WHAT ARE YOU TALKING ABOUT?!

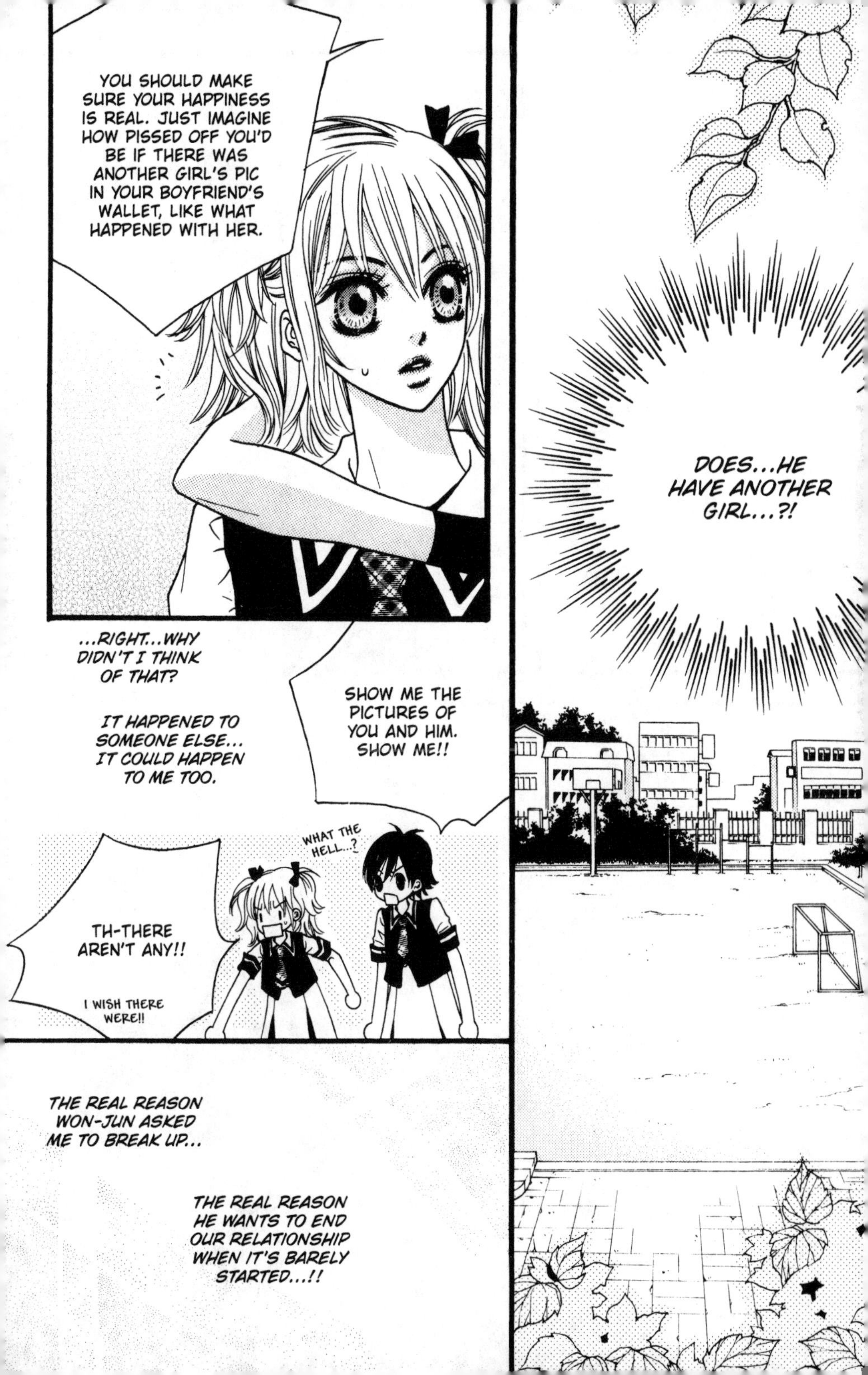
YOU SHOULD MAKE SURE YOUR HAPPINESS IS REAL. JUST IMAGINE HOW PISSED OFF YOU'D BE IF THERE WAS ANOTHER GIRL'S PIC IN YOUR BOYFRIEND'S WALLET, LIKE WHAT HAPPENED WITH HER.
...RIGHT...WHY DIDN'T I THINK OF THAT?
IT HAPPENED TO SOMEONE ELSE... IT COULD HAPPEN TO ME TOO.
SHOW ME THE PICTURES OF YOU AND HIM. SHOW ME!!
WHAT THE HELL...?
TH-THERE AREN'T ANY!!
I WISH THERE WERE!!
THE REAL REASON WON-JUN ASKED ME TO BREAK UP...
THE REAL REASON HE WANTS TO END OUR RELATIONSHIP WHEN IT'S BARELY STARTED...!!
DOES...HE HAVE ANOTHER GIRL...?!

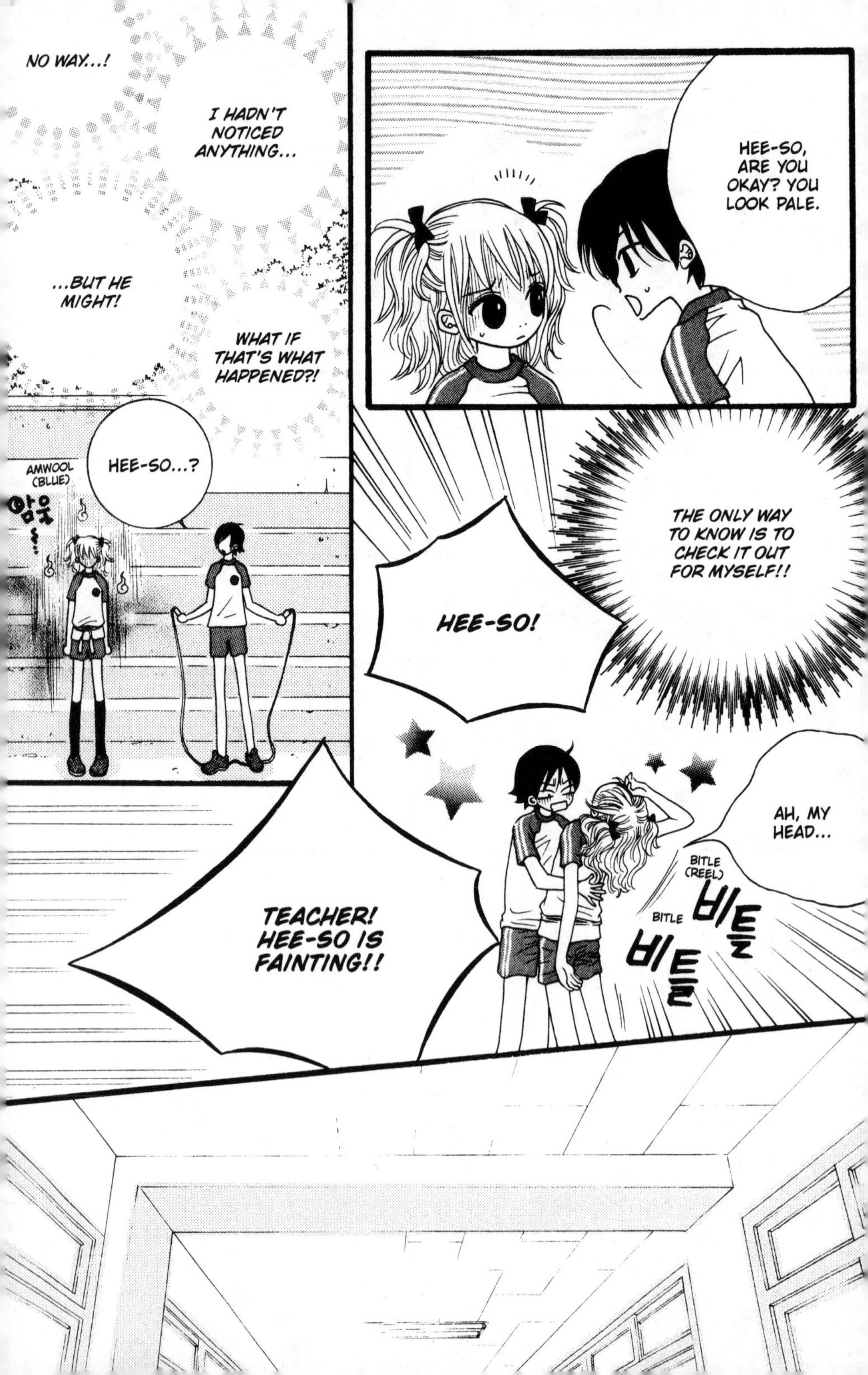
NO WAY...!
I HADN'T NOTICED ANYTHING...
...BUT HE MIGHT!
WHAT IF THAT'S WHAT HAPPENED?!
HEE-SO...?
AMWOOL (BLUE)
암울...
HEE-SO, ARE YOU OKAY? YOU LOOK PALE.
THE ONLY WAY TO KNOW IS TO CHECK IT OUT FOR MYSELF!!
HEE-SO!
TEACHER! HEE-SO IS FAINTING!!
AH, MY HEAD...
BITLE (REEL)
비틀
BITLE
비틀

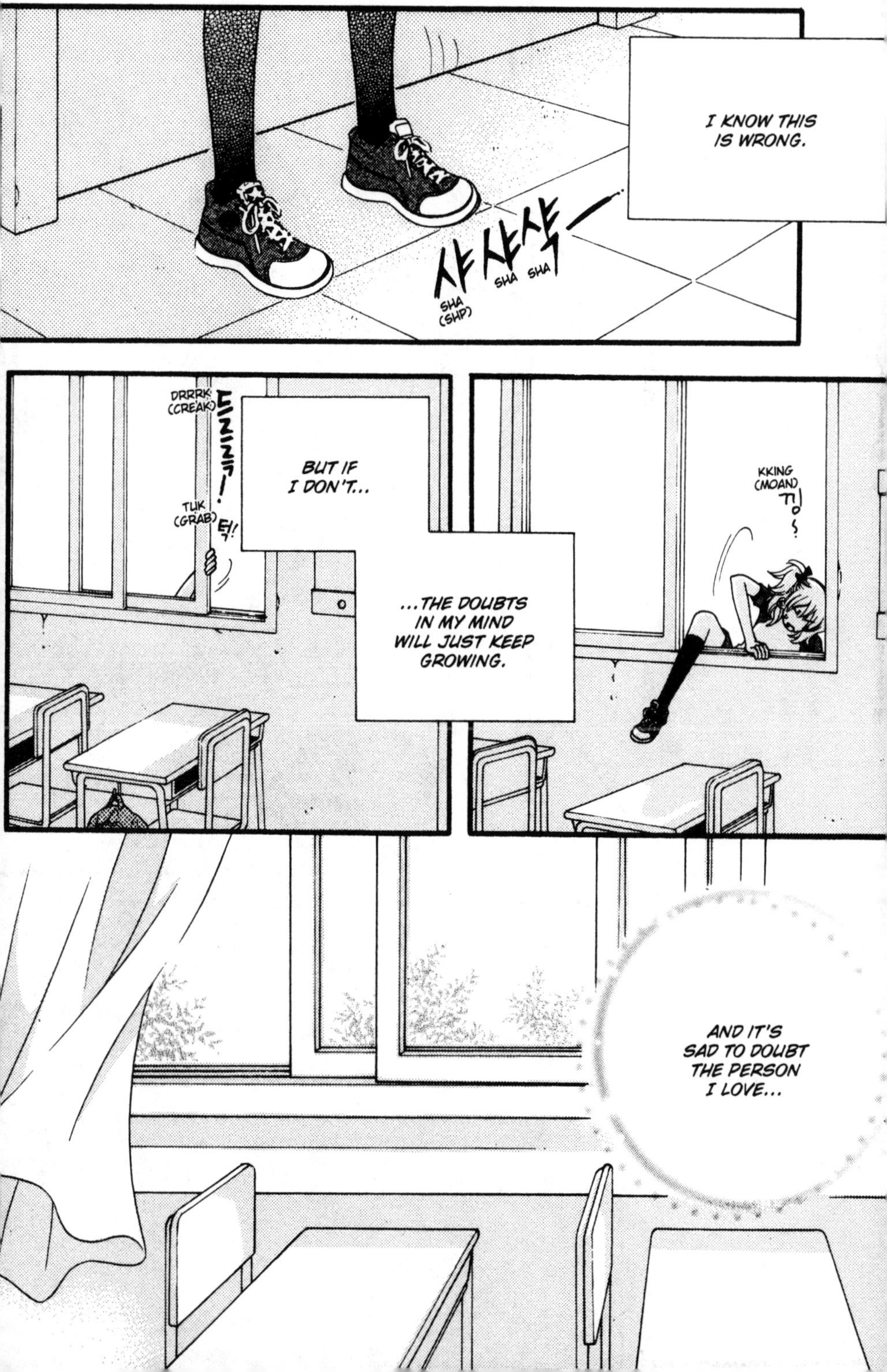
I KNOW THIS IS WRONG.
샤샤샥—
SHA (SHP)
SHA SHA
DRRRK (CREAK)
TUK (GRAB)
턱!
BUT IF I DON'T...
...THE DOUBTS IN MY MIND WILL JUST KEEP GROWING.
KKING (MOAN)
AND IT'S SAD TO DOUBT THE PERSON I LOVE...

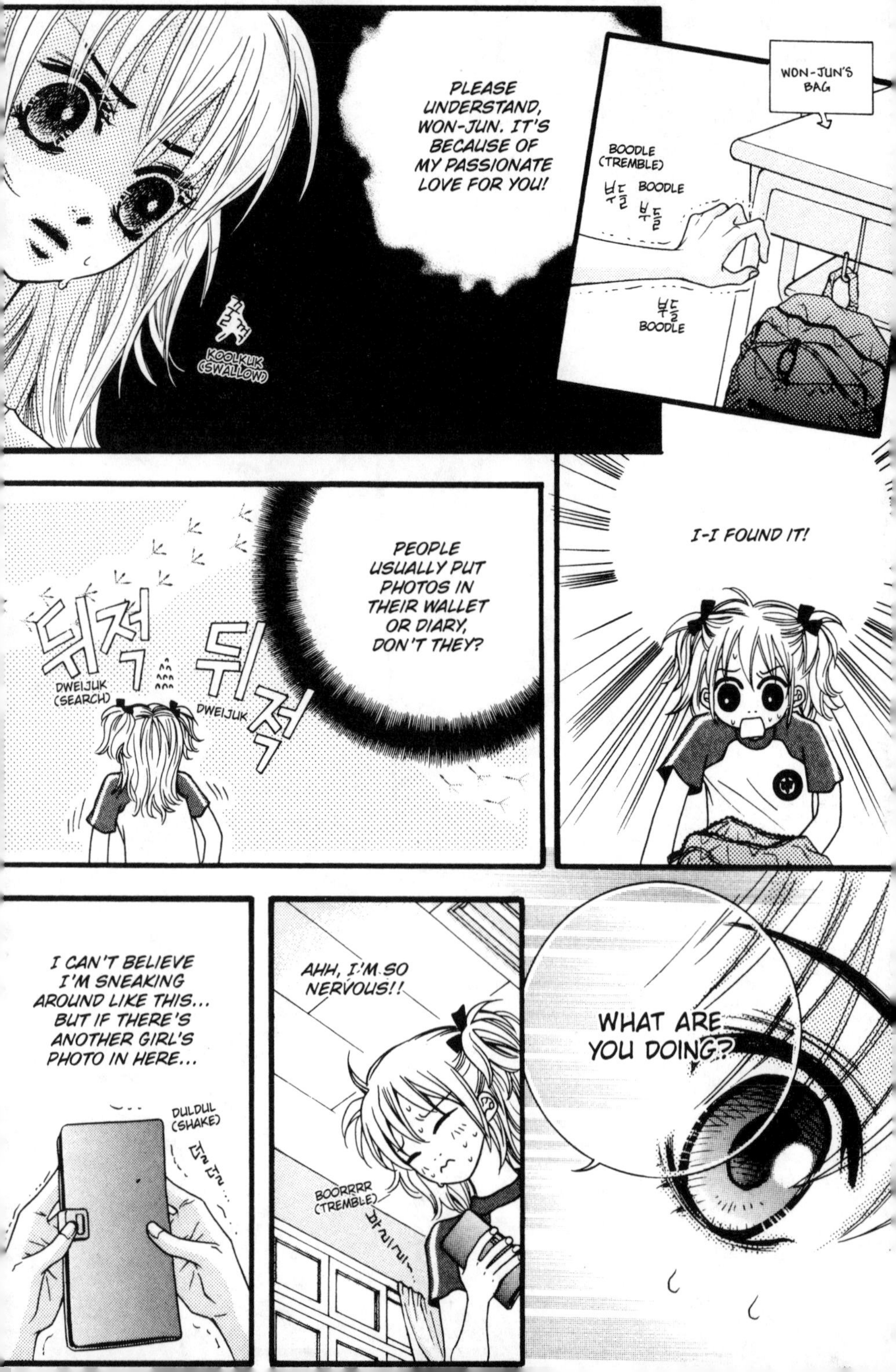
PLEASE UNDERSTAND, WON-JUN. IT'S BECAUSE OF MY PASSIONATE LOVE FOR YOU!
꿀꺽
KOOLKUK (SWALLOW)
WON-JUN'S BAG
BOODLE (TREMBLE)
부들
BOODLE
부들
부들
BOODLE
뒤적
DWEIJUK (SEARCH)
뒤적
DWEIJUK
PEOPLE USUALLY PUT PHOTOS IN THEIR WALLET OR DIARY, DON'T THEY?
I-I FOUND IT!
I CAN'T BELIEVE I'M SNEAKING AROUND LIKE THIS... BUT IF THERE'S ANOTHER GIRL'S PHOTO IN HERE...
DULDUL (SHAKE)
덜덜...
AHH, I'M SO NERVOUS!!
BOORRRR (TREMBLE)
WHAT ARE YOU DOING?

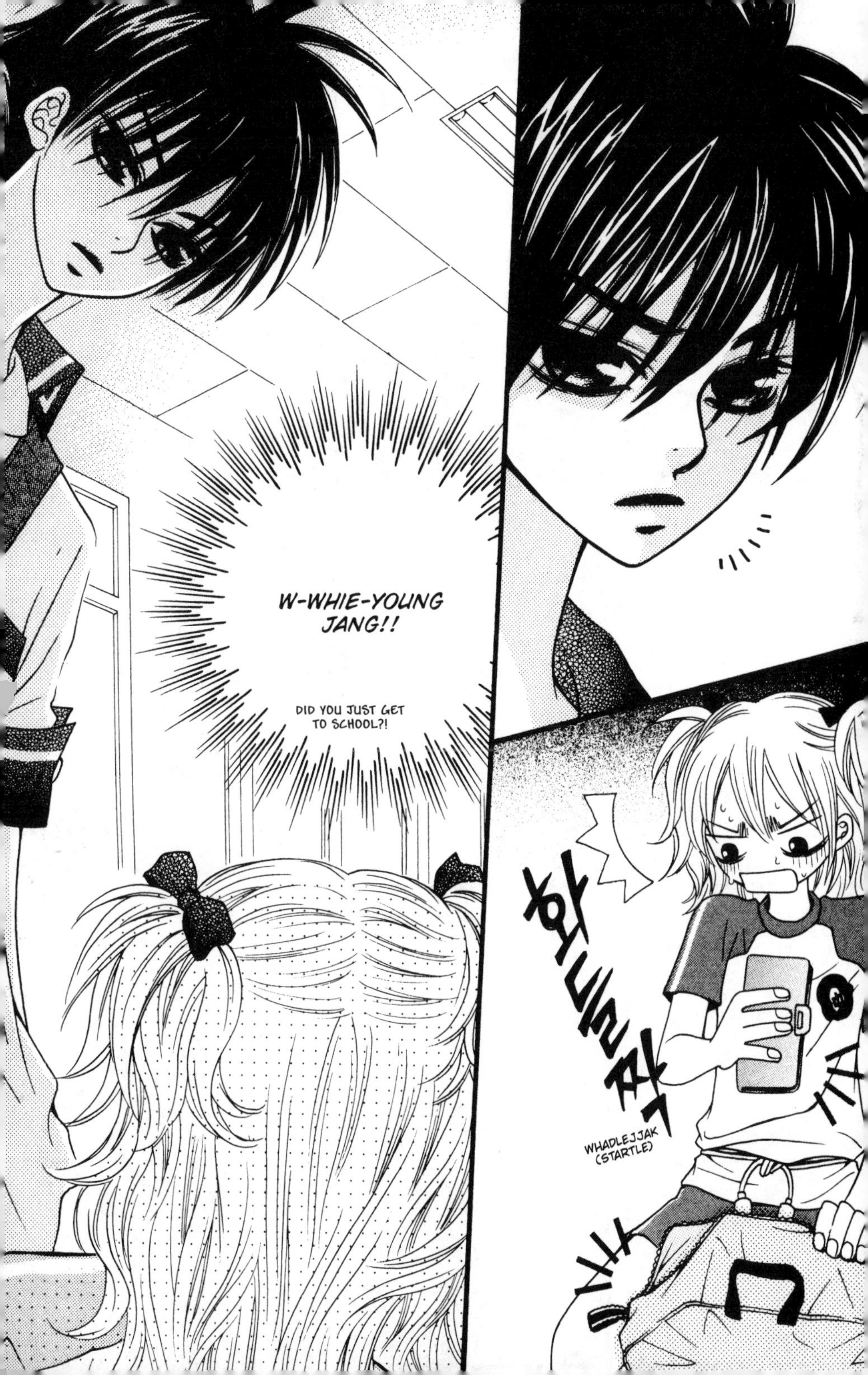
W-WHIE-YOUNG JANG!!
DID YOU JUST GET TO SCHOOL?!
WHADLEJJAK (STARTLE)

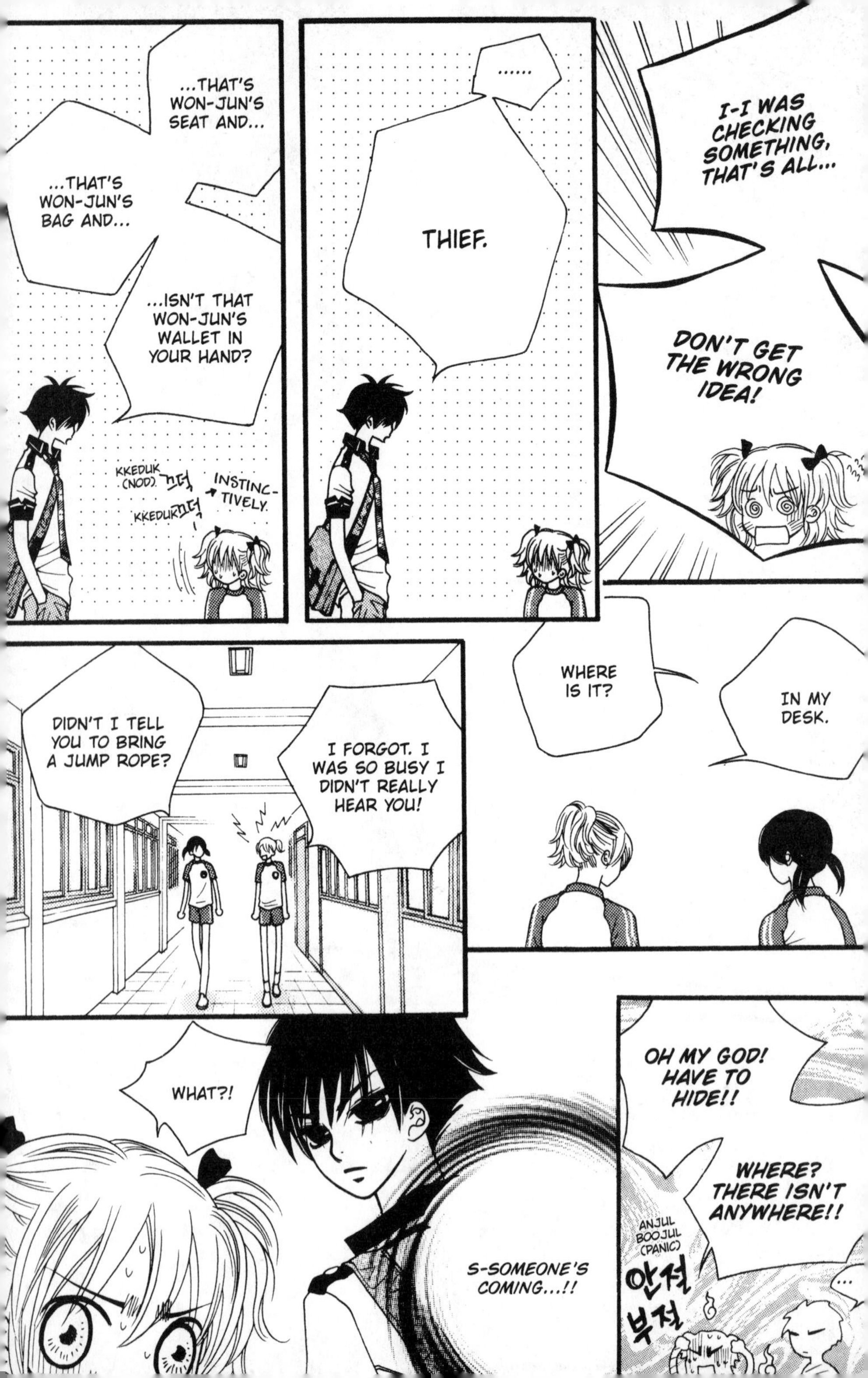

...THAT'S WON-JUN'S SEAT AND...
...THAT'S WON-JUN'S BAG AND...
...ISN'T THAT WON-JUN'S WALLET IN YOUR HAND?
KKEDUK (NOD) 끄덕
KKEDUK 끄덕
INSTINCTIVELY.
......
THIEF.
I-I WAS CHECKING SOMETHING, THAT'S ALL...
DON'T GET THE WRONG IDEA!
DIDN'T I TELL YOU TO BRING A JUMP ROPE?
I FORGOT. I WAS SO BUSY I DIDN'T REALLY HEAR YOU!
WHERE IS IT?
IN MY DESK.
WHAT?!
S-SOMEONE'S COMING...!!
OH MY GOD! HAVE TO HIDE!!
WHERE? THERE ISN'T ANYWHERE!!
ANJUL BOOJUL (PANIC)
안절 부절
...

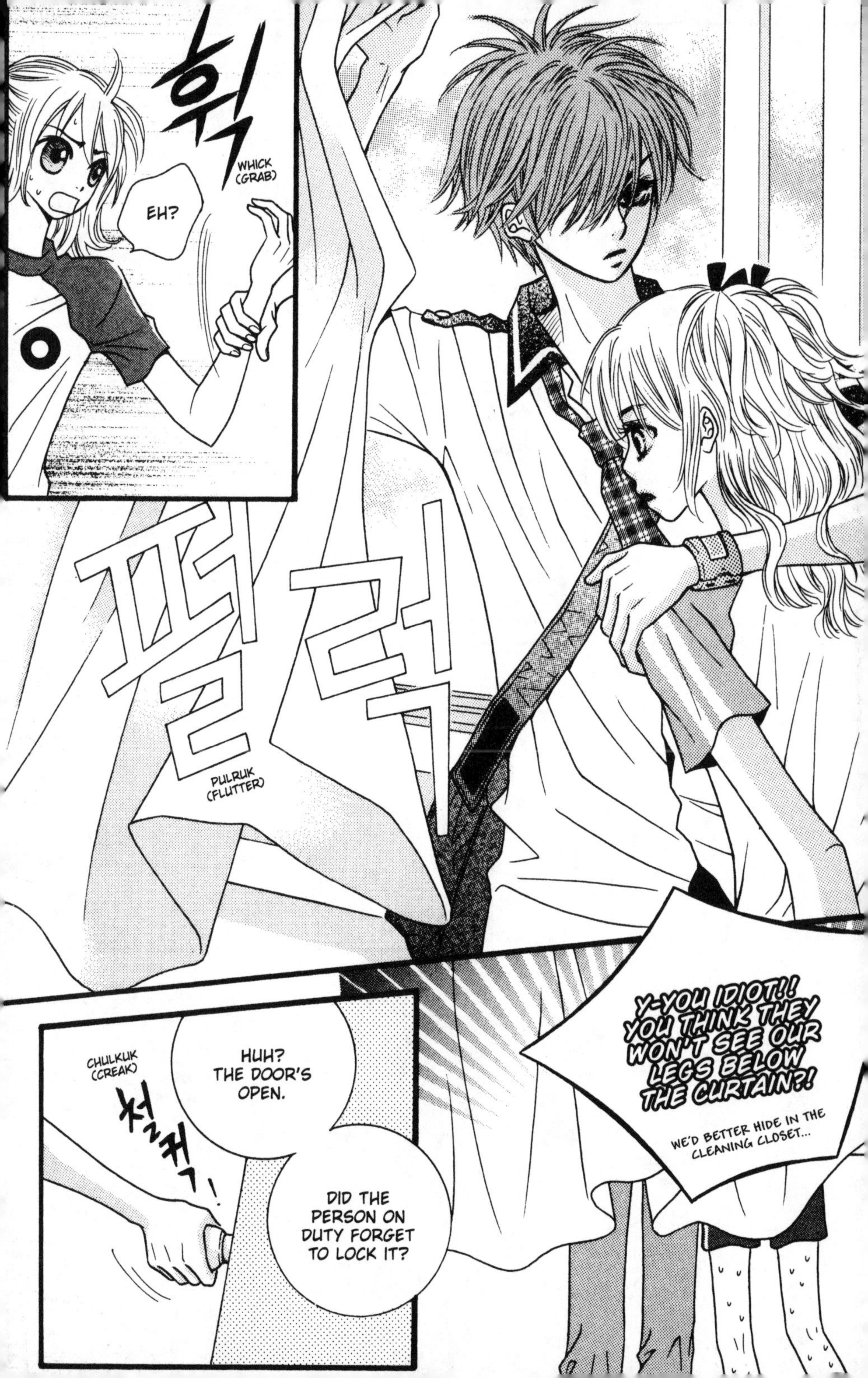

휘
WHICK (GRAB)
EH?
펄럭
PULRUK (FLUTTER)
Y-YOU IDIOT!! YOU THINK THEY WON'T SEE OUR LEGS BELOW THE CURTAIN?!
WE'D BETTER HIDE IN THE CLEANING CLOSET...
HUH? THE DOOR'S OPEN.
DID THE PERSON ON DUTY FORGET TO LOCK IT?
CHULKUK (CREAK)

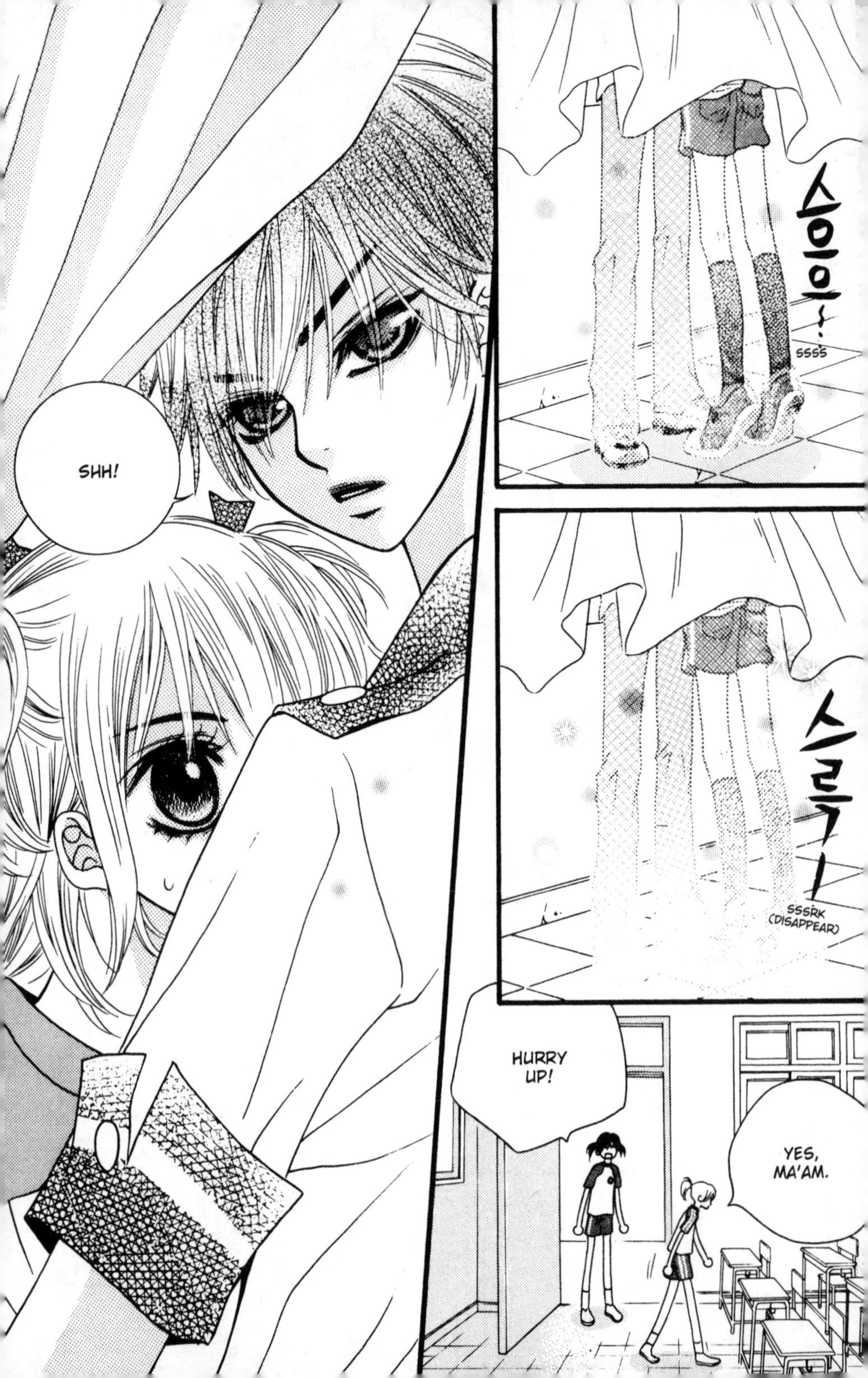
SHH!
스으으~
SSSS
스륵~
SSSRK (DISAPPEAR)
HURRY UP!
YES, MA'AM.

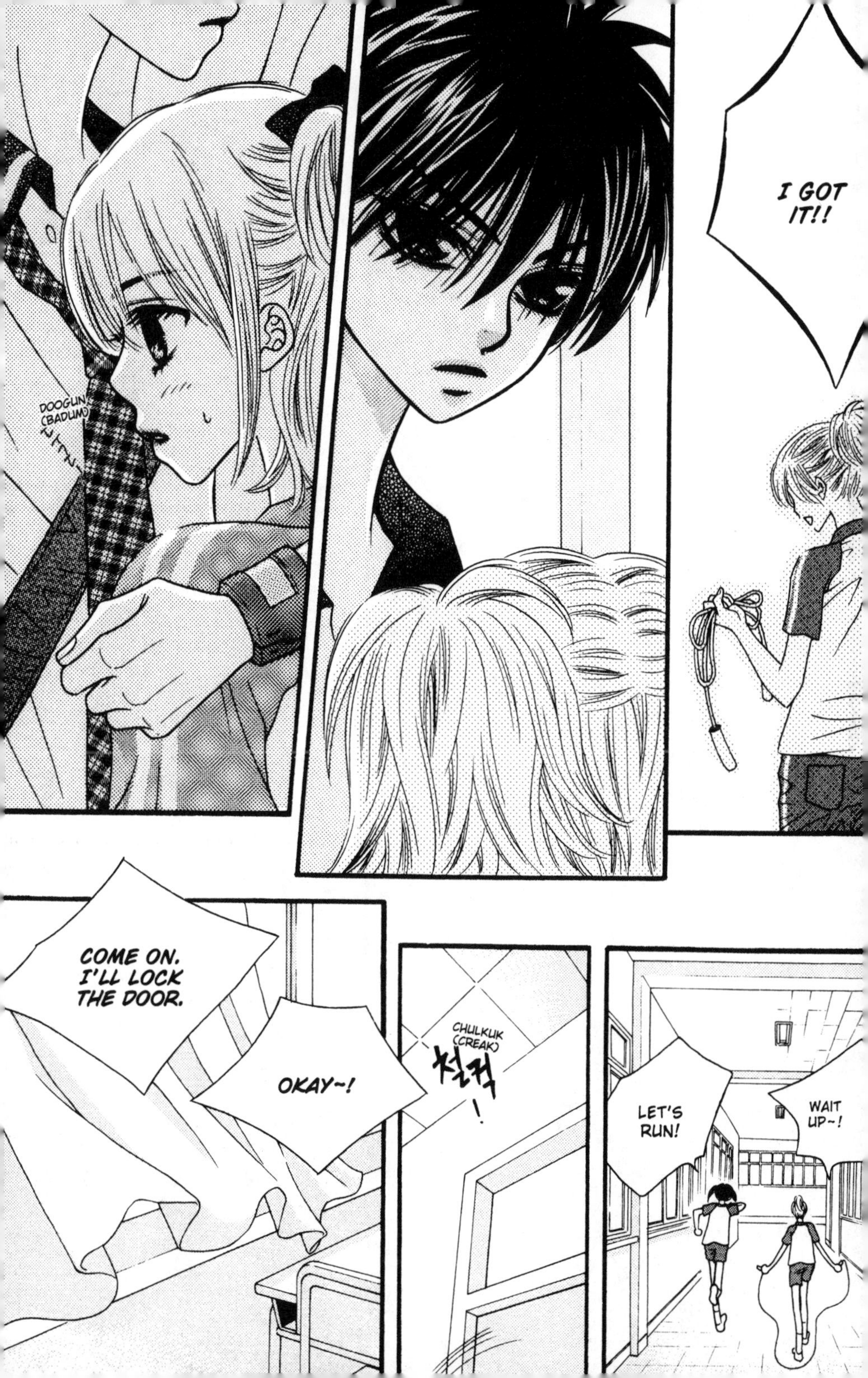
DOOGUN (BADUM)
I GOT IT!!
COME ON. I'LL LOCK THE DOOR.
OKAY~!
CHULKUK (CREAK)
철컥!
LET'S RUN!
WAIT UP~!

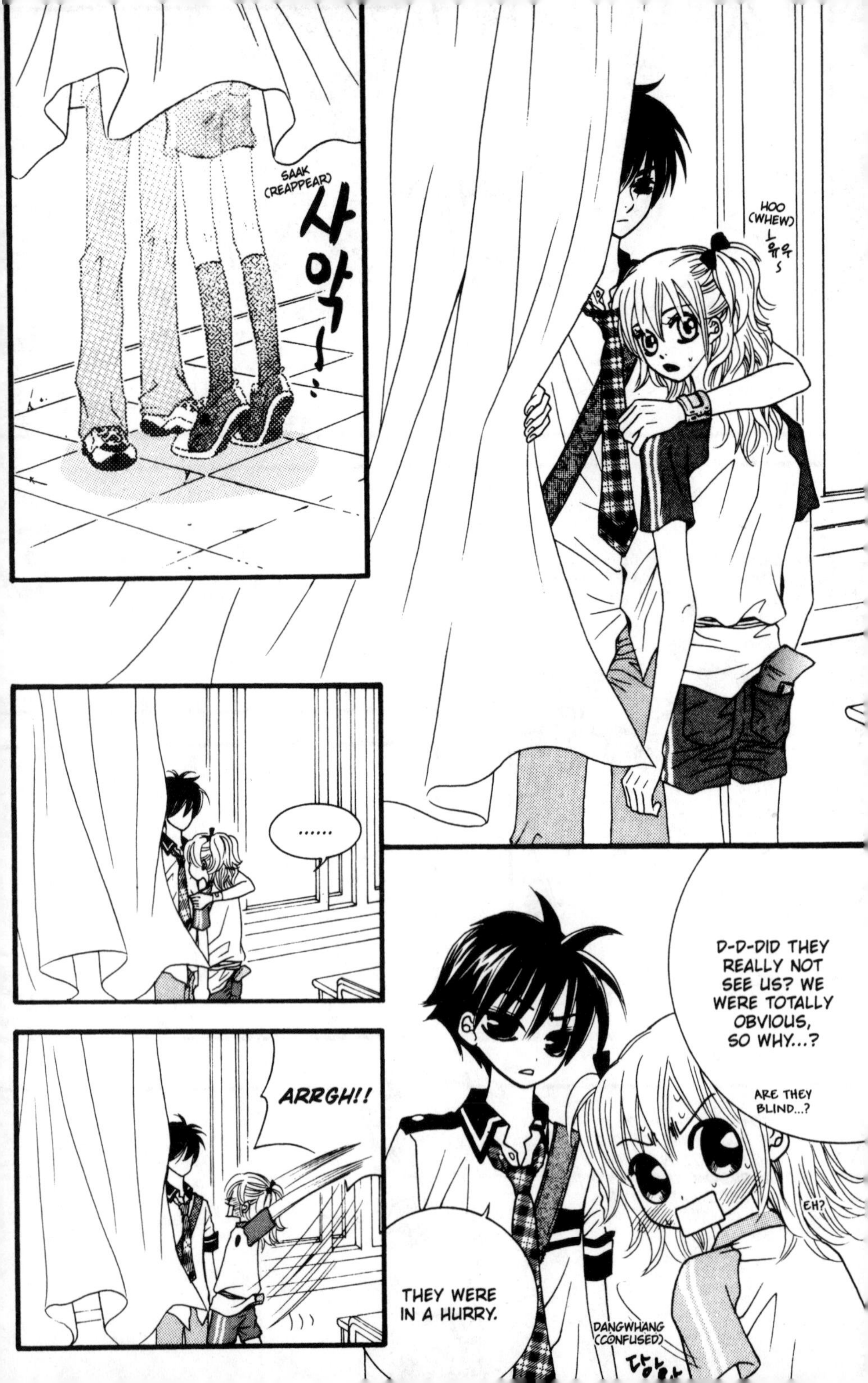
SAAK (REAPPEAR)
사악~
HOO (WHEW)
......
ARRGH!!
D-D-DID THEY REALLY NOT SEE US? WE WERE TOTALLY OBVIOUS, SO WHY...?
ARE THEY BLIND...?
EH?
THEY WERE IN A HURRY.
DANGWHANG (CONFUSED)

TAK (DROP)

AREN'T YOU GONNA GO TO GYM CLASS?

I DON'T HAVE MY GYM CLOTHES.

QUIT BOTHERING ME AND GET ON WITH YOUR OWN BUSINESS.

HE'S DEFINITELY *NOT SWEET* AT ALL!!

SFX: BOWOO (POLIT)

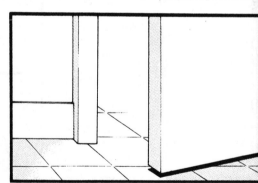

...COME TO THINK OF IT, THE DOOR WAS LOCKED WHEN I GOT INTO THE CLASSROOM...SO HOW'D THAT BASTARD GET IN?

STRANGE KID.

DID HE CLIMB IN THROUGH THE WINDOW LIKE I DID? BUT THEN HOW COME I DIDN'T HEAR ANYTHING?

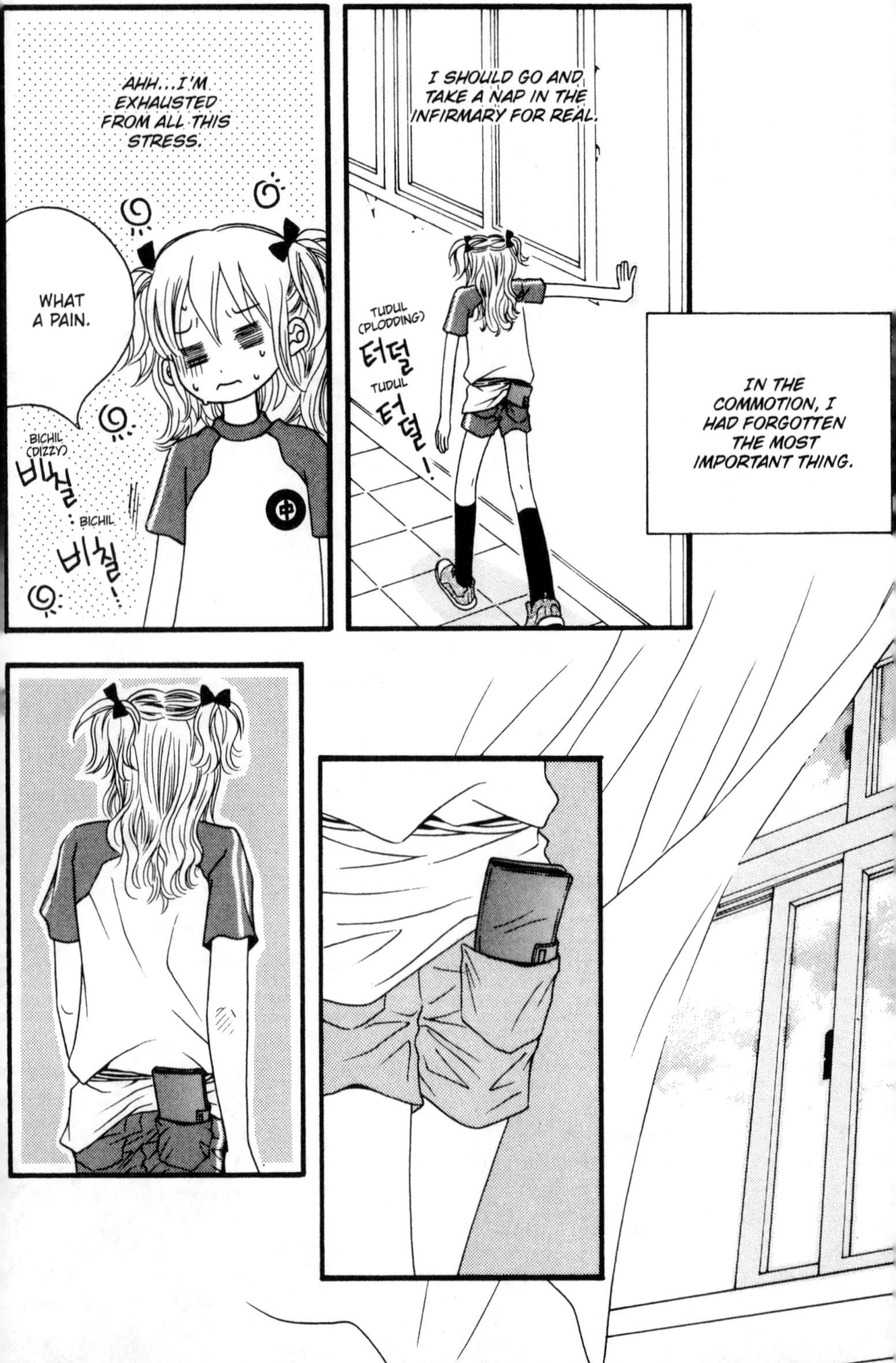
AHH...I'M EXHAUSTED FROM ALL THIS STRESS.
WHAT A PAIN.
BICHIL (DIZZY)
비실
BICHIL
비실
I SHOULD GO AND TAKE A NAP IN THE INFIRMARY FOR REAL.
TUDUL (PLODDING)
터덜
TUDUL
터덜
IN THE COMMOTION, I HAD FORGOTTEN THE MOST IMPORTANT THING.

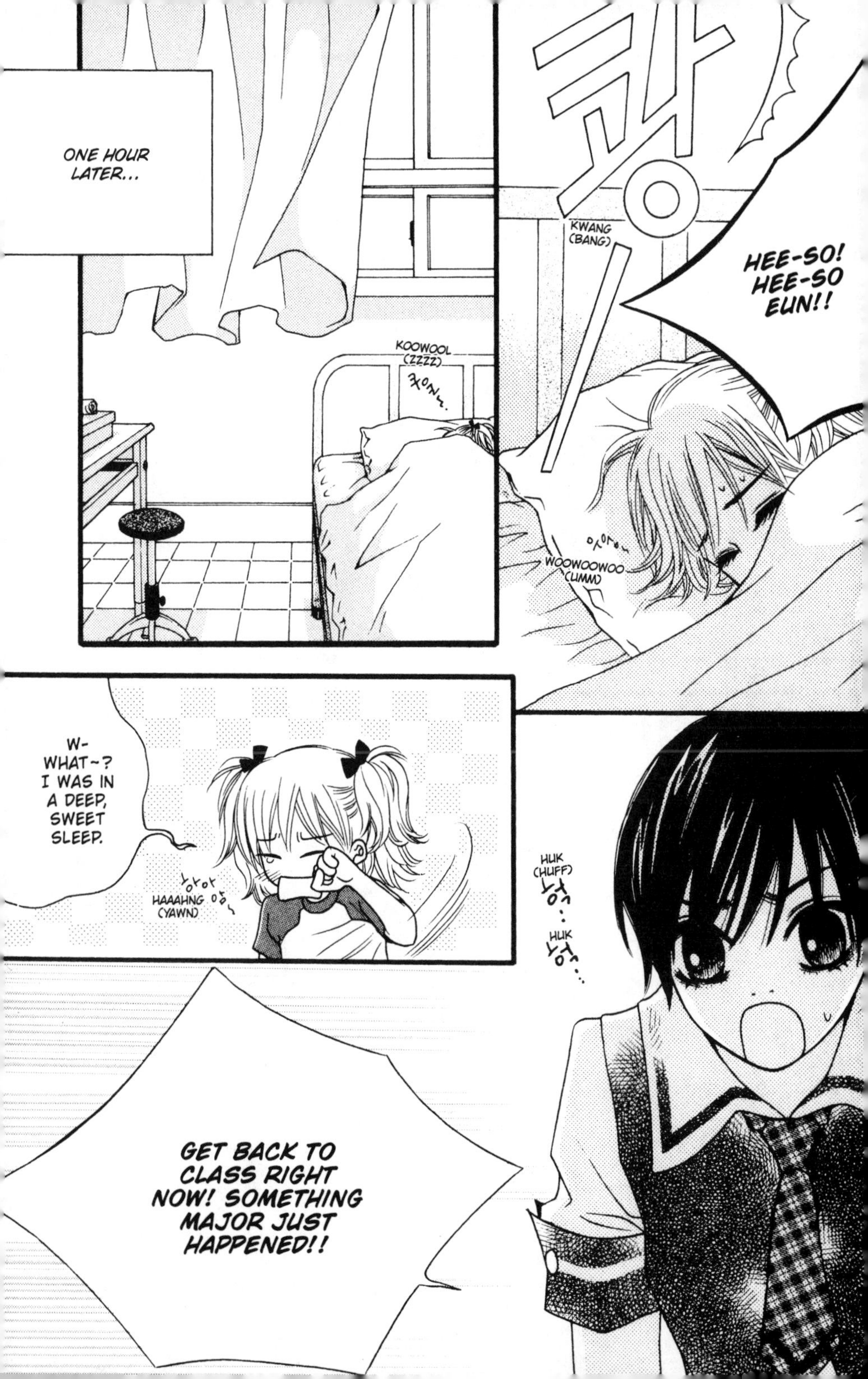
ONE HOUR LATER...
KOOWOOL (ZZZZ)
KWANG (BANG)
HEE-SO! HEE-SO EUN!!
WOOWOOWOO (UMM)
W- WHAT~? I WAS IN A DEEP, SWEET SLEEP.
HAAAHNG (YAWN)
HUK (HUFF)
HUK
GET BACK TO CLASS RIGHT NOW! SOMETHING MAJOR JUST HAPPENED!!

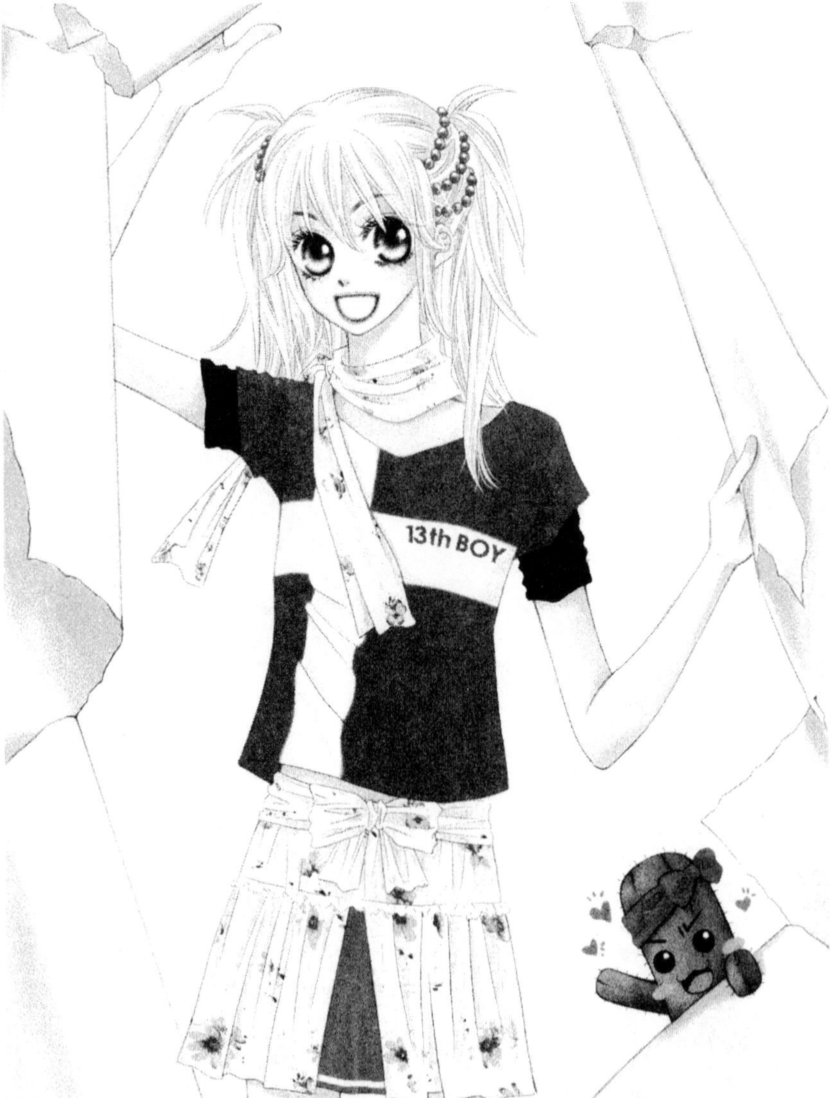
13th BOY

13th Boy

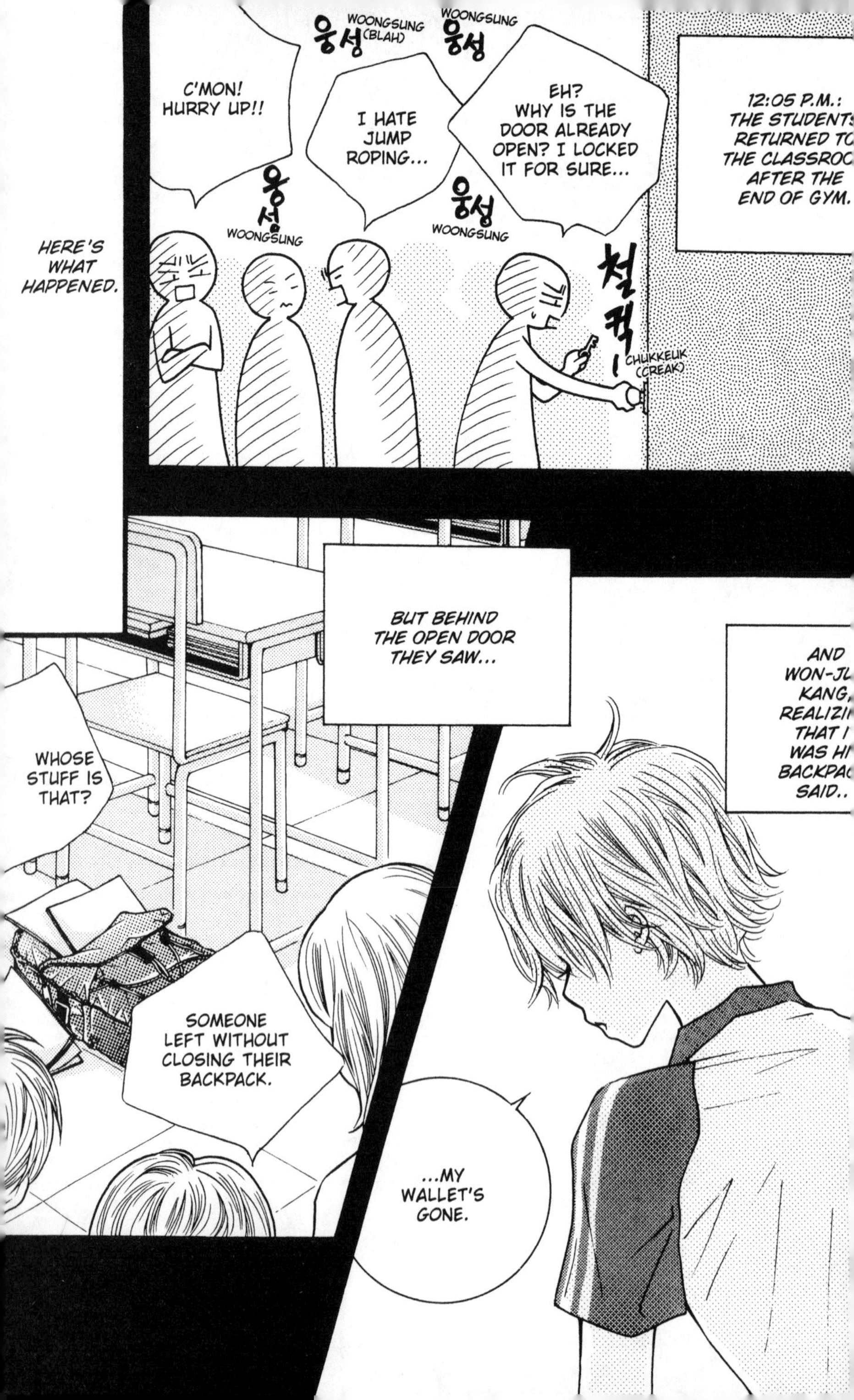
HERE'S WHAT HAPPENED.
C'MON! HURRY UP!!
웅성 WOONGSUNG (BLAH)
웅성 WOONGSUNG
웅성 WOONGSUNG
I HATE JUMP ROPING...
웅성 WOONGSUNG
EH? WHY IS THE DOOR ALREADY OPEN? I LOCKED IT FOR SURE...
철컥! CHUKKEUK (CREAK)
12:05 P.M.: THE STUDENTS RETURNED TO THE CLASSROO AFTER THE END OF GYM.
BUT BEHIND THE OPEN DOOR THEY SAW...
WHOSE STUFF IS THAT?
SOMEONE LEFT WITHOUT CLOSING THEIR BACKPACK.
AND WON-JU KANG, REALIZI THAT I WAS HI BACKPAC SAID..
...MY WALLET'S GONE.

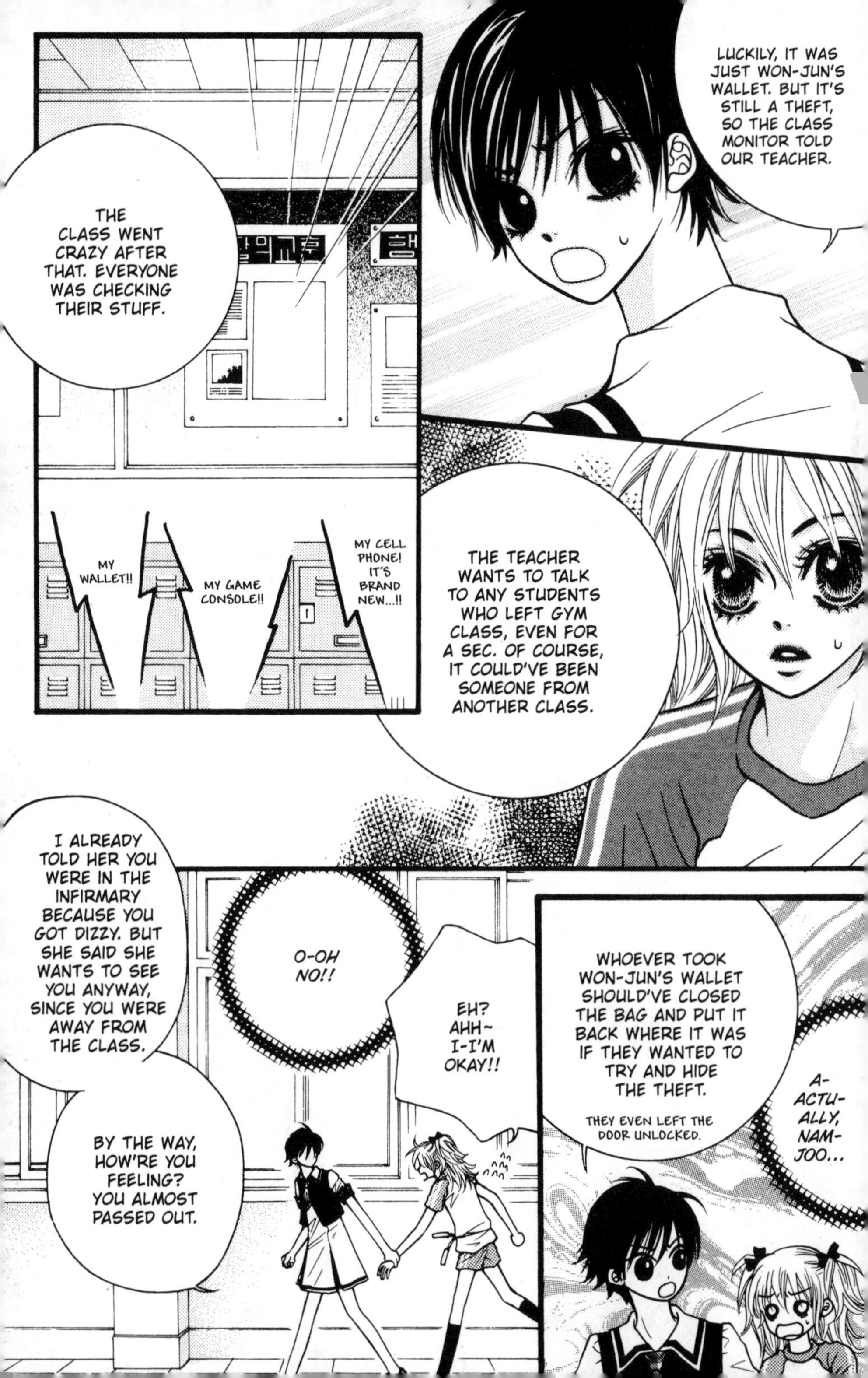

THE CLASS WENT CRAZY AFTER THAT. EVERYONE WAS CHECKING THEIR STUFF.
MY WALLET!!
MY GAME CONSOLE!!
MY CELL PHONE! IT'S BRAND NEW...!!
LUCKILY, IT WAS JUST WON-JUN'S WALLET. BUT IT'S STILL A THEFT, SO THE CLASS MONITOR TOLD OUR TEACHER.
THE TEACHER WANTS TO TALK TO ANY STUDENTS WHO LEFT GYM CLASS, EVEN FOR A SEC. OF COURSE, IT COULD'VE BEEN SOMEONE FROM ANOTHER CLASS.
I ALREADY TOLD HER YOU WERE IN THE INFIRMARY BECAUSE YOU GOT DIZZY. BUT SHE SAID SHE WANTS TO SEE YOU ANYWAY, SINCE YOU WERE AWAY FROM THE CLASS.
BY THE WAY, HOW'RE YOU FEELING? YOU ALMOST PASSED OUT.
O-OH NO!!
EH? AHH~ I-I'M OKAY!!
WHOEVER TOOK WON-JUN'S WALLET SHOULD'VE CLOSED THE BAG AND PUT IT BACK WHERE IT WAS IF THEY WANTED TO TRY AND HIDE THE THEFT.
THEY EVEN LEFT THE DOOR UNLOCKED.
A-ACTU-ALLY, NAM-JOO...

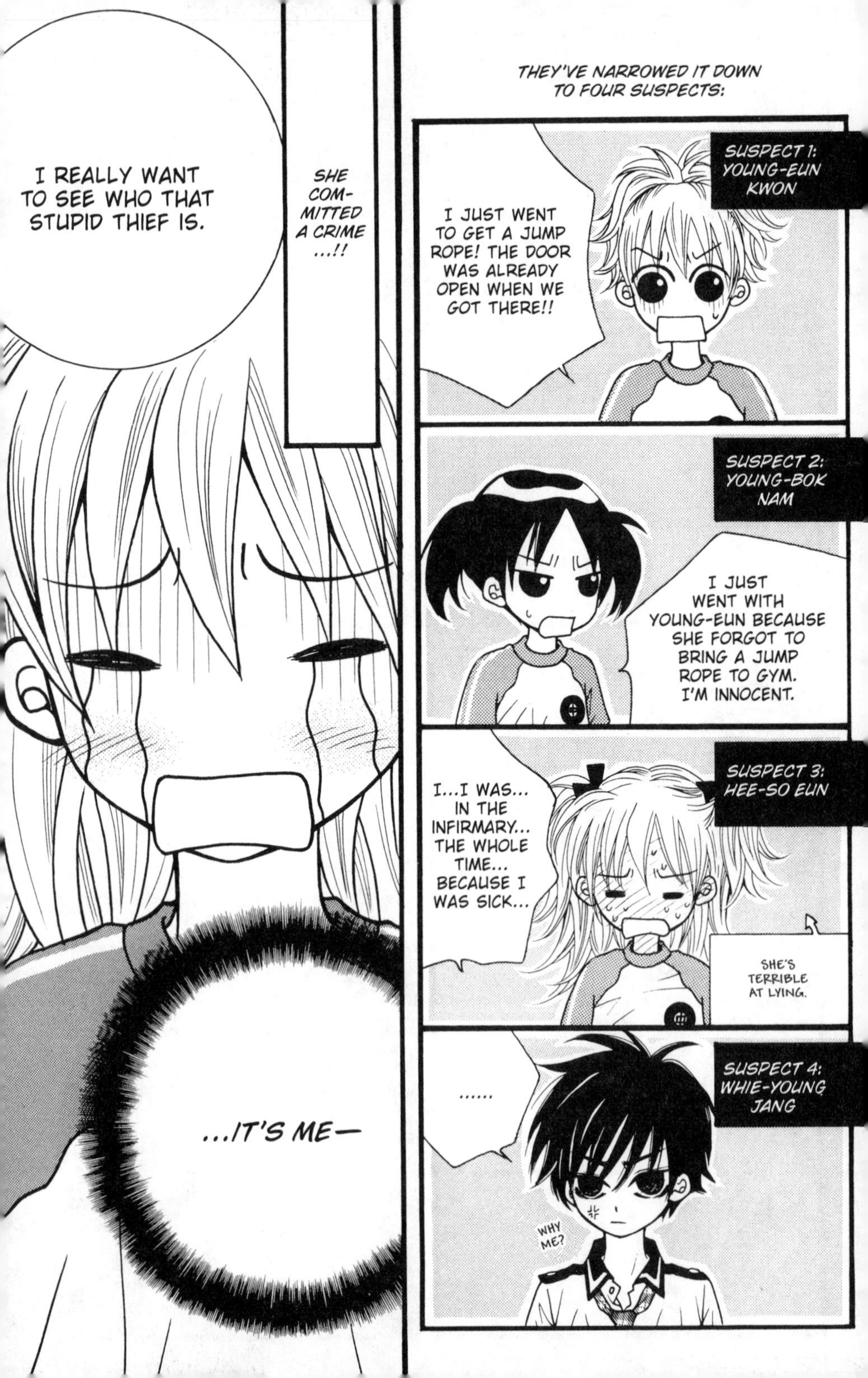
I REALLY WANT TO SEE WHO THAT STUPID THIEF IS.
SHE COM-MITTED A CRIME ...!!
...IT'S ME—
THEY'VE NARROWED IT DOWN TO FOUR SUSPECTS:
SUSPECT 1: YOUNG-EUN KWON
I JUST WENT TO GET A JUMP ROPE! THE DOOR WAS ALREADY OPEN WHEN WE GOT THERE!!
SUSPECT 2: YOUNG-BOK NAM
I JUST WENT WITH YOUNG-EUN BECAUSE SHE FORGOT TO BRING A JUMP ROPE TO GYM. I'M INNOCENT.
SUSPECT 3: HEE-SO EUN
I...I WAS... IN THE INFIRMARY... THE WHOLE TIME... BECAUSE I WAS SICK...
SHE'S TERRIBLE AT LYING.
SUSPECT 4: WHIE-YOUNG JANG
......
WHY ME?

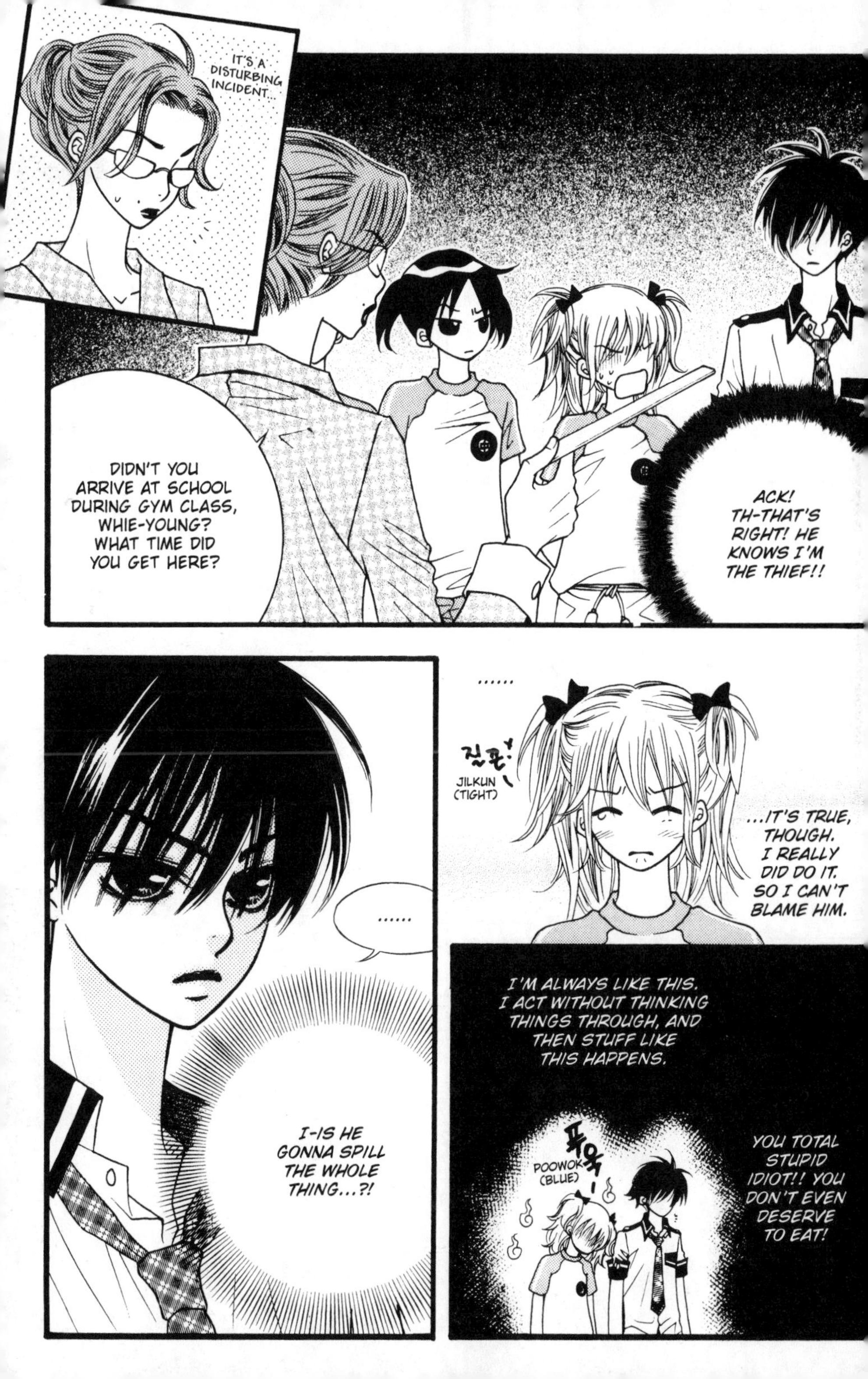
IT'S A DISTURBING INCIDENT...
DIDN'T YOU ARRIVE AT SCHOOL DURING GYM CLASS, WHIE-YOUNG? WHAT TIME DID YOU GET HERE?
ACK! TH-THAT'S RIGHT! HE KNOWS I'M THE THIEF!!
......
I-IS HE GONNA SPILL THE WHOLE THING...?!
......
질끈
JILKUN (TIGHT)
...IT'S TRUE, THOUGH. I REALLY DID DO IT. SO I CAN'T BLAME HIM.
I'M ALWAYS LIKE THIS. I ACT WITHOUT THINKING THINGS THROUGH, AND THEN STUFF LIKE THIS HAPPENS.
푸욱
POOWOK (BLUE)
YOU TOTAL STUPID IDIOT!! YOU DON'T EVEN DESERVE TO EAT!

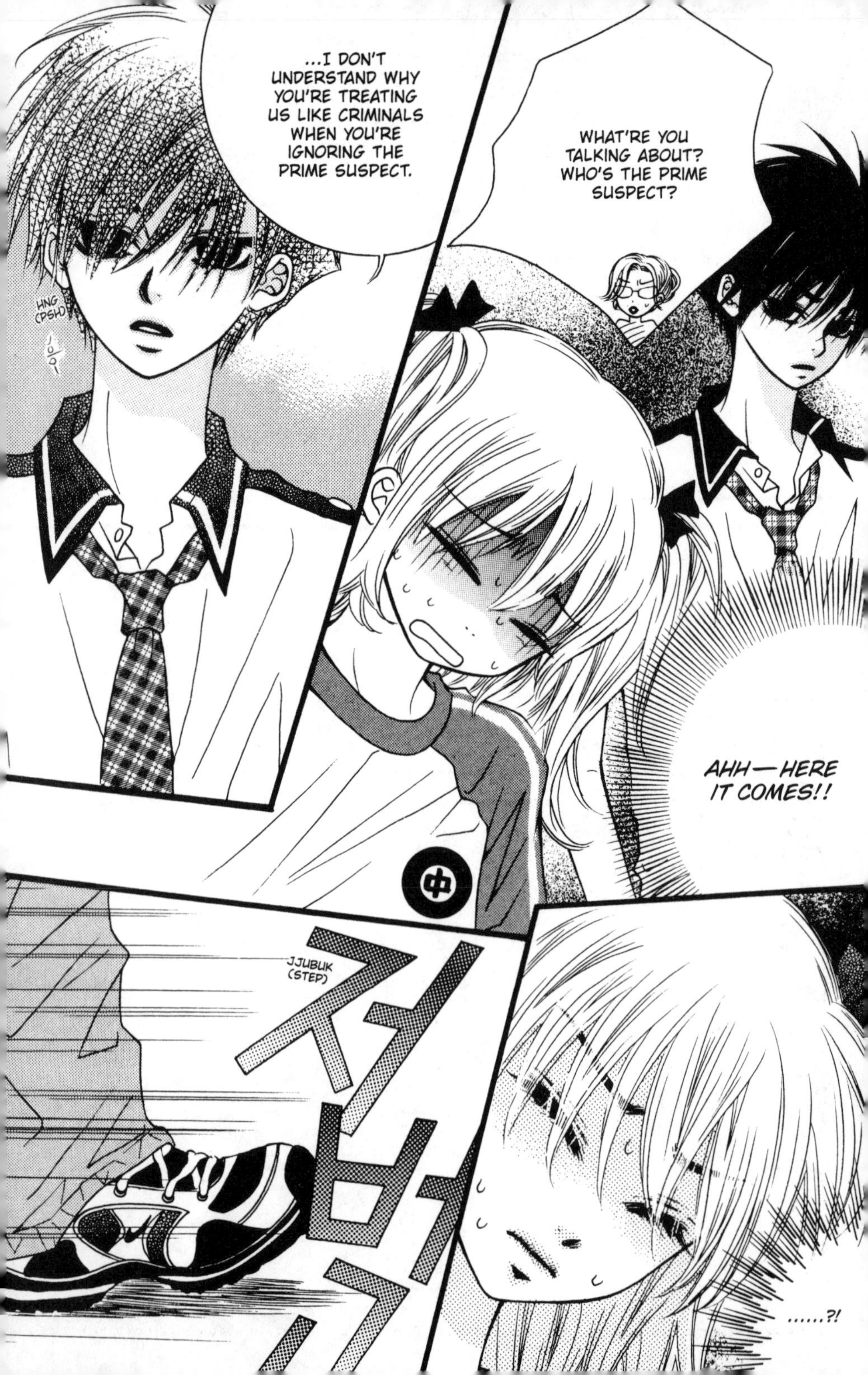
...I DON'T UNDERSTAND WHY YOU'RE TREATING US LIKE CRIMINALS WHEN YOU'RE IGNORING THE PRIME SUSPECT.
HNG (PSH)
WHAT'RE YOU TALKING ABOUT? WHO'S THE PRIME SUSPECT?
AHH—HERE IT COMES!!
JJUBUK (STEP)
......?!

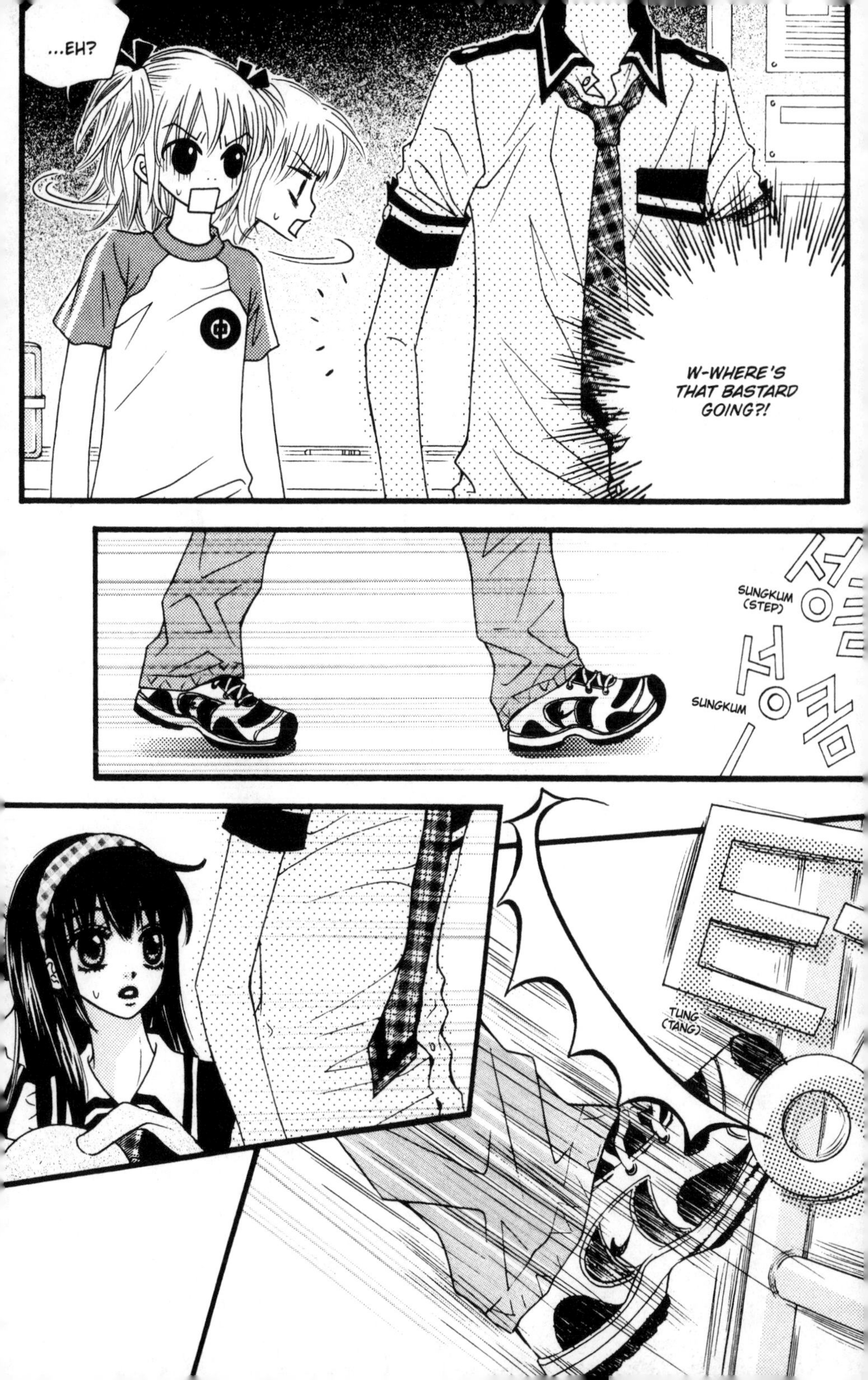
...EH?
W-WHERE'S THAT BASTARD GOING?!
SUNGKUM (STEP)
SUNGKUM
TUNG (TANG)

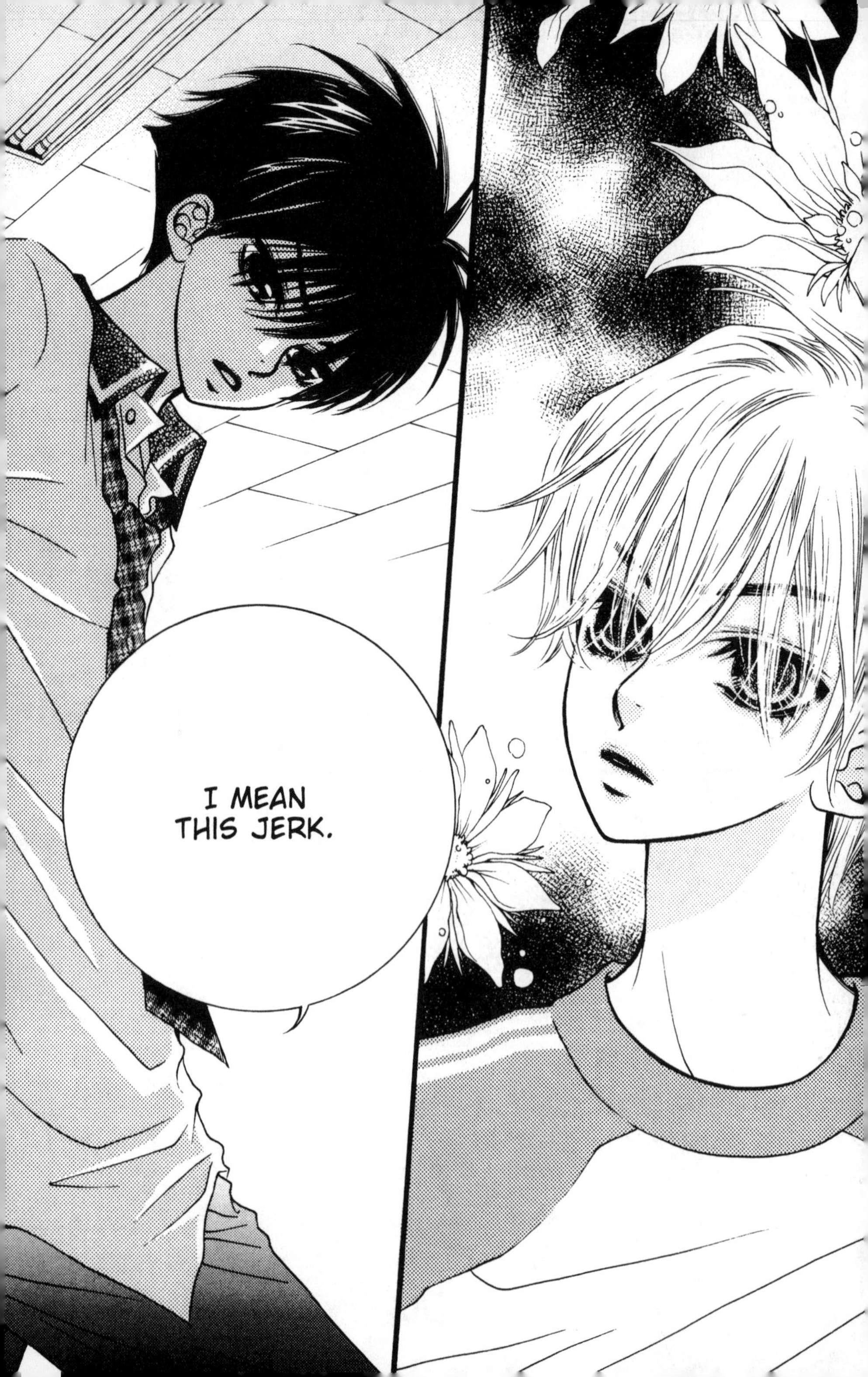
I MEAN THIS JERK.

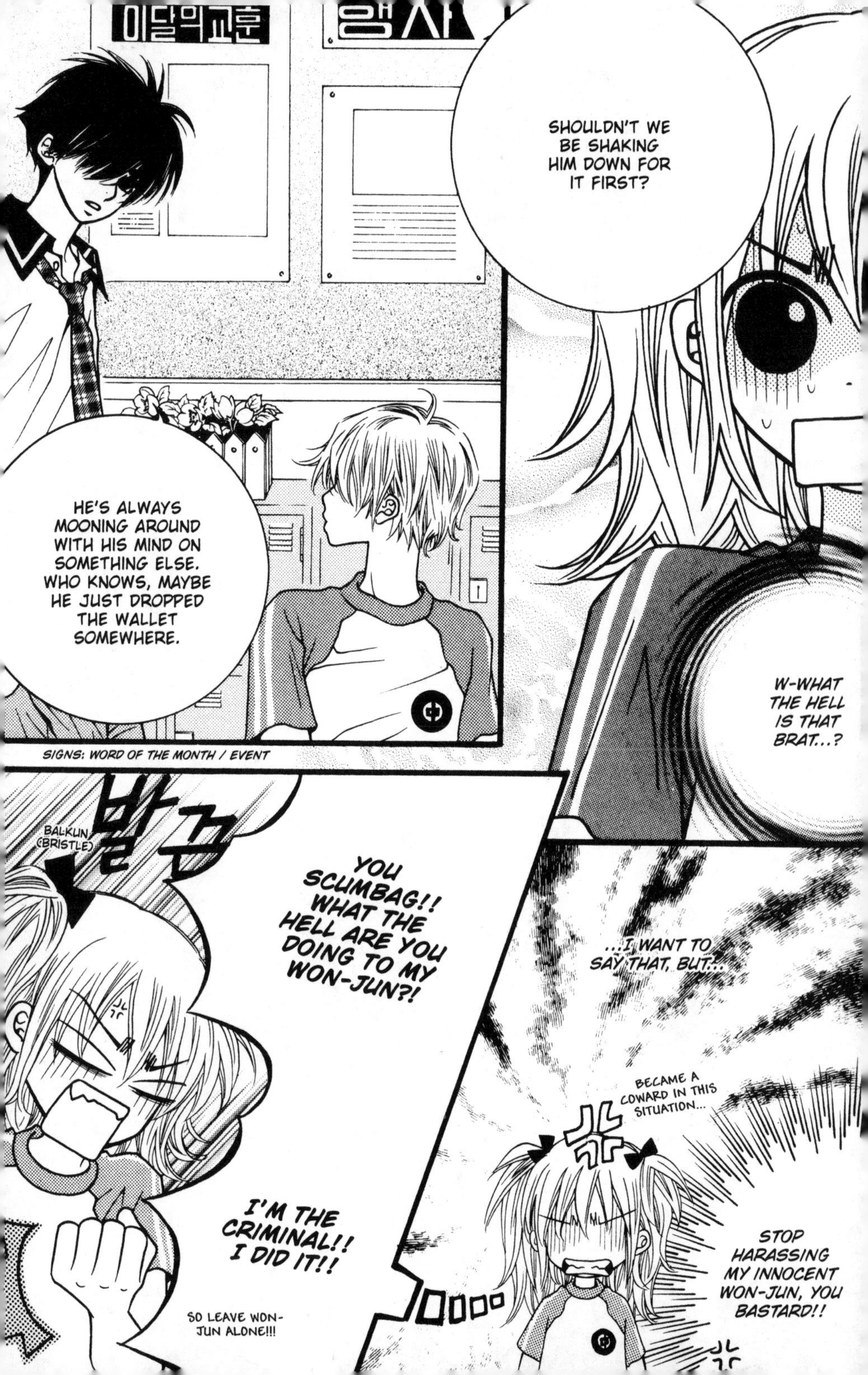
이달의교훈
행사
HE'S ALWAYS MOONING AROUND WITH HIS MIND ON SOMETHING ELSE. WHO KNOWS, MAYBE HE JUST DROPPED THE WALLET SOMEWHERE.
SIGNS: WORD OF THE MONTH / EVENT
SHOULDN'T WE BE SHAKING HIM DOWN FOR IT FIRST?
W-WHAT THE HELL IS THAT BRAT...?
발끈
BALKUN (BRISTLE)
YOU SCUMBAG!! WHAT THE HELL ARE YOU DOING TO MY WON-JUN?!
I'M THE CRIMINAL!! I DID IT!!
SO LEAVE WON-JUN ALONE!!!
...I WANT TO SAY THAT, BUT...
BECAME A COWARD IN THIS SITUATION...
STOP HARASSING MY INNOCENT WON-JUN, YOU BASTARD!!

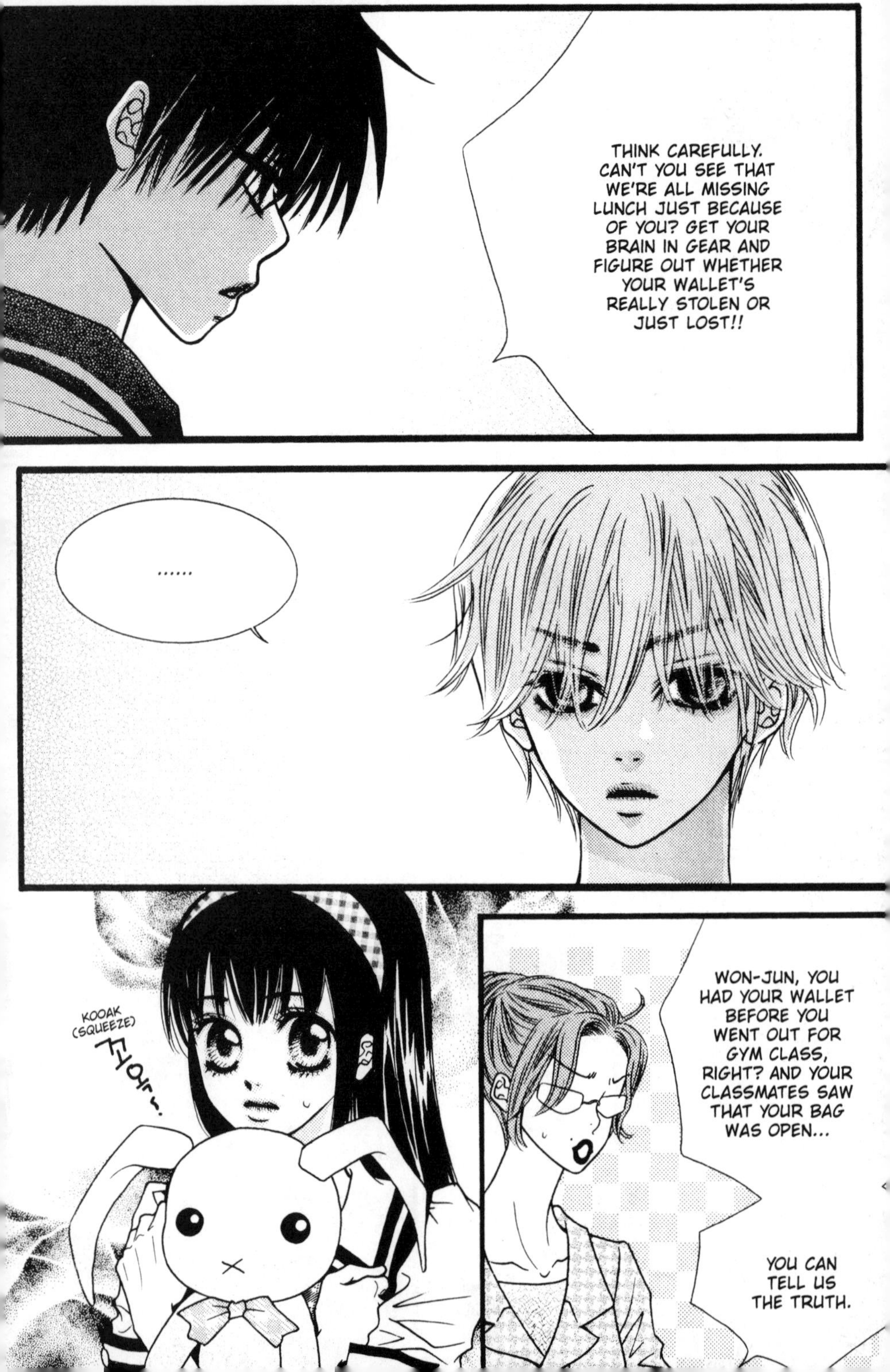
THINK CAREFULLY. CAN'T YOU SEE THAT WE'RE ALL MISSING LUNCH JUST BECAUSE OF YOU? GET YOUR BRAIN IN GEAR AND FIGURE OUT WHETHER YOUR WALLET'S REALLY STOLEN OR JUST LOST!!
......
KOOAK (SQUEEZE)
WON-JUN, YOU HAD YOUR WALLET BEFORE YOU WENT OUT FOR GYM CLASS, RIGHT? AND YOUR CLASSMATES SAW THAT YOUR BAG WAS OPEN...
YOU CAN TELL US THE TRUTH.

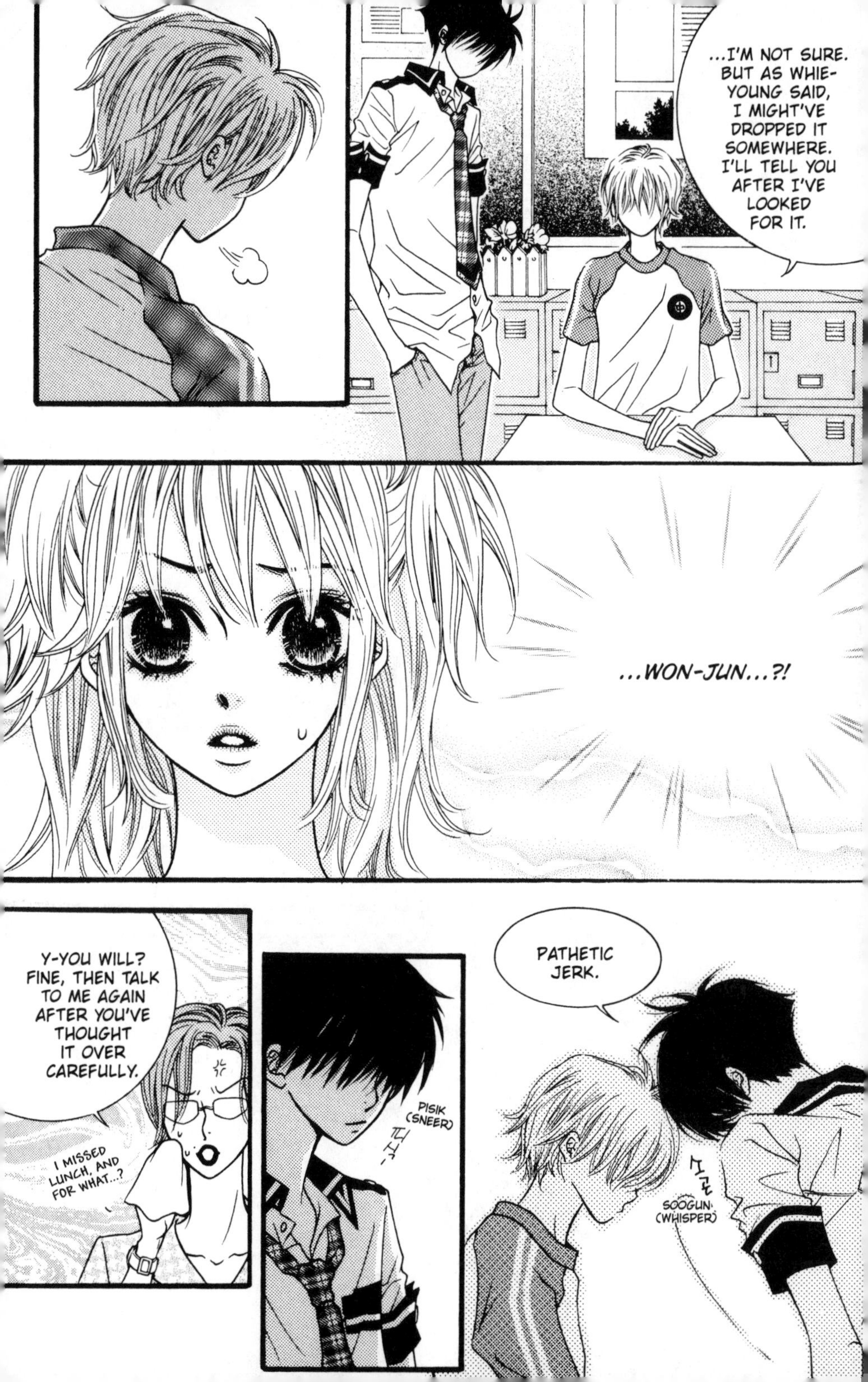
...I'M NOT SURE. BUT AS WHIE-YOUNG SAID, I MIGHT'VE DROPPED IT SOMEWHERE. I'LL TELL YOU AFTER I'VE LOOKED FOR IT.
...WON-JUN...?!
Y-YOU WILL? FINE, THEN TALK TO ME AGAIN AFTER YOU'VE THOUGHT IT OVER CAREFULLY.
I MISSED LUNCH, AND FOR WHAT...?
PISIK (SNEER)
PATHETIC JERK.
SOOGUN (WHISPER)

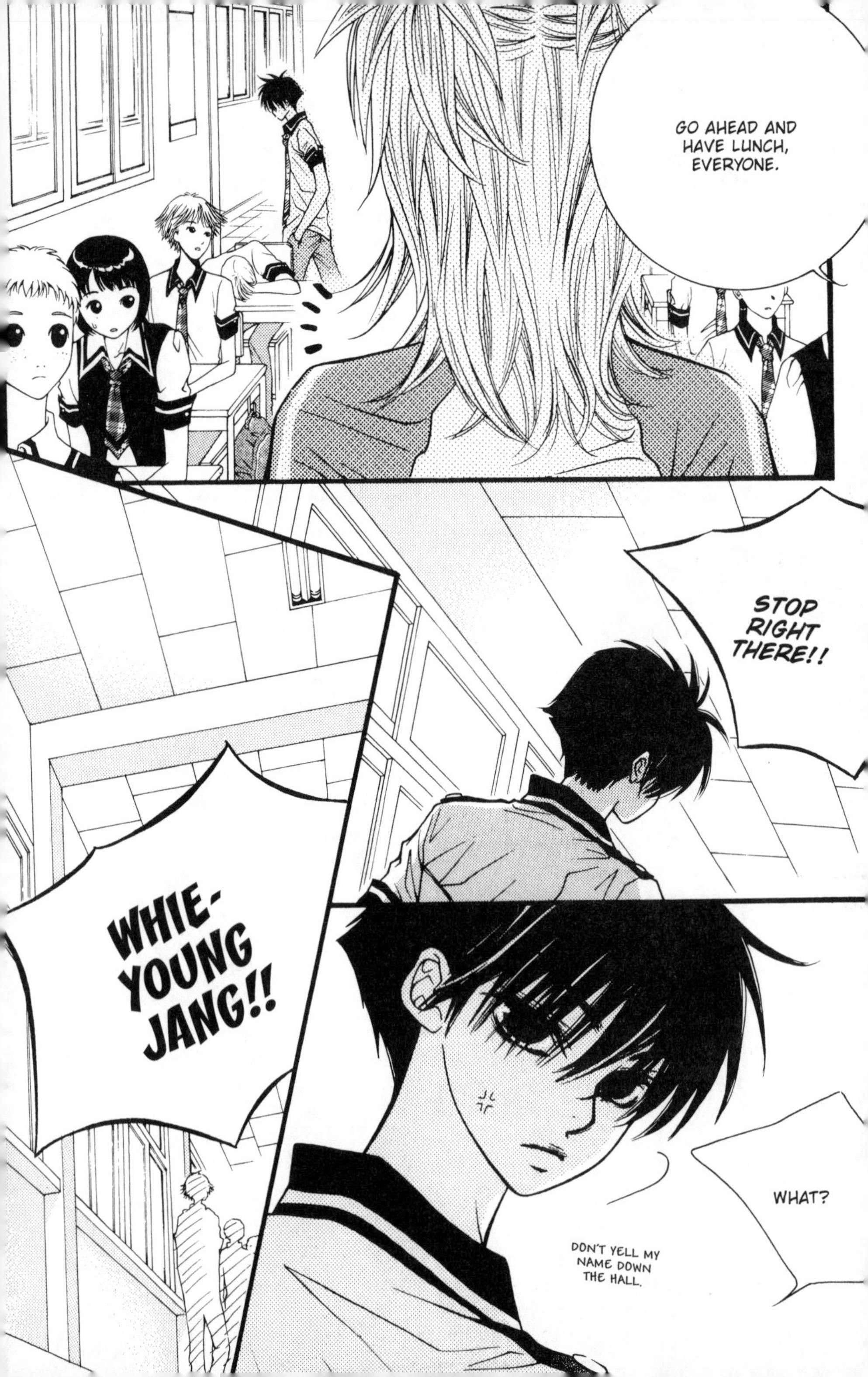
GO AHEAD AND HAVE LUNCH, EVERYONE.
STOP RIGHT THERE!!
WHIE-YOUNG JANG!!
WHAT?
DON'T YELL MY NAME DOWN THE HALL.

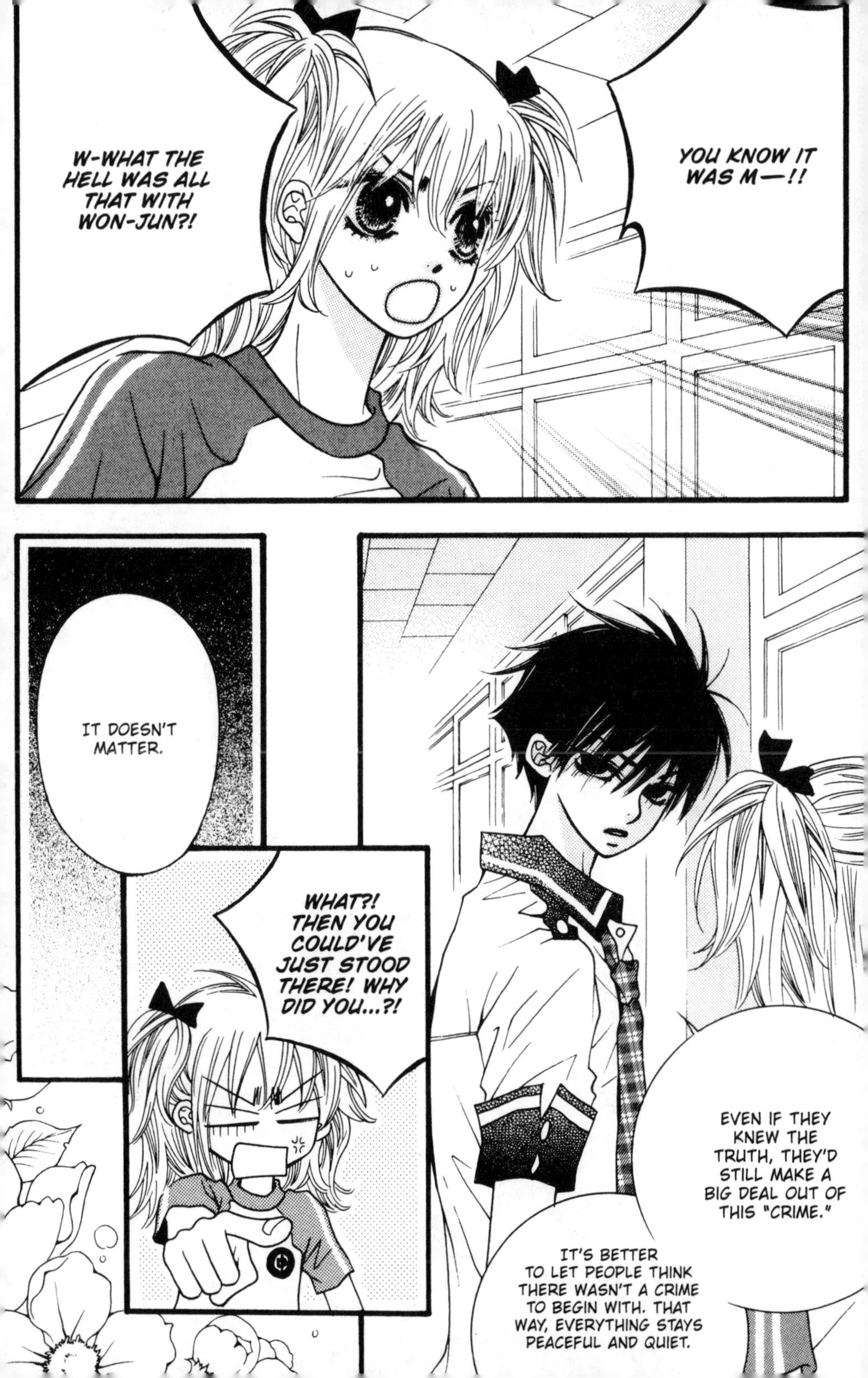
W-WHAT THE HELL WAS ALL THAT WITH WON-JUN?!
YOU KNOW IT WAS M—!!
IT DOESN'T MATTER.
WHAT?! THEN YOU COULD'VE JUST STOOD THERE! WHY DID YOU...?!
EVEN IF THEY KNEW THE TRUTH, THEY'D STILL MAKE A BIG DEAL OUT OF THIS "CRIME."
IT'S BETTER TO LET PEOPLE THINK THERE WASN'T A CRIME TO BEGIN WITH. THAT WAY, EVERYTHING STAYS PEACEFUL AND QUIET.

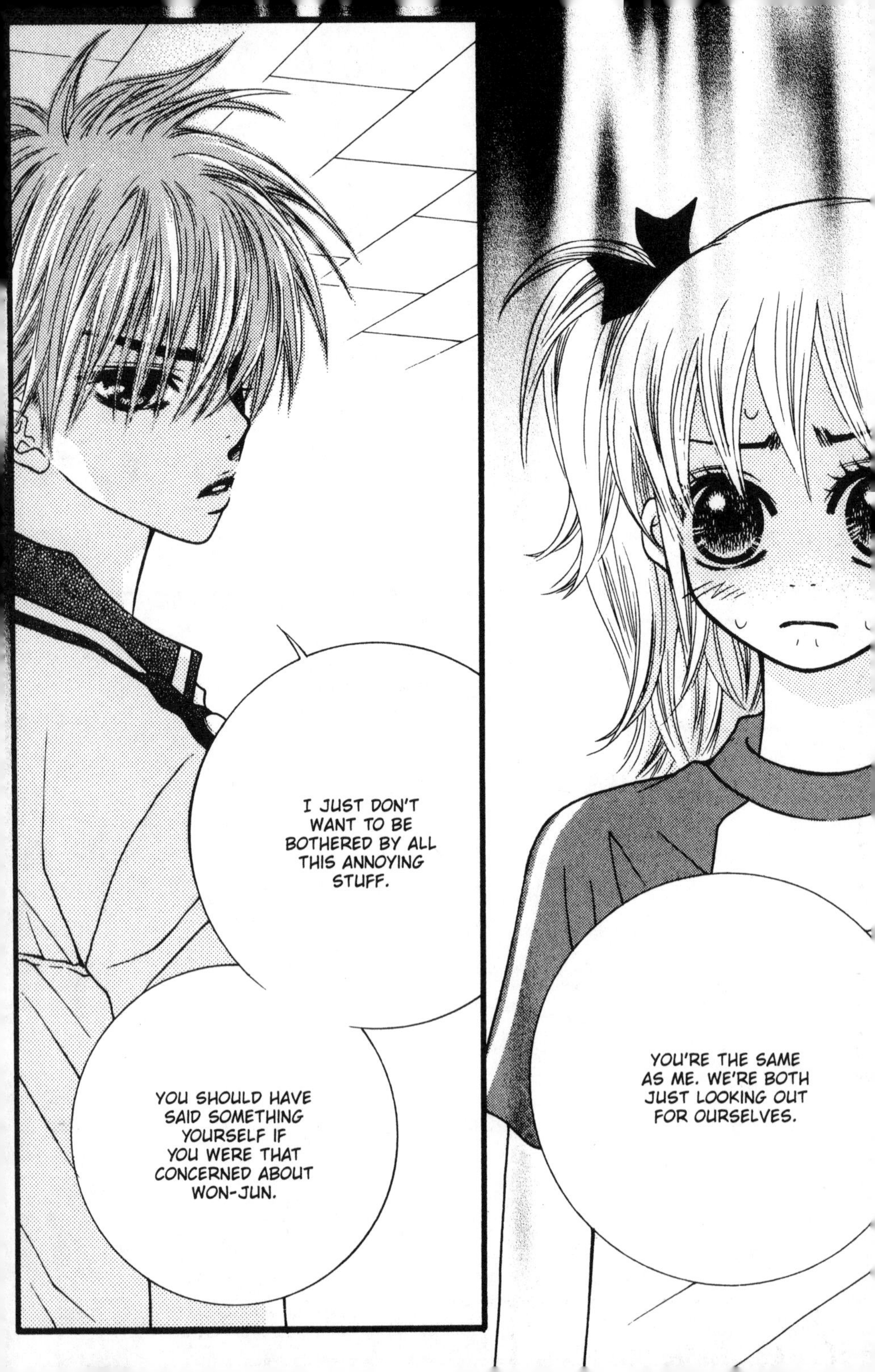
I JUST DON'T WANT TO BE BOTHERED BY ALL THIS ANNOYING STUFF.
YOU SHOULD HAVE SAID SOMETHING YOURSELF IF YOU WERE THAT CONCERNED ABOUT WON-JUN.
YOU'RE THE SAME AS ME. WE'RE BOTH JUST LOOKING OUT FOR OURSELVES.

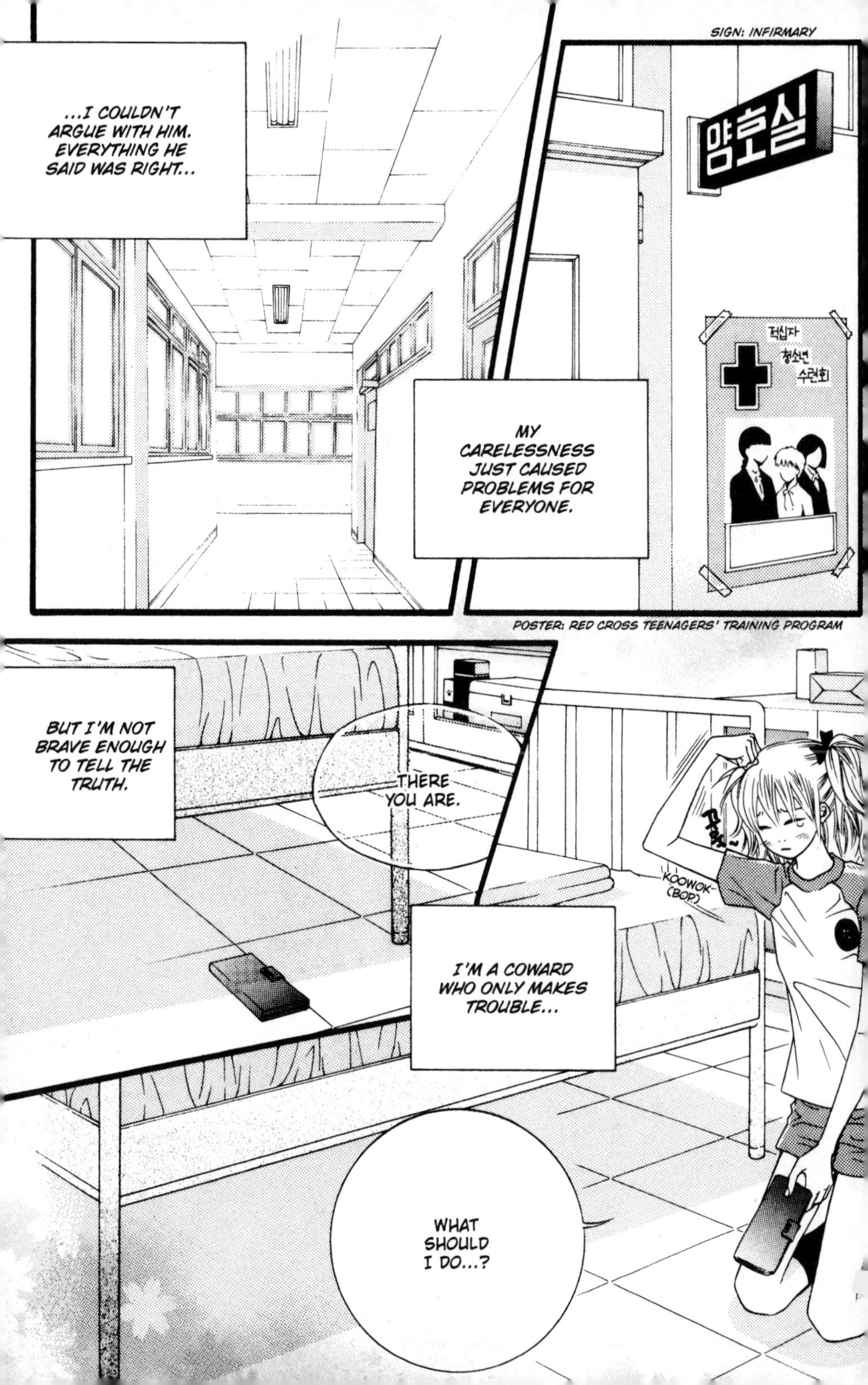
...I COULDN'T ARGUE WITH HIM. EVERYTHING HE SAID WAS RIGHT...
SIGN: INFIRMARY
양호실
MY CARELESSNESS JUST CAUSED PROBLEMS FOR EVERYONE.
적십자 청소년 수련회
POSTER: RED CROSS TEENAGERS' TRAINING PROGRAM
BUT I'M NOT BRAVE ENOUGH TO TELL THE TRUTH.
THERE YOU ARE.
KOOWOK (BOP)
I'M A COWARD WHO ONLY MAKES TROUBLE...
WHAT SHOULD I DO...?

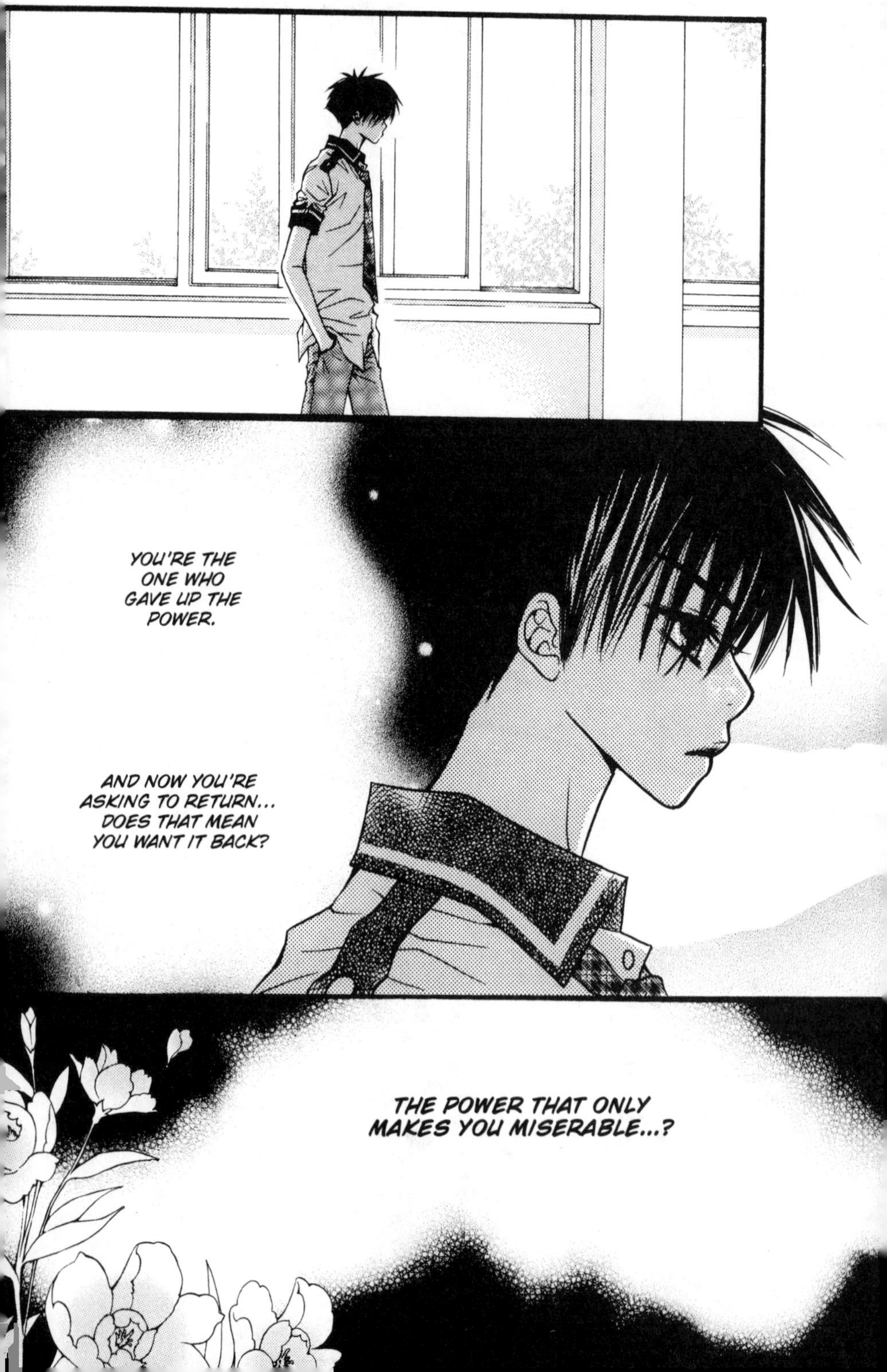
YOU'RE THE ONE WHO GAVE UP THE POWER.
AND NOW YOU'RE ASKING TO RETURN... DOES THAT MEAN YOU WANT IT BACK?
THE POWER THAT ONLY MAKES YOU MISERABLE...?

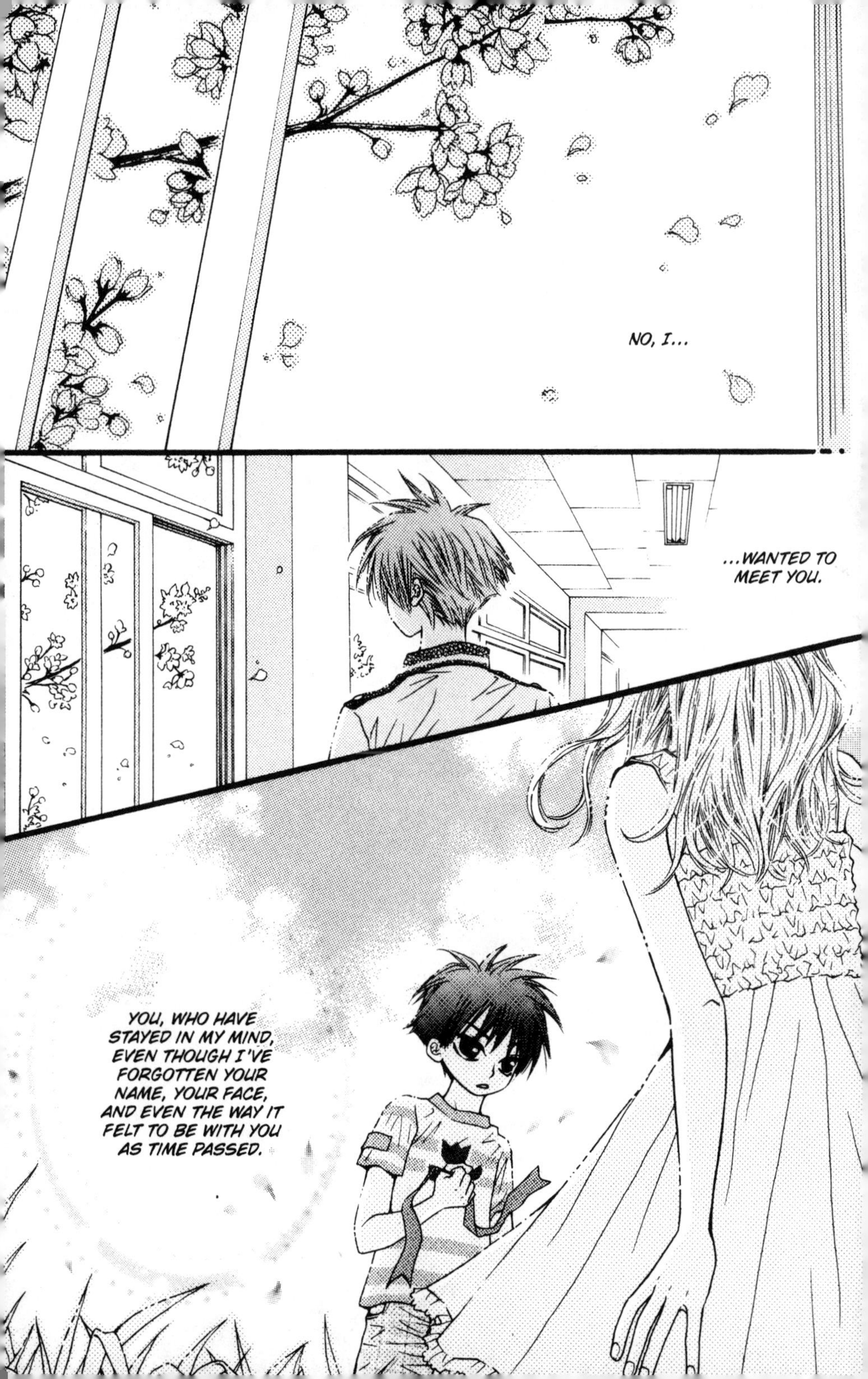
NO, I...
...WANTED TO MEET YOU.
YOU, WHO HAVE STAYED IN MY MIND, EVEN THOUGH I'VE FORGOTTEN YOUR NAME, YOUR FACE, AND EVEN THE WAY IT FELT TO BE WITH YOU AS TIME PASSED.

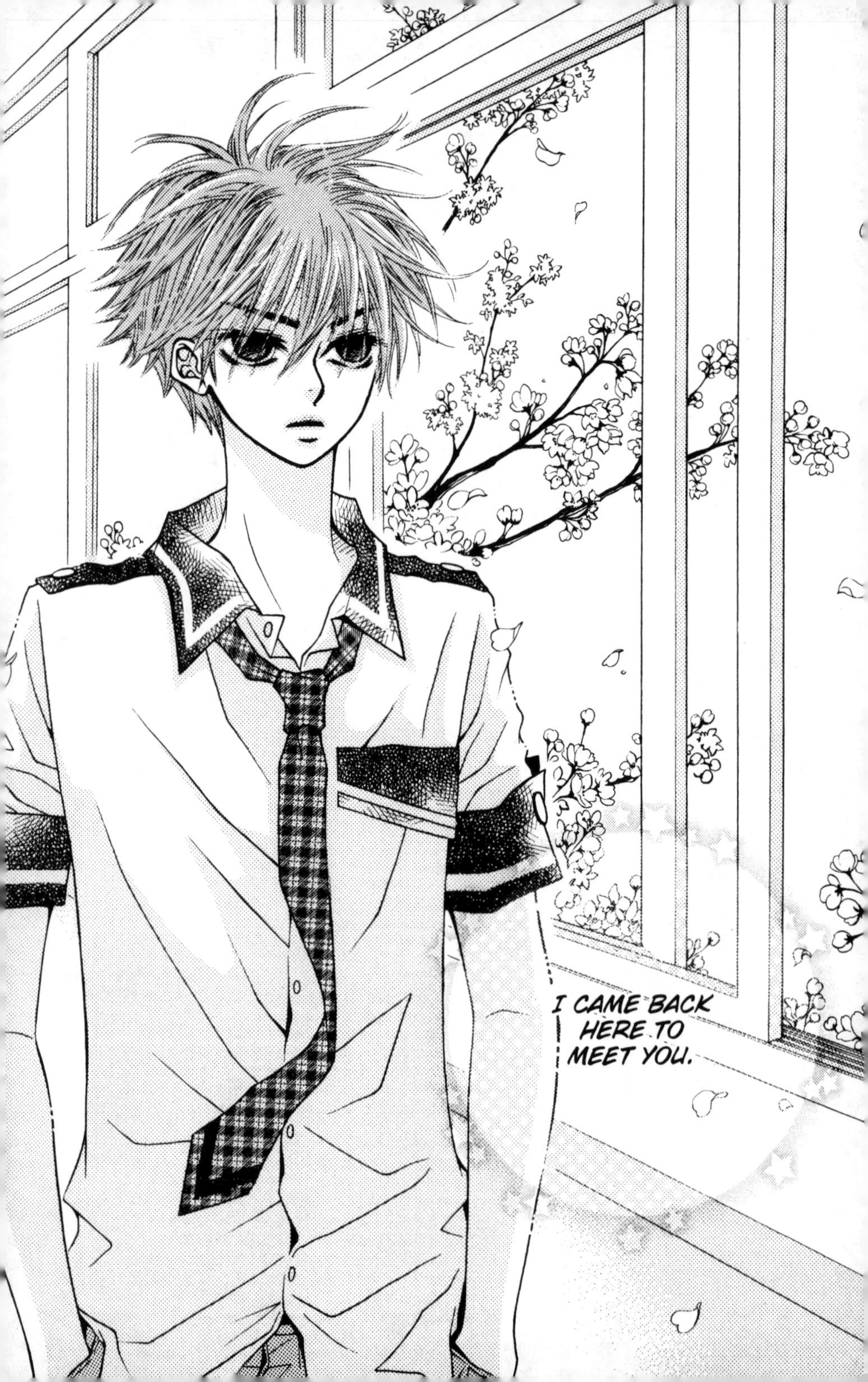
I CAME BACK HERE TO MEET YOU.

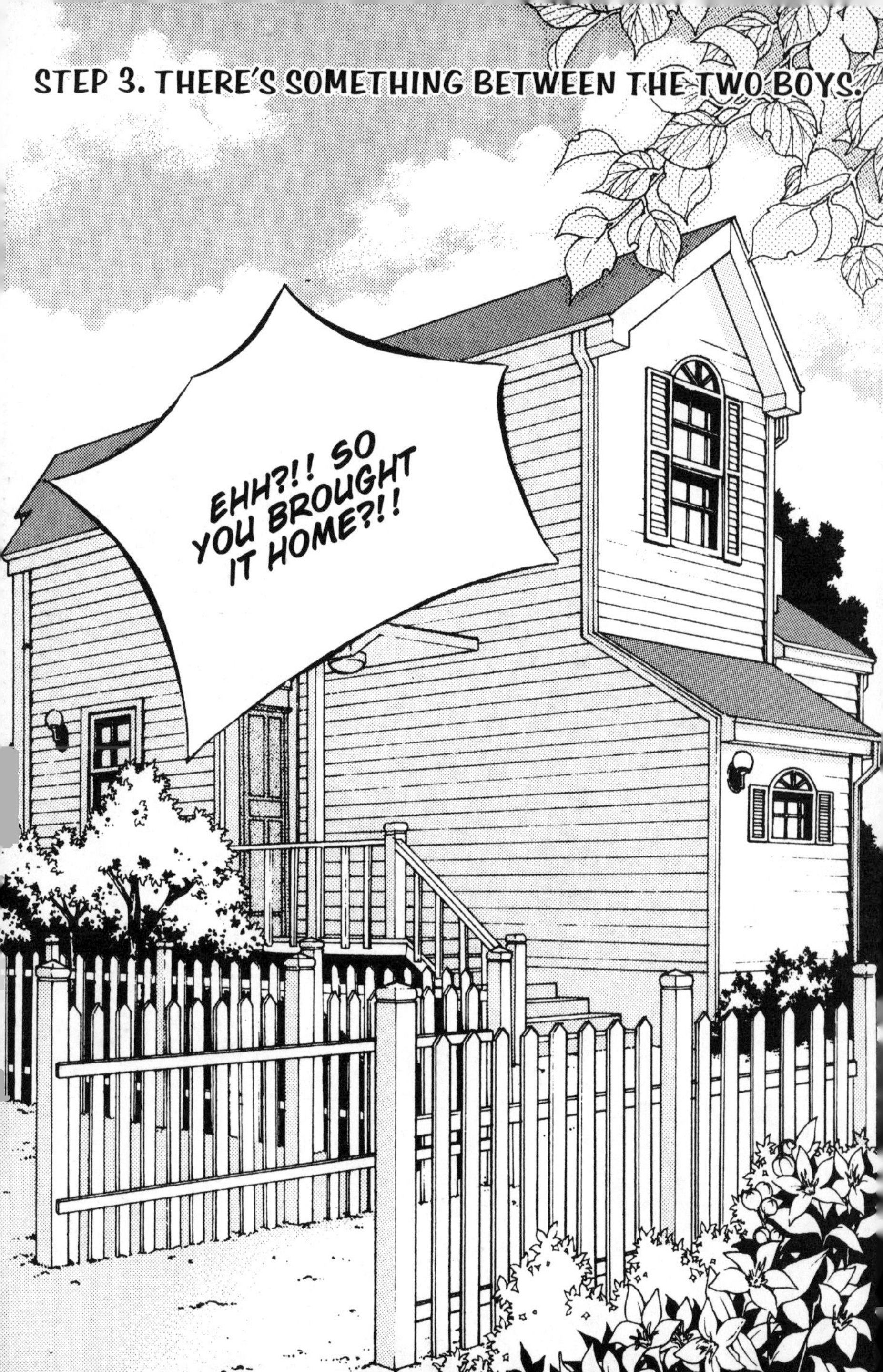
STEP 3. THERE'S SOMETHING BETWEEN THE TWO BOYS.
EHH?!! SO YOU BROUGHT IT HOME?!!

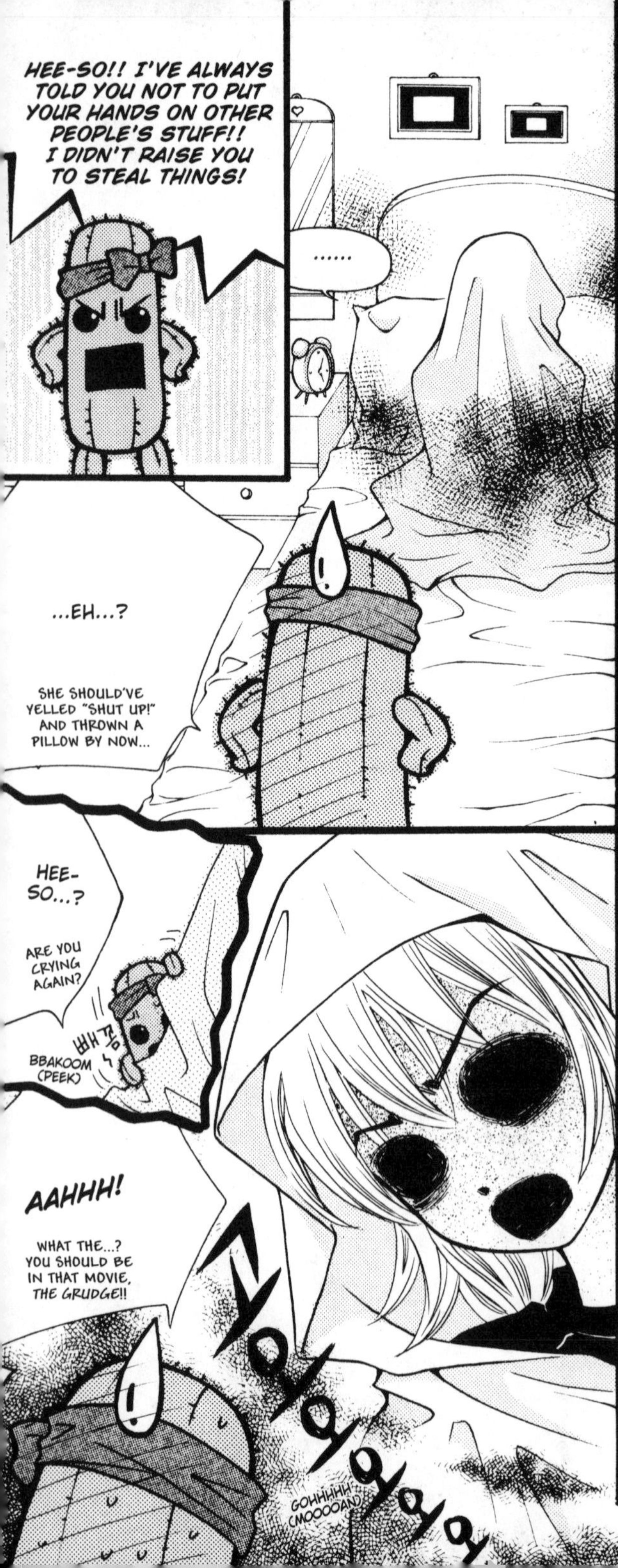
HEE-SO!! I'VE ALWAYS TOLD YOU NOT TO PUT YOUR HANDS ON OTHER PEOPLE'S STUFF!! I DIDN'T RAISE YOU TO STEAL THINGS!
......
...EH...?
SHE SHOULD'VE YELLED "SHUT UP!" AND THROWN A PILLOW BY NOW...
HEE-SO...?
ARE YOU CRYING AGAIN?
BBAKOOM (PEEK)
AAHHH!
WHAT THE...? YOU SHOULD BE IN THAT MOVIE, THE GRUDGE!!
GOHHHHH (MOOOOAN)

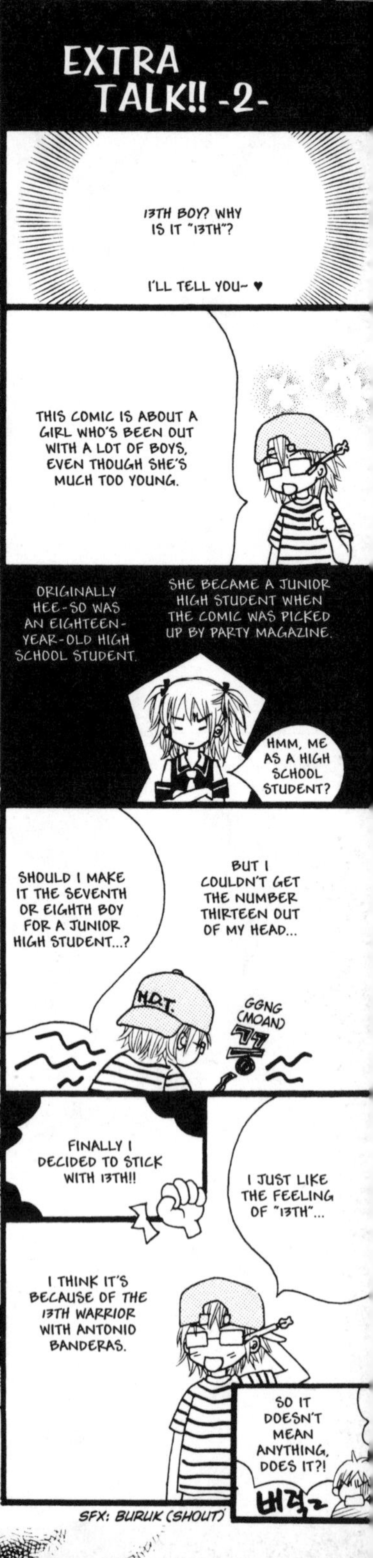
EXTRA TALK!! -2-
13TH BOY? WHY IS IT "13TH"?
I'LL TELL YOU~ ♥
THIS COMIC IS ABOUT A GIRL WHO'S BEEN OUT WITH A LOT OF BOYS, EVEN THOUGH SHE'S MUCH TOO YOUNG.
ORIGINALLY HEE-SO WAS AN EIGHTEEN-YEAR-OLD HIGH SCHOOL STUDENT.
SHE BECAME A JUNIOR HIGH STUDENT WHEN THE COMIC WAS PICKED UP BY PARTY MAGAZINE.
HMM, ME AS A HIGH SCHOOL STUDENT?
SHOULD I MAKE IT THE SEVENTH OR EIGHTH BOY FOR A JUNIOR HIGH STUDENT...?
BUT I COULDN'T GET THE NUMBER THIRTEEN OUT OF MY HEAD...
N.O.T.
GGNG (MOAN)
FINALLY I DECIDED TO STICK WITH 13TH!!
I JUST LIKE THE FEELING OF "13TH"...
I THINK IT'S BECAUSE OF THE 13TH WARRIOR WITH ANTONIO BANDERAS.
SO IT DOESN'T MEAN ANYTHING, DOES IT?!
SFX: BURUK (SHOUT)

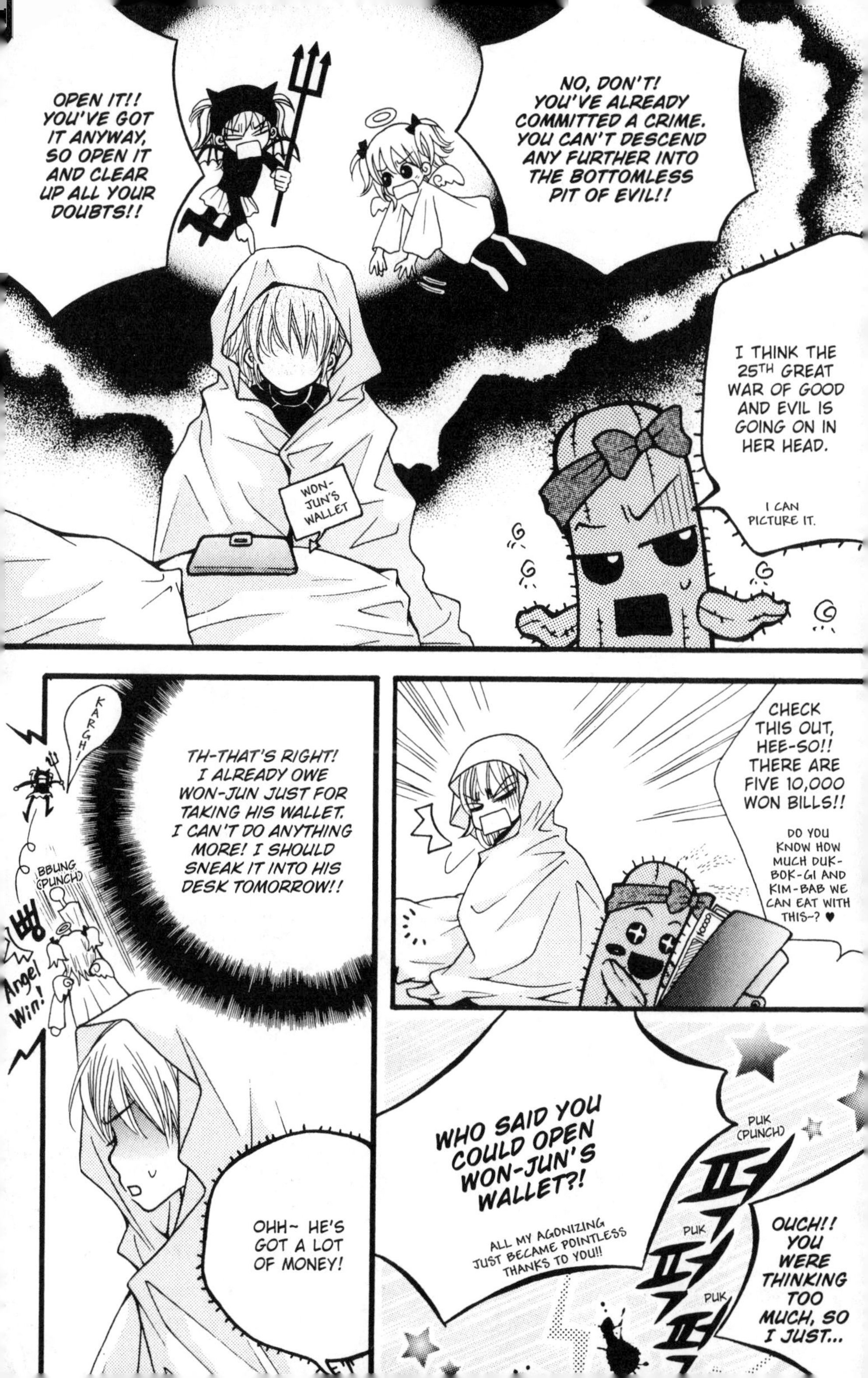
OPEN IT!! YOU'VE GOT IT ANYWAY, SO OPEN IT AND CLEAR UP ALL YOUR DOUBTS!!
NO, DON'T! YOU'VE ALREADY COMMITTED A CRIME. YOU CAN'T DESCEND ANY FURTHER INTO THE BOTTOMLESS PIT OF EVIL!!
WON-JUN'S WALLET
I THINK THE 25TH GREAT WAR OF GOOD AND EVIL IS GOING ON IN HER HEAD.
I CAN PICTURE IT.
KARGH!
TH-THAT'S RIGHT! I ALREADY OWE WON-JUN JUST FOR TAKING HIS WALLET. I CAN'T DO ANYTHING MORE! I SHOULD SNEAK IT INTO HIS DESK TOMORROW!!
BBUNG (PUNCH)
뻥
Angel Win!
OHH~ HE'S GOT A LOT OF MONEY!
CHECK THIS OUT, HEE-SO!! THERE ARE FIVE 10,000 WON BILLS!!
DO YOU KNOW HOW MUCH DUK-BOK-GI AND KIM-BAB WE CAN EAT WITH THIS~? ♥
WHO SAID YOU COULD OPEN WON-JUN'S WALLET?!
ALL MY AGONIZING JUST BECAME POINTLESS THANKS TO YOU!!
PUK (PUNCH)
PUK
PUK
퍽 퍽 퍽
OUCH!! YOU WERE THINKING TOO MUCH, SO I JUST...

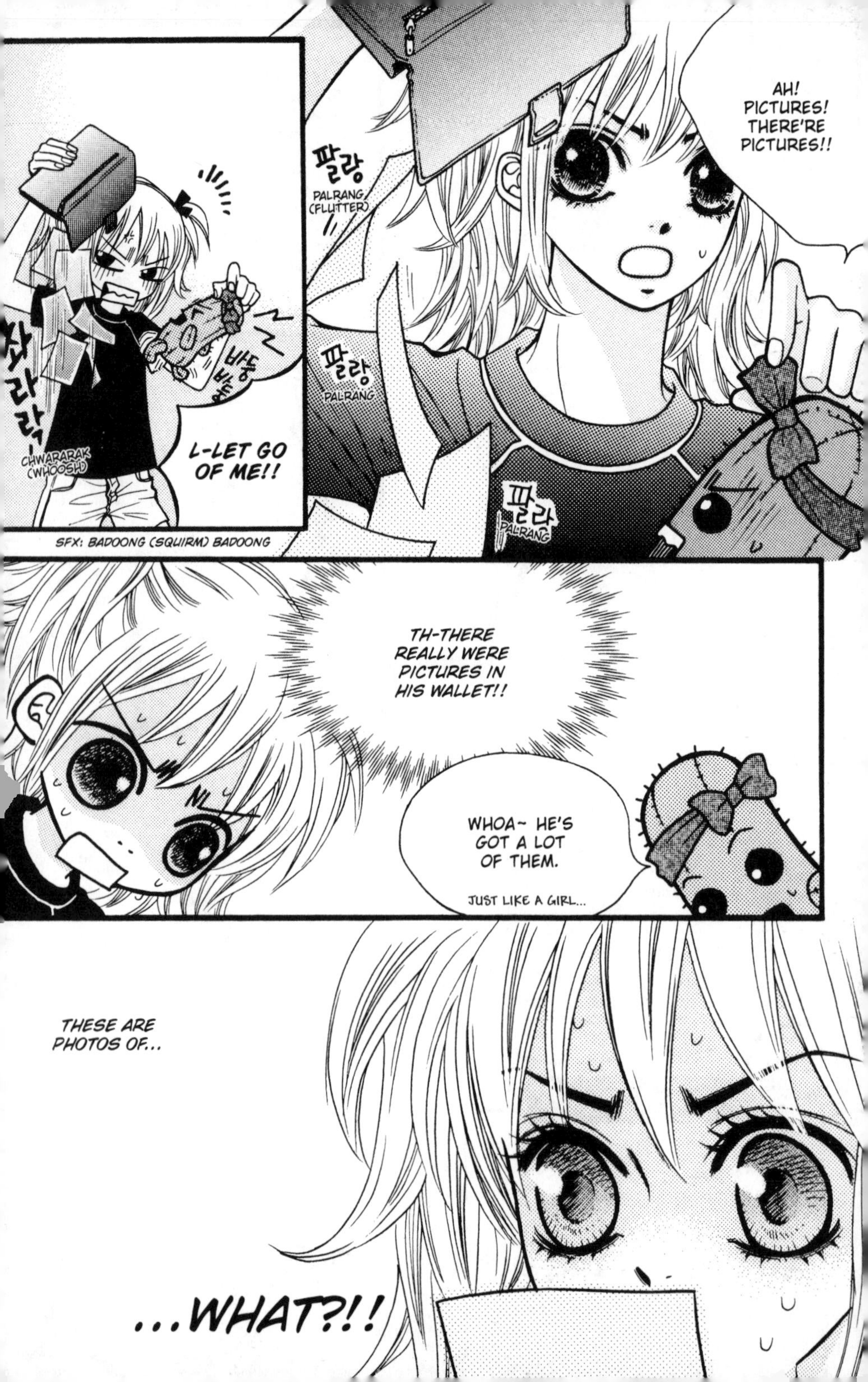

촤라락
CHWARARAK (WHOOSH)
바둥 바둥
L-LET GO OF ME!!
SFX: BADOONG (SQUIRM) BADOONG
팔랑
PALRANG (FLUTTER)
AH! PICTURES! THERE'RE PICTURES!!
팔랑
PALRANG
PALRANG
TH-THERE REALLY WERE PICTURES IN HIS WALLET!!
WHOA~ HE'S GOT A LOT OF THEM.
JUST LIKE A GIRL...
THESE ARE PHOTOS OF...
...WHAT?!!

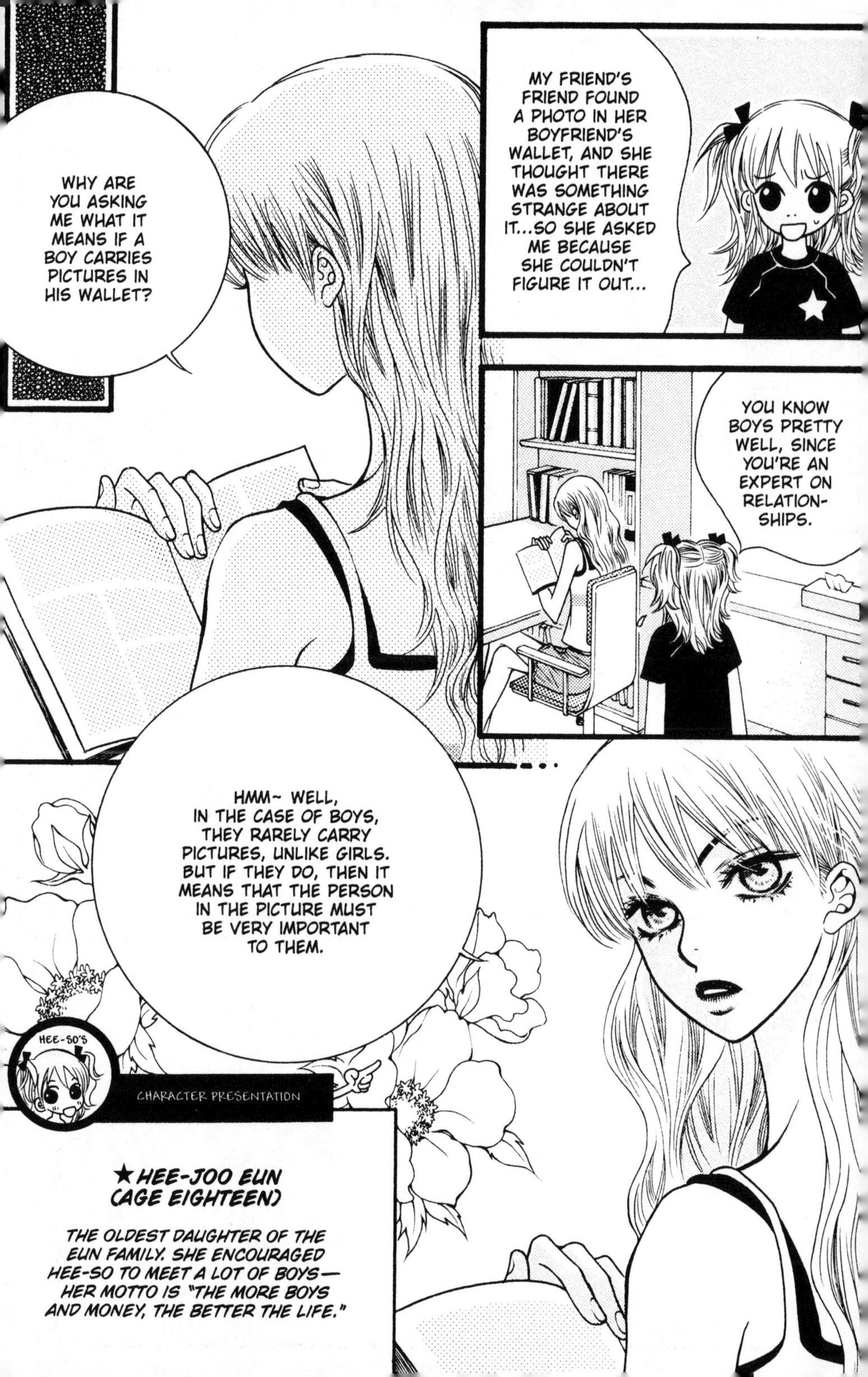
WHY ARE YOU ASKING ME WHAT IT MEANS IF A BOY CARRIES PICTURES IN HIS WALLET?
MY FRIEND'S FRIEND FOUND A PHOTO IN HER BOYFRIEND'S WALLET, AND SHE THOUGHT THERE WAS SOMETHING STRANGE ABOUT IT...SO SHE ASKED ME BECAUSE SHE COULDN'T FIGURE IT OUT...
YOU KNOW BOYS PRETTY WELL, SINCE YOU'RE AN EXPERT ON RELATION-SHIPS.
...
HMM~ WELL, IN THE CASE OF BOYS, THEY RARELY CARRY PICTURES, UNLIKE GIRLS. BUT IF THEY DO, THEN IT MEANS THAT THE PERSON IN THE PICTURE MUST BE VERY IMPORTANT TO THEM.
HEE-SO'S
CHARACTER PRESENTATION
★HEE-JOO EUN (AGE EIGHTEEN)
THE OLDEST DAUGHTER OF THE EUN FAMILY. SHE ENCOURAGED HEE-SO TO MEET A LOT OF BOYS—HER MOTTO IS "THE MORE BOYS AND MONEY, THE BETTER THE LIFE."

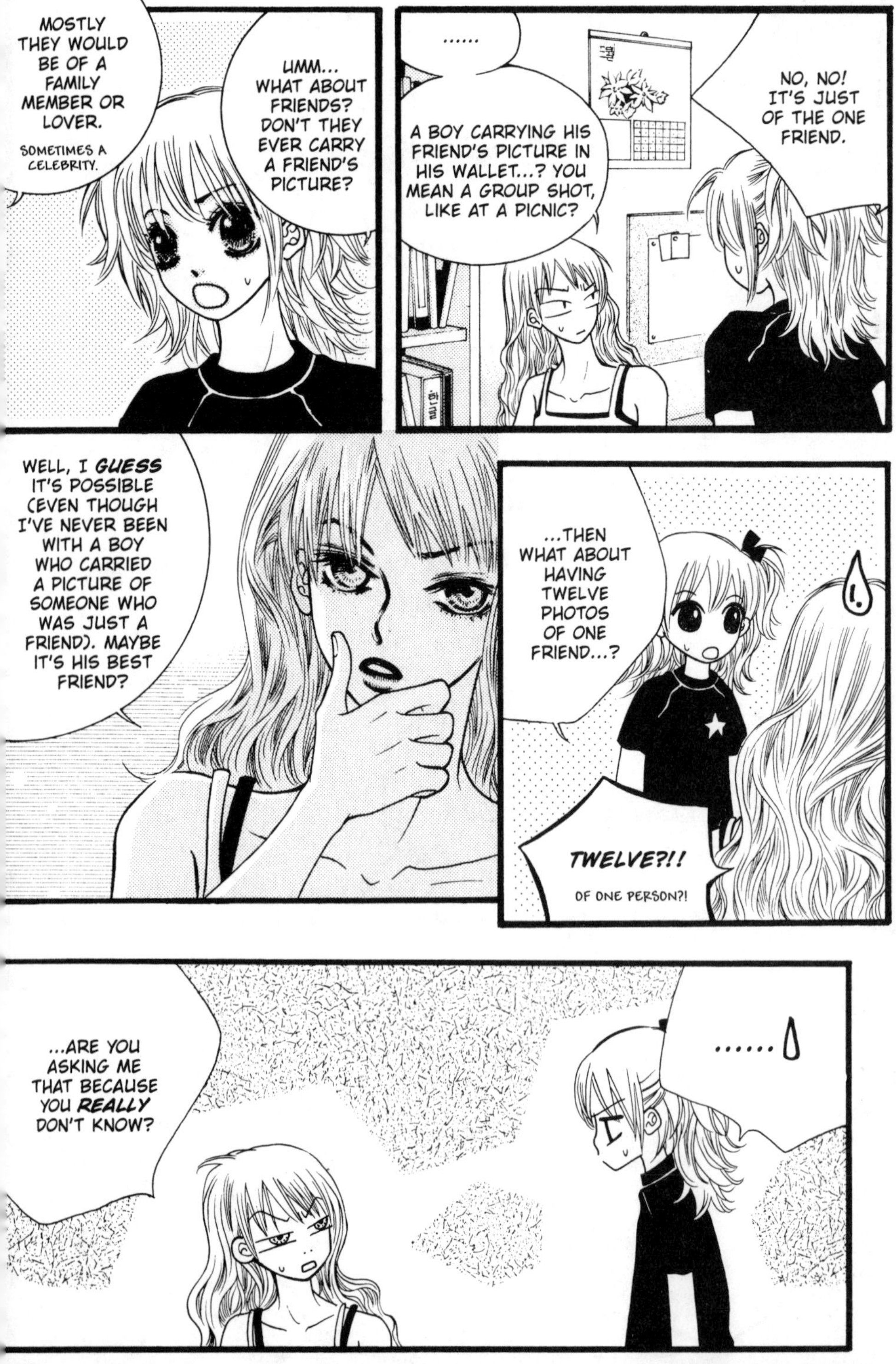
MOSTLY THEY WOULD BE OF A FAMILY MEMBER OR LOVER.
SOMETIMES A CELEBRITY.
UMM... WHAT ABOUT FRIENDS? DON'T THEY EVER CARRY A FRIEND'S PICTURE?
......
A BOY CARRYING HIS FRIEND'S PICTURE IN HIS WALLET...? YOU MEAN A GROUP SHOT, LIKE AT A PICNIC?
NO, NO! IT'S JUST OF THE ONE FRIEND.
WELL, I GUESS IT'S POSSIBLE (EVEN THOUGH I'VE NEVER BEEN WITH A BOY WHO CARRIED A PICTURE OF SOMEONE WHO WAS JUST A FRIEND). MAYBE IT'S HIS BEST FRIEND?
...THEN WHAT ABOUT HAVING TWELVE PHOTOS OF ONE FRIEND...?
TWELVE?!!
OF ONE PERSON?!
...ARE YOU ASKING ME THAT BECAUSE YOU REALLY DON'T KNOW?
......

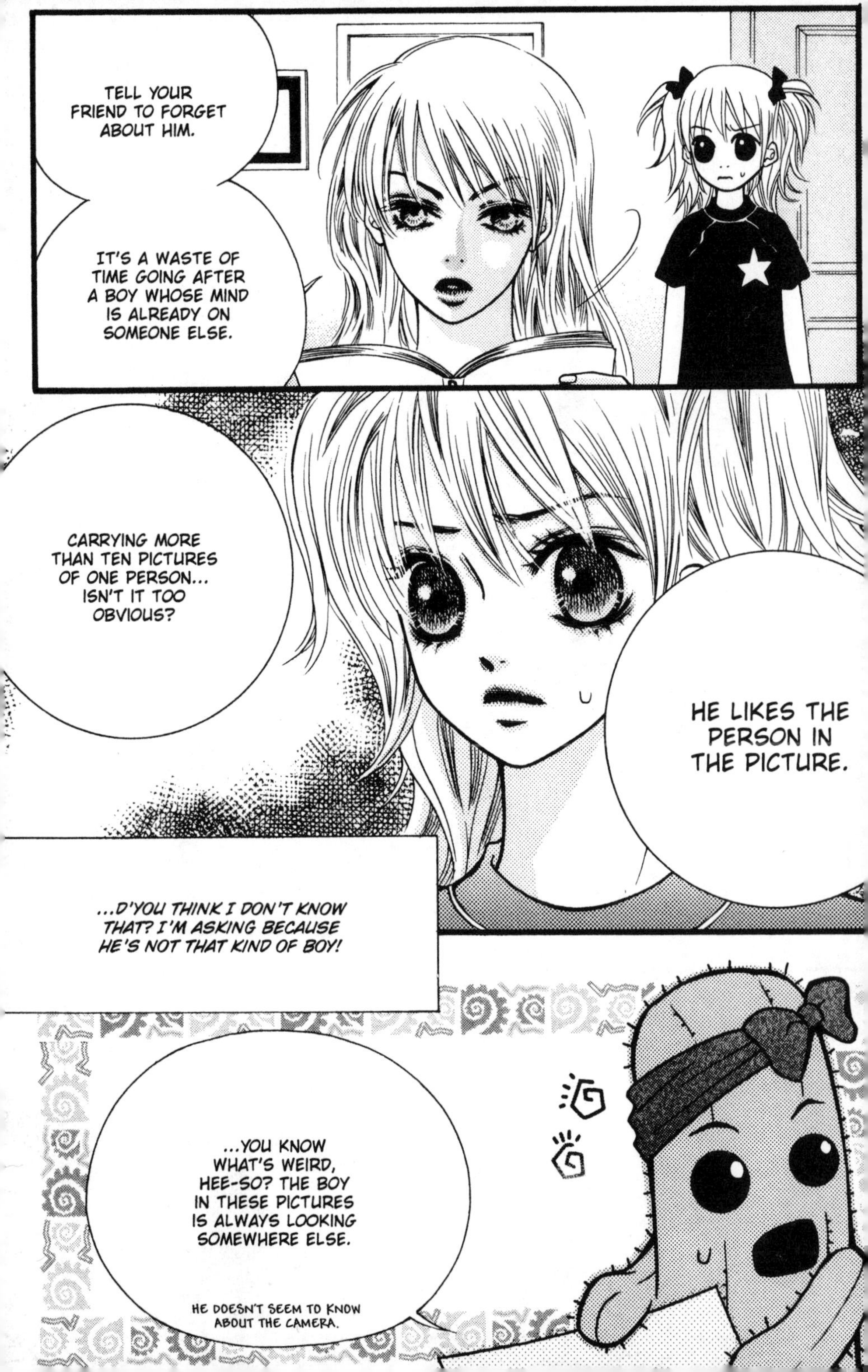
TELL YOUR FRIEND TO FORGET ABOUT HIM.
IT'S A WASTE OF TIME GOING AFTER A BOY WHOSE MIND IS ALREADY ON SOMEONE ELSE.
CARRYING MORE THAN TEN PICTURES OF ONE PERSON... ISN'T IT TOO OBVIOUS?
HE LIKES THE PERSON IN THE PICTURE.
...D'YOU THINK I DON'T KNOW THAT? I'M ASKING BECAUSE HE'S NOT THAT KIND OF BOY!
...YOU KNOW WHAT'S WEIRD, HEE-SO? THE BOY IN THESE PICTURES IS ALWAYS LOOKING SOMEWHERE ELSE.
HE DOESN'T SEEM TO KNOW ABOUT THE CAMERA.

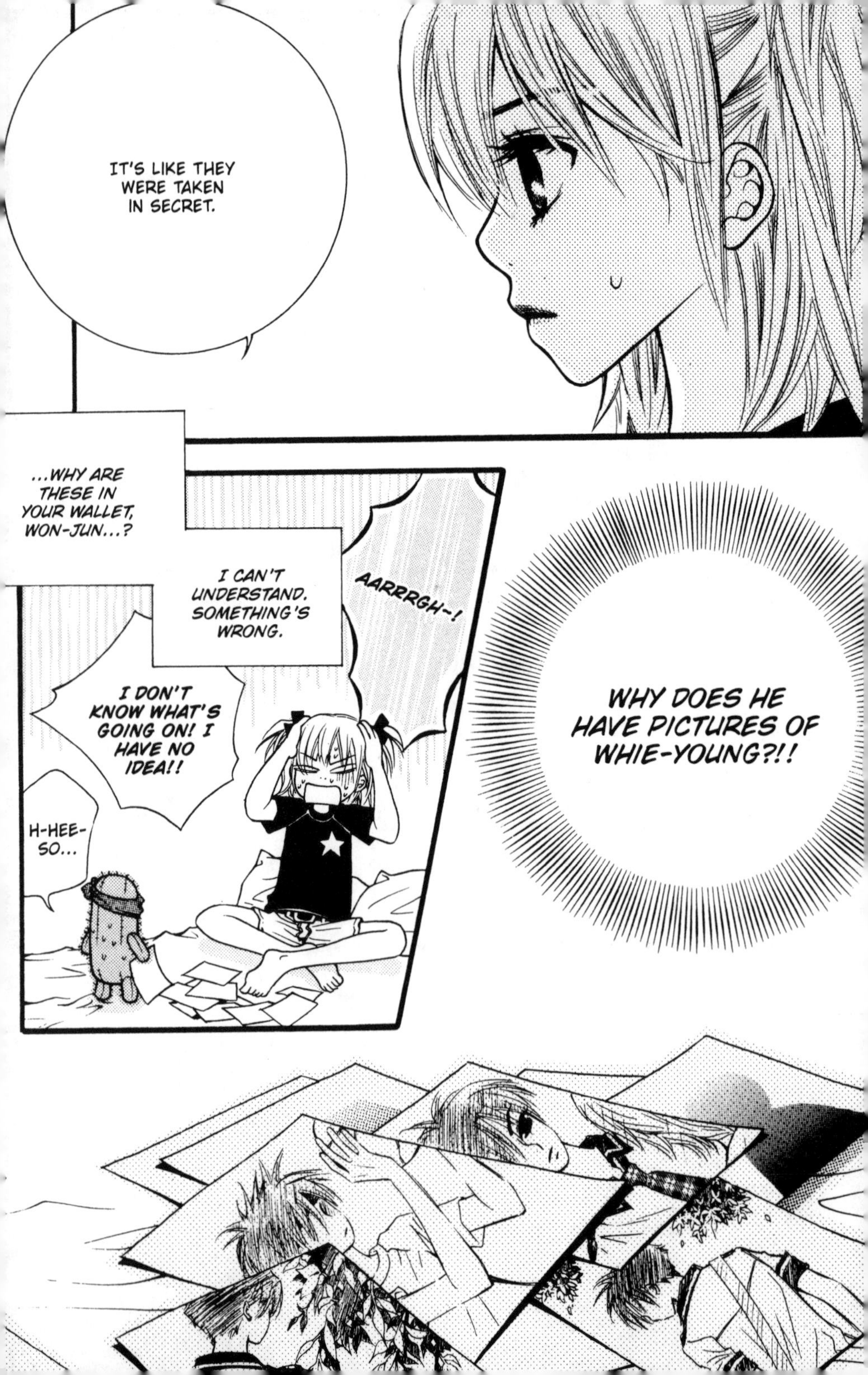
IT'S LIKE THEY WERE TAKEN IN SECRET.
...WHY ARE THESE IN YOUR WALLET, WON-JUN...?
I CAN'T UNDERSTAND. SOMETHING'S WRONG.
AARRRGH~!
I DON'T KNOW WHAT'S GOING ON! I HAVE NO IDEA!!
H-HEE-SO...
WHY DOES HE HAVE PICTURES OF WHIE-YOUNG?!!

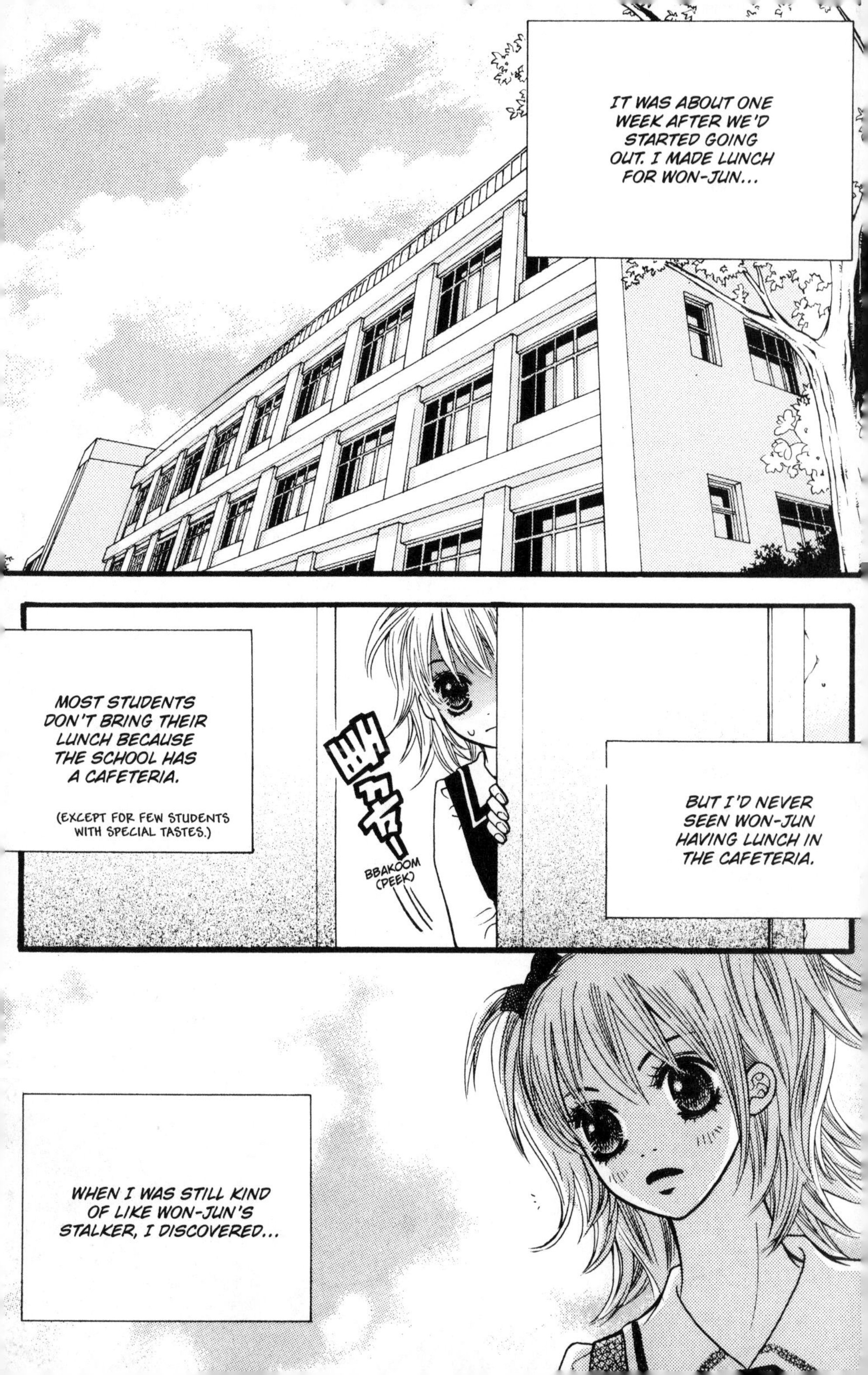
IT WAS ABOUT ONE WEEK AFTER WE'D STARTED GOING OUT. I MADE LUNCH FOR WON-JUN...
MOST STUDENTS DON'T BRING THEIR LUNCH BECAUSE THE SCHOOL HAS A CAFETERIA.
(EXCEPT FOR FEW STUDENTS WITH SPECIAL TASTES.)
BBAKOOM (PEEK)
BUT I'D NEVER SEEN WON-JUN HAVING LUNCH IN THE CAFETERIA.
WHEN I WAS STILL KIND OF LIKE WON-JUN'S STALKER, I DISCOVERED...

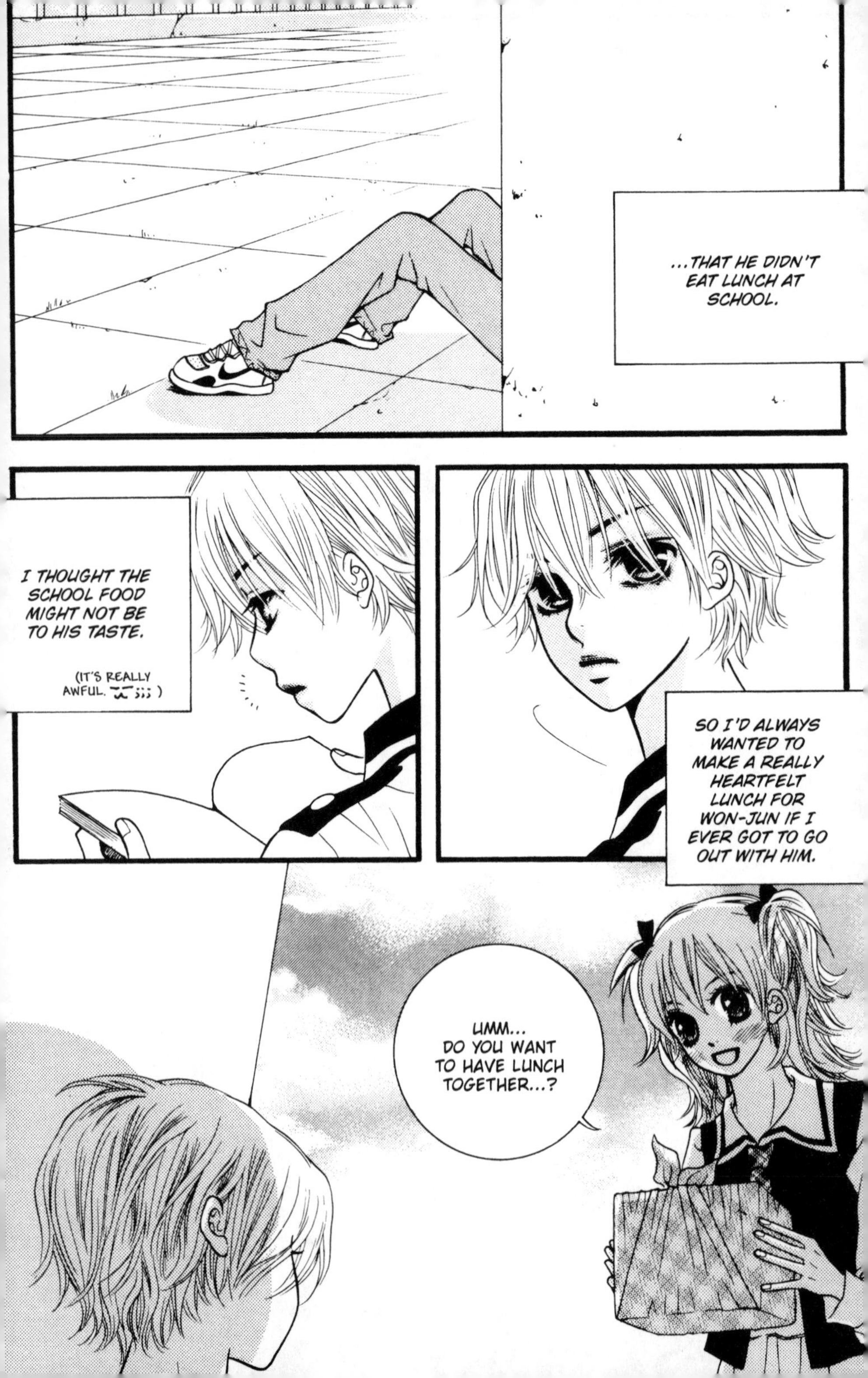
...THAT HE DIDN'T EAT LUNCH AT SCHOOL.
I THOUGHT THE SCHOOL FOOD MIGHT NOT BE TO HIS TASTE.
(IT'S REALLY AWFUL.)
SO I'D ALWAYS WANTED TO MAKE A REALLY HEARTFELT LUNCH FOR WON-JUN IF I EVER GOT TO GO OUT WITH HIM.
UMM... DO YOU WANT TO HAVE LUNCH TOGETHER...?

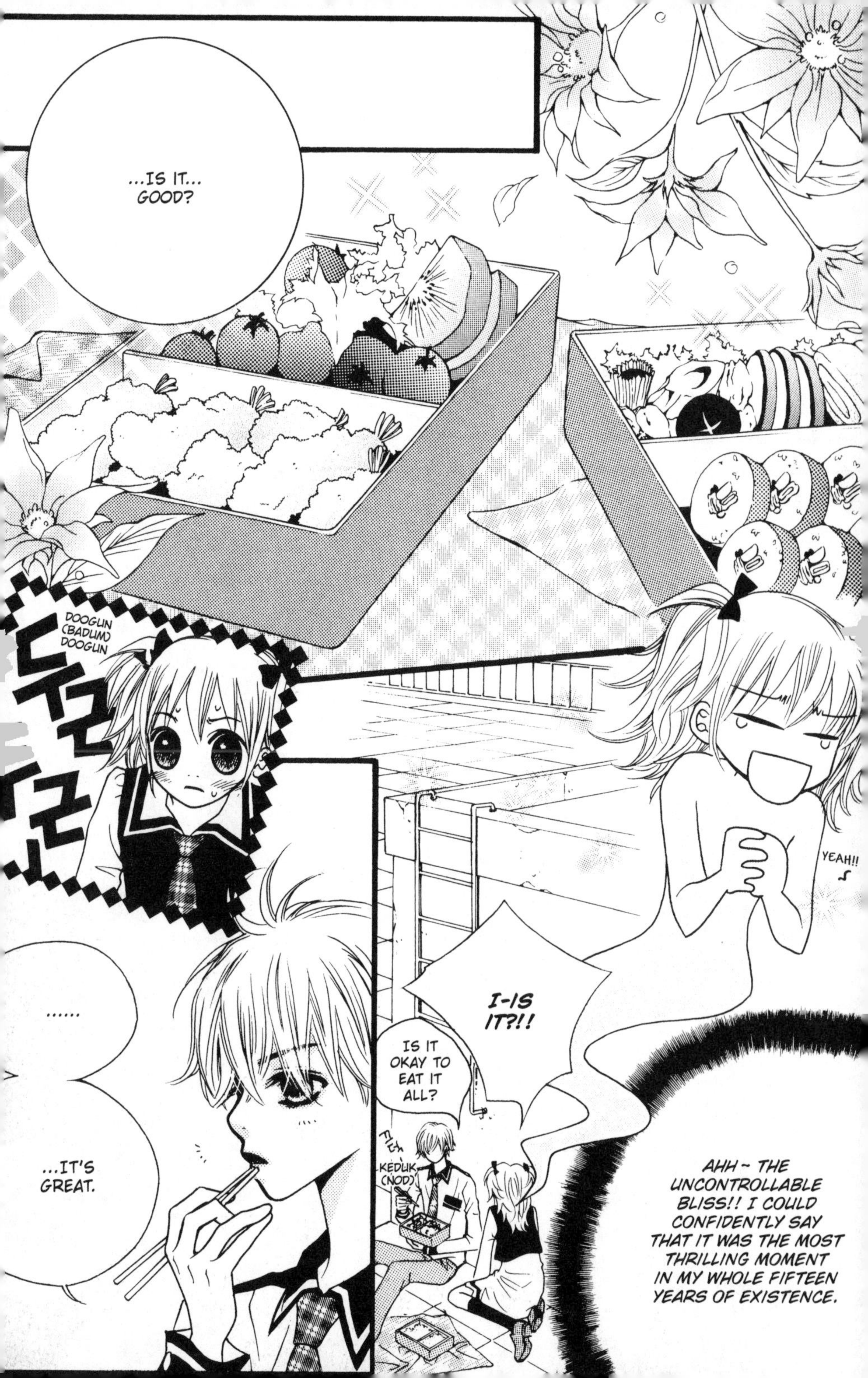
...IS IT... GOOD?
DOOGUN (BADUM) DOOGUN
YEAH!!
......
...IT'S GREAT.
I-IS IT?!!
IS IT OKAY TO EAT IT ALL?
KEDUK (NOD)
AHH~ THE UNCONTROLLABLE BLISS!! I COULD CONFIDENTLY SAY THAT IT WAS THE MOST THRILLING MOMENT IN MY WHOLE FIFTEEN YEARS OF EXISTENCE.

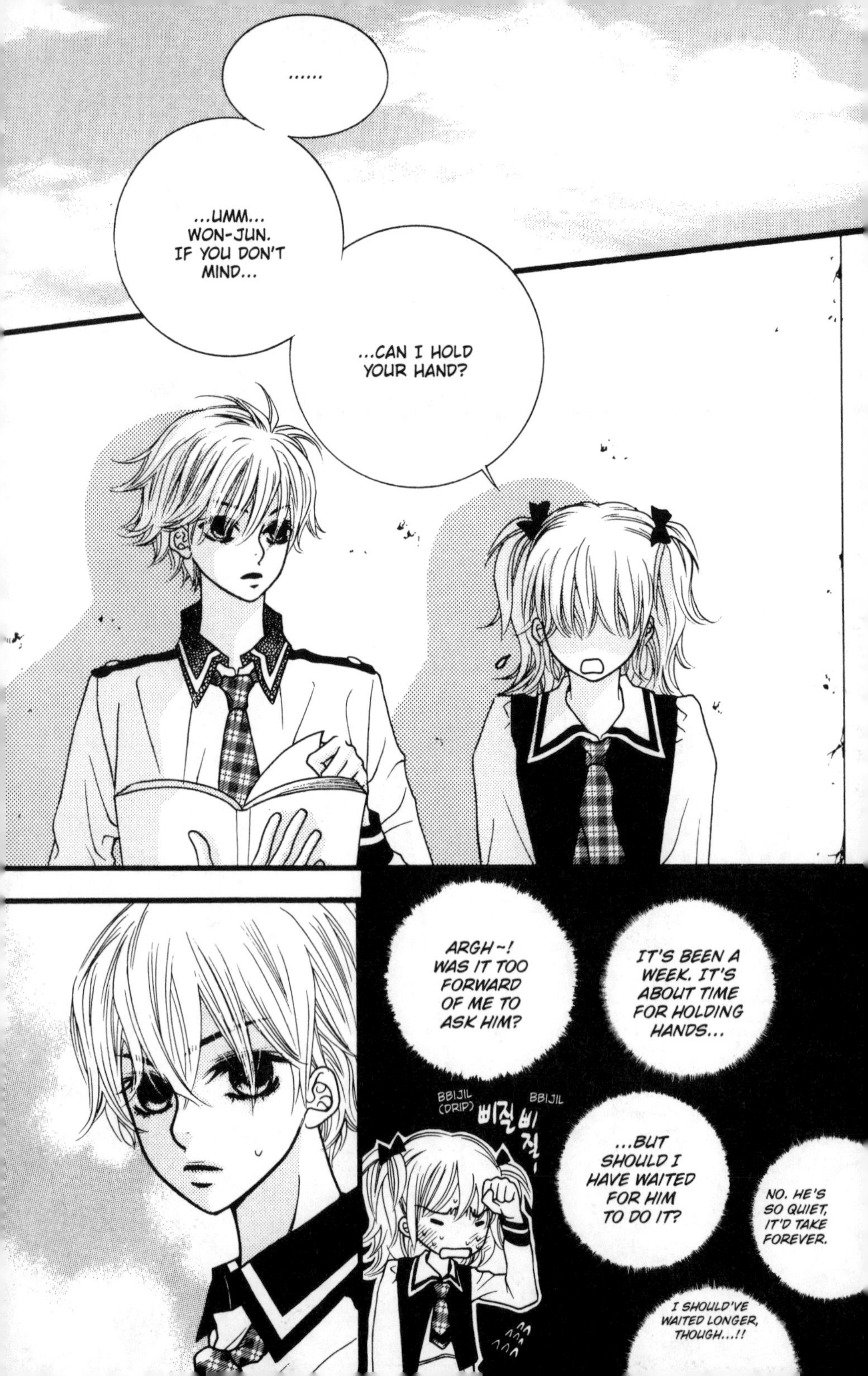
......
...UMM... WON-JUN. IF YOU DON'T MIND...
...CAN I HOLD YOUR HAND?
ARGH~! WAS IT TOO FORWARD OF ME TO ASK HIM?
IT'S BEEN A WEEK. IT'S ABOUT TIME FOR HOLDING HANDS...
BBIJIL (DRIP)
삐질삐질
BBIJIL
...BUT SHOULD I HAVE WAITED FOR HIM TO DO IT?
NO. HE'S SO QUIET, IT'D TAKE FOREVER.
I SHOULD'VE WAITED LONGER, THOUGH...!!

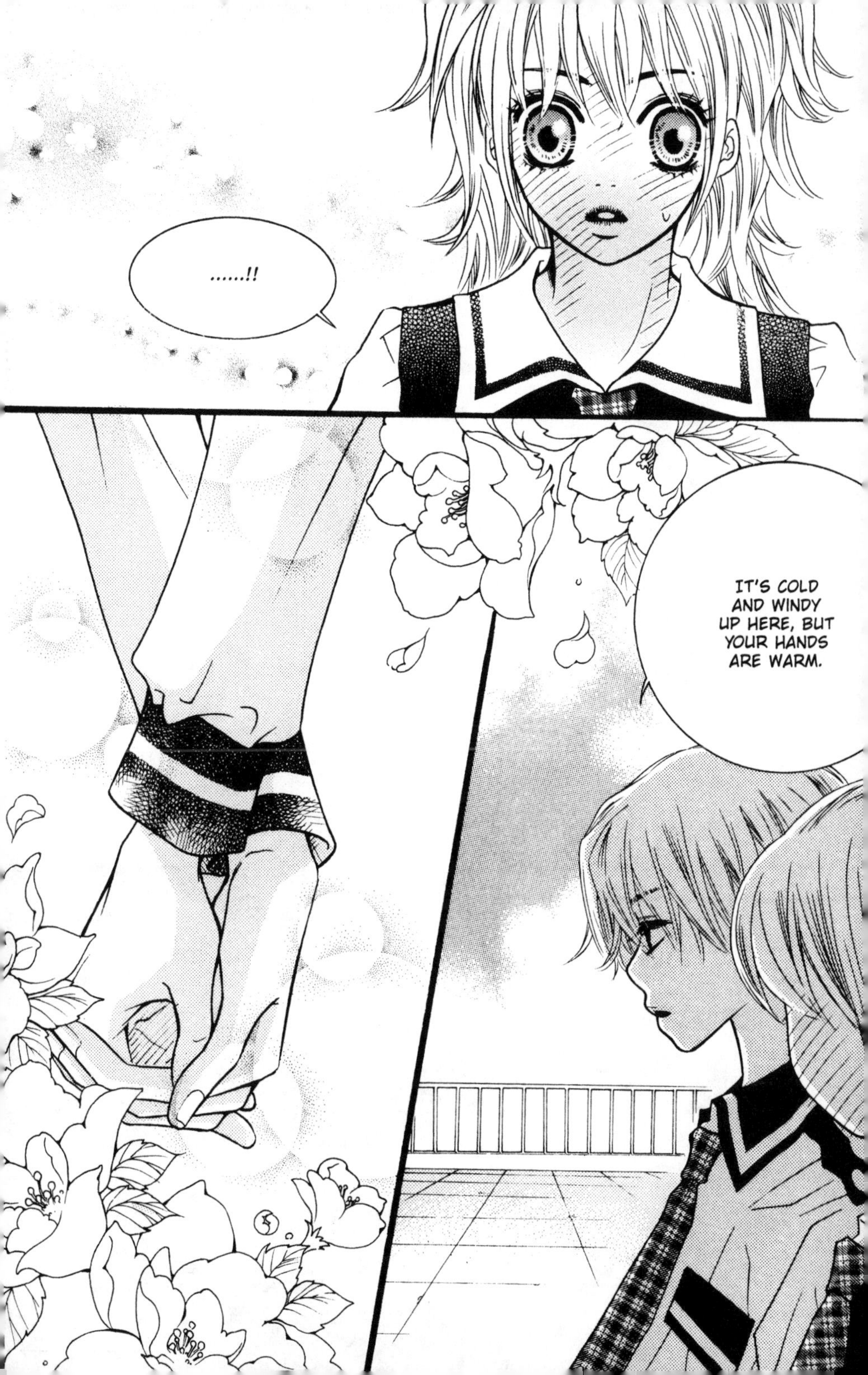
......!!
IT'S COLD AND WINDY UP HERE, BUT YOUR HANDS ARE WARM.

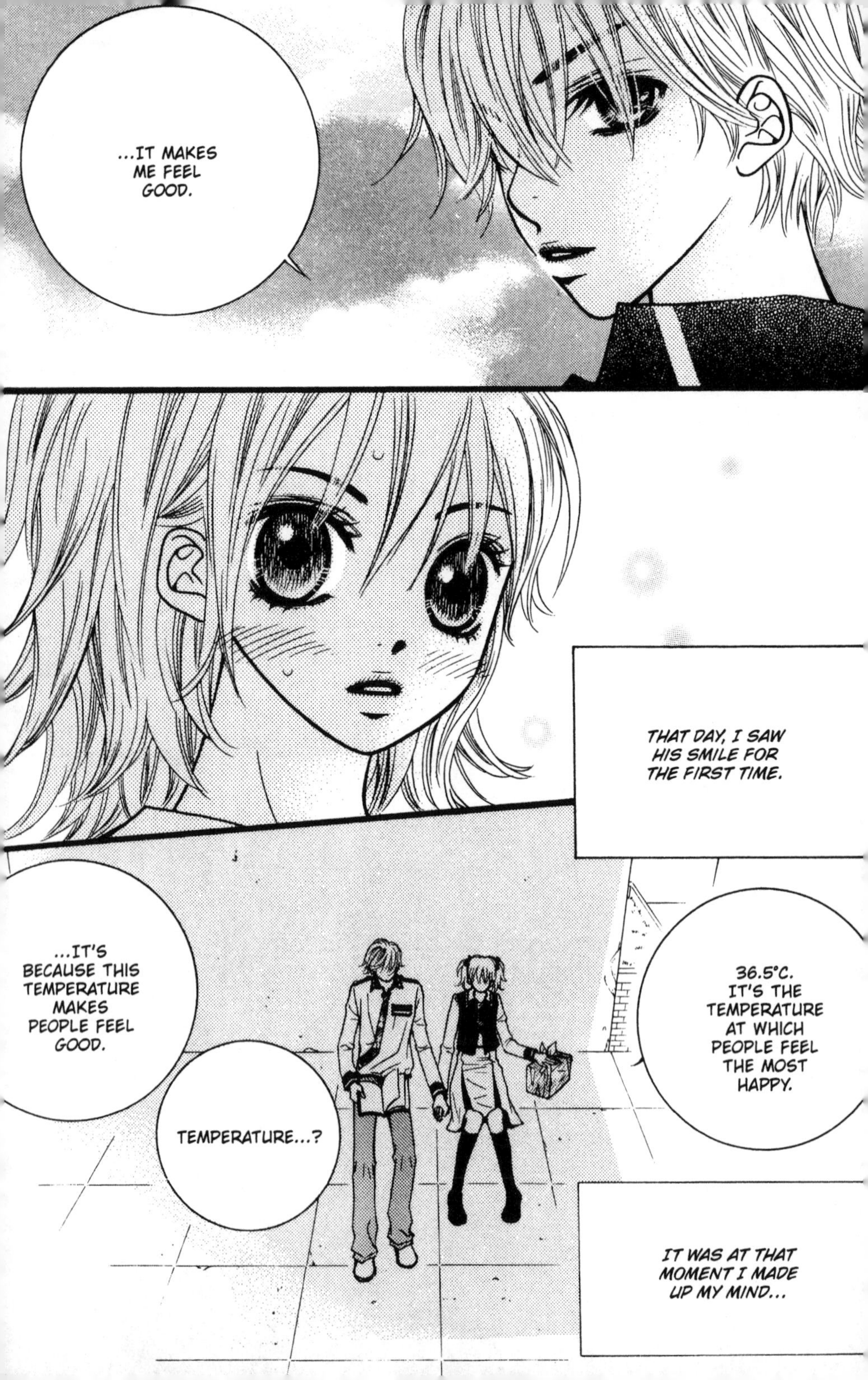
...IT MAKES ME FEEL GOOD.
THAT DAY, I SAW HIS SMILE FOR THE FIRST TIME.
...IT'S BECAUSE THIS TEMPERATURE MAKES PEOPLE FEEL GOOD.
TEMPERATURE...?
36.5°C. IT'S THE TEMPERATURE AT WHICH PEOPLE FEEL THE MOST HAPPY.
IT WAS AT THAT MOMENT I MADE UP MY MIND...

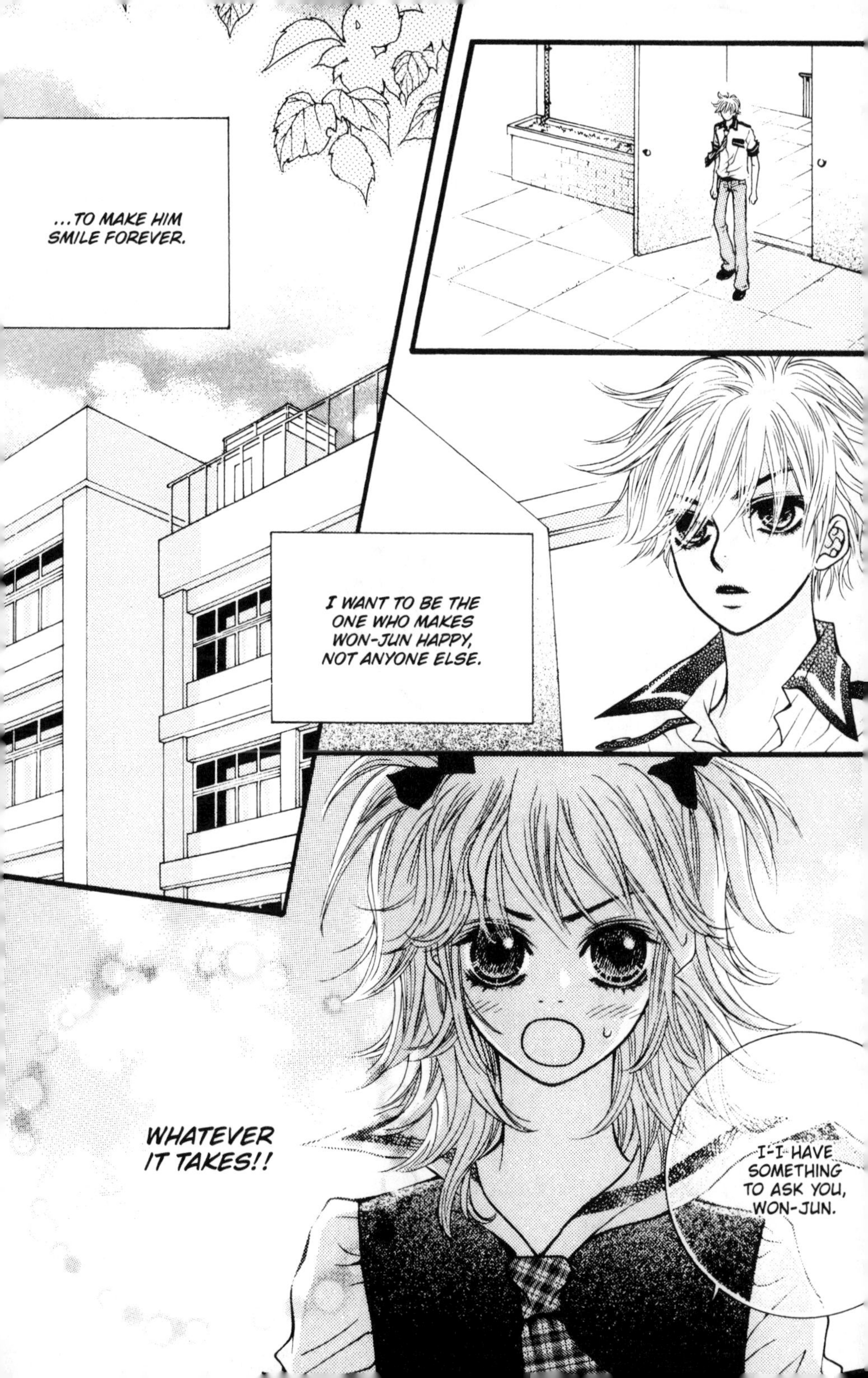
...TO MAKE HIM SMILE FOREVER.
I WANT TO BE THE ONE WHO MAKES WON-JUN HAPPY, NOT ANYONE ELSE.
WHATEVER IT TAKES!!
I-I HAVE SOMETHING TO ASK YOU, WON-JUN.

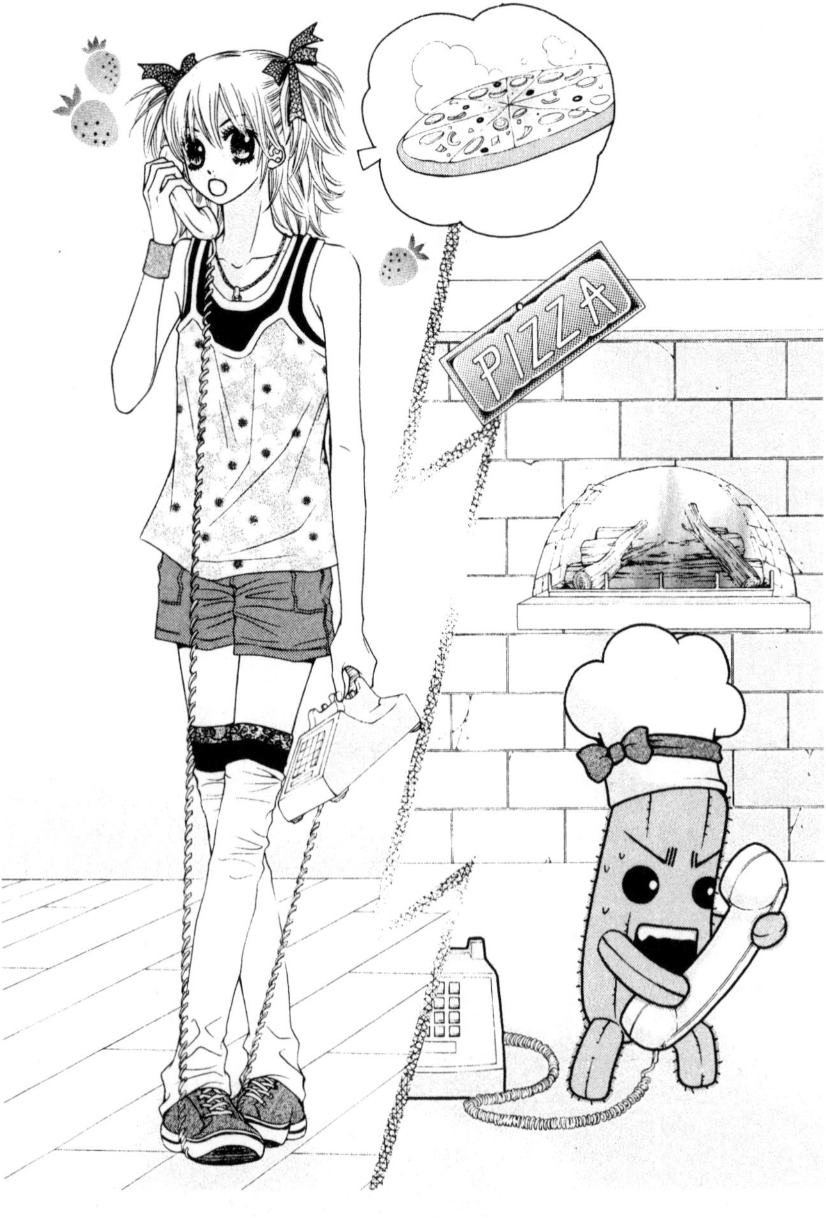
PIZZA

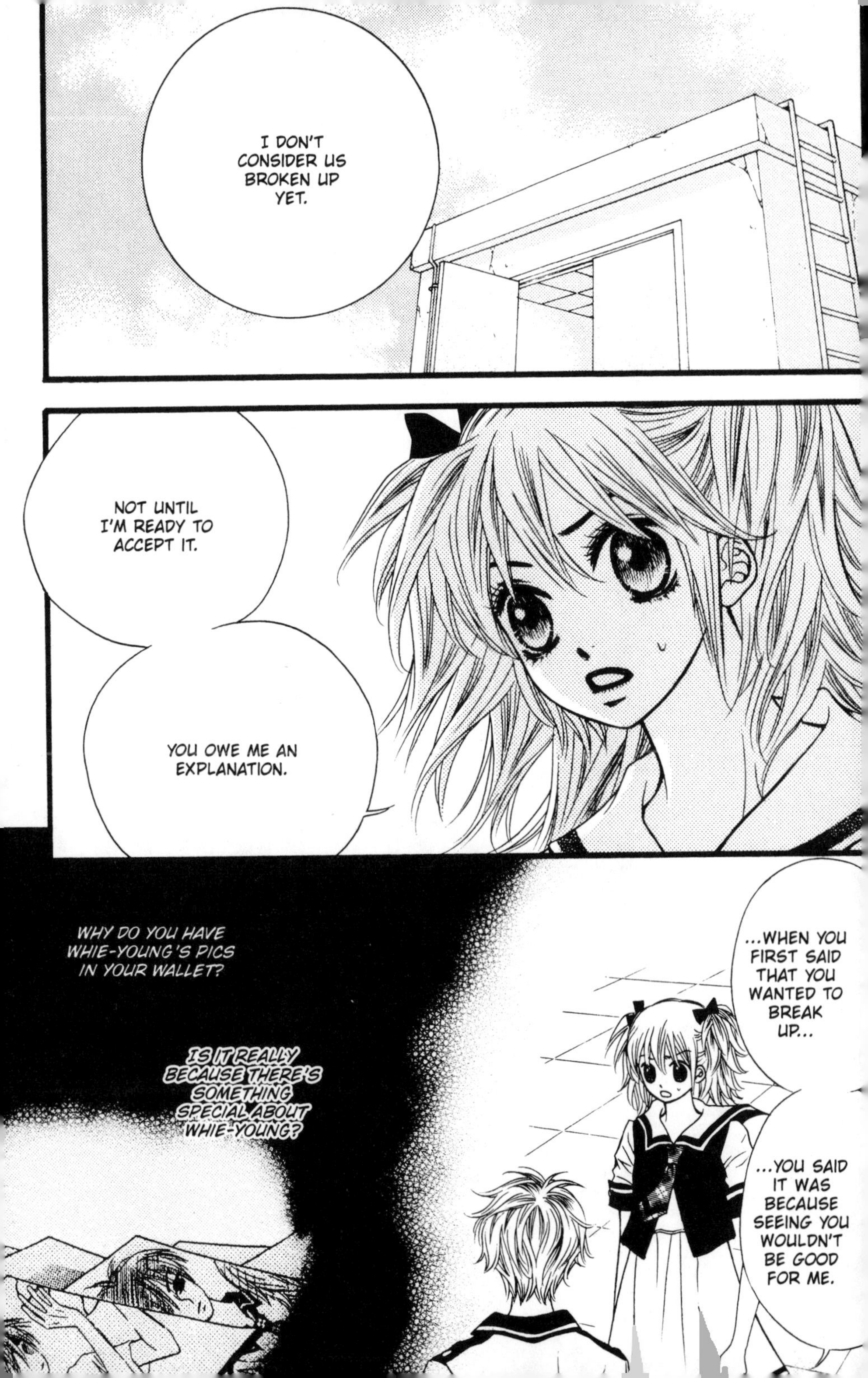
I DON'T CONSIDER US BROKEN UP YET.
NOT UNTIL I'M READY TO ACCEPT IT.
YOU OWE ME AN EXPLANATION.
WHY DO YOU HAVE WHIE-YOUNG'S PICS IN YOUR WALLET?
IS IT REALLY BECAUSE THERE'S SOMETHING SPECIAL ABOUT WHIE-YOUNG?
...WHEN YOU FIRST SAID THAT YOU WANTED TO BREAK UP...
...YOU SAID IT WAS BECAUSE SEEING YOU WOULDN'T BE GOOD FOR ME.

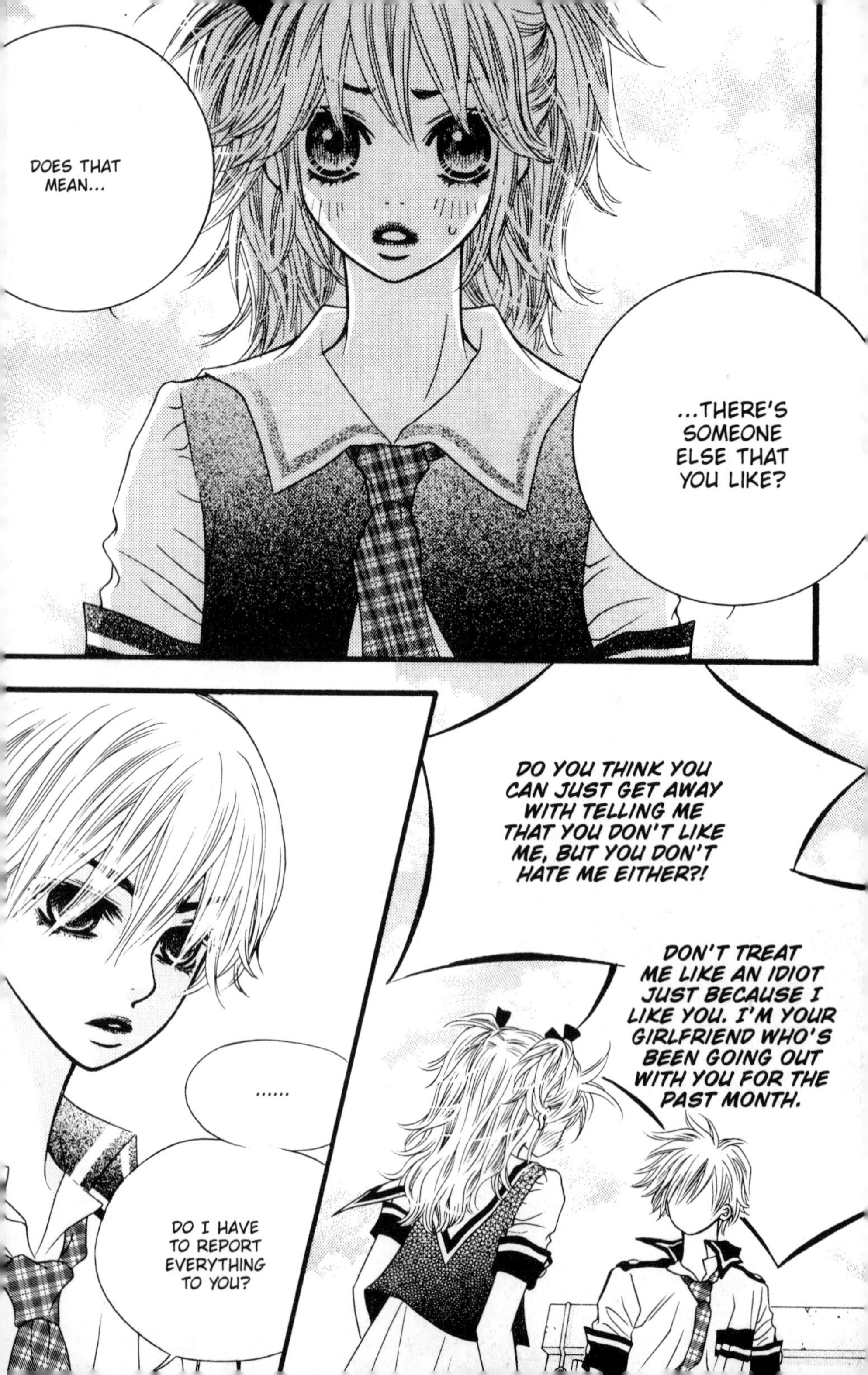
DOES THAT MEAN...
...THERE'S SOMEONE ELSE THAT YOU LIKE?
......
DO I HAVE TO REPORT EVERYTHING TO YOU?
DO YOU THINK YOU CAN JUST GET AWAY WITH TELLING ME THAT YOU DON'T LIKE ME, BUT YOU DON'T HATE ME EITHER?!
DON'T TREAT ME LIKE AN IDIOT JUST BECAUSE I LIKE YOU. I'M YOUR GIRLFRIEND WHO'S BEEN GOING OUT WITH YOU FOR THE PAST MONTH.

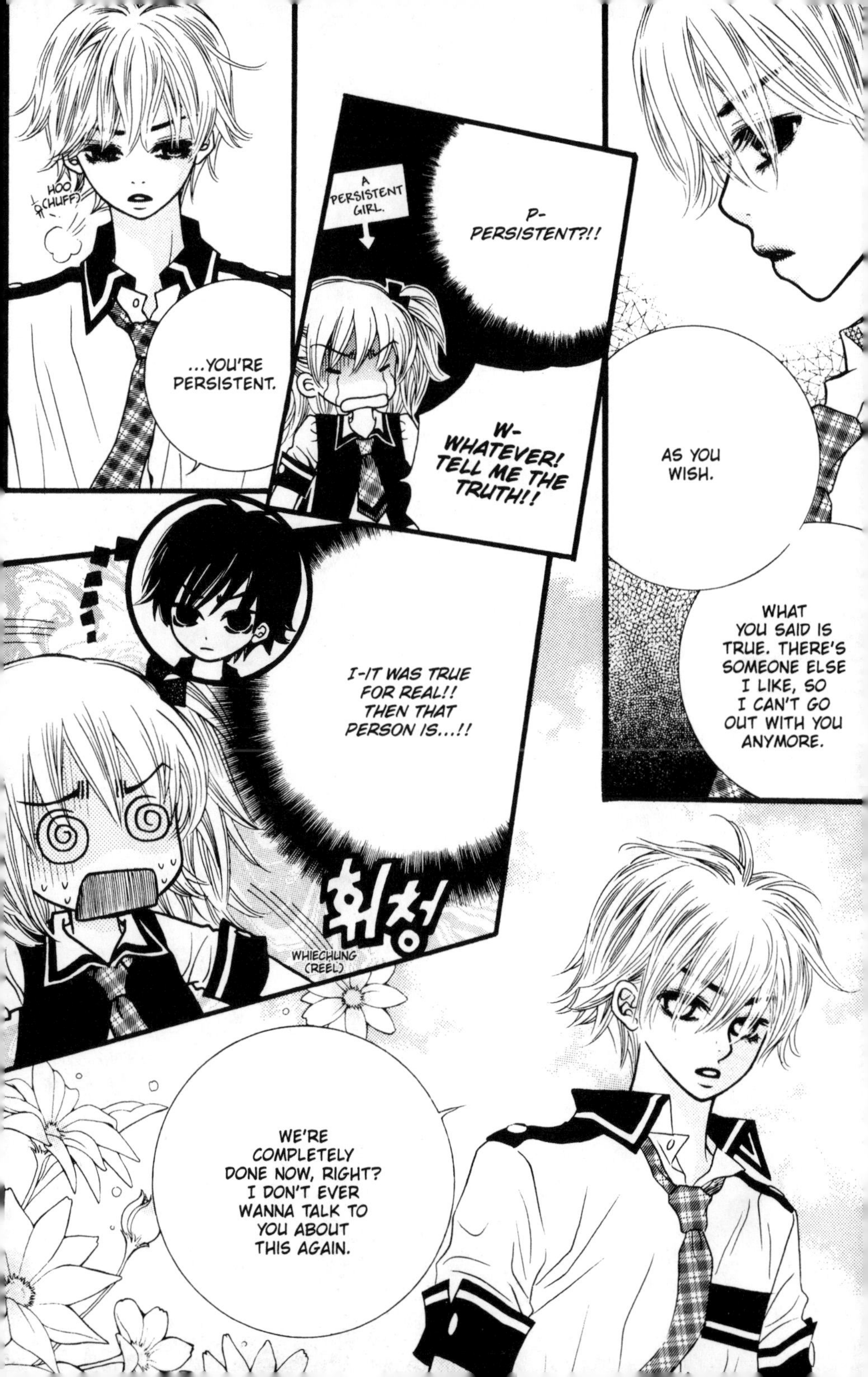
HOO (CHUFF)
...YOU'RE PERSISTENT.
A PERSISTENT GIRL.
P- PERSISTENT?!!
W- WHATEVER! TELL ME THE TRUTH!!
AS YOU WISH.
WHAT YOU SAID IS TRUE. THERE'S SOMEONE ELSE I LIKE, SO I CAN'T GO OUT WITH YOU ANYMORE.
I-IT WAS TRUE FOR REAL!! THEN THAT PERSON IS...!!
휘청
WHIECHUNG (REEL)
WE'RE COMPLETELY DONE NOW, RIGHT? I DON'T EVER WANNA TALK TO YOU ABOUT THIS AGAIN.

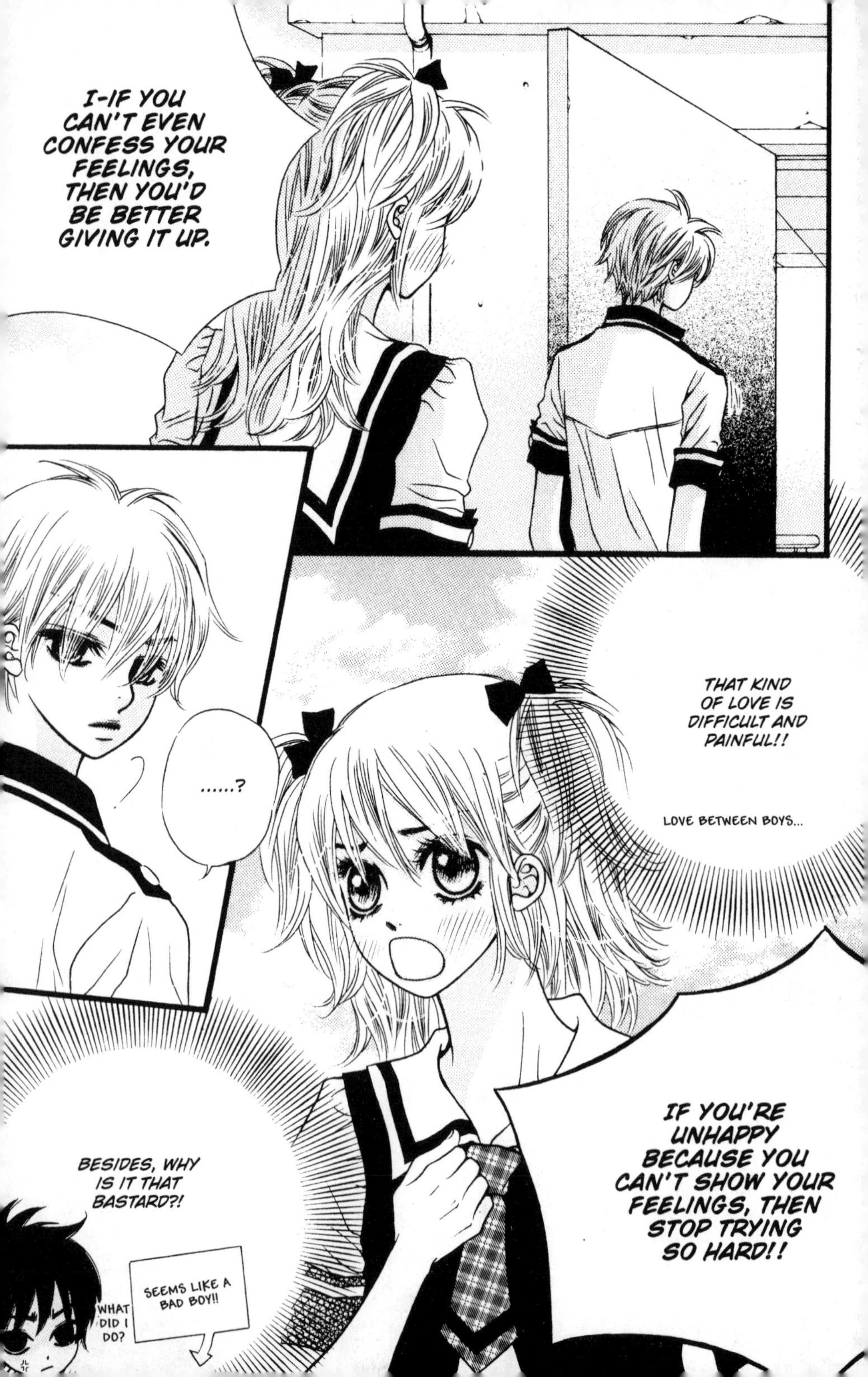
I-IF YOU CAN'T EVEN CONFESS YOUR FEELINGS, THEN YOU'D BE BETTER GIVING IT UP.
......?
THAT KIND OF LOVE IS DIFFICULT AND PAINFUL!!
LOVE BETWEEN BOYS...
BESIDES, WHY IS IT THAT BASTARD?!
SEEMS LIKE A BAD BOY!!
WHAT DID I DO?
IF YOU'RE UNHAPPY BECAUSE YOU CAN'T SHOW YOUR FEELINGS, THEN STOP TRYING SO HARD!!

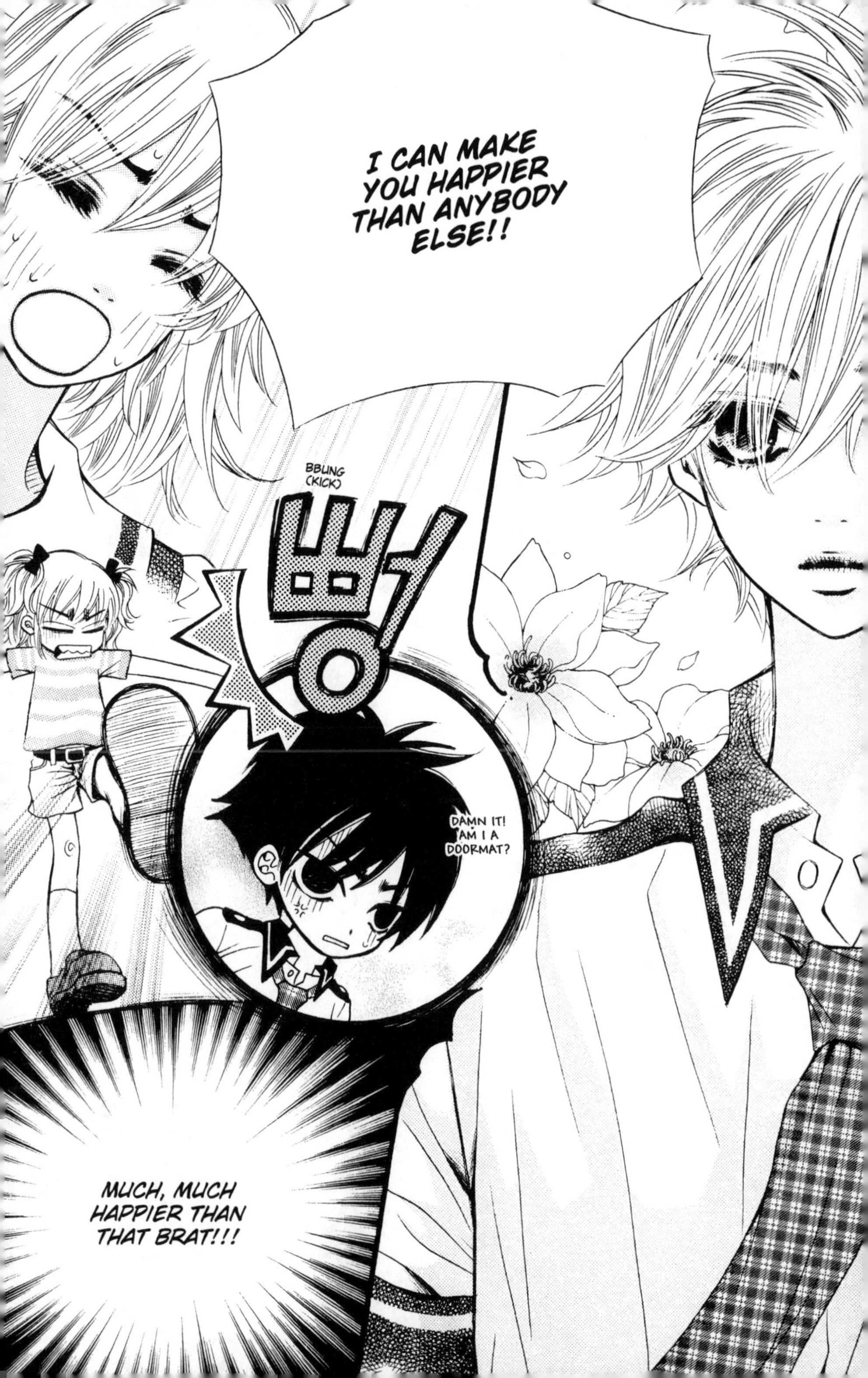
I CAN MAKE YOU HAPPIER THAN ANYBODY ELSE!!
BBUNG (KICK)
뻥
DAMN IT! AM I A DOORMAT?
MUCH, MUCH HAPPIER THAN THAT BRAT!!!

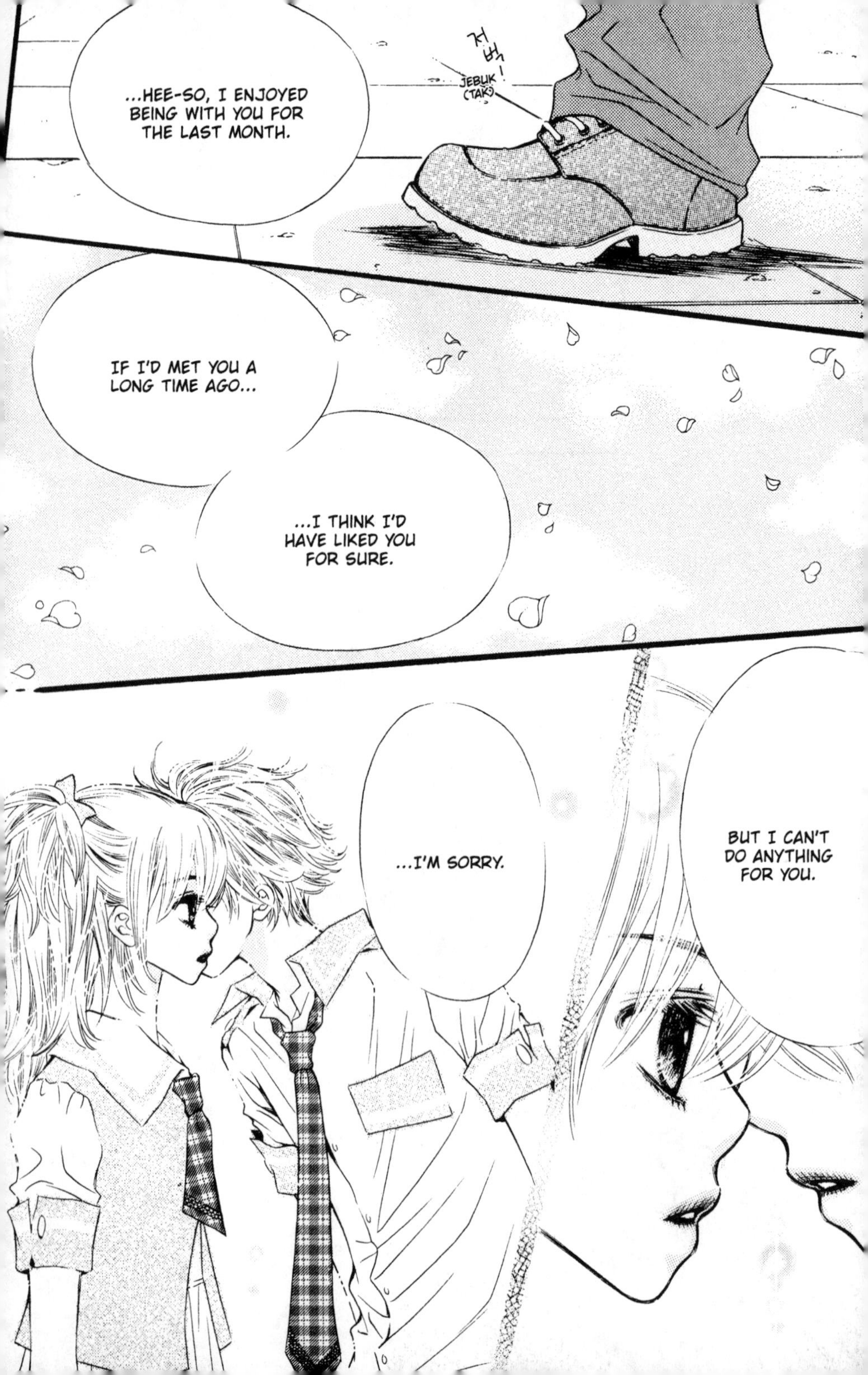

저벅
JEBUK (TAK)
...HEE-SO, I ENJOYED BEING WITH YOU FOR THE LAST MONTH.
IF I'D MET YOU A LONG TIME AGO...
...I THINK I'D HAVE LIKED YOU FOR SURE.
...I'M SORRY.
BUT I CAN'T DO ANYTHING FOR YOU.

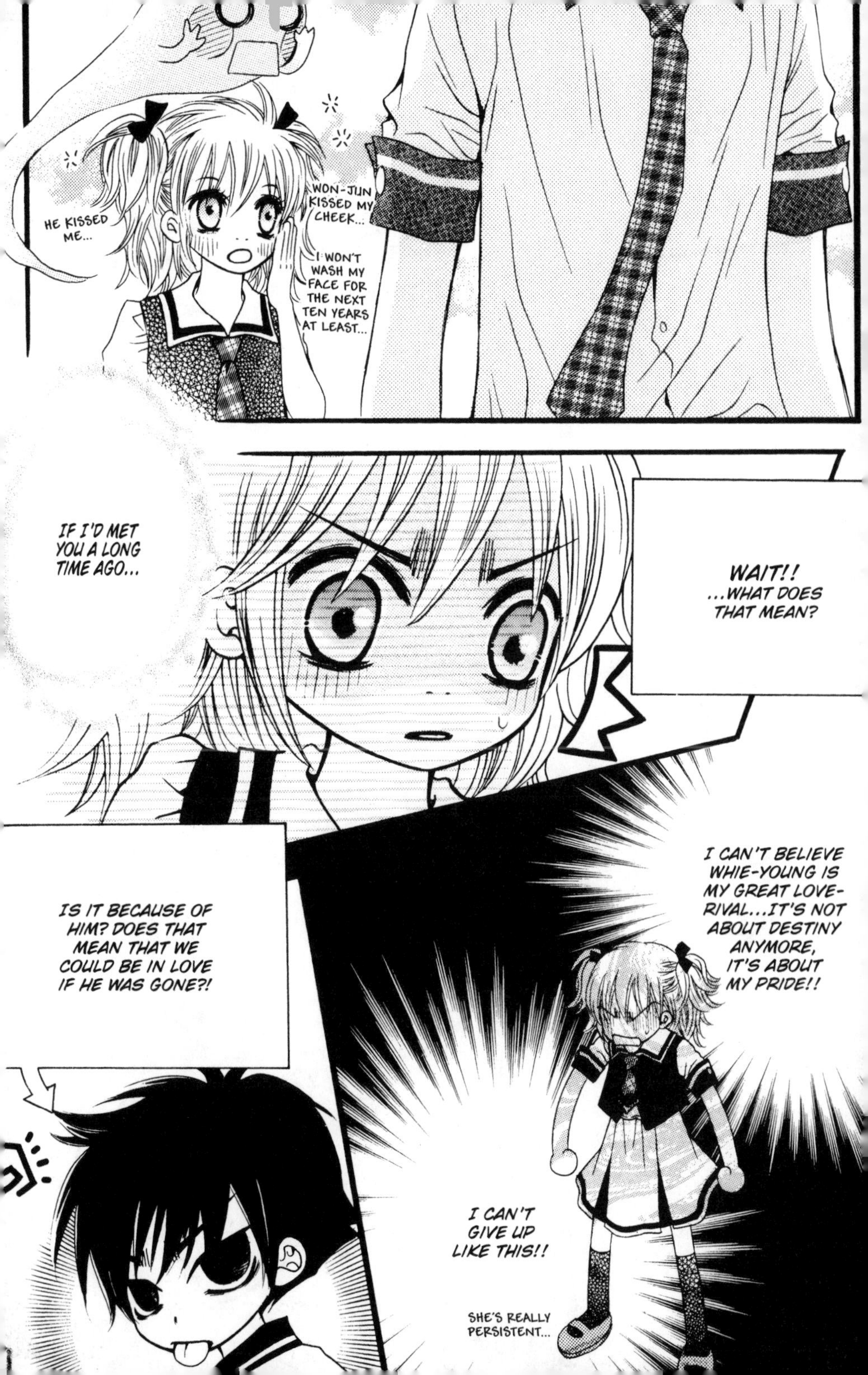
HE KISSED ME...
WON-JUN KISSED MY CHEEK...
I WON'T WASH MY FACE FOR THE NEXT TEN YEARS AT LEAST...
IF I'D MET YOU A LONG TIME AGO...
WAIT!! ...WHAT DOES THAT MEAN?
IS IT BECAUSE OF HIM? DOES THAT MEAN THAT WE COULD BE IN LOVE IF HE WAS GONE?!
I CAN'T BELIEVE WHIE-YOUNG IS MY GREAT LOVE-RIVAL...IT'S NOT ABOUT DESTINY ANYMORE, IT'S ABOUT MY PRIDE!!
I CAN'T GIVE UP LIKE THIS!!
SHE'S REALLY PERSISTENT...

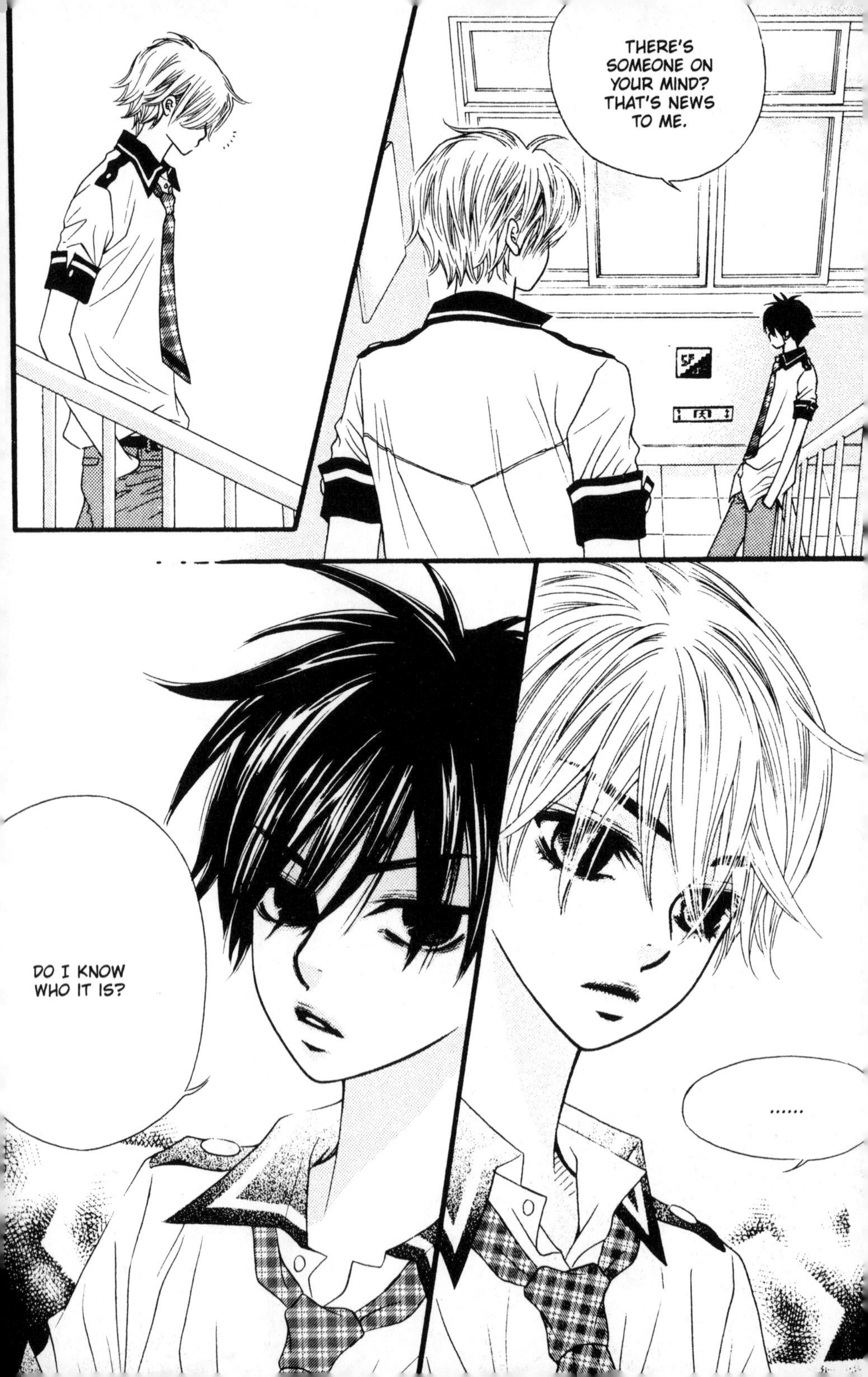
THERE'S SOMEONE ON YOUR MIND? THAT'S NEWS TO ME.
DO I KNOW WHO IT IS?
......

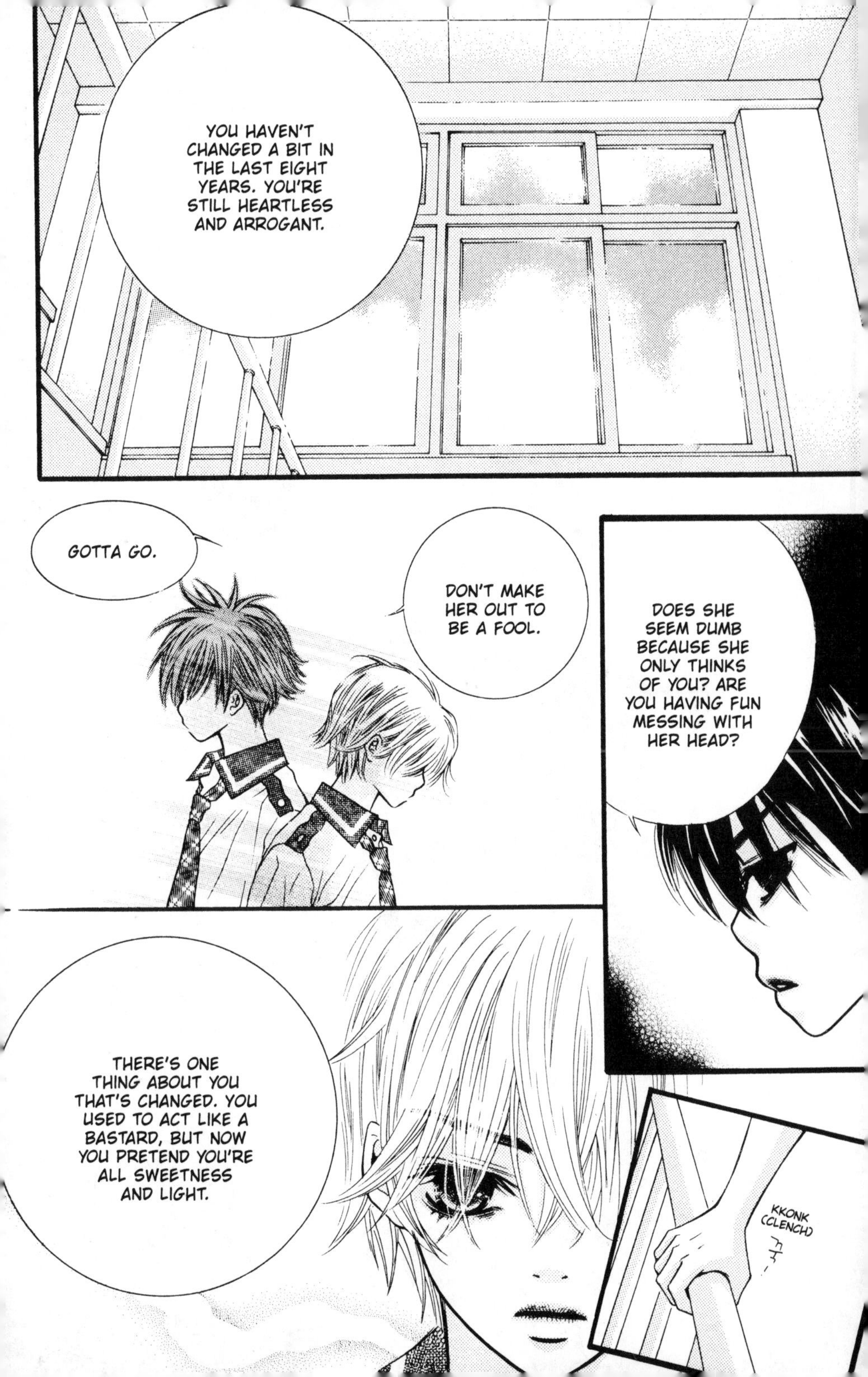
YOU HAVEN'T CHANGED A BIT IN THE LAST EIGHT YEARS. YOU'RE STILL HEARTLESS AND ARROGANT.
GOTTA GO.
DON'T MAKE HER OUT TO BE A FOOL.
DOES SHE SEEM DUMB BECAUSE SHE ONLY THINKS OF YOU? ARE YOU HAVING FUN MESSING WITH HER HEAD?
THERE'S ONE THING ABOUT YOU THAT'S CHANGED. YOU USED TO ACT LIKE A BASTARD, BUT NOW YOU PRETEND YOU'RE ALL SWEETNESS AND LIGHT.
KKONK (CLENCH)

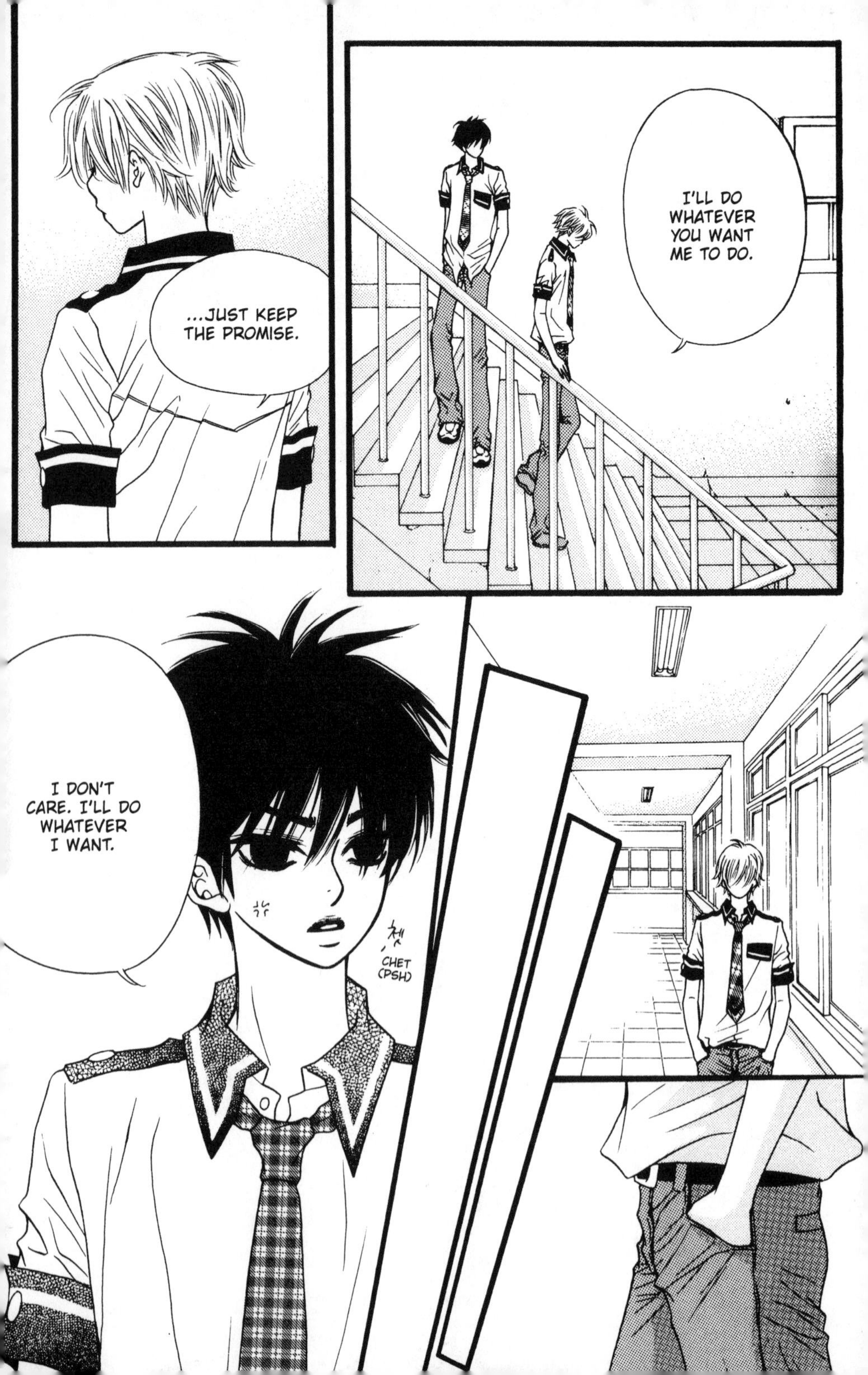
...JUST KEEP THE PROMISE.
I'LL DO WHATEVER YOU WANT ME TO DO.
I DON'T CARE. I'LL DO WHATEVER I WANT.
칫
CHET (PSH)

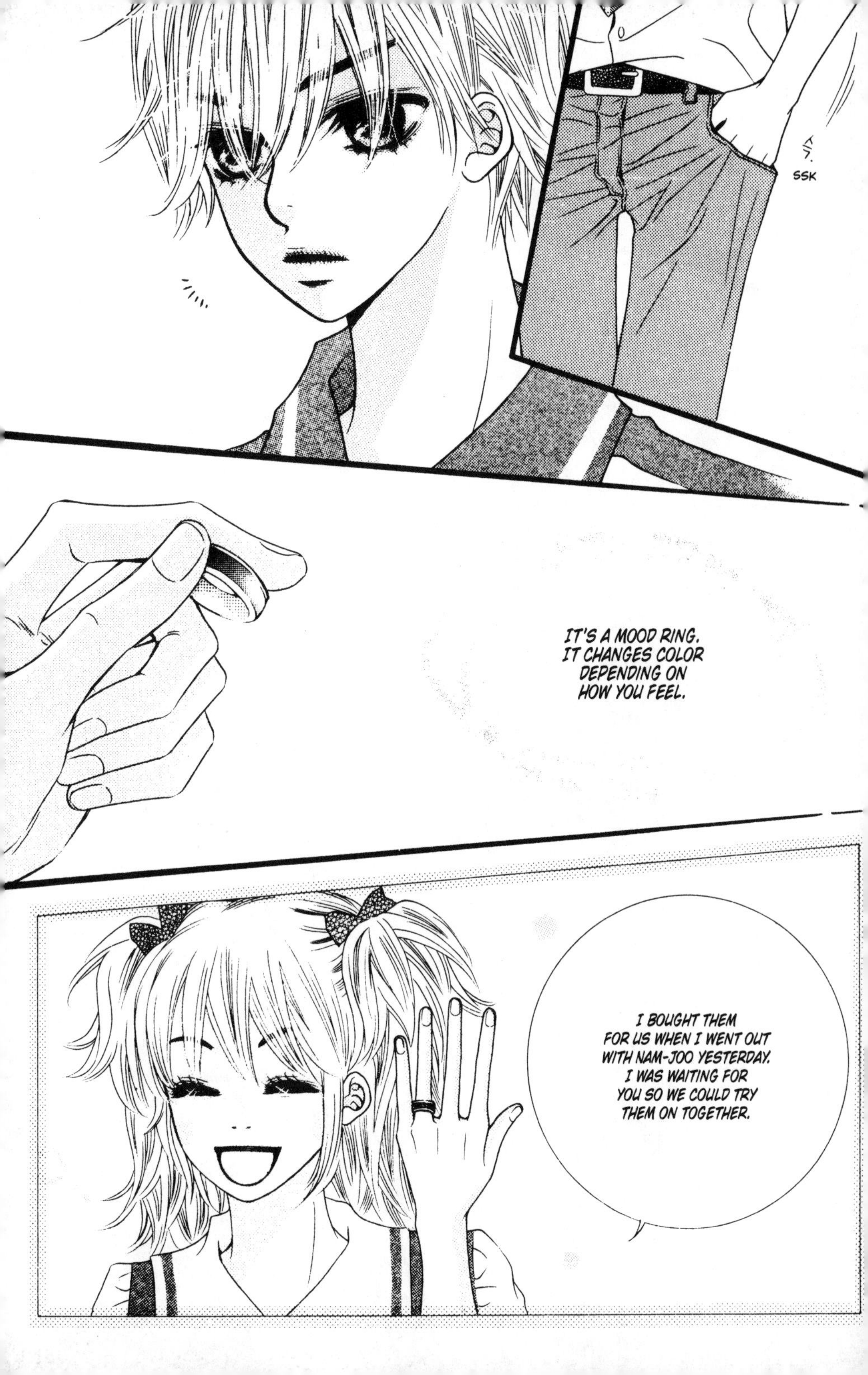
SSK
IT'S A MOOD RING. IT CHANGES COLOR DEPENDING ON HOW YOU FEEL.
I BOUGHT THEM FOR US WHEN I WENT OUT WITH NAM-JOO YESTERDAY. I WAS WAITING FOR YOU SO WE COULD TRY THEM ON TOGETHER.

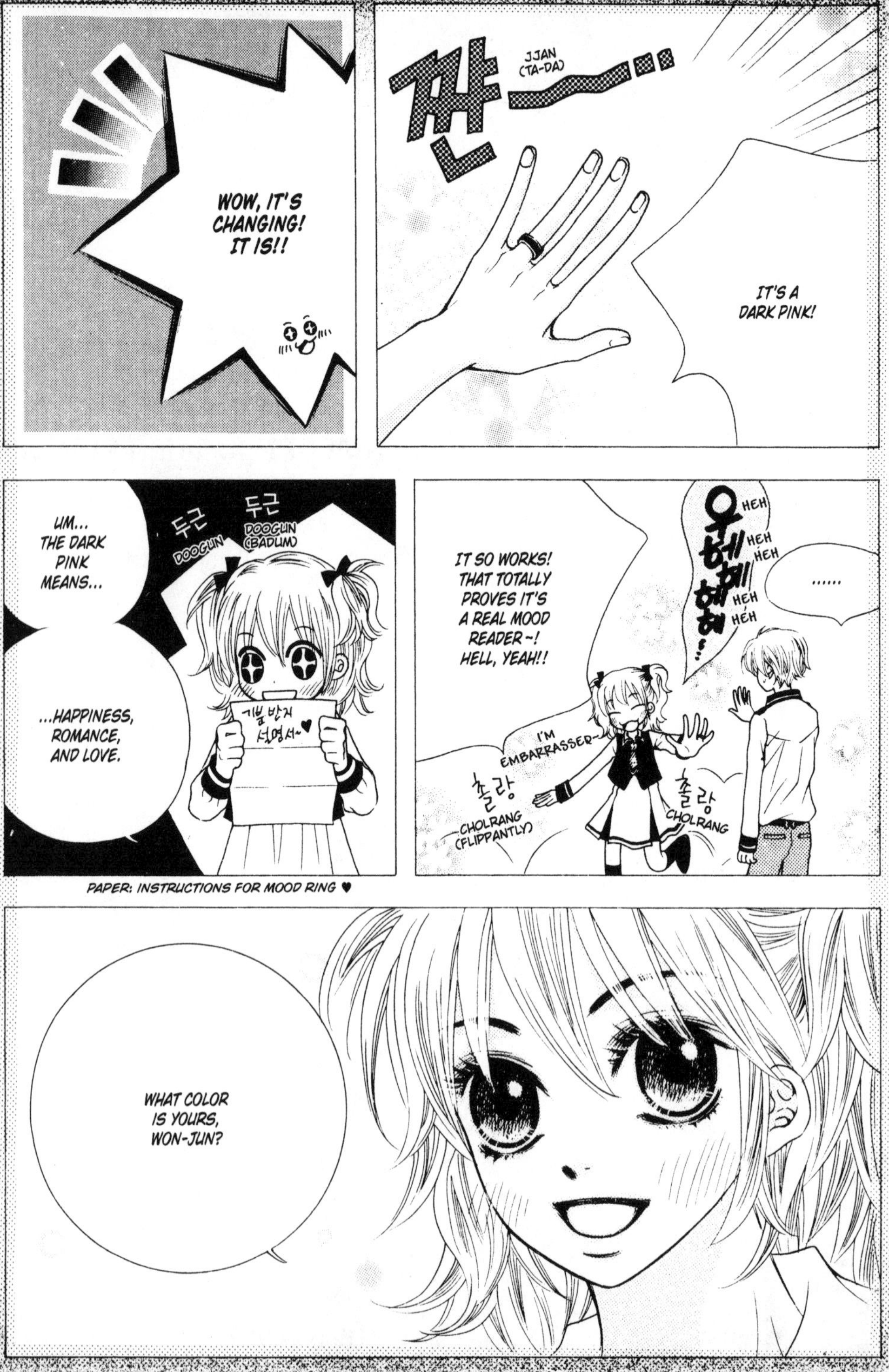
WOW, IT'S CHANGING! IT IS!!
짠~~
JJAN (TA-DA)
IT'S A DARK PINK!
UM... THE DARK PINK MEANS...
두근 두근
DOOGUN DOOGUN (BADUM)
기분 반지 설명서~♥
...HAPPINESS, ROMANCE, AND LOVE.
IT SO WORKS! THAT TOTALLY PROVES IT'S A REAL MOOD READER~! HELL, YEAH!!
우헤헤헤...
HEH HEH HEH HEH HEH
......
I'M EMBARRASSED~
촐랑
CHOLRANG (FLIPPANTLY)
촐랑
CHOLRANG
PAPER: INSTRUCTIONS FOR MOOD RING ♥
WHAT COLOR IS YOURS, WON-JUN?

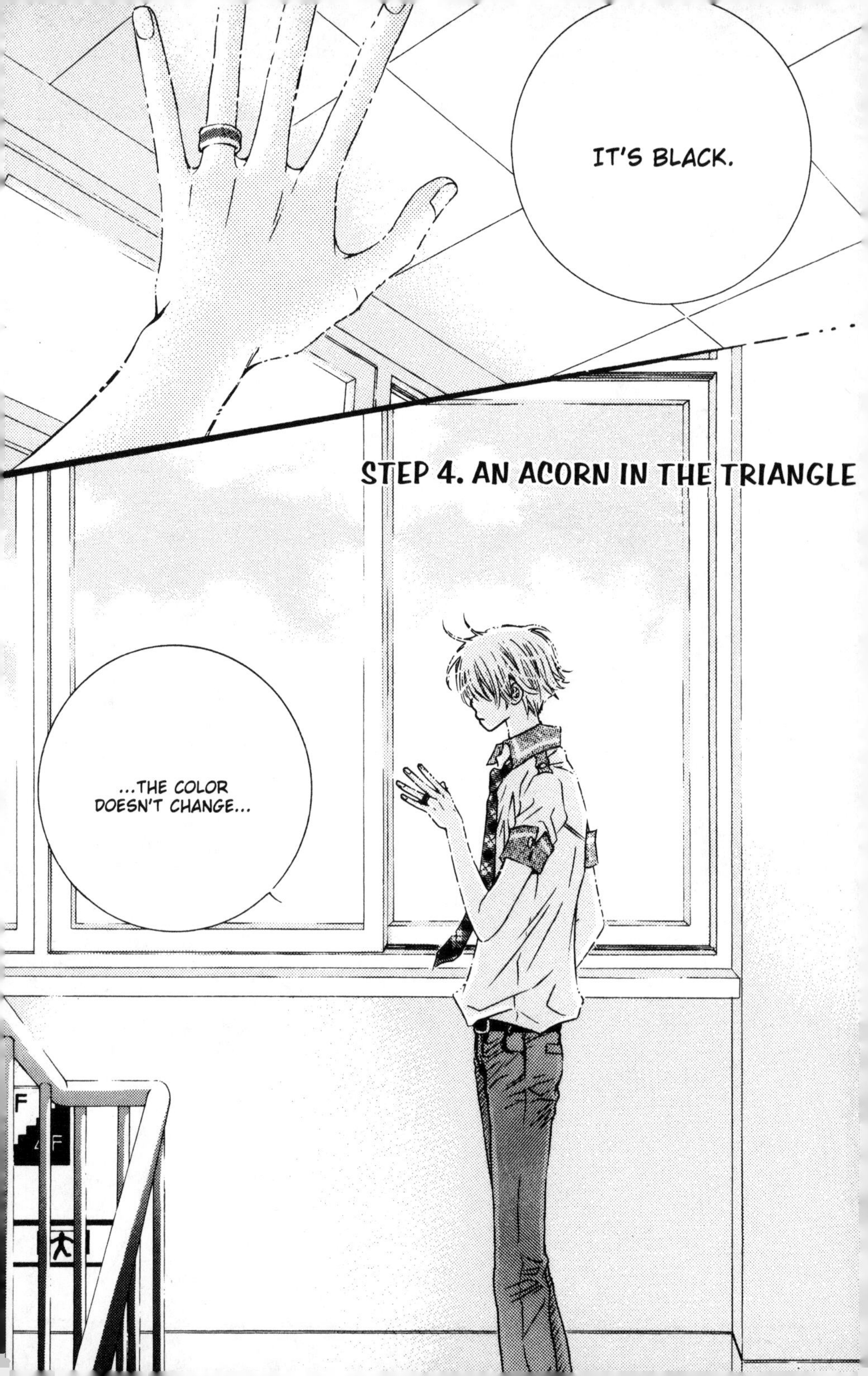
IT'S BLACK.
STEP 4. AN ACORN IN THE TRIANGLE
...THE COLOR DOESN'T CHANGE...
4F

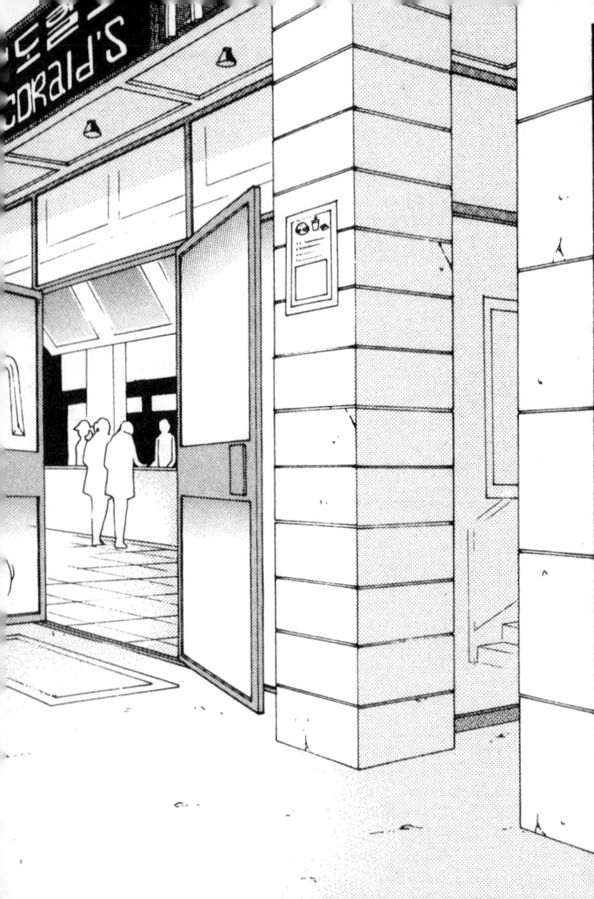

CDONALD'S

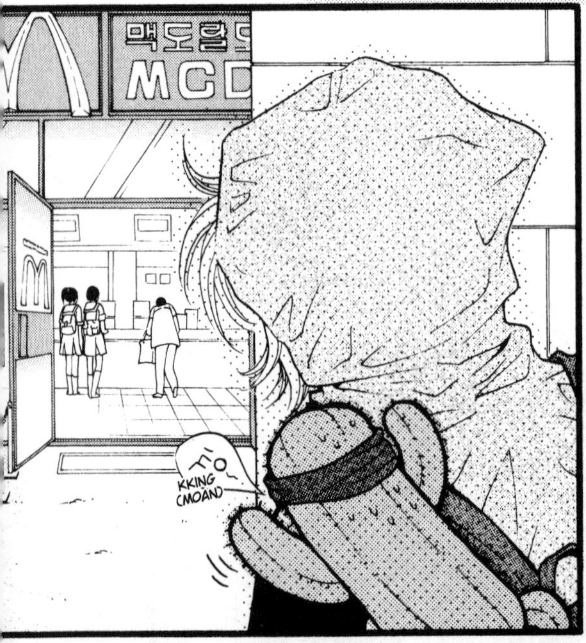

MCD
KKING
(MOAN)

EXTRA TALK! -3-

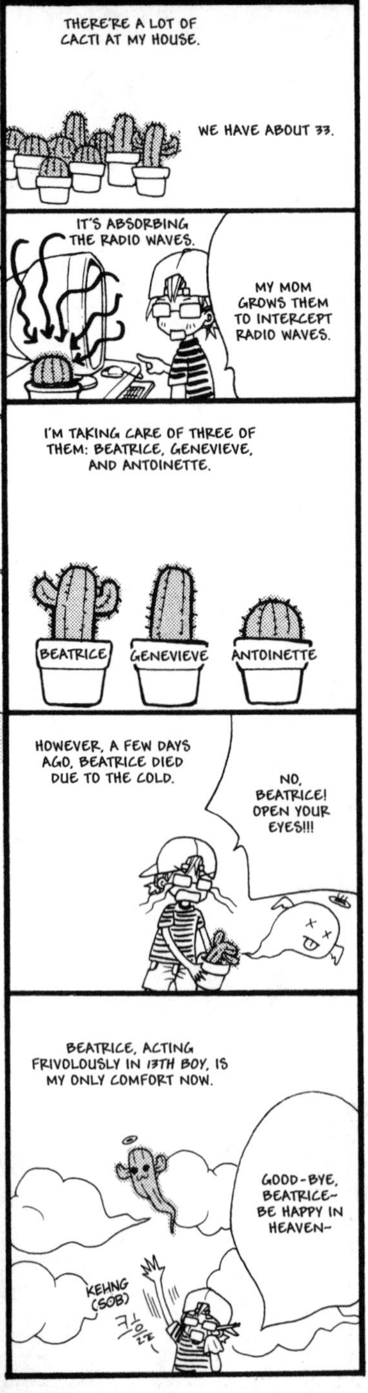

THERE'RE A LOT OF CACTI AT MY HOUSE.
WE HAVE ABOUT 33.
IT'S ABSORBING THE RADIO WAVES.
MY MOM GROWS THEM TO INTERCEPT RADIO WAVES.
I'M TAKING CARE OF THREE OF THEM: BEATRICE, GENEVIEVE, AND ANTOINETTE.
BEATRICE
GENEVIEVE
ANTOINETTE
HOWEVER, A FEW DAYS AGO, BEATRICE DIED DUE TO THE COLD.
NO, BEATRICE! OPEN YOUR EYES!!!
BEATRICE, ACTING FRIVOLOUSLY IN 13TH BOY, IS MY ONLY COMFORT NOW.
GOOD-BYE, BEATRICE~ BE HAPPY IN HEAVEN~
KEHNG
(SOB)

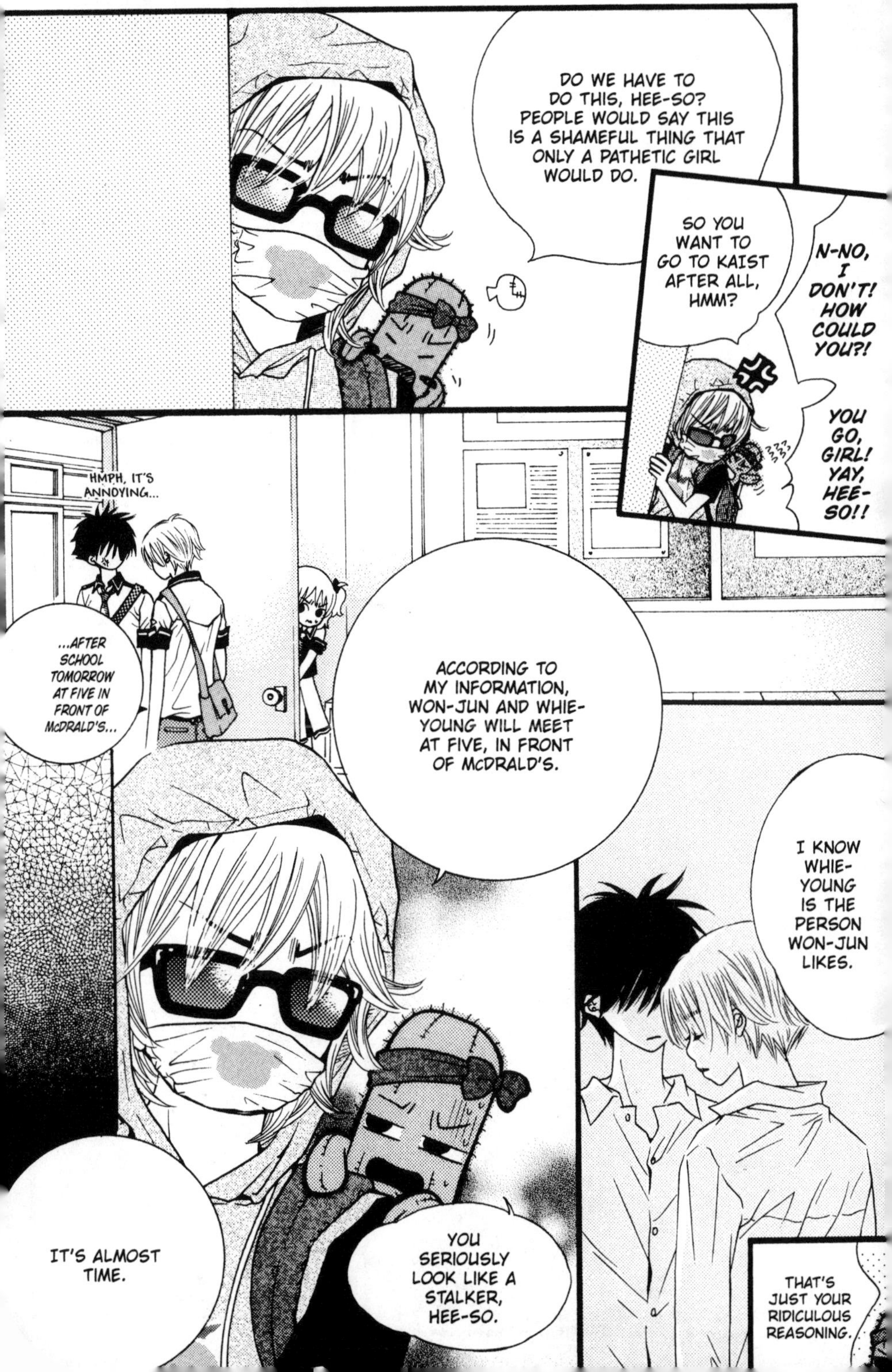
DO WE HAVE TO DO THIS, HEE-SO? PEOPLE WOULD SAY THIS IS A SHAMEFUL THING THAT ONLY A PATHETIC GIRL WOULD DO.
SO YOU WANT TO GO TO KAIST AFTER ALL, HMM?
N-NO, I DON'T! HOW COULD YOU?!
YOU GO, GIRL! YAY, HEE-SO!!
HMPH, IT'S ANNOYING...
...AFTER SCHOOL TOMORROW AT FIVE IN FRONT OF McDRALD'S...
ACCORDING TO MY INFORMATION, WON-JUN AND WHIE-YOUNG WILL MEET AT FIVE, IN FRONT OF McDRALD'S.
IT'S ALMOST TIME.
YOU SERIOUSLY LOOK LIKE A STALKER, HEE-SO.
I KNOW WHIE-YOUNG IS THE PERSON WON-JUN LIKES.
THAT'S JUST YOUR RIDICULOUS REASONING.

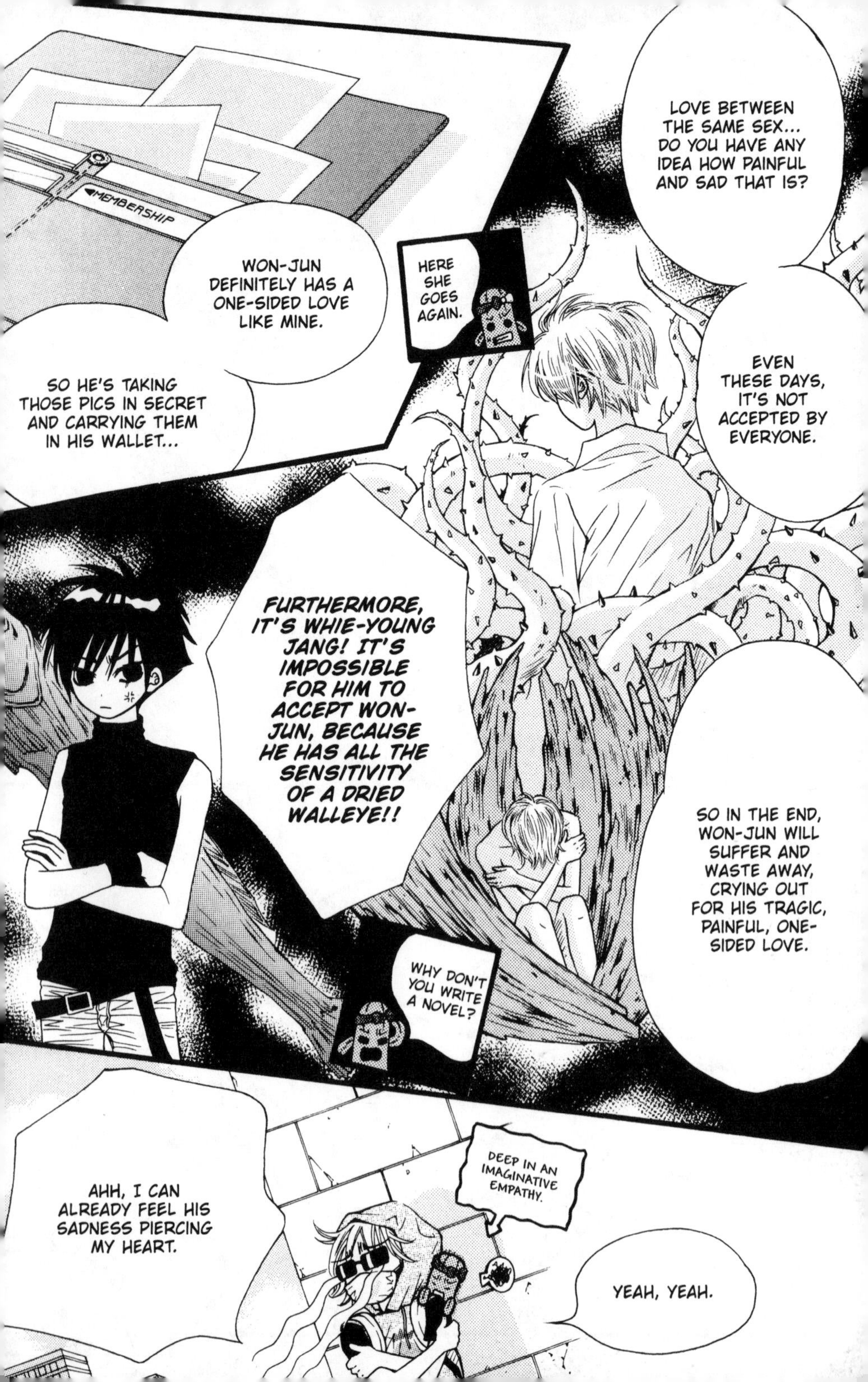

◀MEMBERSHIP
WON-JUN DEFINITELY HAS A ONE-SIDED LOVE LIKE MINE.
SO HE'S TAKING THOSE PICS IN SECRET AND CARRYING THEM IN HIS WALLET...
FURTHERMORE, IT'S WHIE-YOUNG JANG! IT'S IMPOSSIBLE FOR HIM TO ACCEPT WON-JUN, BECAUSE HE HAS ALL THE SENSITIVITY OF A DRIED WALLEYE!!
LOVE BETWEEN THE SAME SEX... DO YOU HAVE ANY IDEA HOW PAINFUL AND SAD THAT IS?
HERE SHE GOES AGAIN.
EVEN THESE DAYS, IT'S NOT ACCEPTED BY EVERYONE.
SO IN THE END, WON-JUN WILL SUFFER AND WASTE AWAY, CRYING OUT FOR HIS TRAGIC, PAINFUL, ONE-SIDED LOVE.
WHY DON'T YOU WRITE A NOVEL?
AHH, I CAN ALREADY FEEL HIS SADNESS PIERCING MY HEART.
DEEP IN AN IMAGINATIVE EMPATHY.
YEAH, YEAH.

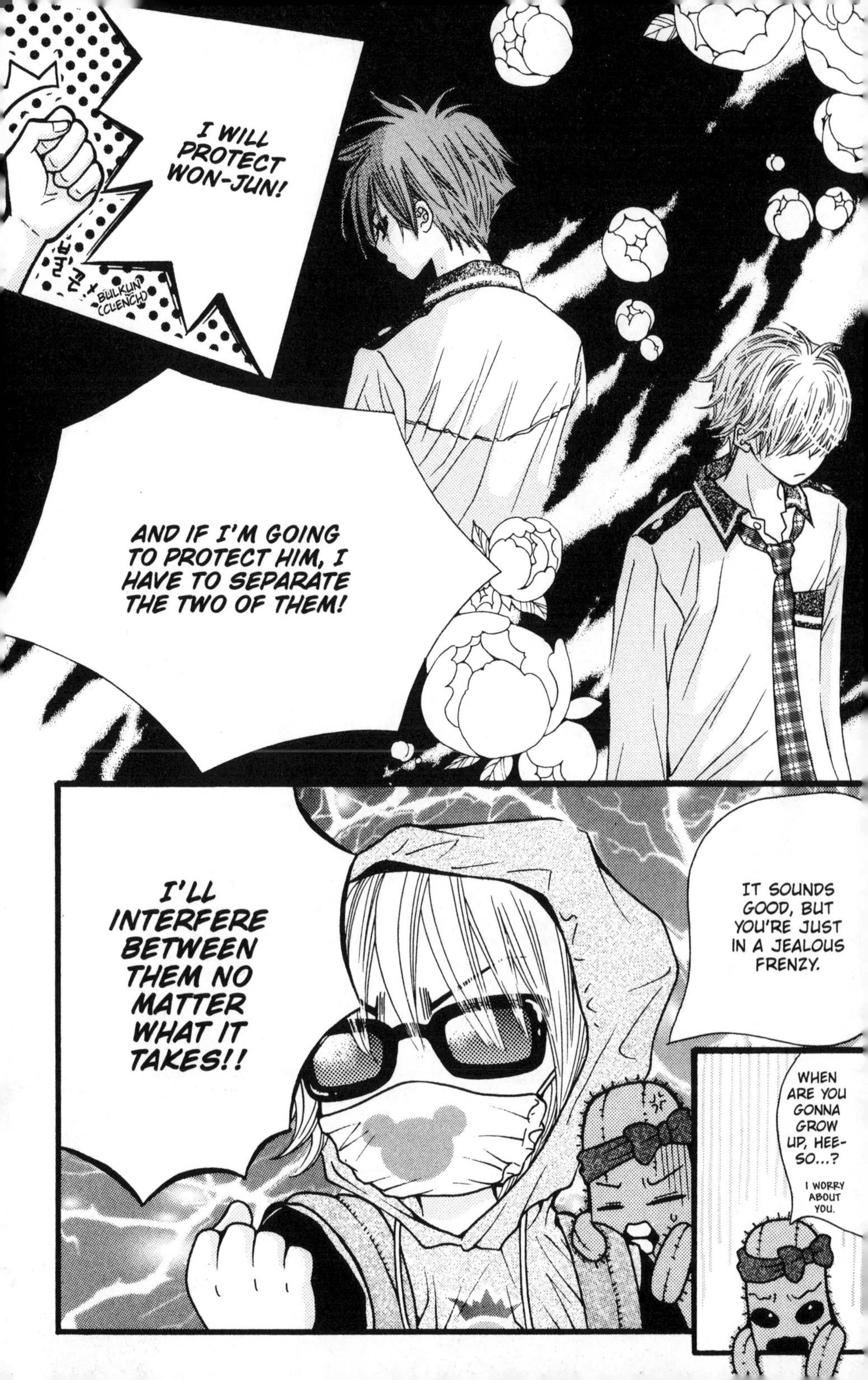
I WILL PROTECT WON-JUN!
BULKUN (CLENCH)
AND IF I'M GOING TO PROTECT HIM, I HAVE TO SEPARATE THE TWO OF THEM!
I'LL INTERFERE BETWEEN THEM NO MATTER WHAT IT TAKES!!
IT SOUNDS GOOD, BUT YOU'RE JUST IN A JEALOUS FRENZY.
WHEN ARE YOU GONNA GROW UP, HEE-SO...?
I WORRY ABOUT YOU.

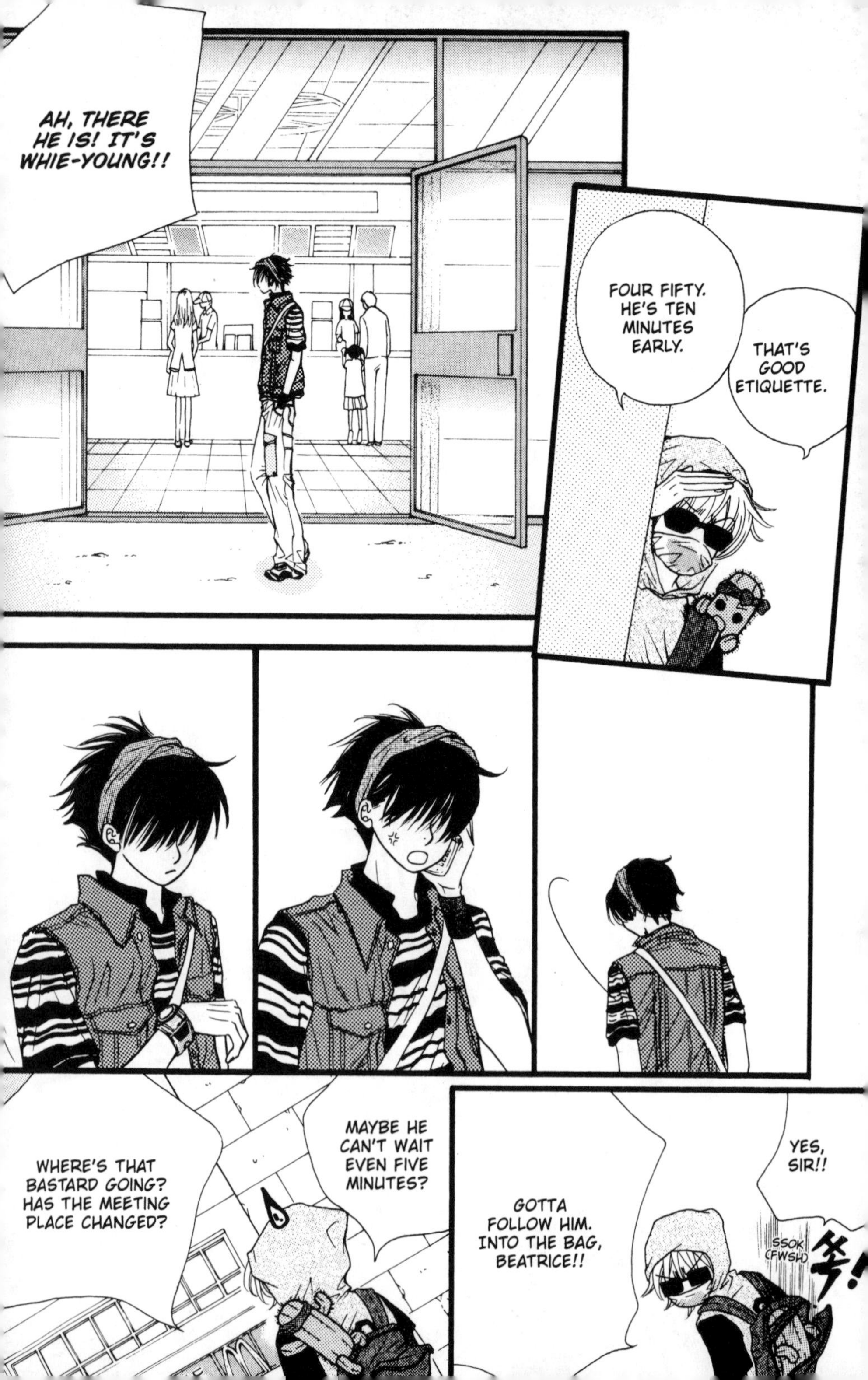
AH, THERE HE IS! IT'S WHIE-YOUNG!!
FOUR FIFTY. HE'S TEN MINUTES EARLY.
THAT'S GOOD ETIQUETTE.
WHERE'S THAT BASTARD GOING? HAS THE MEETING PLACE CHANGED?
MAYBE HE CAN'T WAIT EVEN FIVE MINUTES?
GOTTA FOLLOW HIM. INTO THE BAG, BEATRICE!!
YES, SIR!!
SSOK (FWSH)

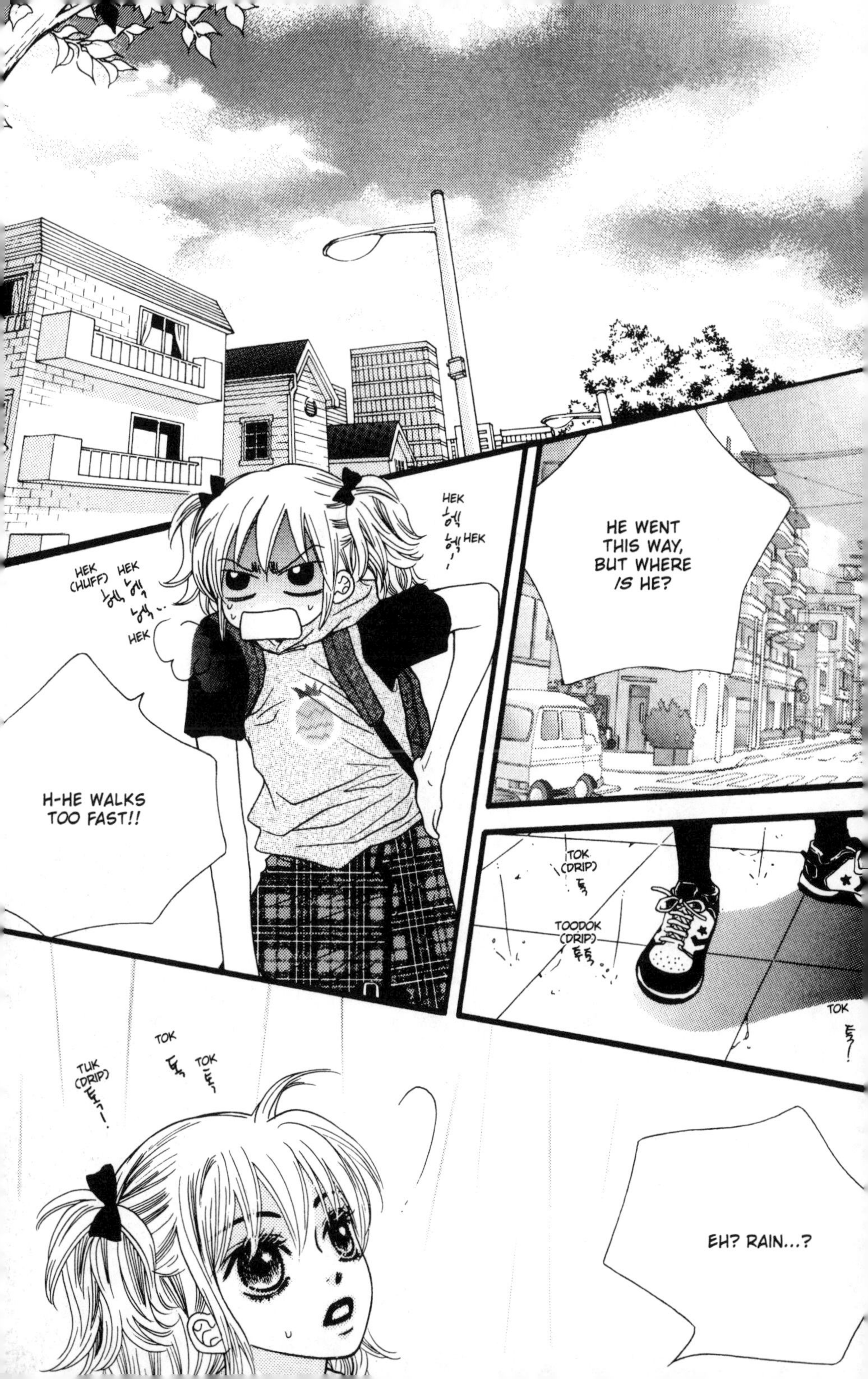
HEK (HUFF) HEK
HEK
HEK
HEK
H-HE WALKS TOO FAST!!
HE WENT THIS WAY, BUT WHERE IS HE?
TOK (DRIP)
TOODOK (DRIP)
TOK
TUK (DRIP)
TOK
TOK
EH? RAIN...?

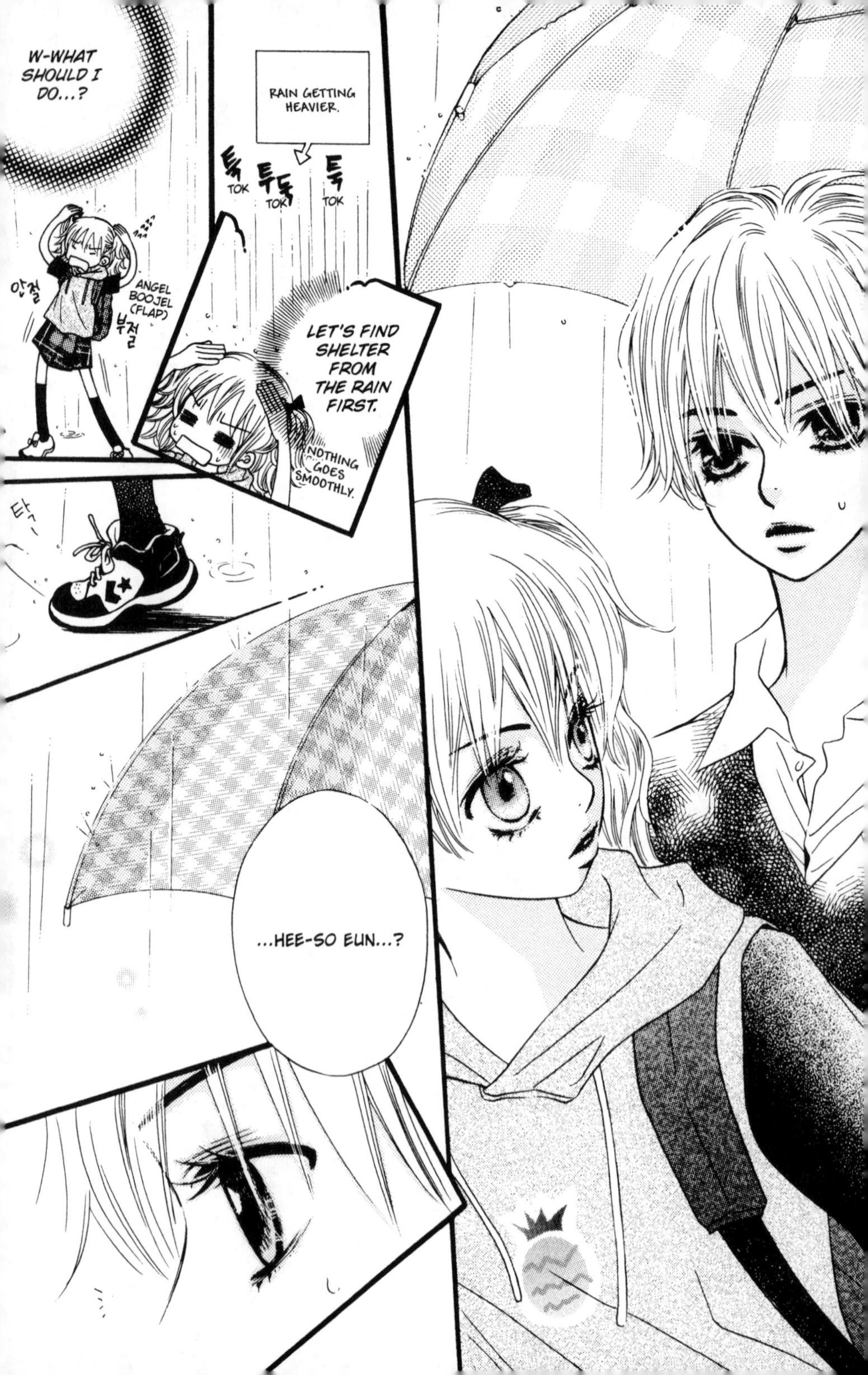
W-WHAT SHOULD I DO...?
RAIN GETTING HEAVIER.
툭 TOK
투둑 TOK
툭 TOK
안절 ANGEL BOOJEL (FLAP) 부절
LET'S FIND SHELTER FROM THE RAIN FIRST.
NOTHING GOES SMOOTHLY.
탁
...HEE-SO EUN...?

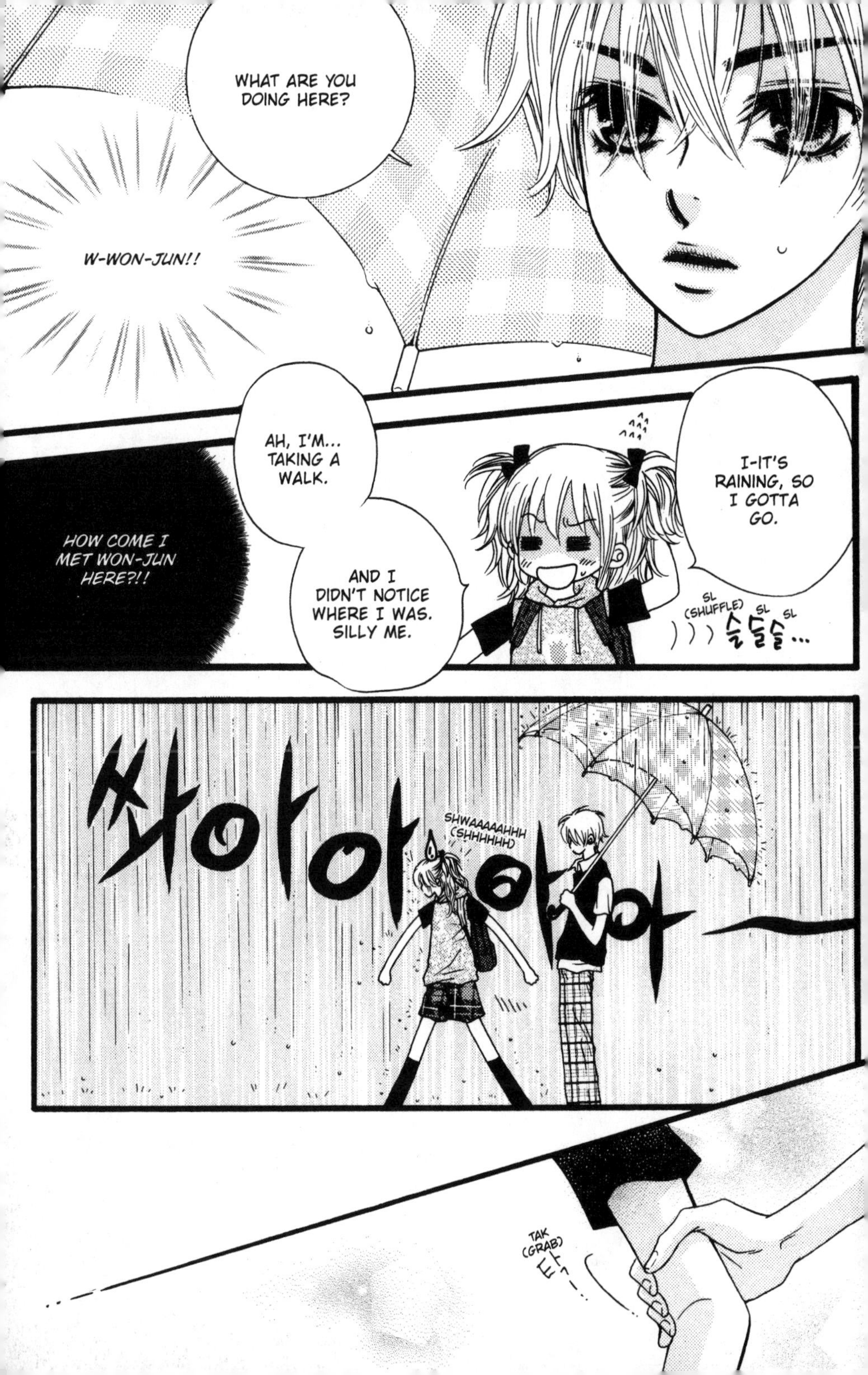
WHAT ARE YOU DOING HERE?
W-WON-JUN!!
HOW COME I MET WON-JUN HERE?!!
AH, I'M... TAKING A WALK.
AND I DIDN'T NOTICE WHERE I WAS. SILLY ME.
I-IT'S RAINING, SO I GOTTA GO.
SL (SHUFFLE) SL SL
슬슬슬...
싸아아아—
SHWAAAAAHHH (SHHHHHHH)
TAK (GRAB)
탁...

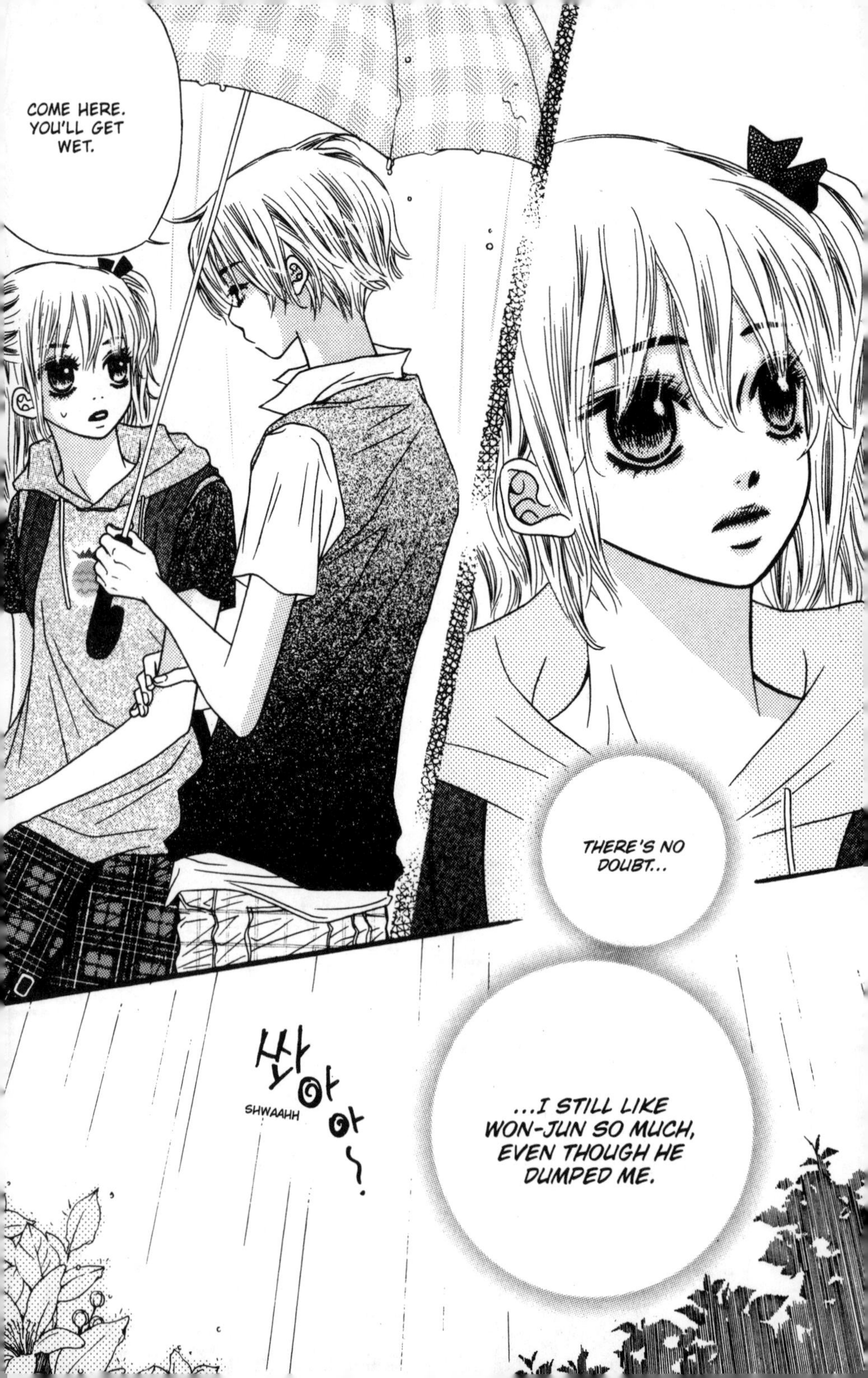
COME HERE. YOU'LL GET WET.
THERE'S NO DOUBT...
쏴아아~
SHWAAHH
...I STILL LIKE WON-JUN SO MUCH, EVEN THOUGH HE DUMPED ME.

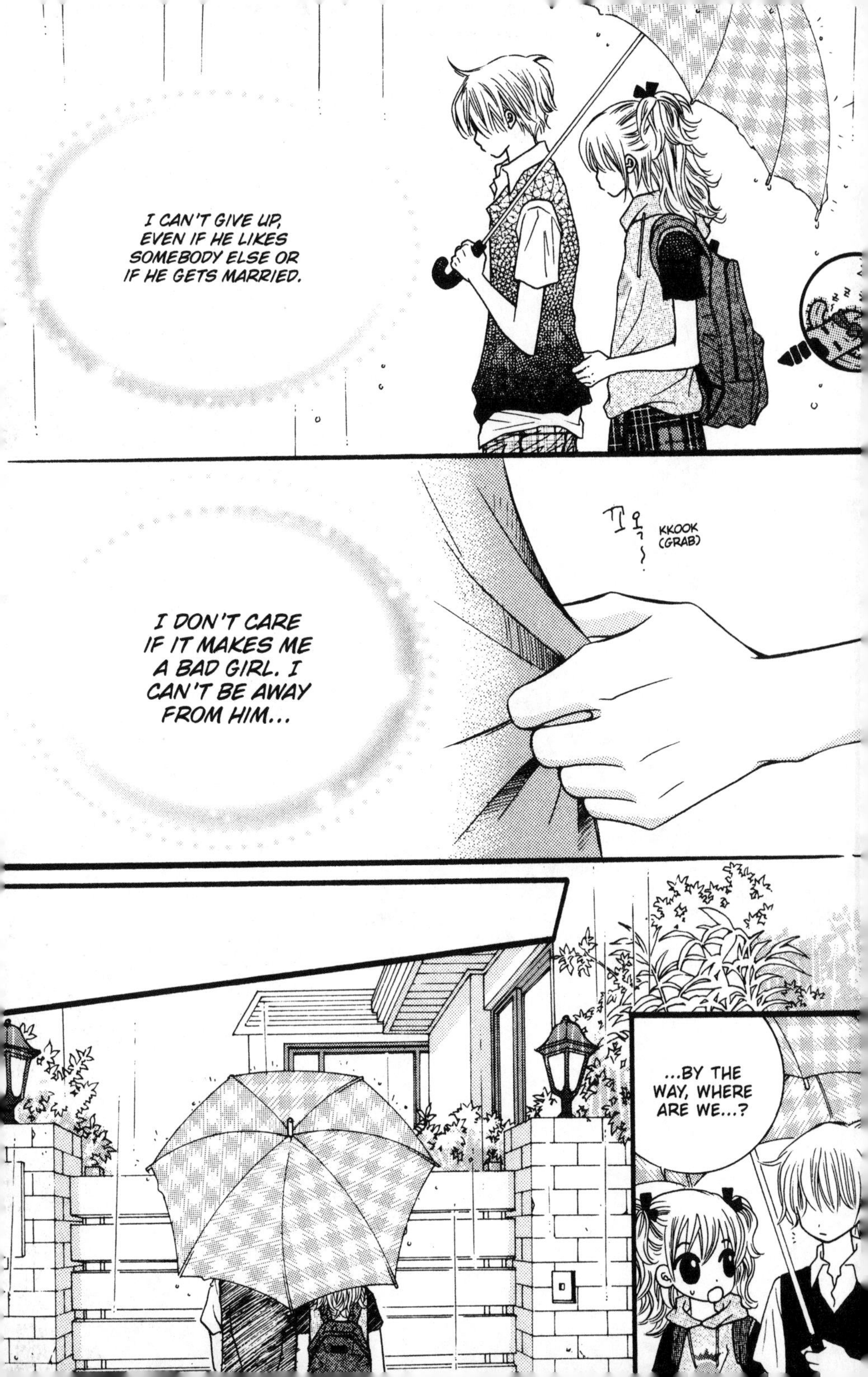
I CAN'T GIVE UP, EVEN IF HE LIKES SOMEBODY ELSE OR IF HE GETS MARRIED.
I DON'T CARE IF IT MAKES ME A BAD GIRL. I CAN'T BE AWAY FROM HIM...
KKOOK (GRAB)
...BY THE WAY, WHERE ARE WE...?

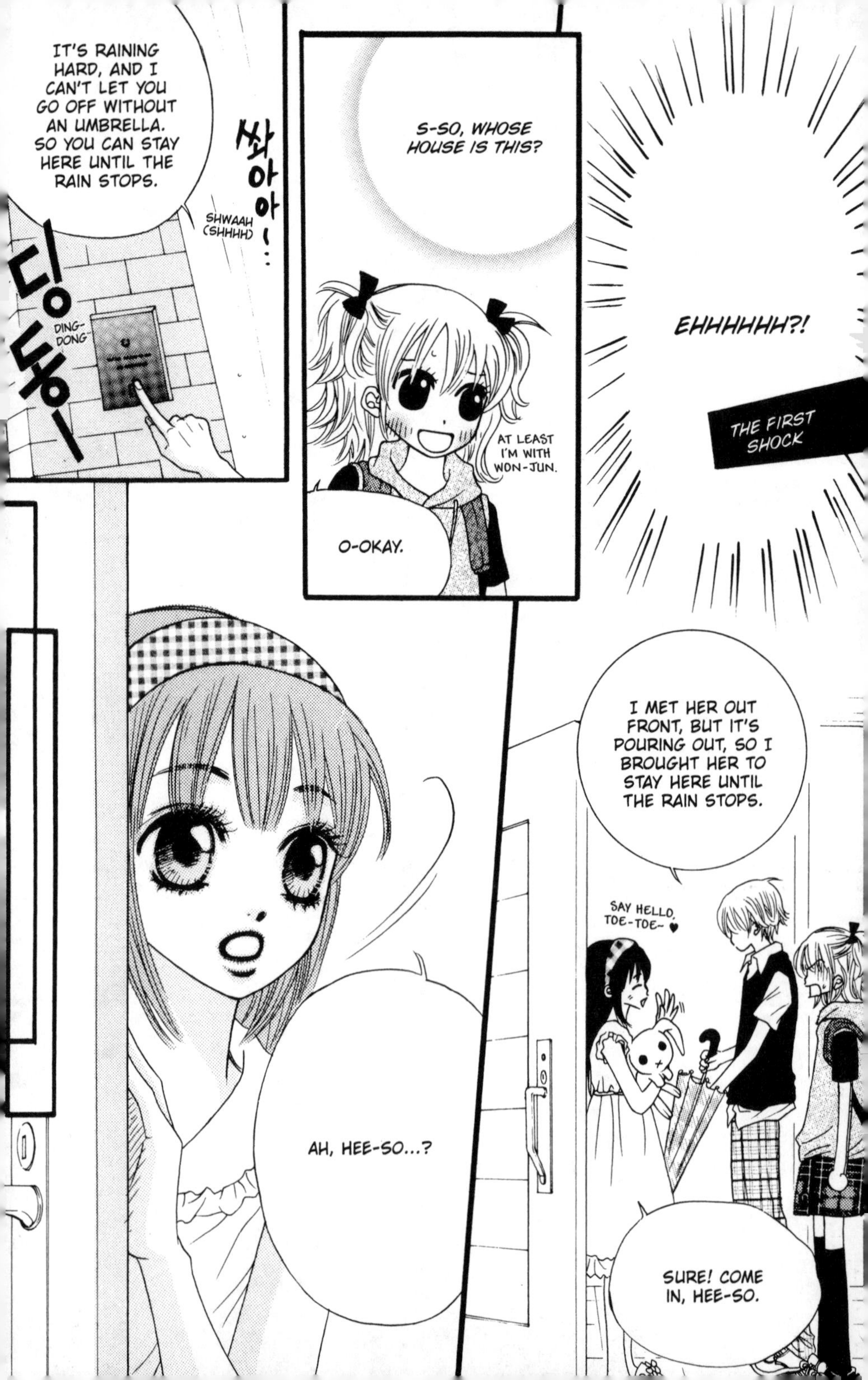

IT'S RAINING HARD, AND I CAN'T LET YOU GO OFF WITHOUT AN UMBRELLA. SO YOU CAN STAY HERE UNTIL THE RAIN STOPS.
쏴아아
SHWAAH (SHHHH)
딩동
DING-DONG
S-SO, WHOSE HOUSE IS THIS?
AT LEAST I'M WITH WON-JUN.
O-OKAY.
EHHHHHH?!
THE FIRST SHOCK
AH, HEE-SO...?
I MET HER OUT FRONT, BUT IT'S POURING OUT, SO I BROUGHT HER TO STAY HERE UNTIL THE RAIN STOPS.
SAY HELLO, TOE-TOE~ ♥
SURE! COME IN, HEE-SO.

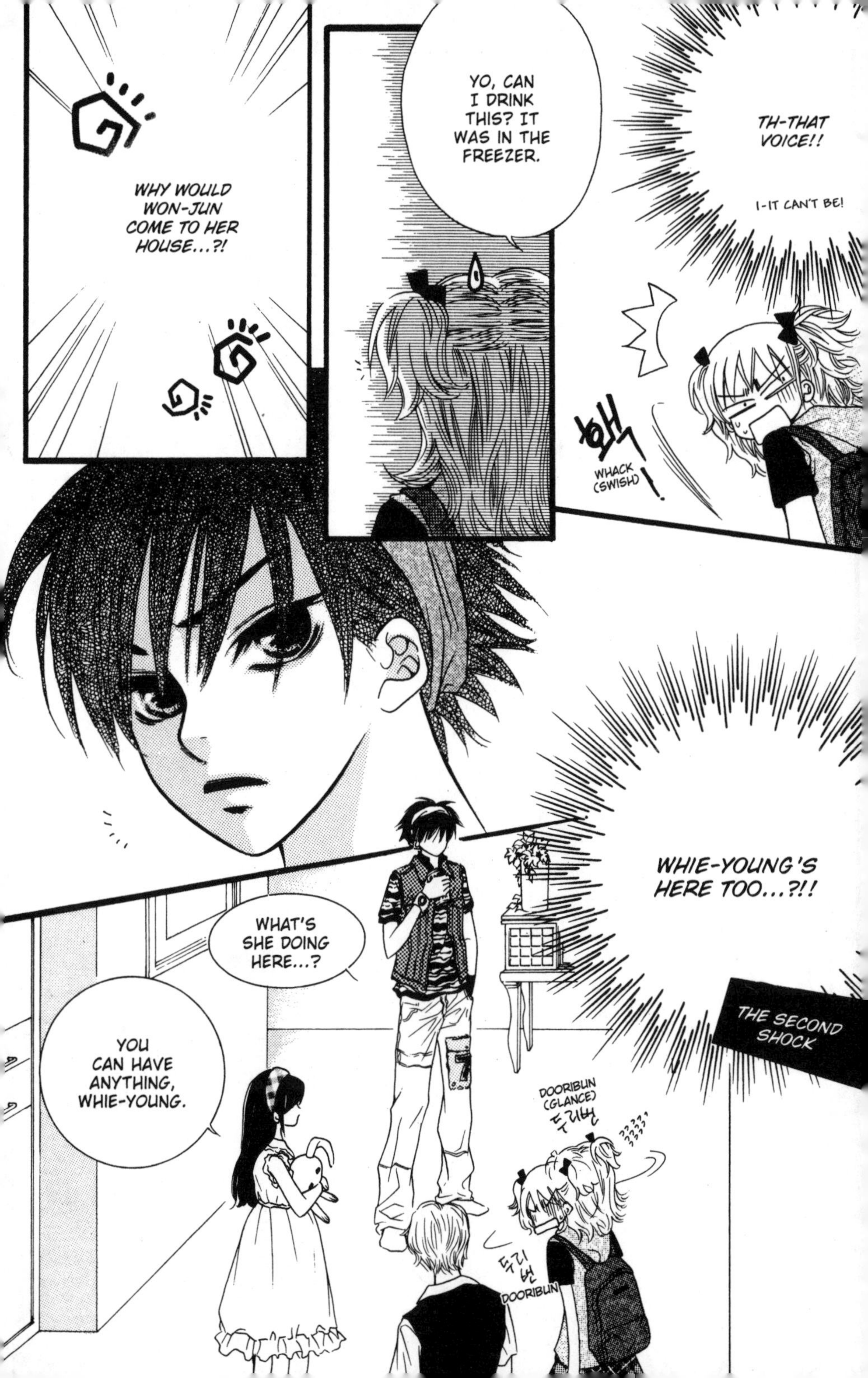
WHY WOULD WON-JUN COME TO HER HOUSE...?!
YO, CAN I DRINK THIS? IT WAS IN THE FREEZER.
TH-THAT VOICE!!
I-IT CAN'T BE!
홱
WHACK (SWISH)
WHIE-YOUNG'S HERE TOO...?!!
WHAT'S SHE DOING HERE...?
YOU CAN HAVE ANYTHING, WHIE-YOUNG.
THE SECOND SHOCK
DOORIBUN (GLANCE)
두리번
두리번
DOORIBUN

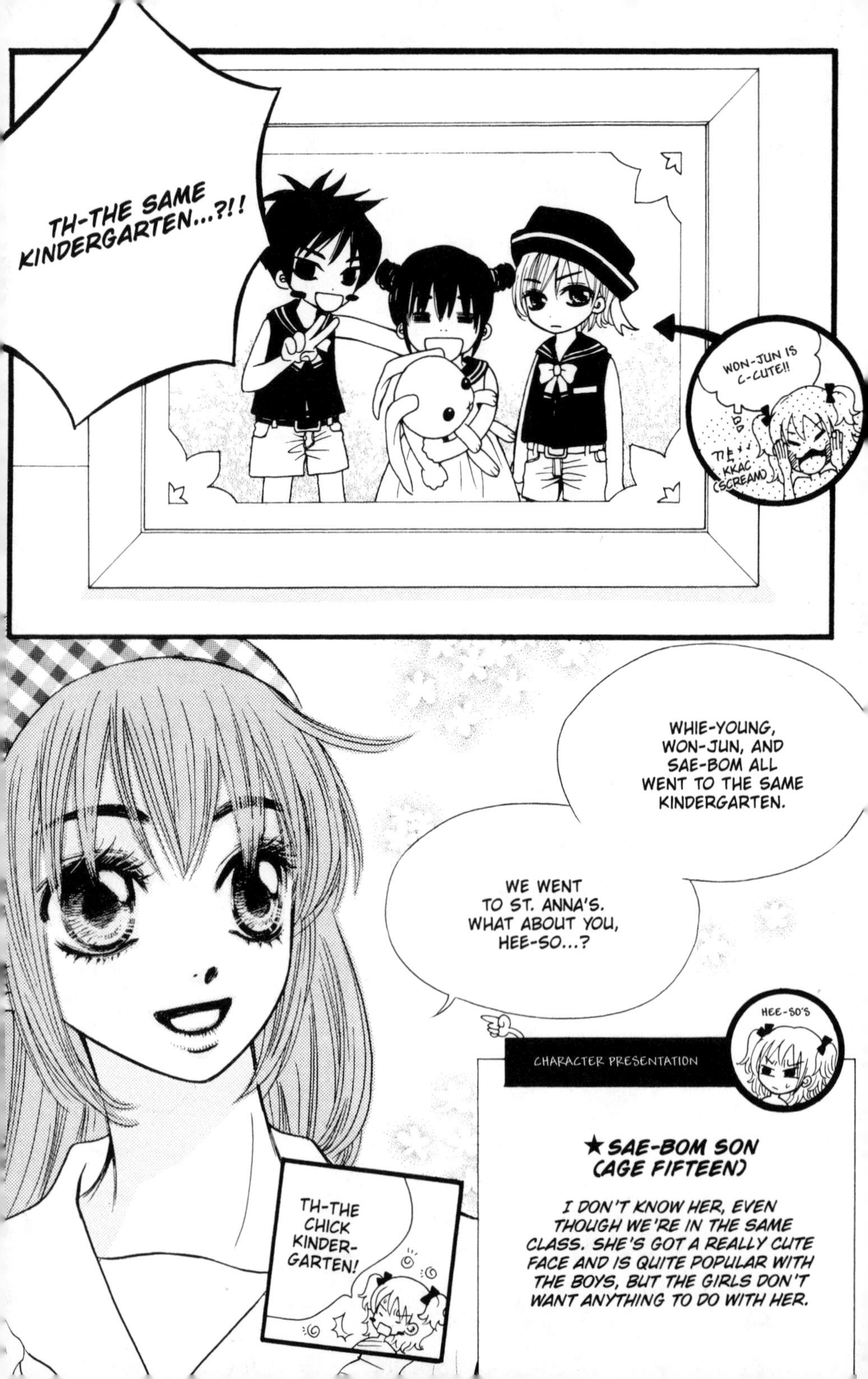
TH-THE SAME KINDERGARTEN...?!!
WON-JUN IS C-CUTE!!
꺅
KKAC (SCREAM)
WHIE-YOUNG, WON-JUN, AND SAE-BOM ALL WENT TO THE SAME KINDERGARTEN.
WE WENT TO ST. ANNA'S. WHAT ABOUT YOU, HEE-SO...?
HEE-SO'S
CHARACTER PRESENTATION
★SAE-BOM SON (AGE FIFTEEN)
I DON'T KNOW HER, EVEN THOUGH WE'RE IN THE SAME CLASS. SHE'S GOT A REALLY CUTE FACE AND IS QUITE POPULAR WITH THE BOYS, BUT THE GIRLS DON'T WANT ANYTHING TO DO WITH HER.
TH-THE CHICK KINDER-GARTEN!

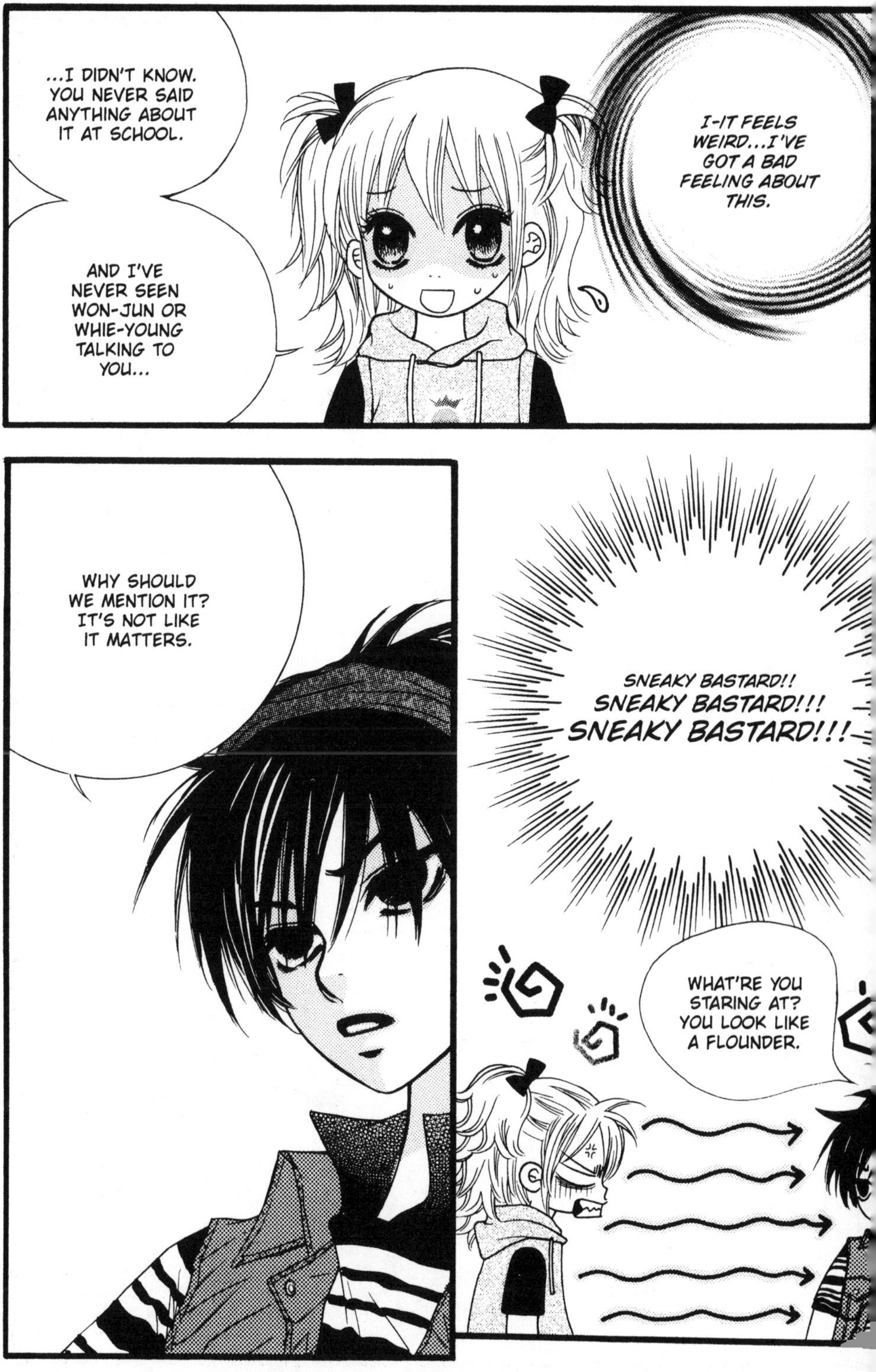
...I DIDN'T KNOW. YOU NEVER SAID ANYTHING ABOUT IT AT SCHOOL.
AND I'VE NEVER SEEN WON-JUN OR WHIE-YOUNG TALKING TO YOU...
I-IT FEELS WEIRD...I'VE GOT A BAD FEELING ABOUT THIS.
WHY SHOULD WE MENTION IT? IT'S NOT LIKE IT MATTERS.
SNEAKY BASTARD!!
SNEAKY BASTARD!!!
SNEAKY BASTARD!!!
WHAT'RE YOU STARING AT? YOU LOOK LIKE A FLOUNDER.

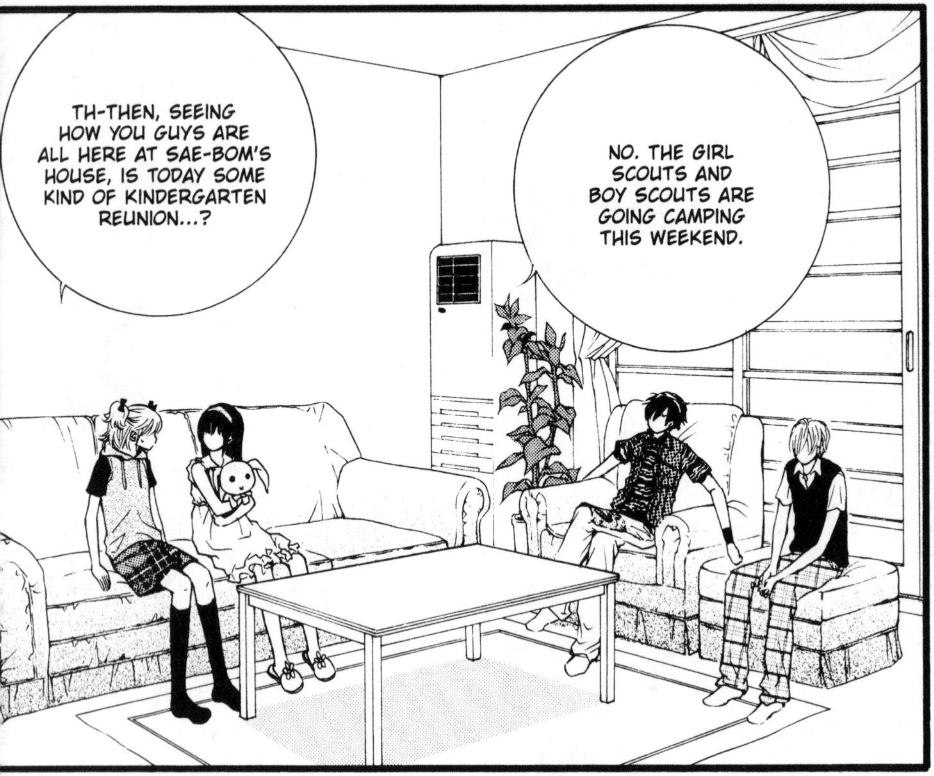
TH-THEN, SEEING HOW YOU GUYS ARE ALL HERE AT SAE-BOM'S HOUSE, IS TODAY SOME KIND OF KINDERGARTEN REUNION...?
NO. THE GIRL SCOUTS AND BOY SCOUTS ARE GOING CAMPING THIS WEEKEND.
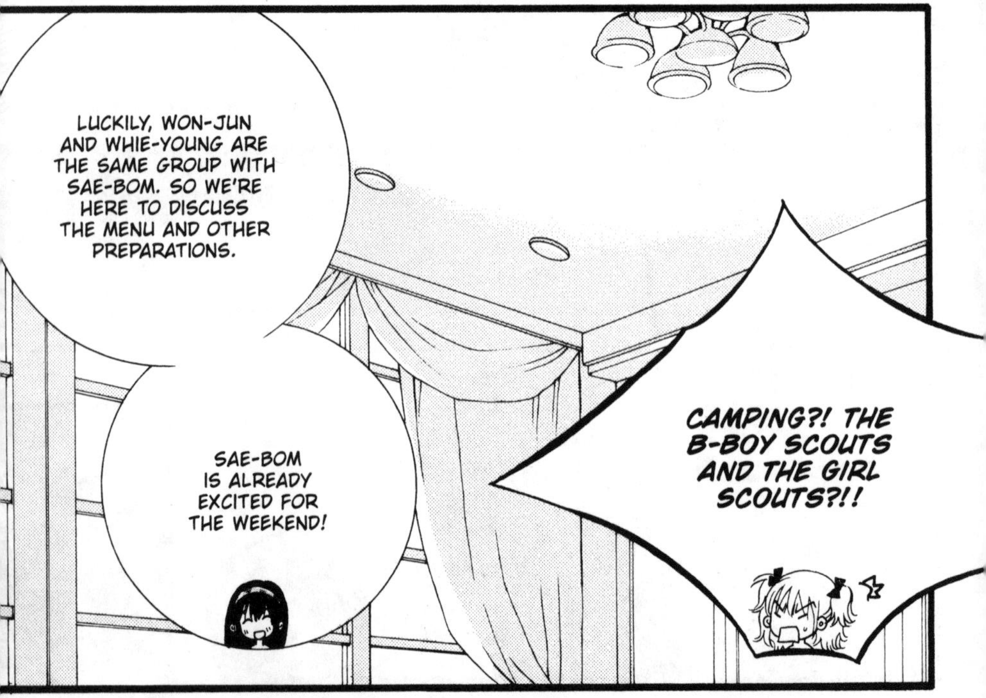
LUCKILY, WON-JUN AND WHIE-YOUNG ARE THE SAME GROUP WITH SAE-BOM. SO WE'RE HERE TO DISCUSS THE MENU AND OTHER PREPARATIONS.
SAE-BOM IS ALREADY EXCITED FOR THE WEEKEND!
CAMPING?! THE B-BOY SCOUTS AND THE GIRL SCOUTS?!!

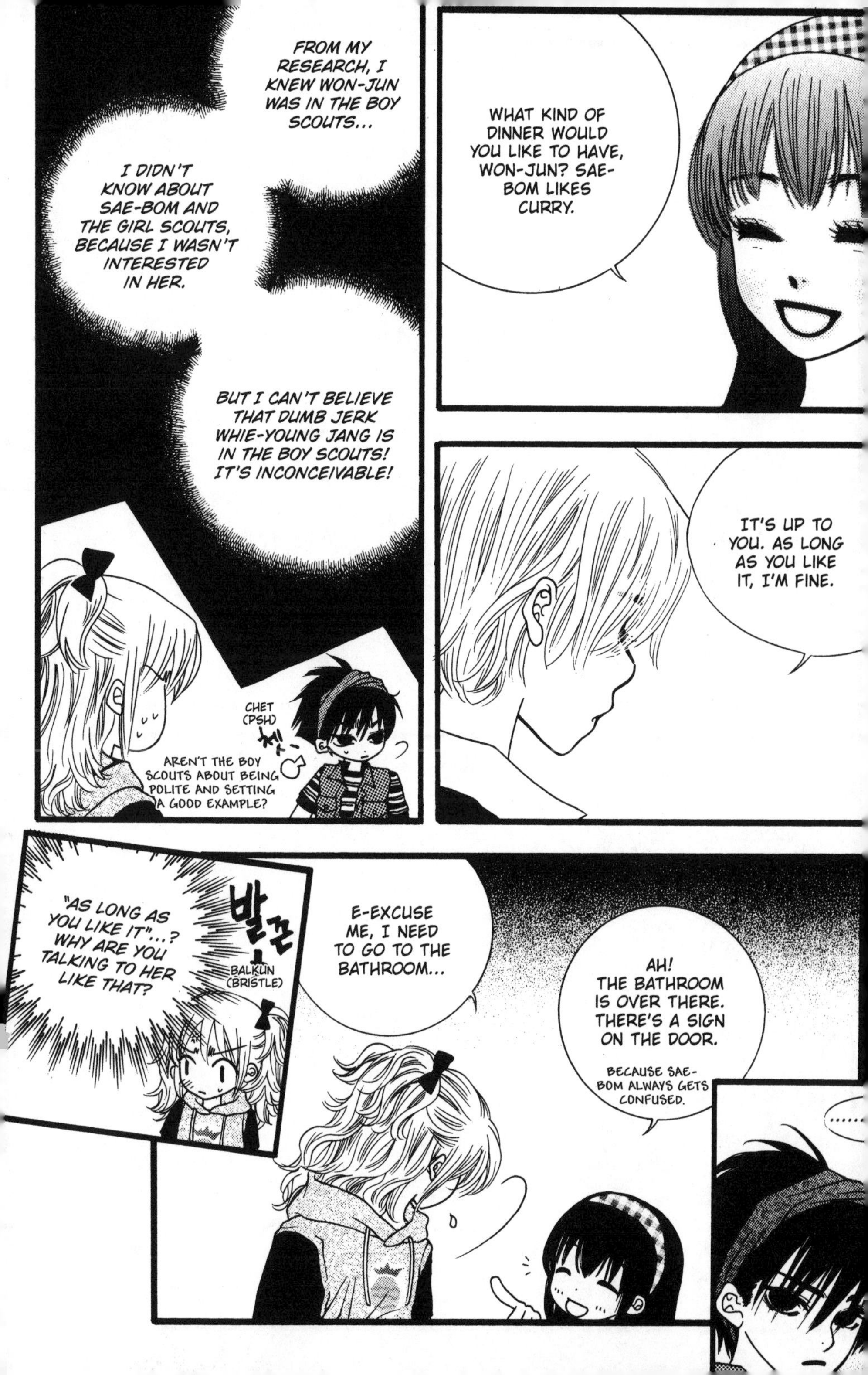
FROM MY RESEARCH, I KNEW WON-JUN WAS IN THE BOY SCOUTS...
I DIDN'T KNOW ABOUT SAE-BOM AND THE GIRL SCOUTS, BECAUSE I WASN'T INTERESTED IN HER.
BUT I CAN'T BELIEVE THAT DUMB JERK WHIE-YOUNG JANG IS IN THE BOY SCOUTS! IT'S INCONCEIVABLE!
CHET (PSH)
AREN'T THE BOY SCOUTS ABOUT BEING POLITE AND SETTING A GOOD EXAMPLE?
WHAT KIND OF DINNER WOULD YOU LIKE TO HAVE, WON-JUN? SAE-BOM LIKES CURRY.
IT'S UP TO YOU. AS LONG AS YOU LIKE IT, I'M FINE.
"AS LONG AS YOU LIKE IT"...? WHY ARE YOU TALKING TO HER LIKE THAT?
발끈
BALKUN (BRISTLE)
E-EXCUSE ME, I NEED TO GO TO THE BATHROOM...
AH! THE BATHROOM IS OVER THERE. THERE'S A SIGN ON THE DOOR.
BECAUSE SAE-BOM ALWAYS GETS CONFUSED.
......

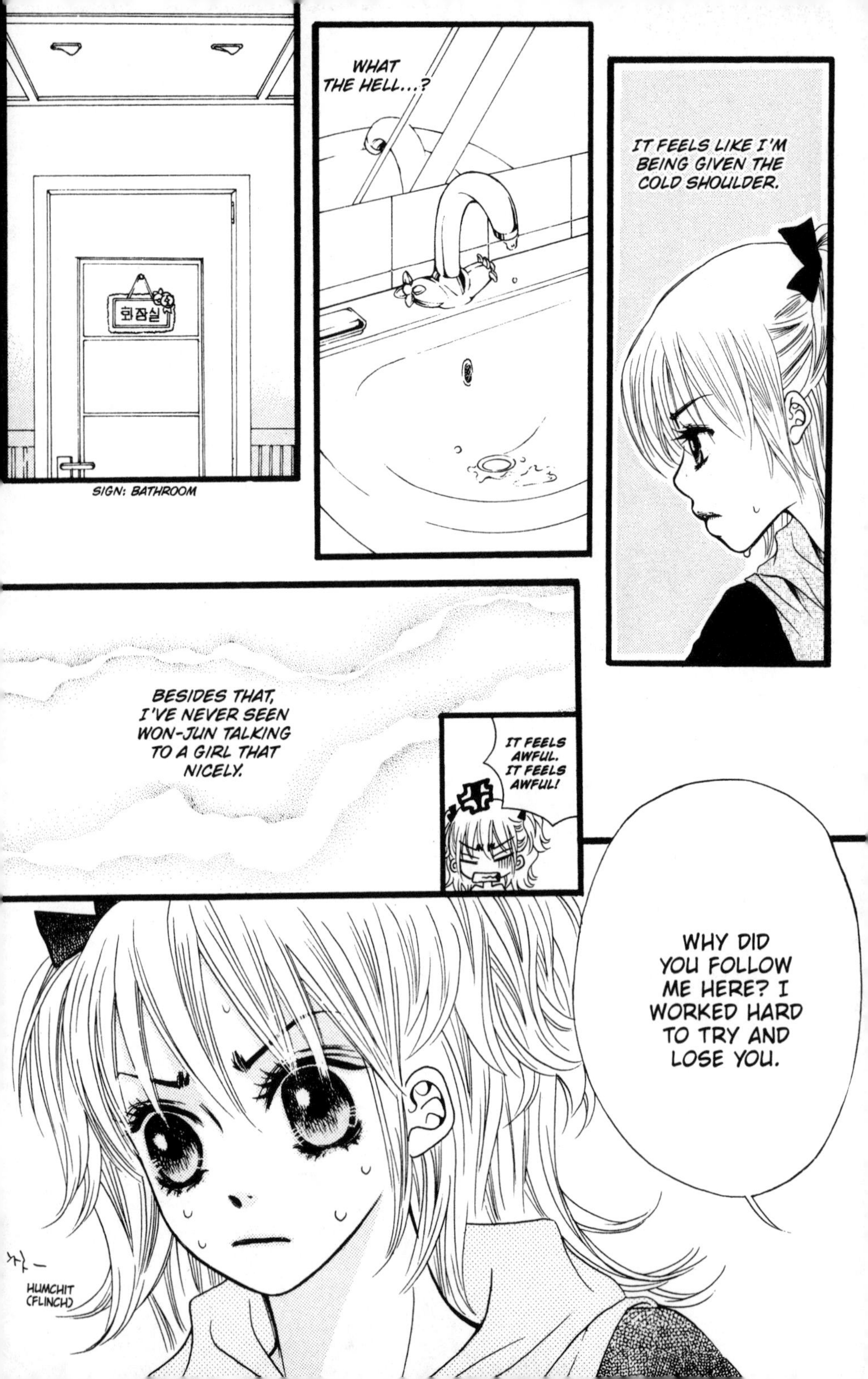
SIGN: BATHROOM
WHAT THE HELL...?
IT FEELS LIKE I'M BEING GIVEN THE COLD SHOULDER.
BESIDES THAT, I'VE NEVER SEEN WON-JUN TALKING TO A GIRL THAT NICELY.
IT FEELS AWFUL. IT FEELS AWFUL!
WHY DID YOU FOLLOW ME HERE? I WORKED HARD TO TRY AND LOSE YOU.
HUMCHIT (FLINCH)

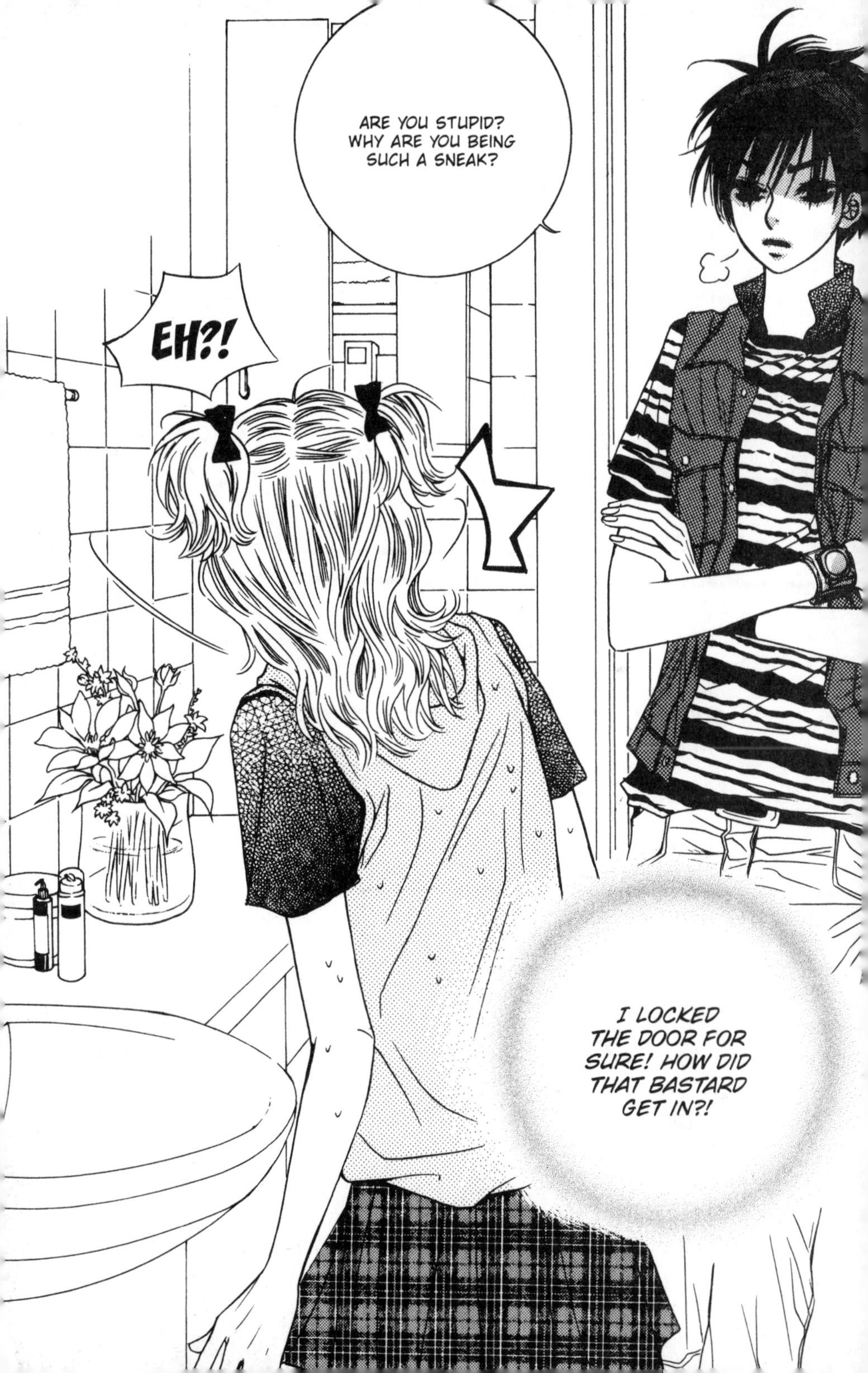
ARE YOU STUPID? WHY ARE YOU BEING SUCH A SNEAK?
EH?!
I LOCKED THE DOOR FOR SURE! HOW DID THAT BASTARD GET IN?!

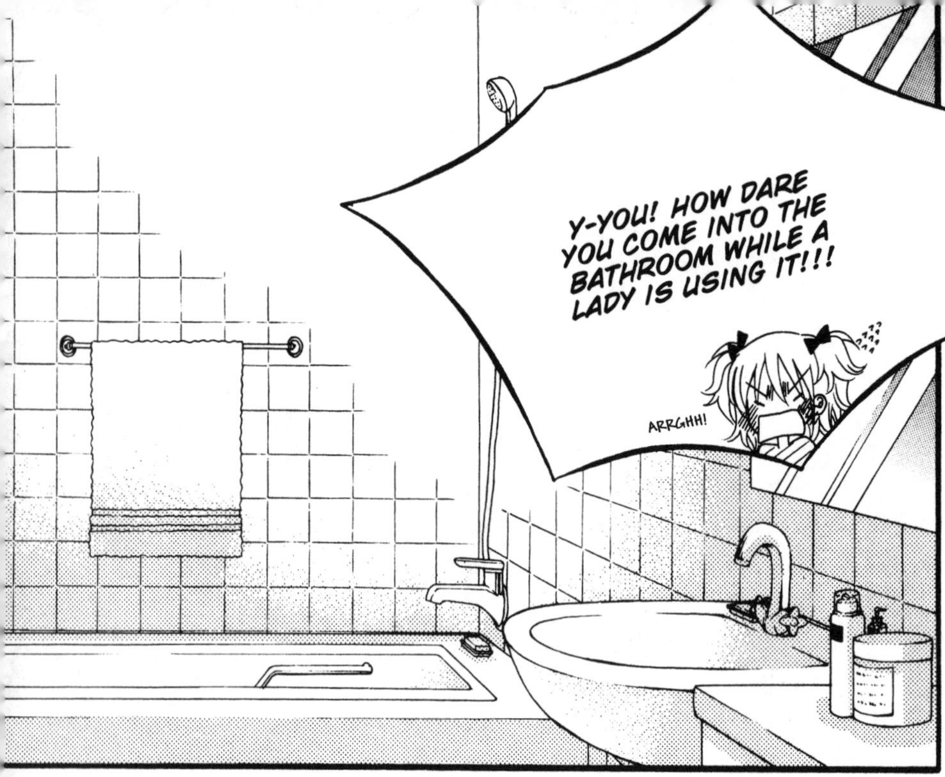
Y-YOU! HOW DARE YOU COME INTO THE BATHROOM WHILE A LADY IS USING IT!!!
ARRGHH!

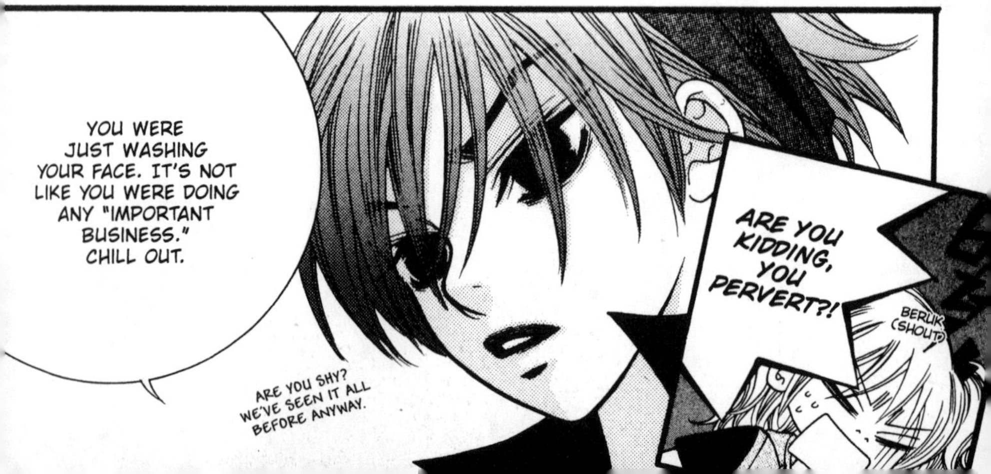
YOU WERE JUST WASHING YOUR FACE. IT'S NOT LIKE YOU WERE DOING ANY "IMPORTANT BUSINESS." CHILL OUT.
ARE YOU SHY? WE'VE SEEN IT ALL BEFORE ANYWAY.
ARE YOU KIDDING, YOU PERVERT?!
BERUK (SHOUT)

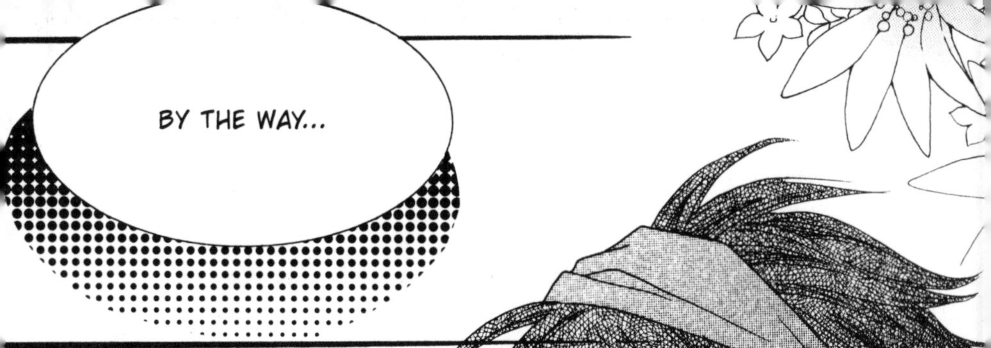
BY THE WAY...

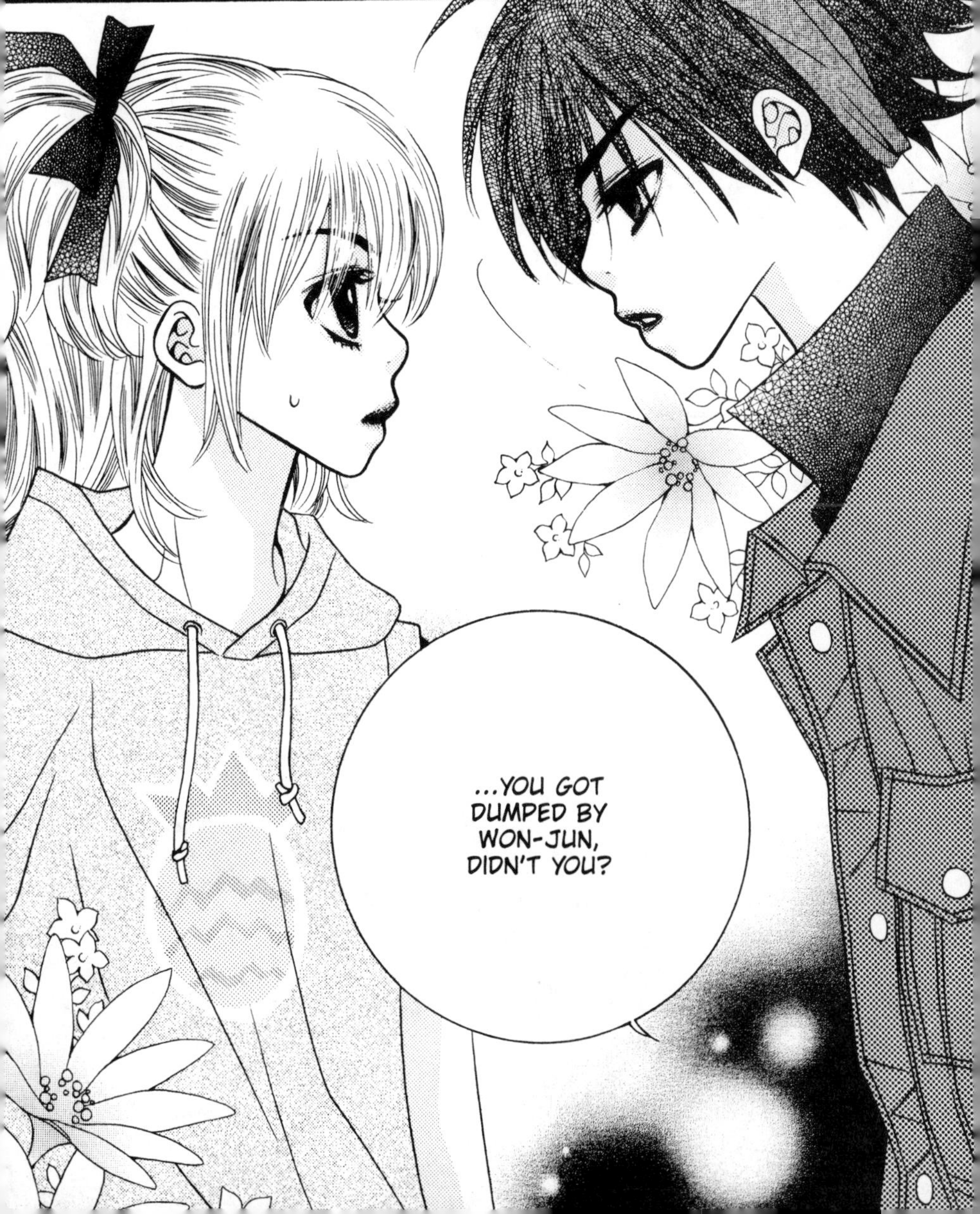
...YOU GOT DUMPED BY WON-JUN, DIDN'T YOU?

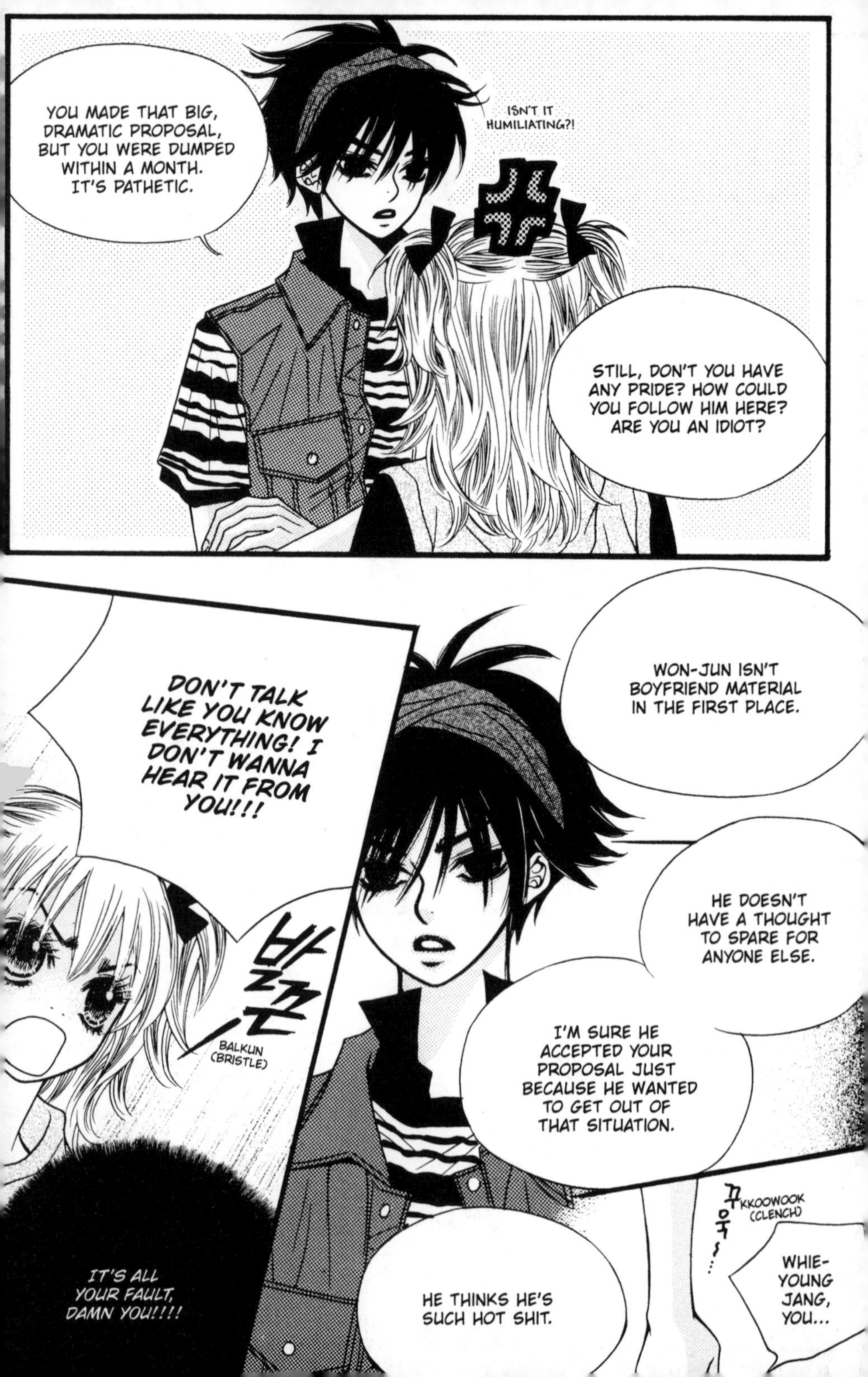
YOU MADE THAT BIG, DRAMATIC PROPOSAL, BUT YOU WERE DUMPED WITHIN A MONTH. IT'S PATHETIC.
ISN'T IT HUMILIATING?!
STILL, DON'T YOU HAVE ANY PRIDE? HOW COULD YOU FOLLOW HIM HERE? ARE YOU AN IDIOT?
DON'T TALK LIKE YOU KNOW EVERYTHING! I DON'T WANNA HEAR IT FROM YOU!!!
발끈
BALKUN (BRISTLE)
IT'S ALL YOUR FAULT, DAMN YOU!!!!
WON-JUN ISN'T BOYFRIEND MATERIAL IN THE FIRST PLACE.
HE DOESN'T HAVE A THOUGHT TO SPARE FOR ANYONE ELSE.
I'M SURE HE ACCEPTED YOUR PROPOSAL JUST BECAUSE HE WANTED TO GET OUT OF THAT SITUATION.
HE THINKS HE'S SUCH HOT SHIT.
꾸욱
KKOOWOOK (CLENCH)
WHIE-YOUNG JANG, YOU...

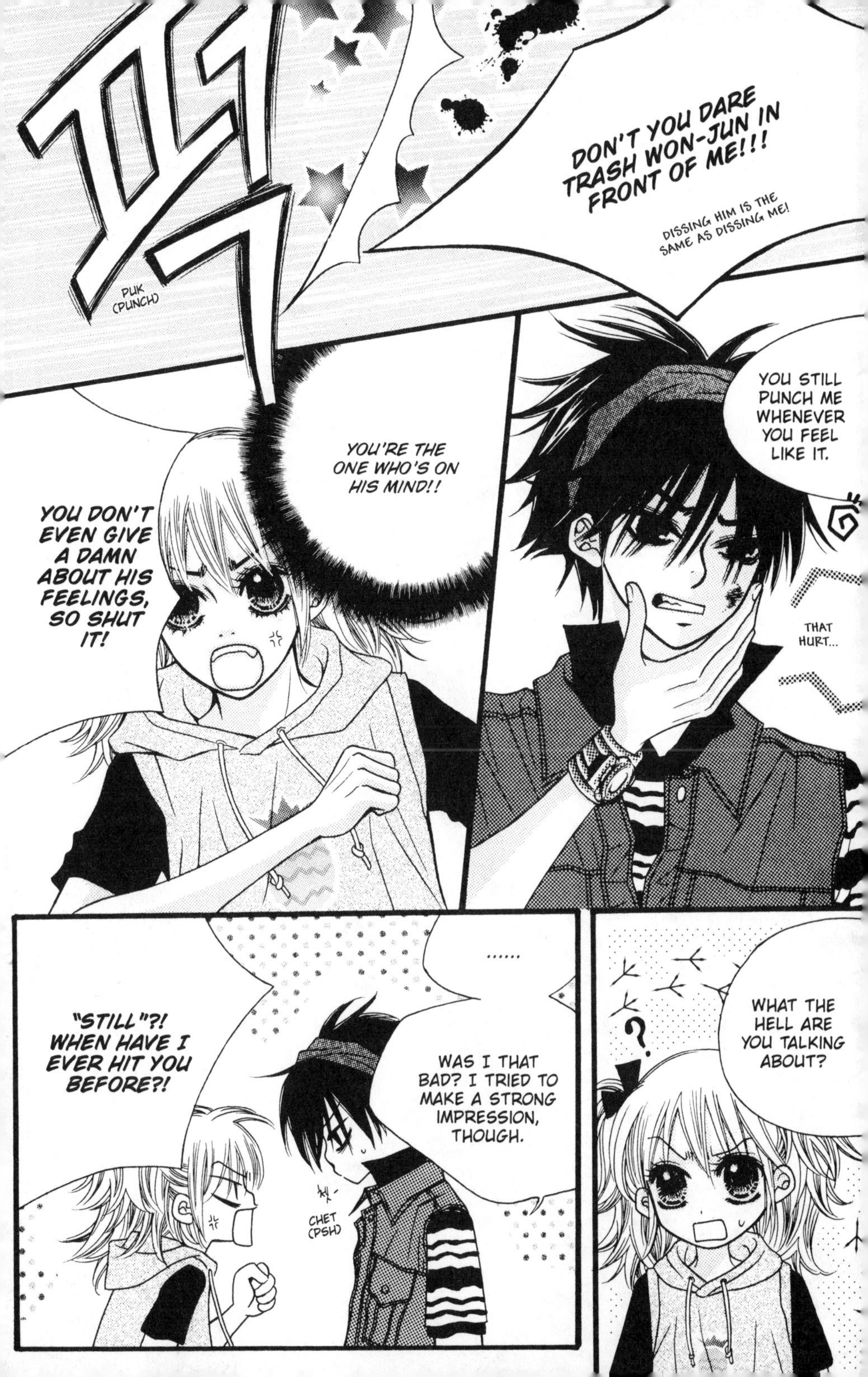
PUK (PUNCH)
DON'T YOU DARE TRASH WON-JUN IN FRONT OF ME!!!
DISSING HIM IS THE SAME AS DISSING ME!
YOU'RE THE ONE WHO'S ON HIS MIND!!
YOU DON'T EVEN GIVE A DAMN ABOUT HIS FEELINGS, SO SHUT IT!
YOU STILL PUNCH ME WHENEVER YOU FEEL LIKE IT.
THAT HURT...
"STILL"?! WHEN HAVE I EVER HIT YOU BEFORE?!
......
WAS I THAT BAD? I TRIED TO MAKE A STRONG IMPRESSION, THOUGH.
칫
CHET (PSH)
WHAT THE HELL ARE YOU TALKING ABOUT?

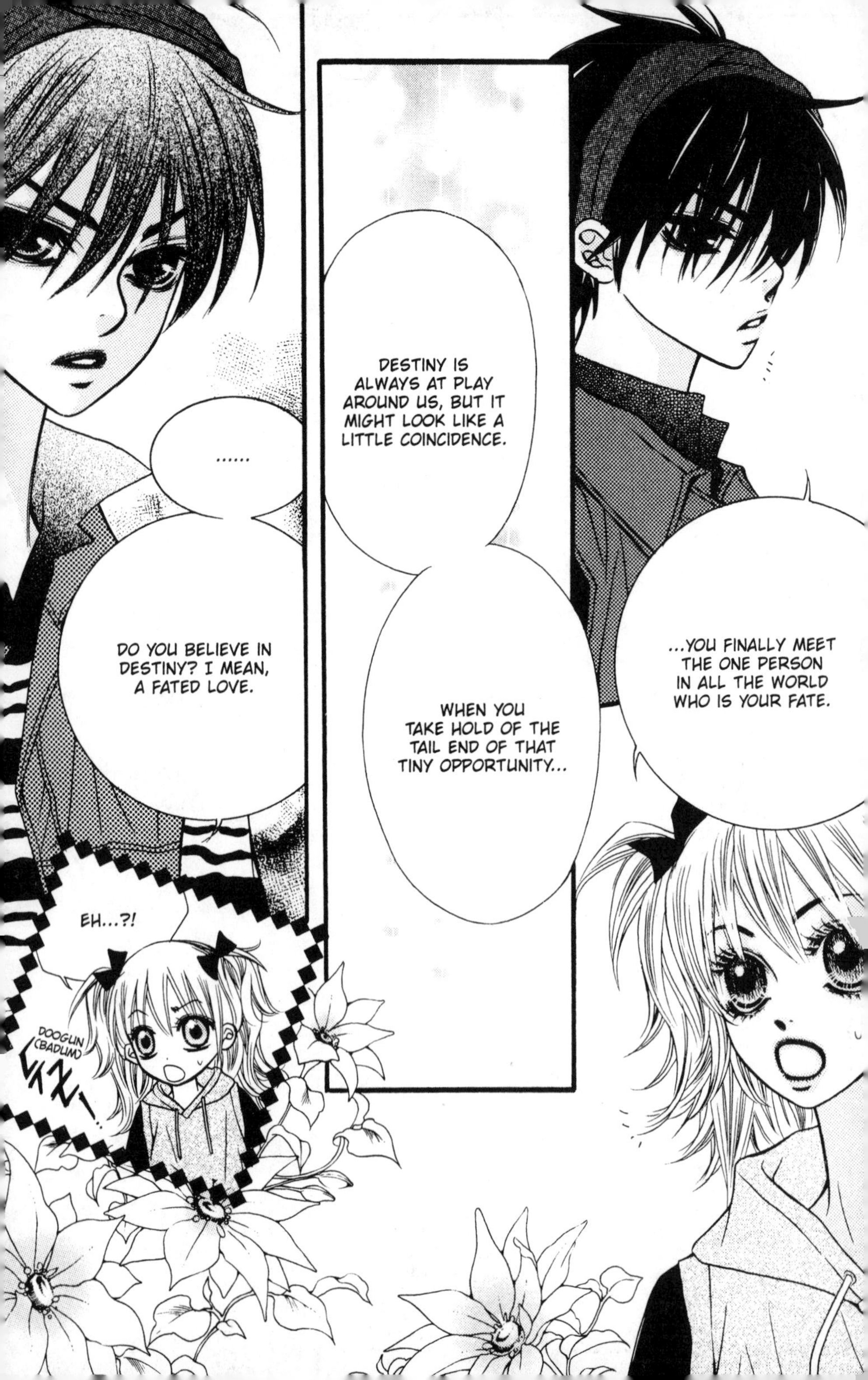
......
DO YOU BELIEVE IN DESTINY? I MEAN, A FATED LOVE.
DESTINY IS ALWAYS AT PLAY AROUND US, BUT IT MIGHT LOOK LIKE A LITTLE COINCIDENCE.
WHEN YOU TAKE HOLD OF THE TAIL END OF THAT TINY OPPORTUNITY...
...YOU FINALLY MEET THE ONE PERSON IN ALL THE WORLD WHO IS YOUR FATE.
EH...?!
DOOGUN (BADUM)

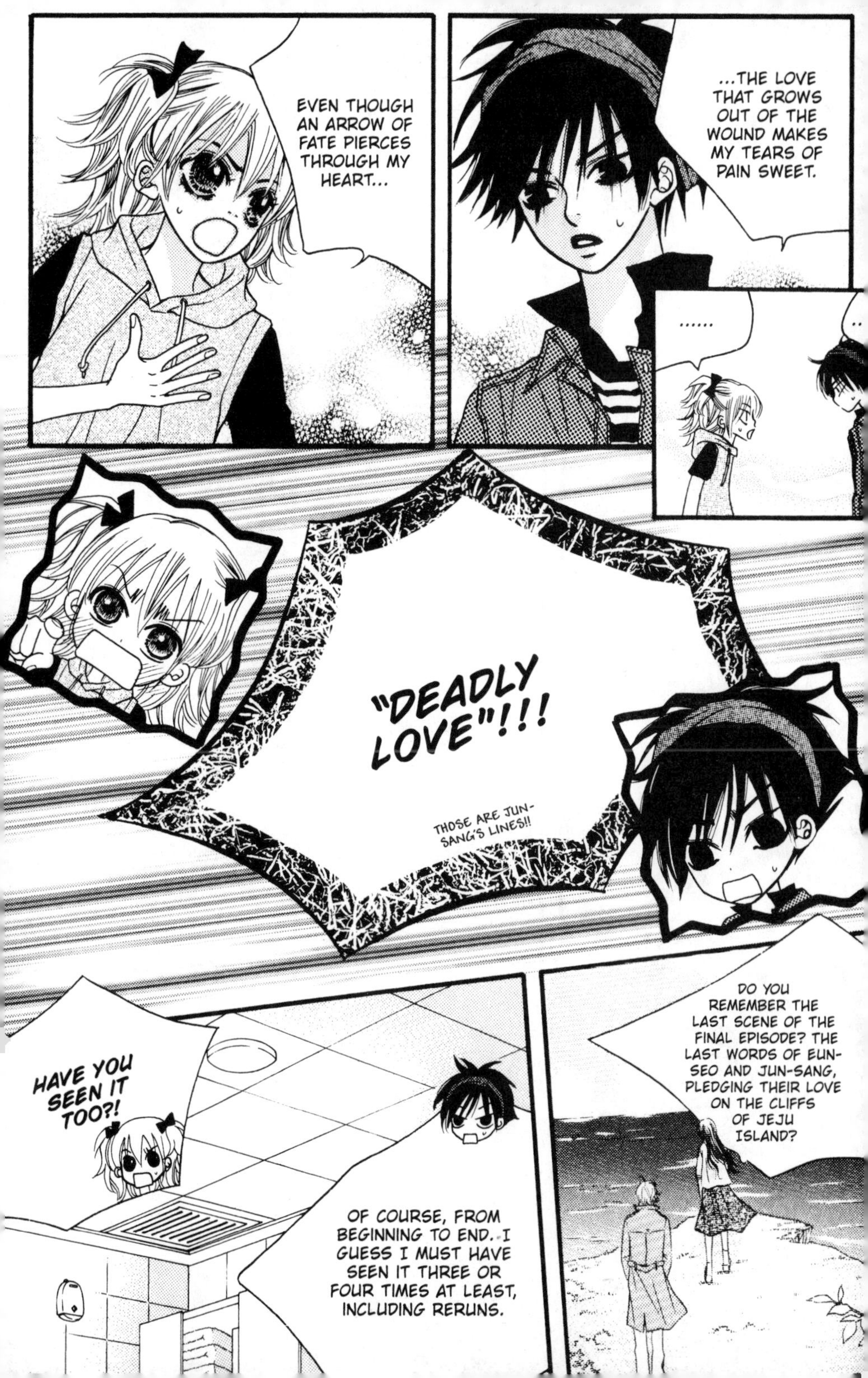
EVEN THOUGH AN ARROW OF FATE PIERCES THROUGH MY HEART...
...THE LOVE THAT GROWS OUT OF THE WOUND MAKES MY TEARS OF PAIN SWEET.
......
..
"DEADLY LOVE"!!!
THOSE ARE JUN-SANG'S LINES!!
HAVE YOU SEEN IT TOO?!
OF COURSE, FROM BEGINNING TO END. I GUESS I MUST HAVE SEEN IT THREE OR FOUR TIMES AT LEAST, INCLUDING RERUNS.
DO YOU REMEMBER THE LAST SCENE OF THE FINAL EPISODE? THE LAST WORDS OF EUN-SEO AND JUN-SANG, PLEDGING THEIR LOVE ON THE CLIFFS OF JEJU ISLAND?

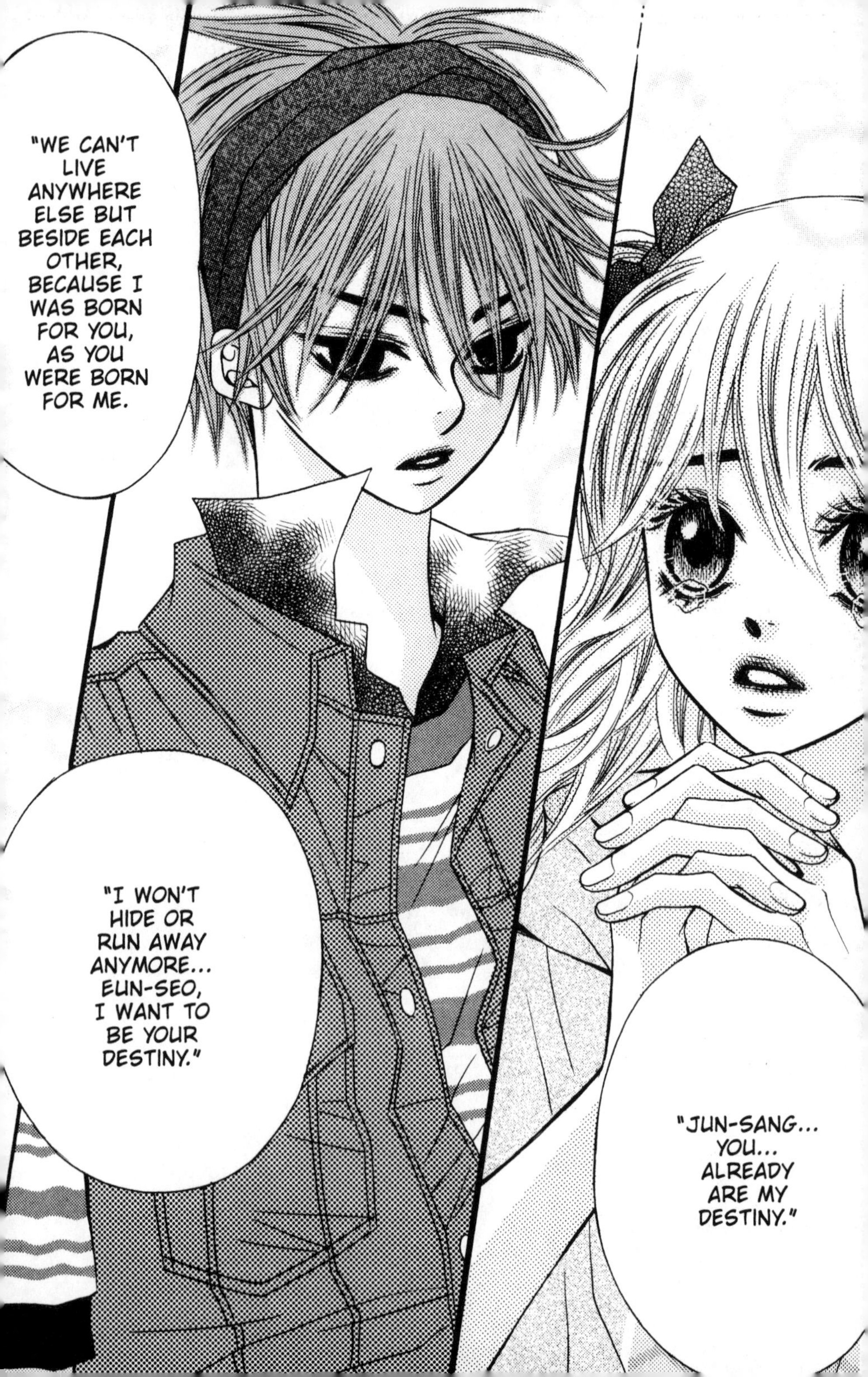
"WE CAN'T LIVE ANYWHERE ELSE BUT BESIDE EACH OTHER, BECAUSE I WAS BORN FOR YOU, AS YOU WERE BORN FOR ME.
"I WON'T HIDE OR RUN AWAY ANYMORE... EUN-SEO, I WANT TO BE YOUR DESTINY."
"JUN-SANG... YOU... ALREADY ARE MY DESTINY."

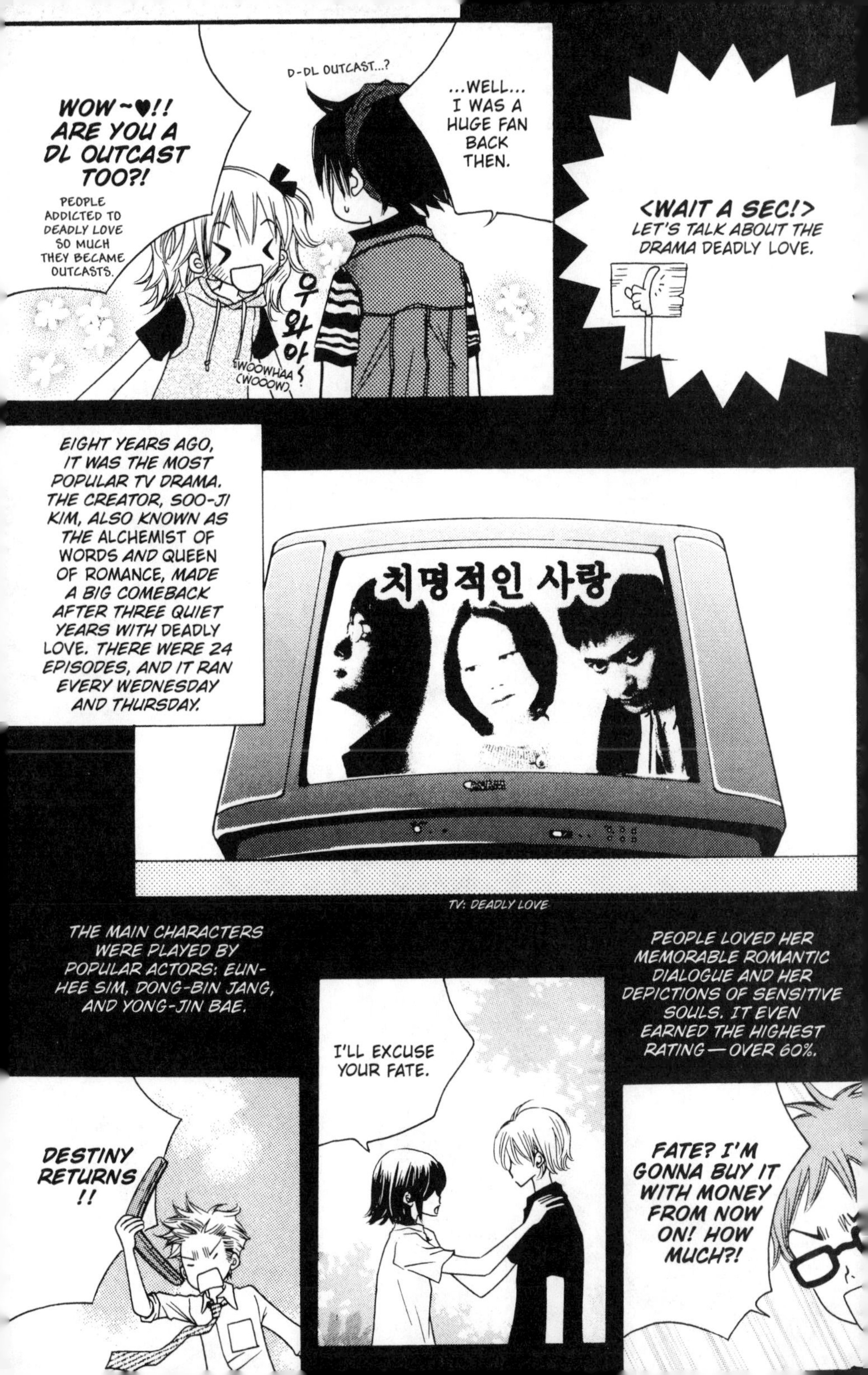

WOW~♥!! ARE YOU A DL OUTCAST TOO?!
PEOPLE ADDICTED TO DEADLY LOVE SO MUCH THEY BECAME OUTCASTS.
우와아~
WOOWHAA (WOOOW)
D-DL OUTCAST...?
...WELL... I WAS A HUGE FAN BACK THEN.
<WAIT A SEC!>
LET'S TALK ABOUT THE DRAMA DEADLY LOVE.
EIGHT YEARS AGO, IT WAS THE MOST POPULAR TV DRAMA. THE CREATOR, SOO-JI KIM, ALSO KNOWN AS THE ALCHEMIST OF WORDS AND QUEEN OF ROMANCE, MADE A BIG COMEBACK AFTER THREE QUIET YEARS WITH DEADLY LOVE. THERE WERE 24 EPISODES, AND IT RAN EVERY WEDNESDAY AND THURSDAY.
치명적인 사랑
TV: DEADLY LOVE
THE MAIN CHARACTERS WERE PLAYED BY POPULAR ACTORS: EUN-HEE SIM, DONG-BIN JANG, AND YONG-JIN BAE.
I'LL EXCUSE YOUR FATE.
PEOPLE LOVED HER MEMORABLE ROMANTIC DIALOGUE AND HER DEPICTIONS OF SENSITIVE SOULS. IT EVEN EARNED THE HIGHEST RATING—OVER 60%.
DESTINY RETURNS !!
FATE? I'M GONNA BUY IT WITH MONEY FROM NOW ON! HOW MUCH?!

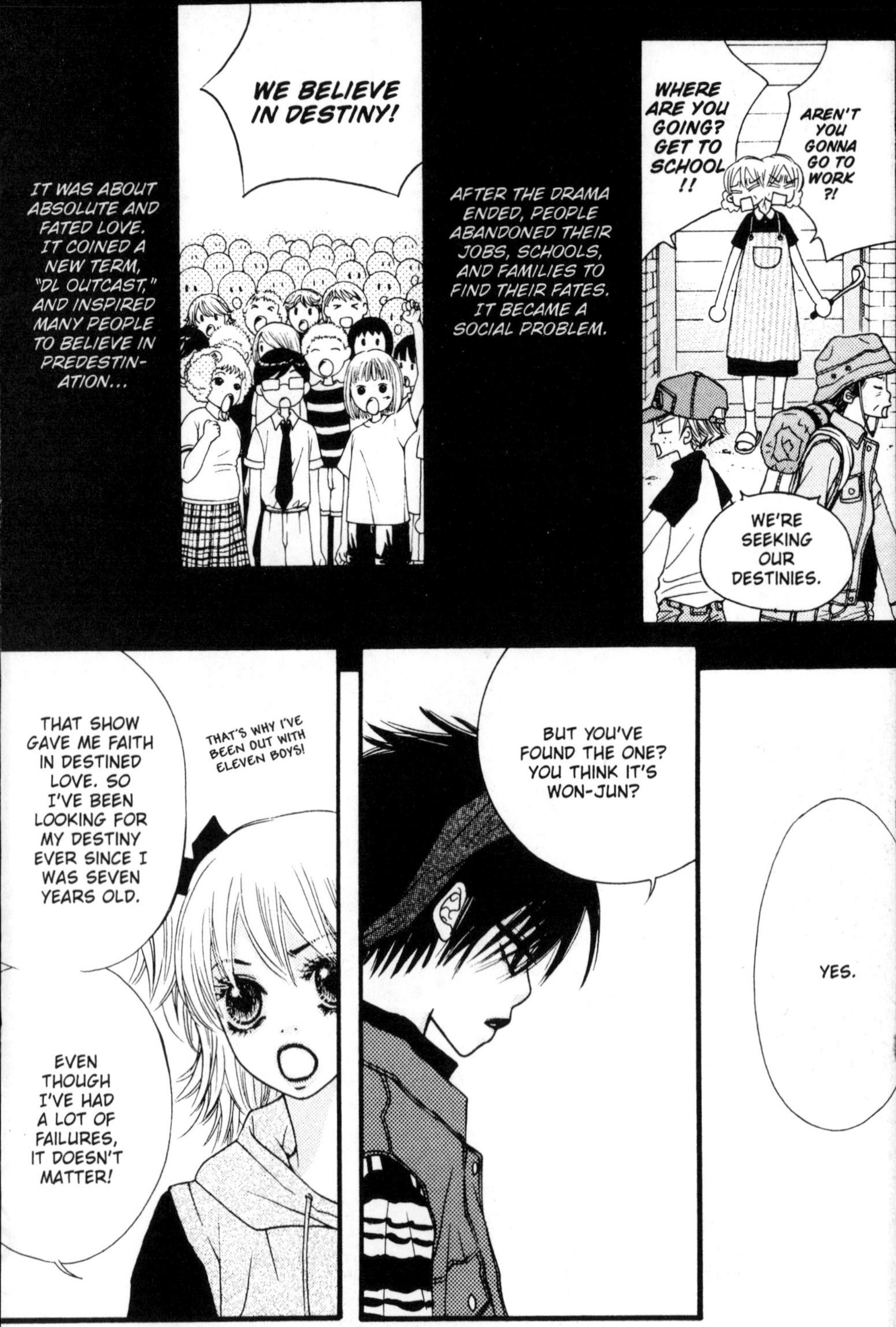
IT WAS ABOUT ABSOLUTE AND FATED LOVE. IT COINED A NEW TERM, "DL OUTCAST," AND INSPIRED MANY PEOPLE TO BELIEVE IN PREDESTIN-ATION...
WE BELIEVE IN DESTINY!
AFTER THE DRAMA ENDED, PEOPLE ABANDONED THEIR JOBS, SCHOOLS, AND FAMILIES TO FIND THEIR FATES. IT BECAME A SOCIAL PROBLEM.
WHERE ARE YOU GOING? GET TO SCHOOL!!
AREN'T YOU GONNA GO TO WORK?!
WE'RE SEEKING OUR DESTINIES.
THAT SHOW GAVE ME FAITH IN DESTINED LOVE. SO I'VE BEEN LOOKING FOR MY DESTINY EVER SINCE I WAS SEVEN YEARS OLD.
THAT'S WHY I'VE BEEN OUT WITH ELEVEN BOYS!
EVEN THOUGH I'VE HAD A LOT OF FAILURES, IT DOESN'T MATTER!
BUT YOU'VE FOUND THE ONE? YOU THINK IT'S WON-JUN?
YES.

WHAT ABOUT YOU? AFTER SEEING THAT SHOW, HAVEN'T YOU THOUGHT ABOUT LOOKING FOR YOUR SPECIAL SOMEONE?

......

BUT HE DUMPED YOU. AREN'T YOU BARKING UP THE WRONG TREE?

NO, I'M NOT! THE COUPLE IN THE DRAMA BROKE UP TOO, AND THEN FIVE YEARS LATER THEY REALIZED THEY WERE MEANT FOR ONE ANOTHER.

HNG CHUMPH

I CAN WAIT. I WON'T GIVE UP NO MATTER HOW MANY TIMES I'M DUMPED!!

HE'S PICKIN WIT

......

YOU ARE PERSISTENT.

DON'T YOU DARE SAY I'M PERSISTENT!!!

IT'S THE SECOND TIME!!

FINE. LET'S SEE IF HE'S YOUR DESTINY.

W-WHAT THE?!!

TAK (GRAB)

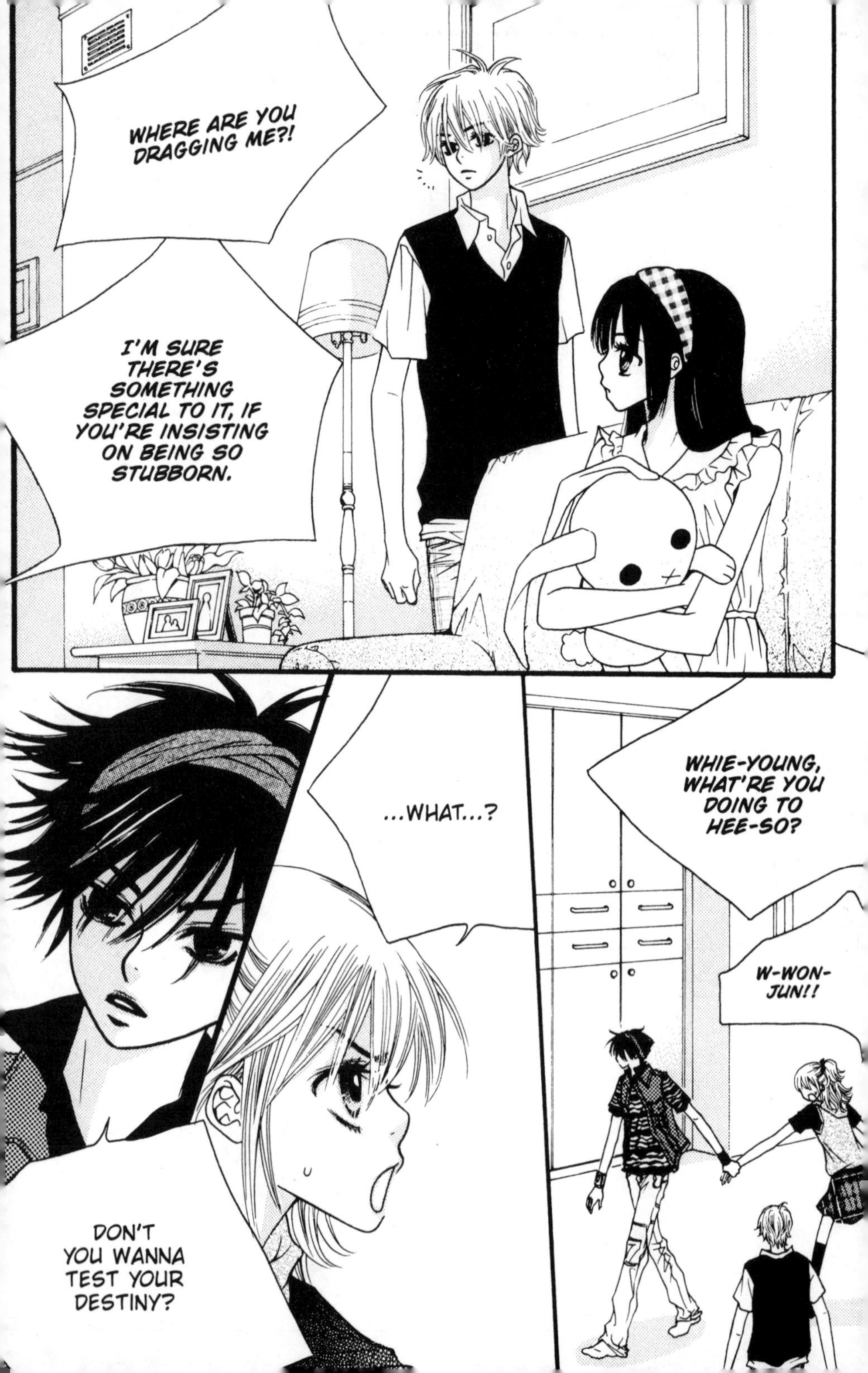
WHERE ARE YOU DRAGGING ME?!
I'M SURE THERE'S SOMETHING SPECIAL TO IT, IF YOU'RE INSISTING ON BEING SO STUBBORN.
...WHAT...?
DON'T YOU WANNA TEST YOUR DESTINY?
WHIE-YOUNG, WHAT'RE YOU DOING TO HEE-SO?
W-WON-JUN!!

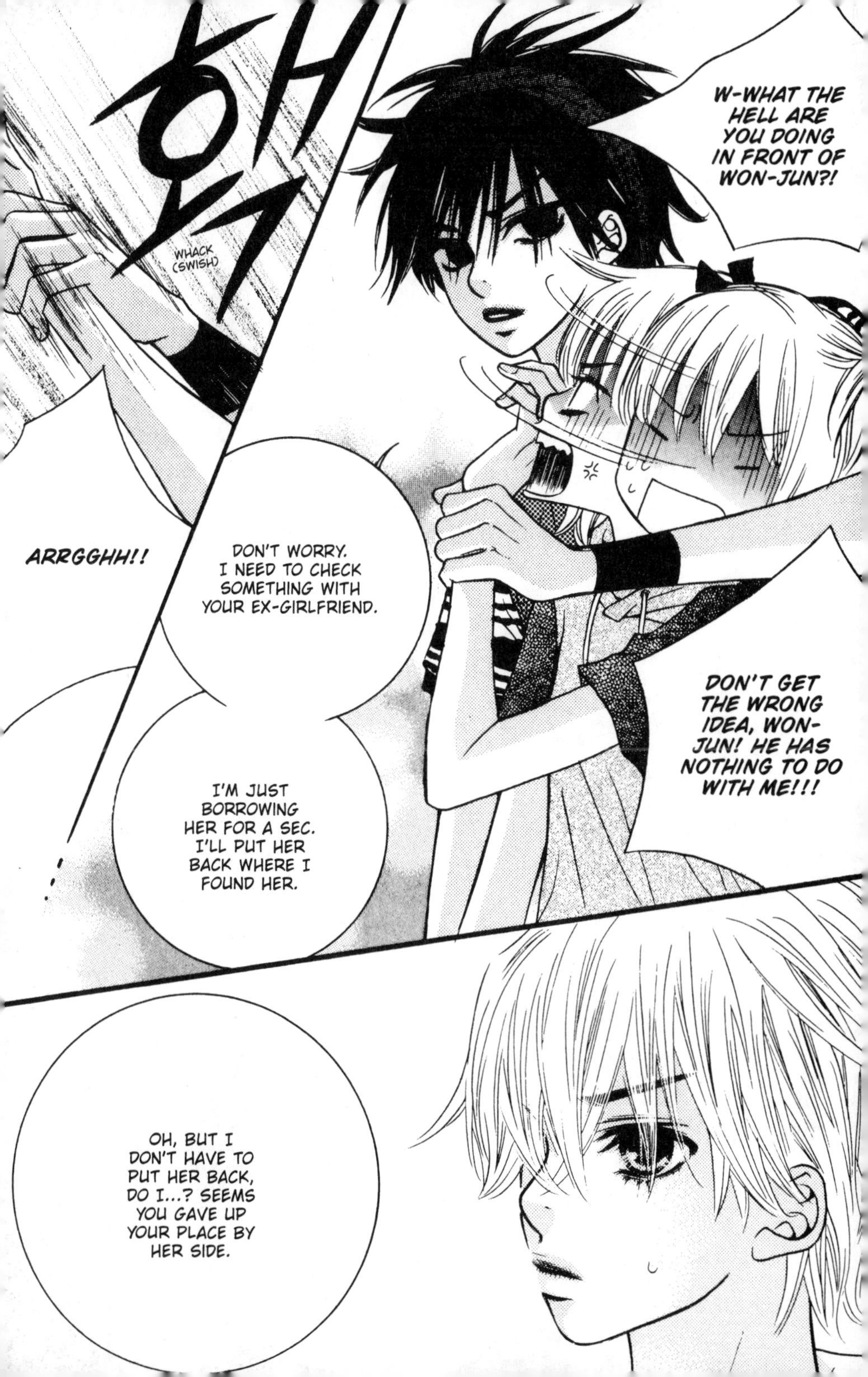
WHACK (SWISH)
ARRGGHH!!
...
W-WHAT THE HELL ARE YOU DOING IN FRONT OF WON-JUN?!
DON'T WORRY. I NEED TO CHECK SOMETHING WITH YOUR EX-GIRLFRIEND.
I'M JUST BORROWING HER FOR A SEC. I'LL PUT HER BACK WHERE I FOUND HER.
DON'T GET THE WRONG IDEA, WON-JUN! HE HAS NOTHING TO DO WITH ME!!!
OH, BUT I DON'T HAVE TO PUT HER BACK, DO I...? SEEMS YOU GAVE UP YOUR PLACE BY HER SIDE.

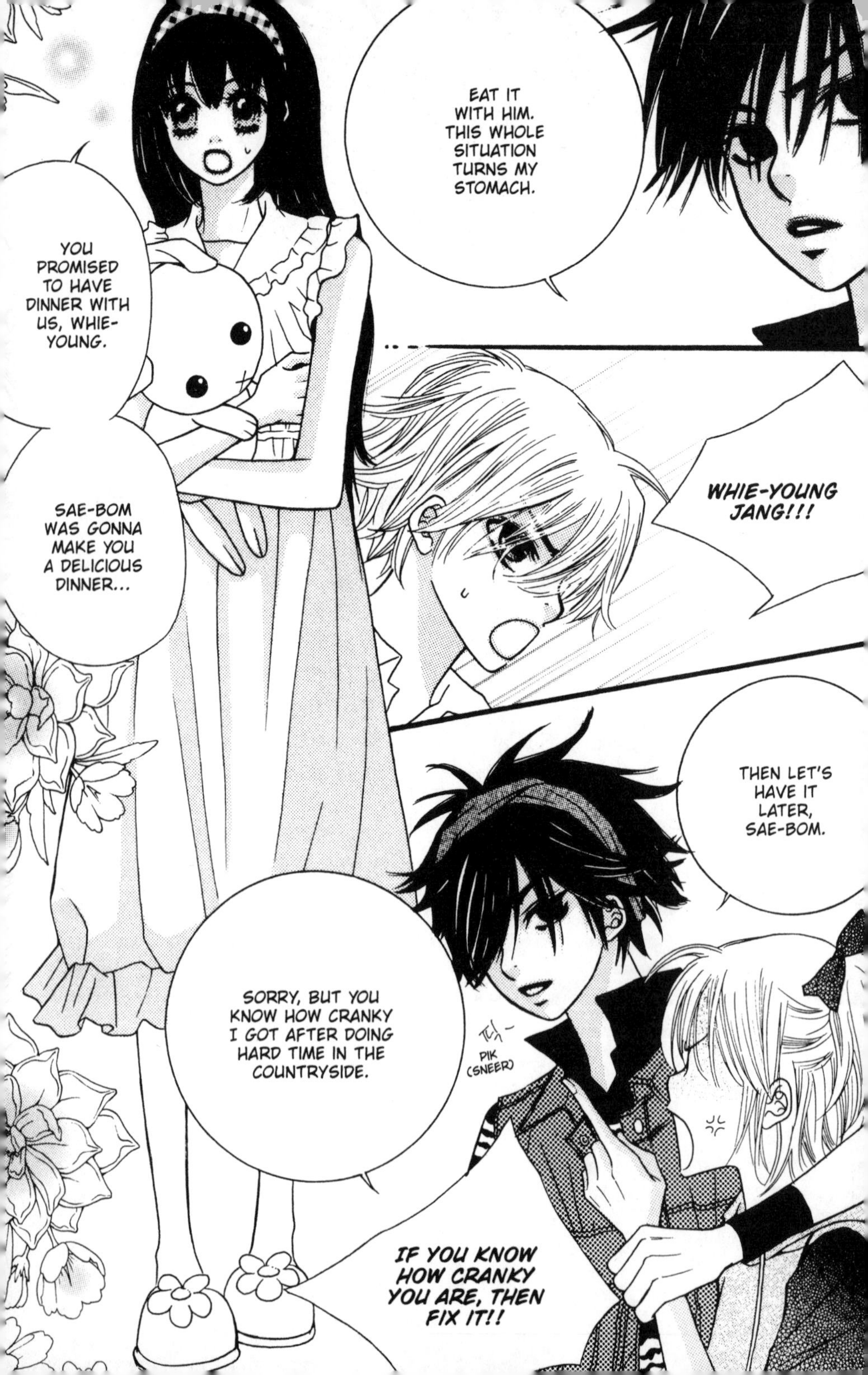
YOU PROMISED TO HAVE DINNER WITH US, WHIE-YOUNG.
SAE-BOM WAS GONNA MAKE YOU A DELICIOUS DINNER...
EAT IT WITH HIM. THIS WHOLE SITUATION TURNS MY STOMACH.
WHIE-YOUNG JANG!!!
THEN LET'S HAVE IT LATER, SAE-BOM.
SORRY, BUT YOU KNOW HOW CRANKY I GOT AFTER DOING HARD TIME IN THE COUNTRYSIDE.
PIK (SNEER)
IF YOU KNOW HOW CRANKY YOU ARE, THEN FIX IT!!

WE GOTTA GO, THEN.

GET AWAY FROM ME!! I HAVE TO GET MY BAG!!

BEATRICE IS IN THERE!

BESIDES, I CAN'T LEAVE WON-JUN ALONE WITH SAE-BOM!

ZZ ZZ

T'S NOISY.

......

WHIE-YOUNG...

IT'S OKAY. YOU'LL BE CAMPING WITH HIM IN A FEW DAYS. YOU'LL HAVE PLENTY OF TIME THEN.

RIGHT! AND ON THAT TRIP, I'LL BE STAYING OVERNIGHT WITH WHIE-YOUNG~!!

KKOOK (SQUEEZE)
끄옥

HE'S GONE... SAE-BOM WAS SO EXCITED...ABOUT HAVING DINNER WITH WHIE-YOUNG...

...UMM...DID YOU BREAK UP WITH HEE-SO...?

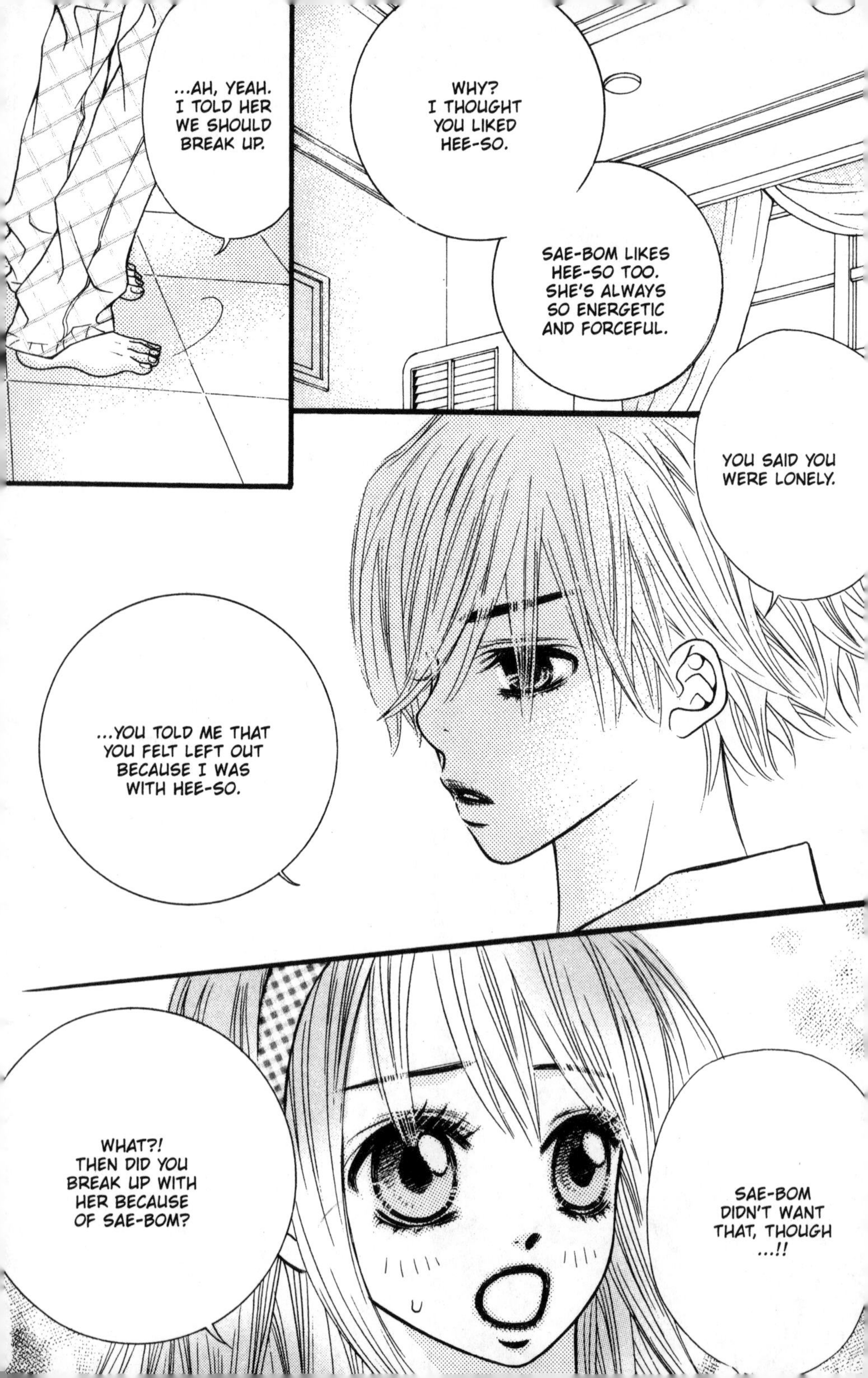
...AH, YEAH. I TOLD HER WE SHOULD BREAK UP.
WHY? I THOUGHT YOU LIKED HEE-SO.
SAE-BOM LIKES HEE-SO TOO. SHE'S ALWAYS SO ENERGETIC AND FORCEFUL.
YOU SAID YOU WERE LONELY.
...YOU TOLD ME THAT YOU FELT LEFT OUT BECAUSE I WAS WITH HEE-SO.
WHAT?! THEN DID YOU BREAK UP WITH HER BECAUSE OF SAE-BOM?
SAE-BOM DIDN'T WANT THAT, THOUGH ...!!

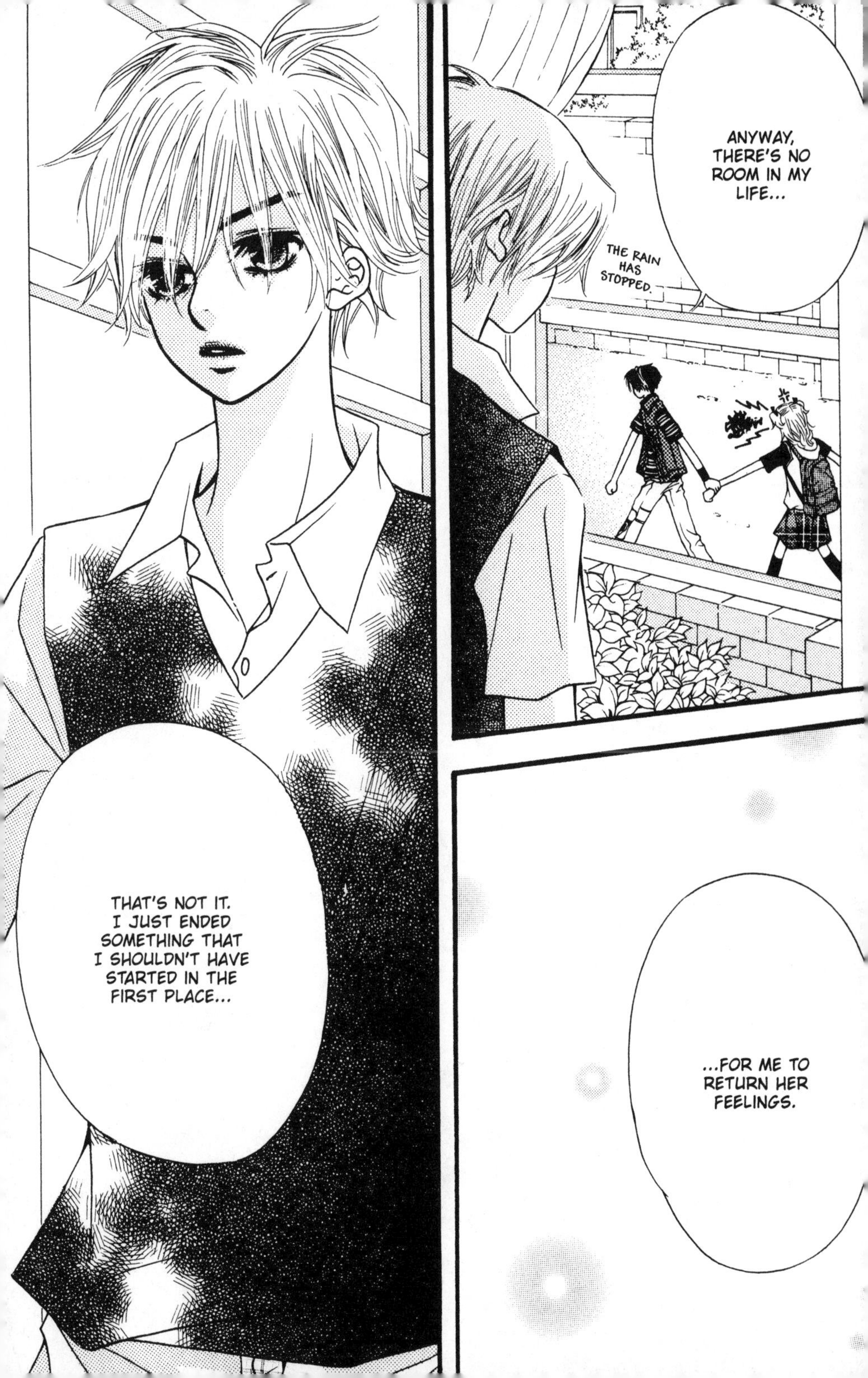
THAT'S NOT IT. I JUST ENDED SOMETHING THAT I SHOULDN'T HAVE STARTED IN THE FIRST PLACE...
ANYWAY, THERE'S NO ROOM IN MY LIFE...
THE RAIN HAS STOPPED.
...FOR ME TO RETURN HER FEELINGS.

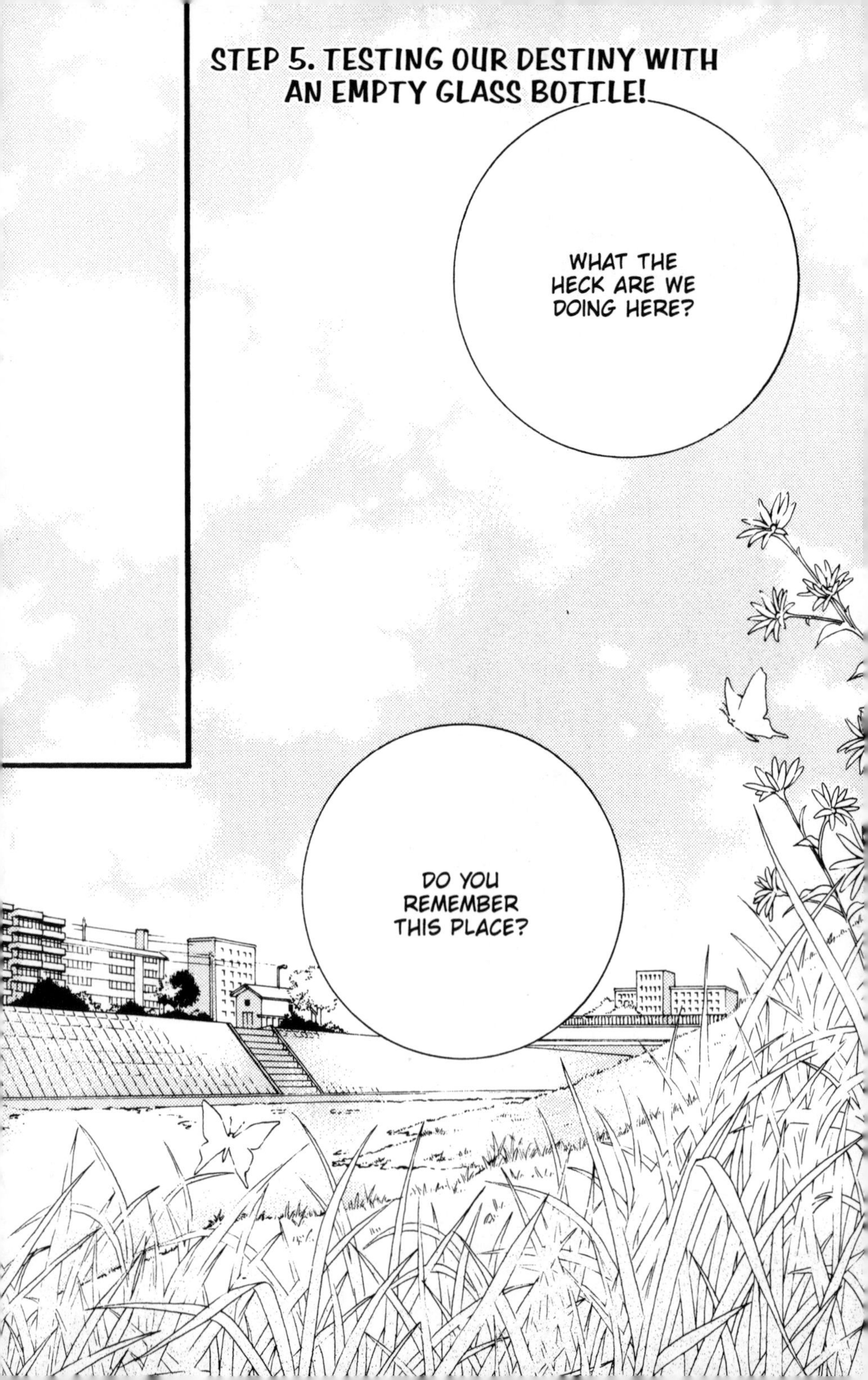
STEP 5. TESTING OUR DESTINY WITH AN EMPTY GLASS BOTTLE!
WHAT THE HECK ARE WE DOING HERE?
DO YOU REMEMBER THIS PLACE?

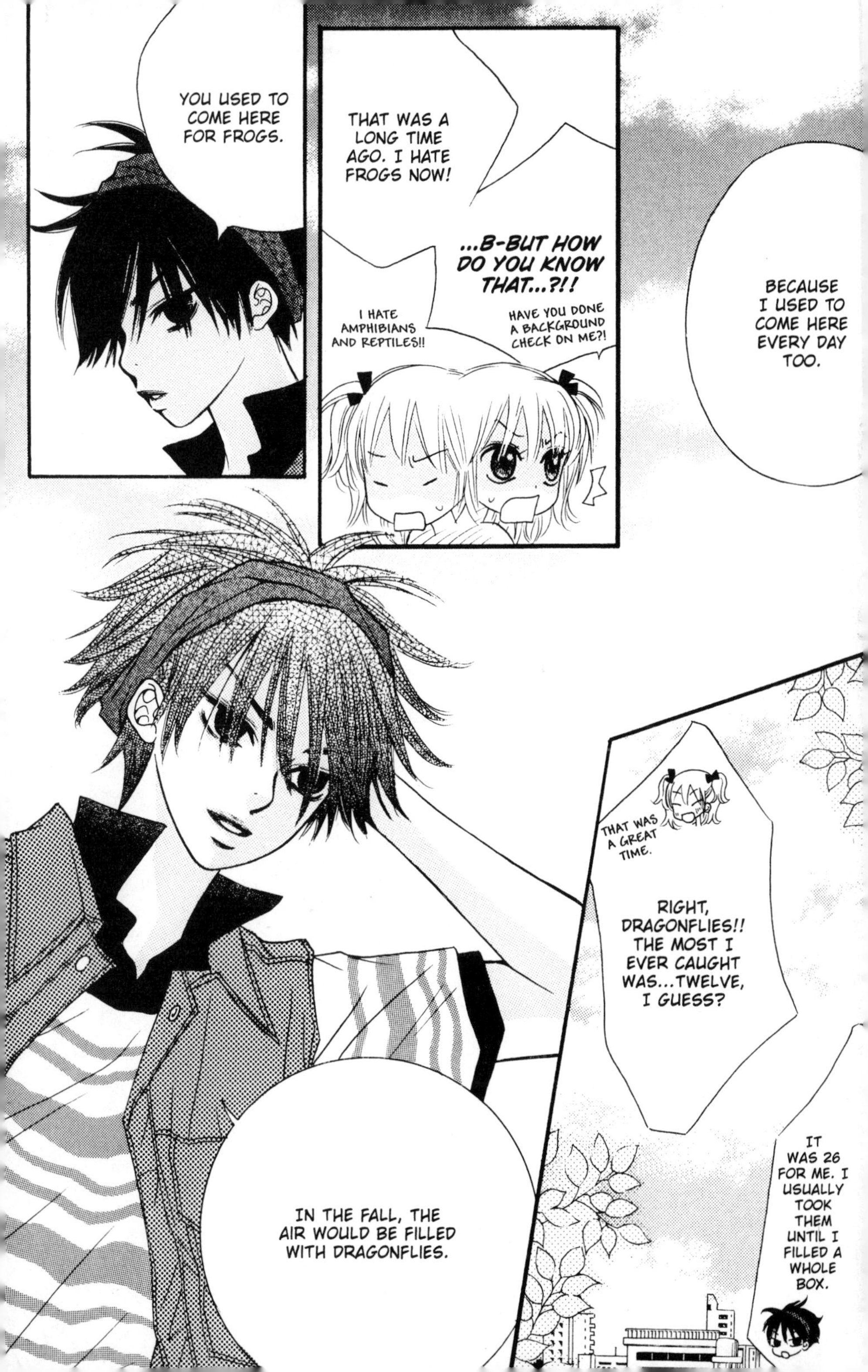
YOU USED TO COME HERE FOR FROGS.
THAT WAS A LONG TIME AGO. I HATE FROGS NOW!
...B-BUT HOW DO YOU KNOW THAT...?!!
I HATE AMPHIBIANS AND REPTILES!!
HAVE YOU DONE A BACKGROUND CHECK ON ME?!
BECAUSE I USED TO COME HERE EVERY DAY TOO.
IN THE FALL, THE AIR WOULD BE FILLED WITH DRAGONFLIES.
THAT WAS A GREAT TIME.
RIGHT, DRAGONFLIES!! THE MOST I EVER CAUGHT WAS...TWELVE, I GUESS?
IT WAS 26 FOR ME. I USUALLY TOOK THEM UNTIL I FILLED A WHOLE BOX.

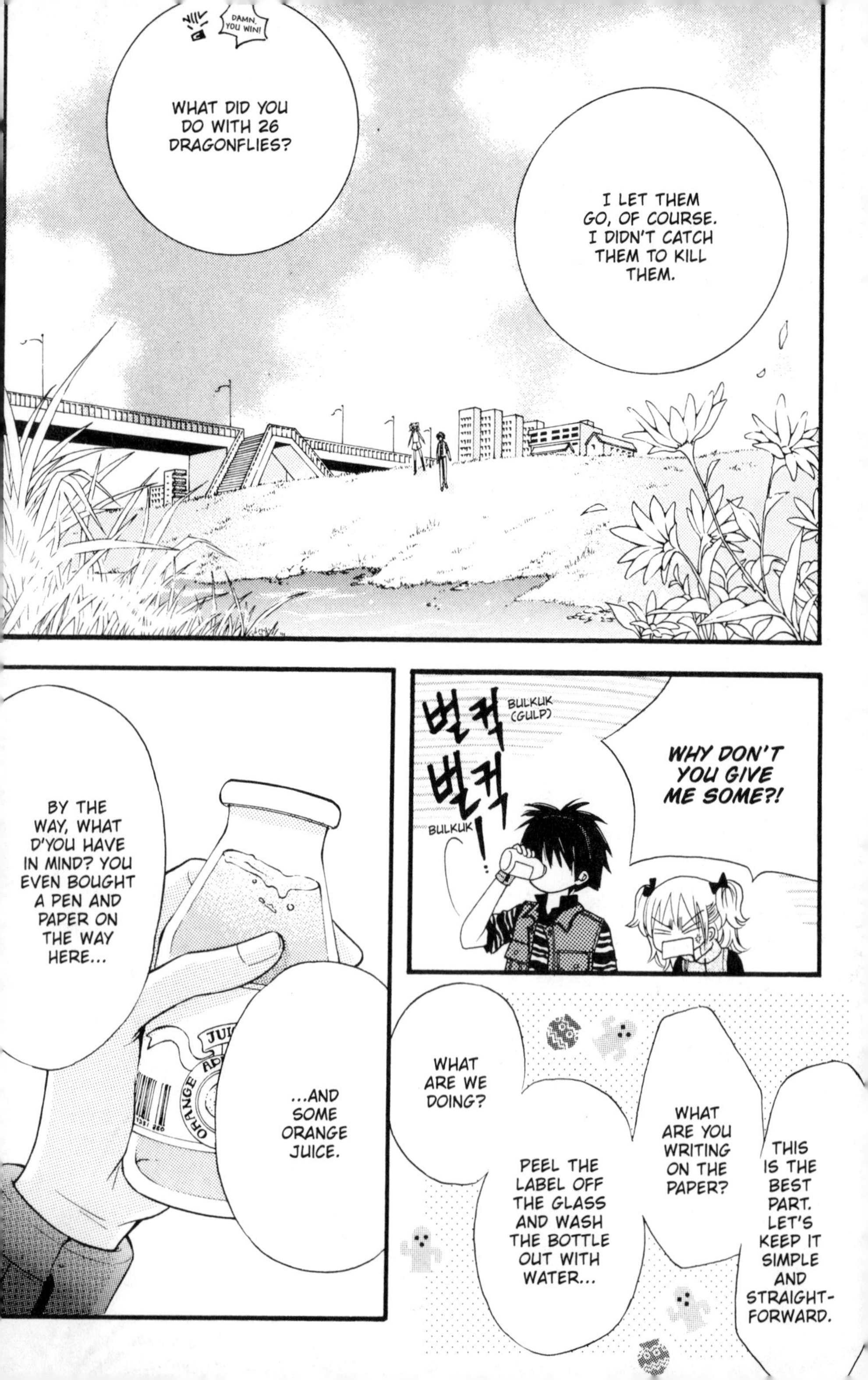
DAMN, YOU WIN!
WHAT DID YOU DO WITH 26 DRAGONFLIES?
I LET THEM GO, OF COURSE. I DIDN'T CATCH THEM TO KILL THEM.
BY THE WAY, WHAT D'YOU HAVE IN MIND? YOU EVEN BOUGHT A PEN AND PAPER ON THE WAY HERE...
...AND SOME ORANGE JUICE.
벌컥 벌컥
BULKUK (GULP)
BULKUK
WHY DON'T YOU GIVE ME SOME?!
WHAT ARE WE DOING?
PEEL THE LABEL OFF THE GLASS AND WASH THE BOTTLE OUT WITH WATER...
WHAT ARE YOU WRITING ON THE PAPER?
THIS IS THE BEST PART. LET'S KEEP IT SIMPLE AND STRAIGHT-FORWARD.

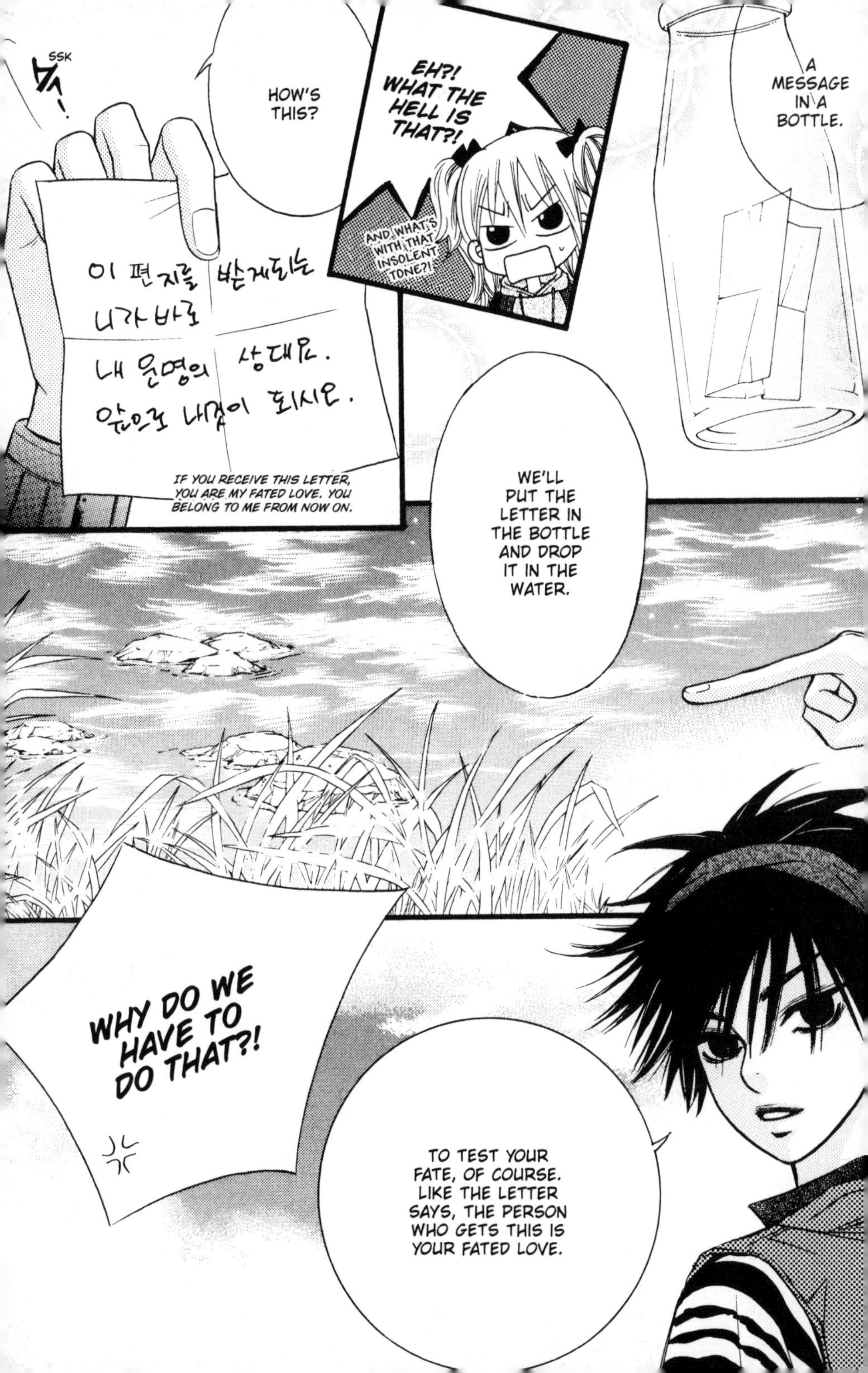
SSK
HOW'S THIS?
이 편지를 받게되는 니가 바로 내 운명의 상대요. 앞으로 내것이 되시오.
IF YOU RECEIVE THIS LETTER, YOU ARE MY FATED LOVE. YOU BELONG TO ME FROM NOW ON.
EH?! WHAT THE HELL IS THAT?!
AND WHAT'S WITH THAT INSOLENT TONE?!
A MESSAGE IN A BOTTLE.
WE'LL PUT THE LETTER IN THE BOTTLE AND DROP IT IN THE WATER.
WHY DO WE HAVE TO DO THAT?!
TO TEST YOUR FATE, OF COURSE. LIKE THE LETTER SAYS, THE PERSON WHO GETS THIS IS YOUR FATED LOVE.

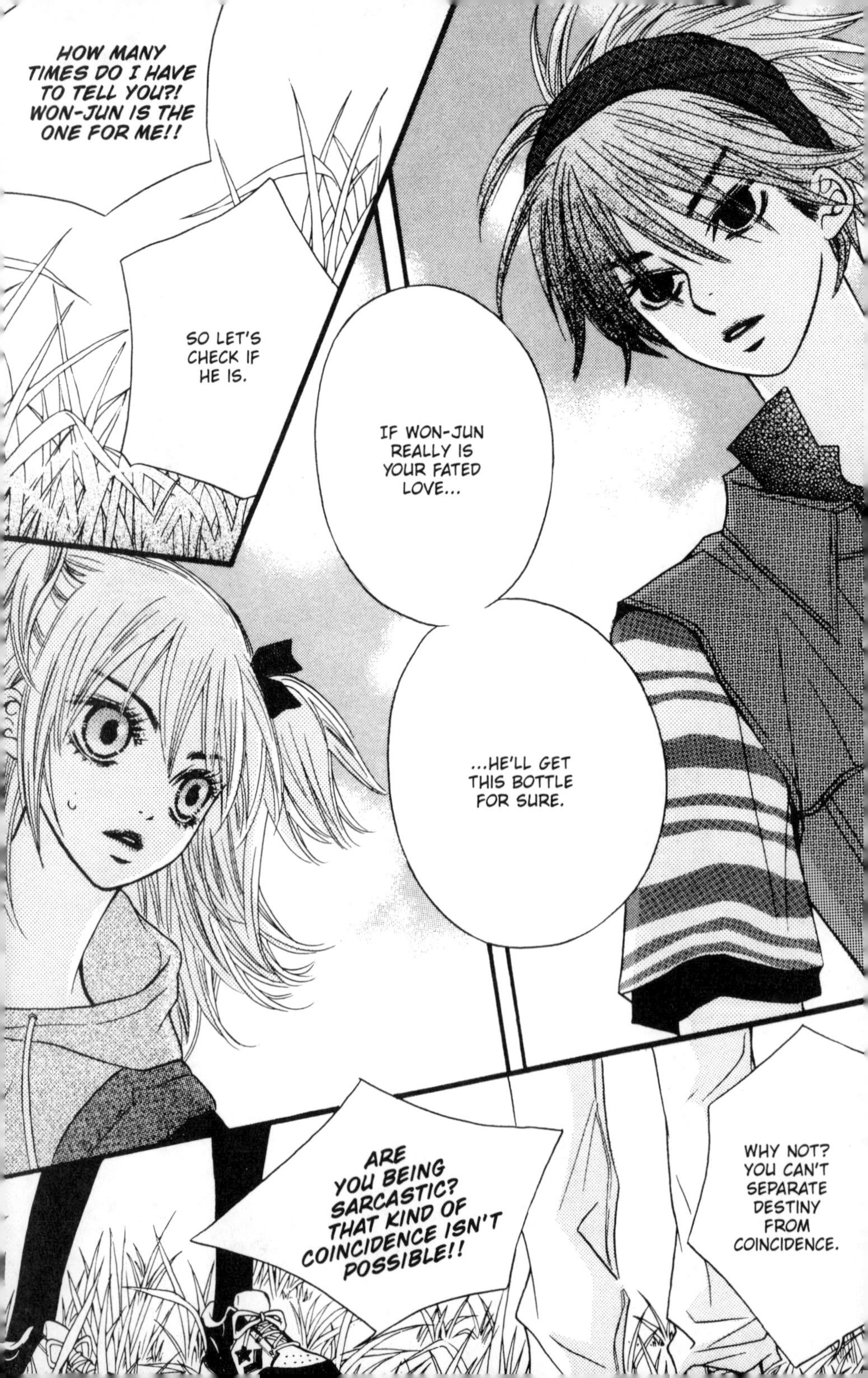
HOW MANY TIMES DO I HAVE TO TELL YOU?! WON-JUN IS THE ONE FOR ME!!
SO LET'S CHECK IF HE IS.
IF WON-JUN REALLY IS YOUR FATED LOVE...
...HE'LL GET THIS BOTTLE FOR SURE.
ARE YOU BEING SARCASTIC? THAT KIND OF COINCIDENCE ISN'T POSSIBLE!!
WHY NOT? YOU CAN'T SEPARATE DESTINY FROM COINCIDENCE.

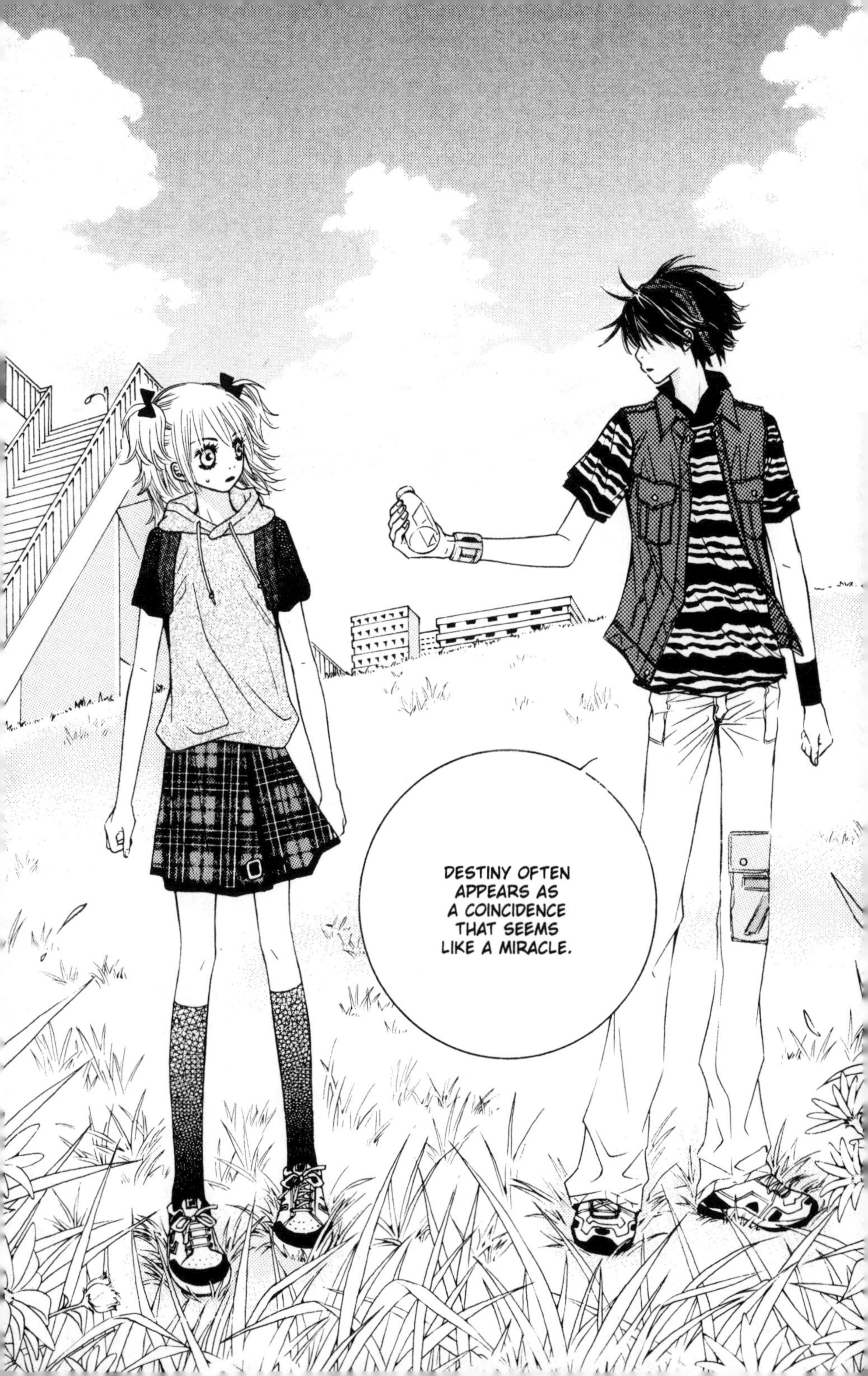
DESTINY OFTEN APPEARS AS A COINCIDENCE THAT SEEMS LIKE A MIRACLE.

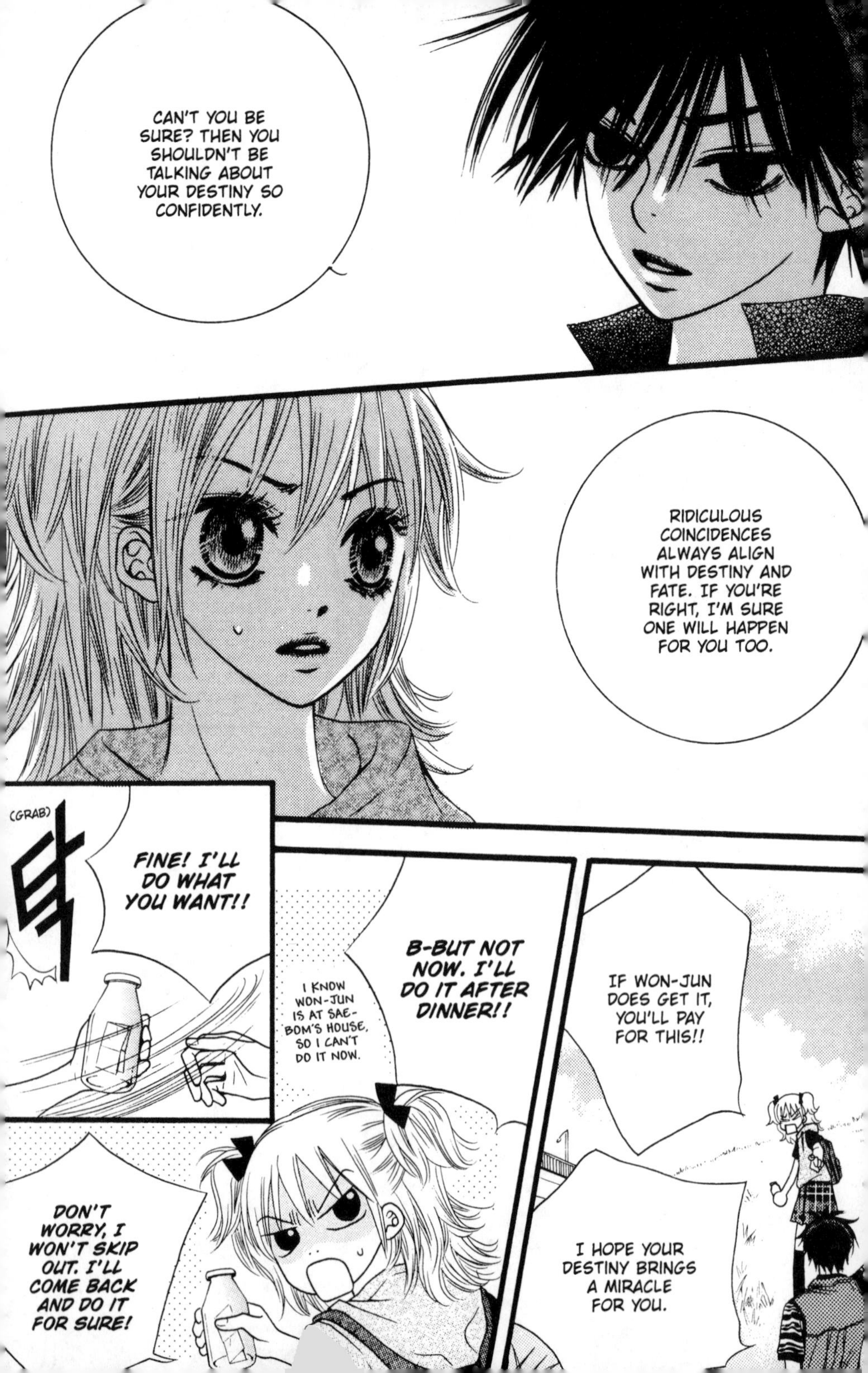
CAN'T YOU BE SURE? THEN YOU SHOULDN'T BE TALKING ABOUT YOUR DESTINY SO CONFIDENTLY.
RIDICULOUS COINCIDENCES ALWAYS ALIGN WITH DESTINY AND FATE. IF YOU'RE RIGHT, I'M SURE ONE WILL HAPPEN FOR YOU TOO.
(GRAB)
탁
FINE! I'LL DO WHAT YOU WANT!!
B-BUT NOT NOW. I'LL DO IT AFTER DINNER!!
I KNOW WON-JUN IS AT SAE-BOM'S HOUSE, SO I CAN'T DO IT NOW.
DON'T WORRY, I WON'T SKIP OUT. I'LL COME BACK AND DO IT FOR SURE!
IF WON-JUN DOES GET IT, YOU'LL PAY FOR THIS!!
I HOPE YOUR DESTINY BRINGS A MIRACLE FOR YOU.

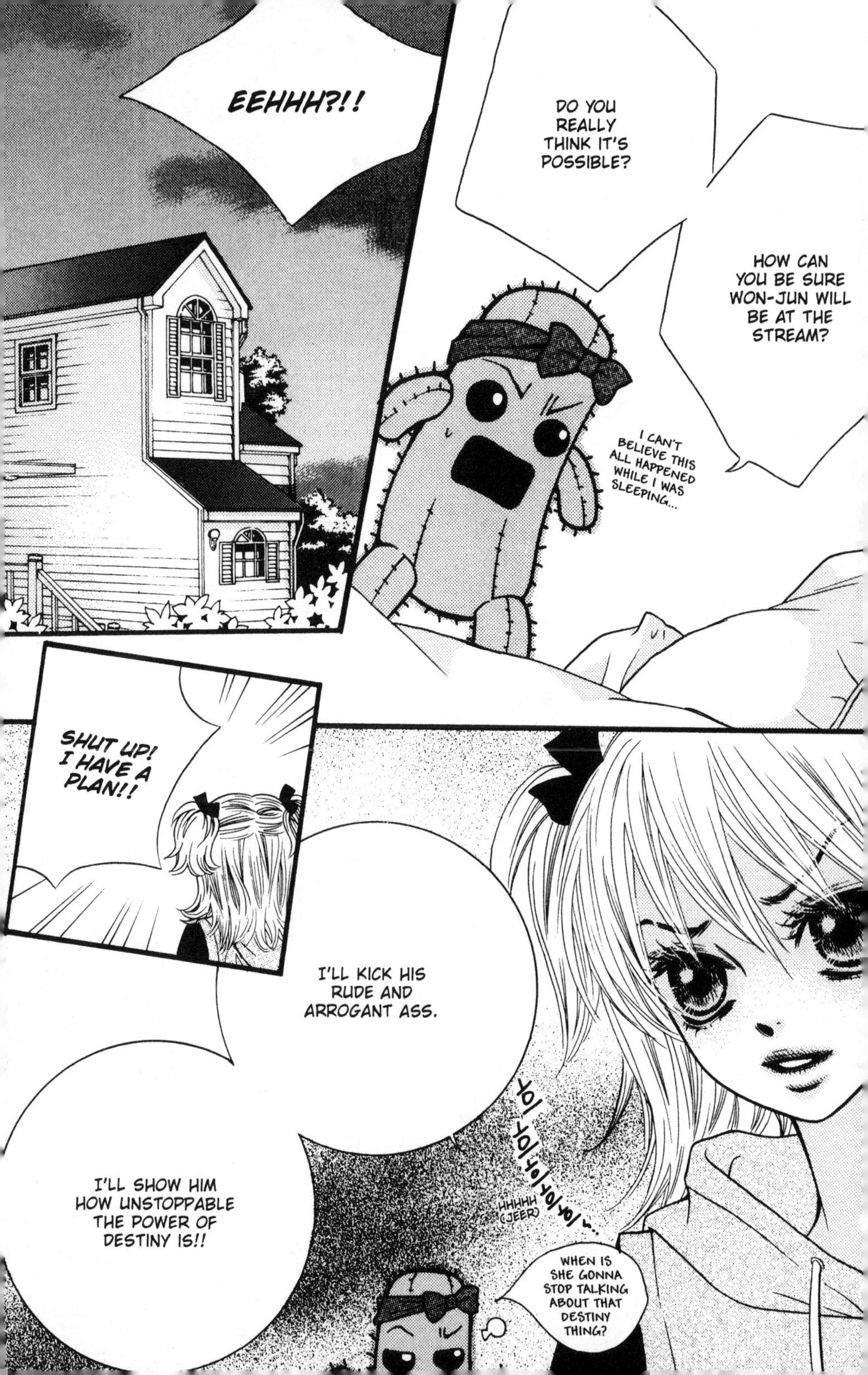
EEHHH?!!
DO YOU REALLY THINK IT'S POSSIBLE?
HOW CAN YOU BE SURE WON-JUN WILL BE AT THE STREAM?
I CAN'T BELIEVE THIS ALL HAPPENED WHILE I WAS SLEEPING...
SHUT UP! I HAVE A PLAN!!
I'LL KICK HIS RUDE AND ARROGANT ASS.
I'LL SHOW HIM HOW UNSTOPPABLE THE POWER OF DESTINY IS!!
YO! YO! YO! YO! YO! YO! YO!~...
HHHHH (JEER)
WHEN IS SHE GONNA STOP TALKING ABOUT THAT DESTINY THING?

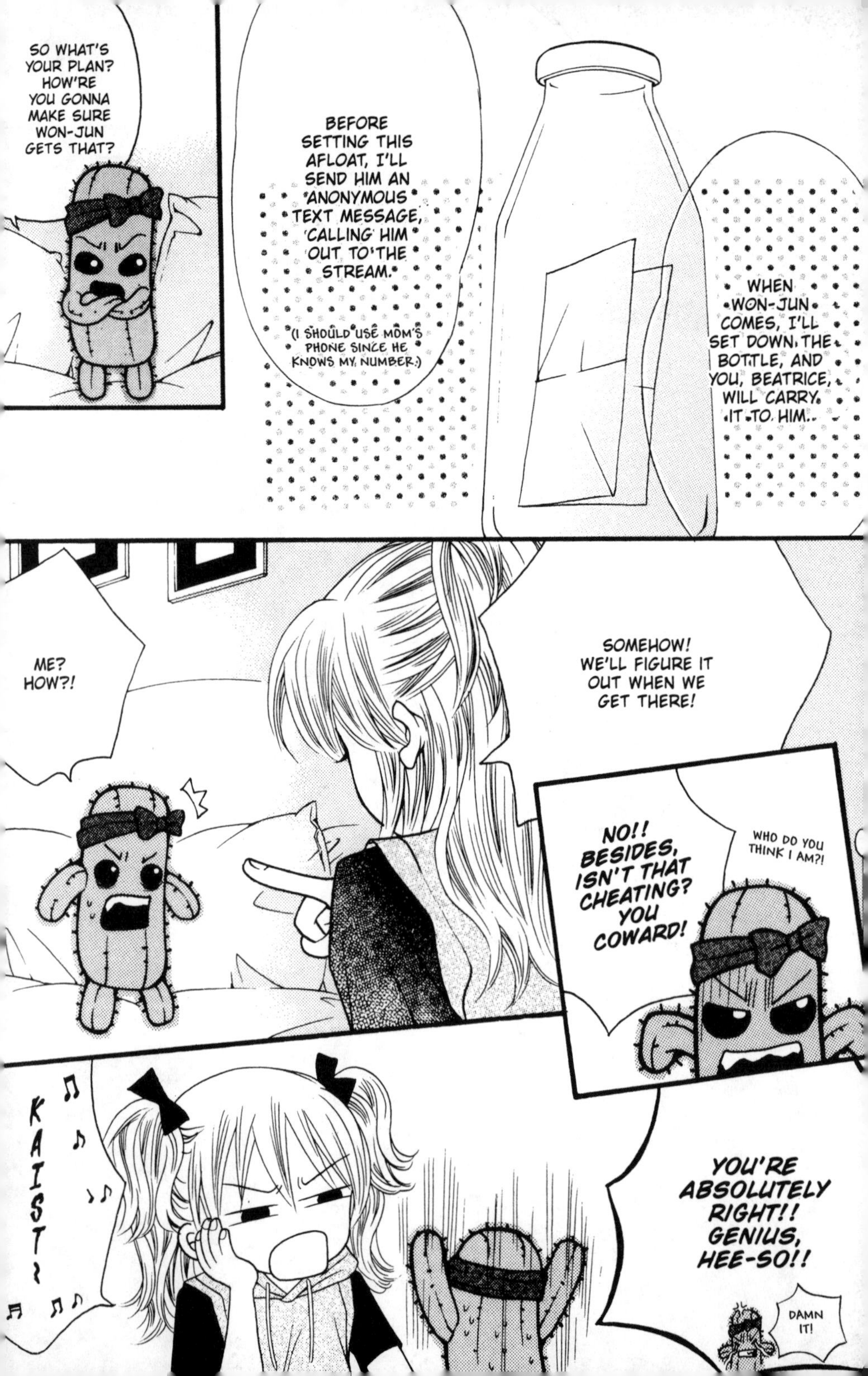
SO WHAT'S YOUR PLAN? HOW'RE YOU GONNA MAKE SURE WON-JUN GETS THAT?
BEFORE SETTING THIS AFLOAT, I'LL SEND HIM AN ANONYMOUS TEXT MESSAGE, CALLING HIM OUT TO THE STREAM.
(I SHOULD USE MOM'S PHONE SINCE HE KNOWS MY NUMBER.)
WHEN WON-JUN COMES, I'LL SET DOWN THE BOTTLE, AND YOU, BEATRICE, WILL CARRY IT TO HIM.
ME? HOW?!
SOMEHOW! WE'LL FIGURE IT OUT WHEN WE GET THERE!
NO!! BESIDES, ISN'T THAT CHEATING? YOU COWARD!
WHO DO YOU THINK I AM?!
KAIST~
YOU'RE ABSOLUTELY RIGHT!! GENIUS, HEE-SO!!
DAMN IT!

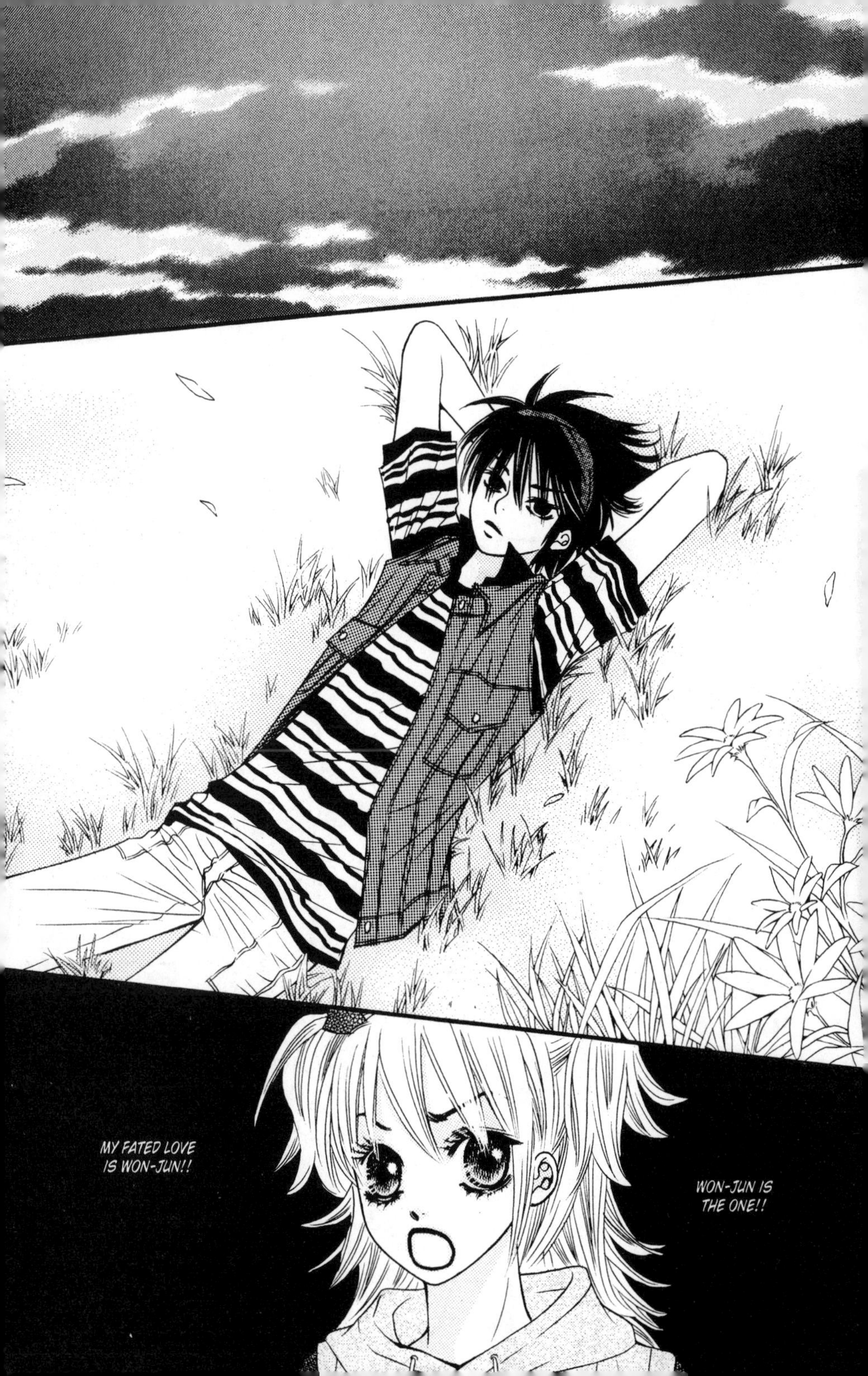
MY FATED LOVE IS WON-JUN!!
WON-JUN IS THE ONE!!

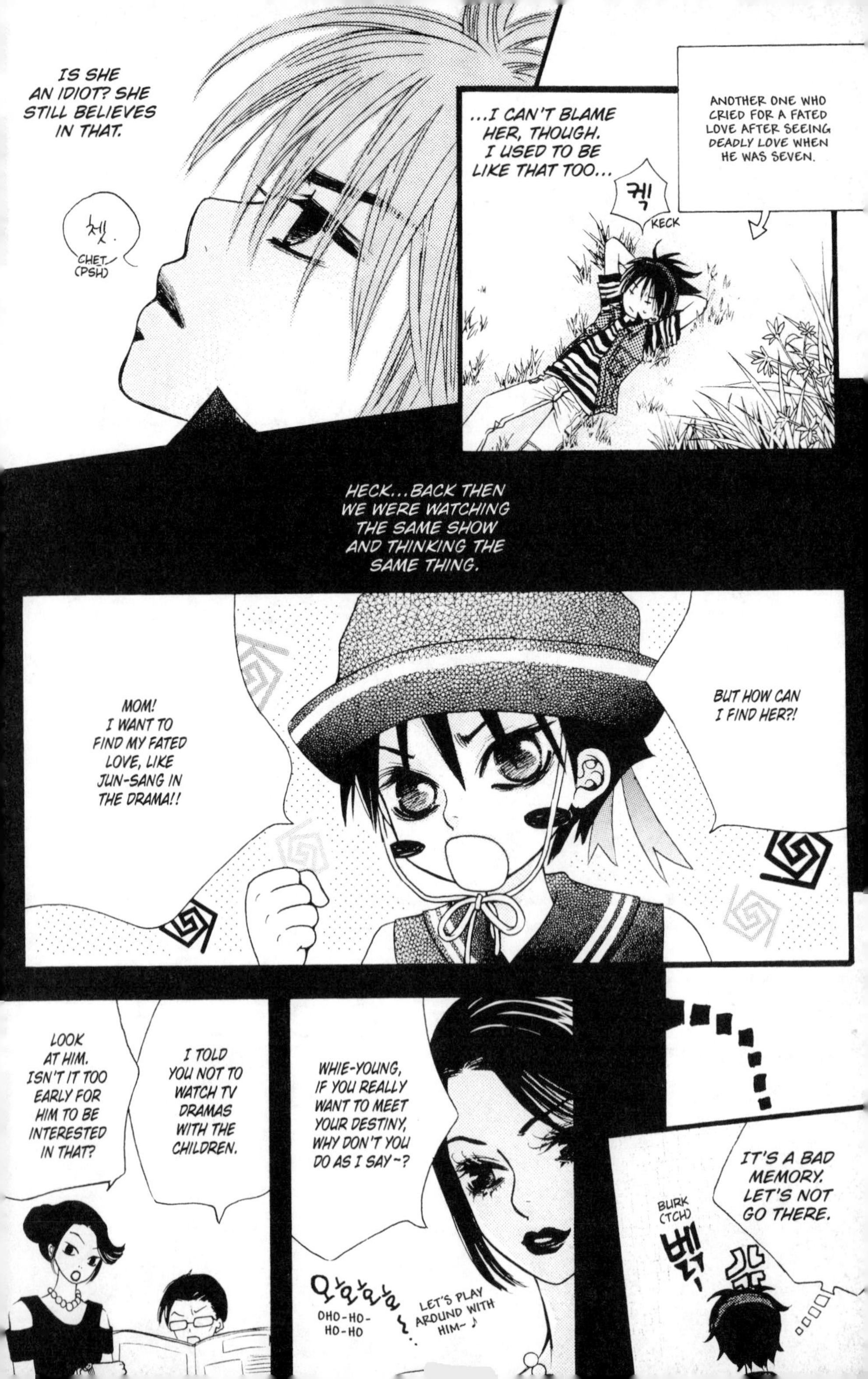
IS SHE AN IDIOT? SHE STILL BELIEVES IN THAT.
쳇.
CHET (PSH)
...I CAN'T BLAME HER, THOUGH. I USED TO BE LIKE THAT TOO...
켁
KECK
ANOTHER ONE WHO CRIED FOR A FATED LOVE AFTER SEEING DEADLY LOVE WHEN HE WAS SEVEN.
HECK...BACK THEN WE WERE WATCHING THE SAME SHOW AND THINKING THE SAME THING.
MOM! I WANT TO FIND MY FATED LOVE, LIKE JUN-SANG IN THE DRAMA!!
BUT HOW CAN I FIND HER?!
LOOK AT HIM. ISN'T IT TOO EARLY FOR HIM TO BE INTERESTED IN THAT?
I TOLD YOU NOT TO WATCH TV DRAMAS WITH THE CHILDREN.
WHIE-YOUNG, IF YOU REALLY WANT TO MEET YOUR DESTINY, WHY DON'T YOU DO AS I SAY~?
OHO-HO-HO-HO
LET'S PLAY AROUND WITH HIM~♪
IT'S A BAD MEMORY. LET'S NOT GO THERE.
BURK (TCH)

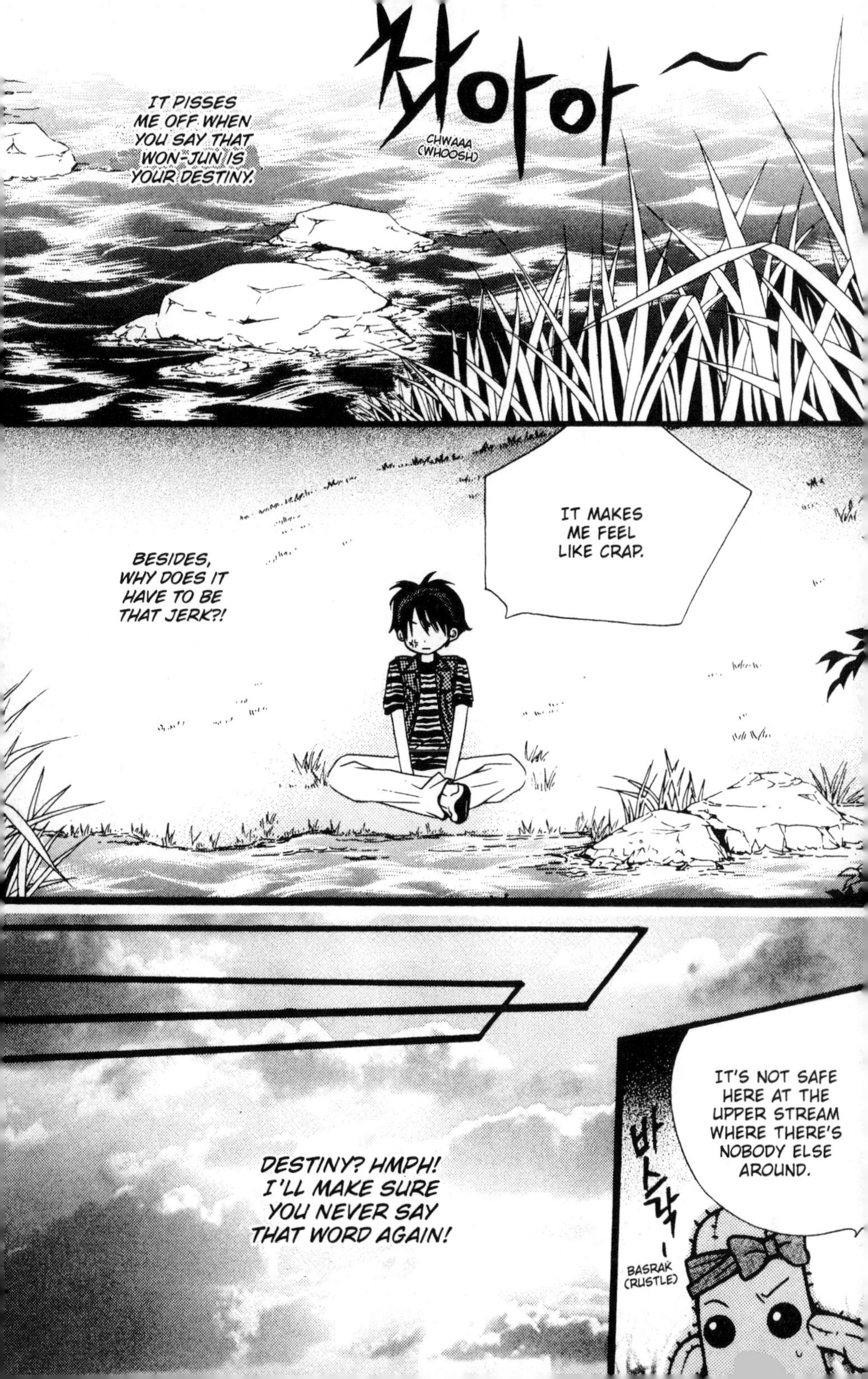
IT PISSES ME OFF WHEN YOU SAY THAT WON-JUN IS YOUR DESTINY.
CHWAAA (WHOOSH)
IT MAKES ME FEEL LIKE CRAP.
BESIDES, WHY DOES IT HAVE TO BE THAT JERK?!
DESTINY? HMPH! I'LL MAKE SURE YOU NEVER SAY THAT WORD AGAIN!
IT'S NOT SAFE HERE AT THE UPPER STREAM WHERE THERE'S NOBODY ELSE AROUND.
BASRAK (RUSTLE)

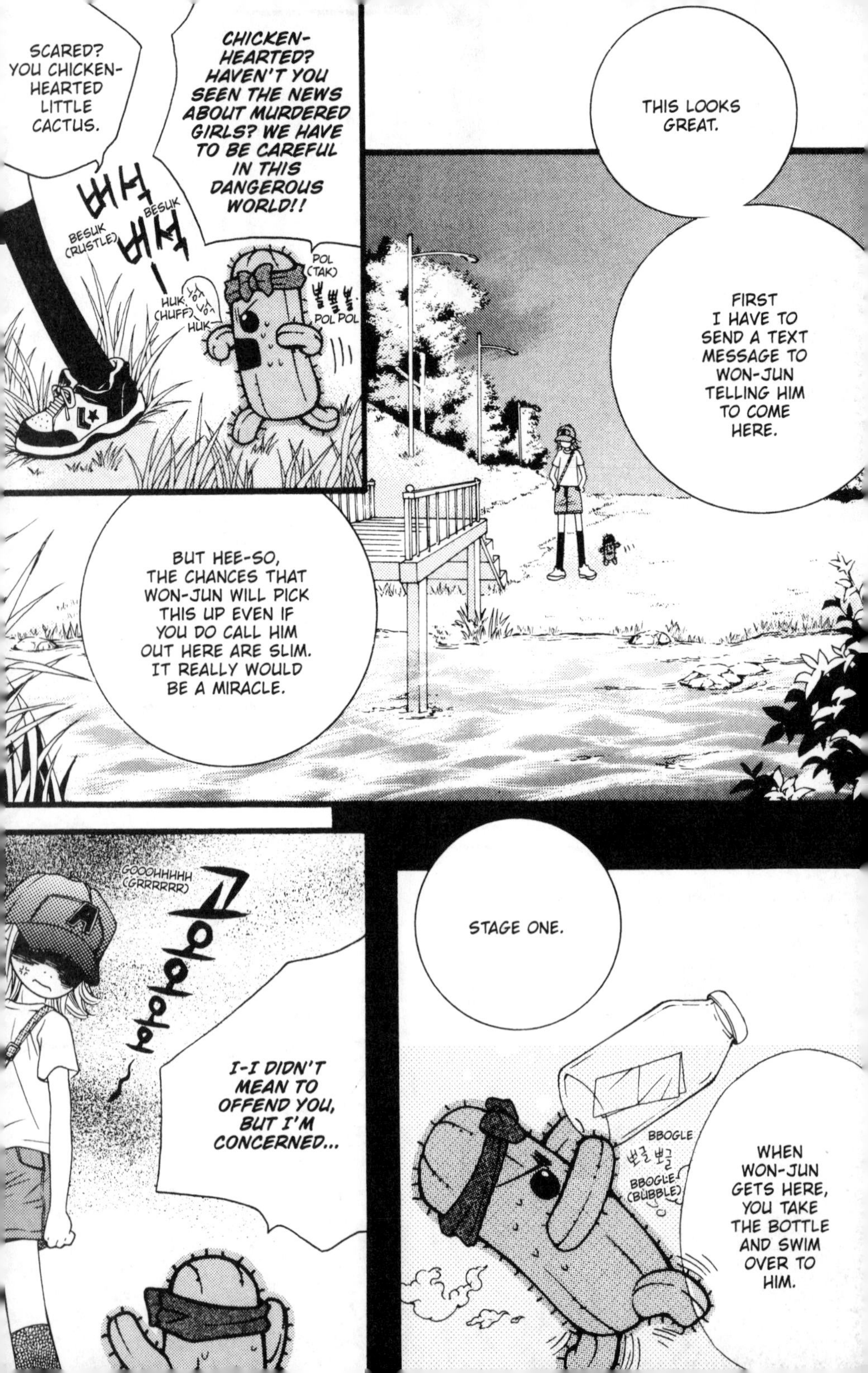
SCARED? YOU CHICKEN-HEARTED LITTLE CACTUS.
CHICKEN-HEARTED? HAVEN'T YOU SEEN THE NEWS ABOUT MURDERED GIRLS? WE HAVE TO BE CAREFUL IN THIS DANGEROUS WORLD!!
버석 버석
BESUK (RUSTLE)
BESUK
헉 헉
HUK (HUFF)
HUK
POL (TAK)
POL POL
THIS LOOKS GREAT.
FIRST I HAVE TO SEND A TEXT MESSAGE TO WON-JUN TELLING HIM TO COME HERE.
BUT HEE-SO, THE CHANCES THAT WON-JUN WILL PICK THIS UP EVEN IF YOU DO CALL HIM OUT HERE ARE SLIM. IT REALLY WOULD BE A MIRACLE.
GOOOHHHHH (GRRRRRR)
I-I DIDN'T MEAN TO OFFEND YOU, BUT I'M CONCERNED...
STAGE ONE.
BBOGLE
뽀글 뽀글
BBOGLE (BUBBLE)
WHEN WON-JUN GETS HERE, YOU TAKE THE BOTTLE AND SWIM OVER TO HIM.

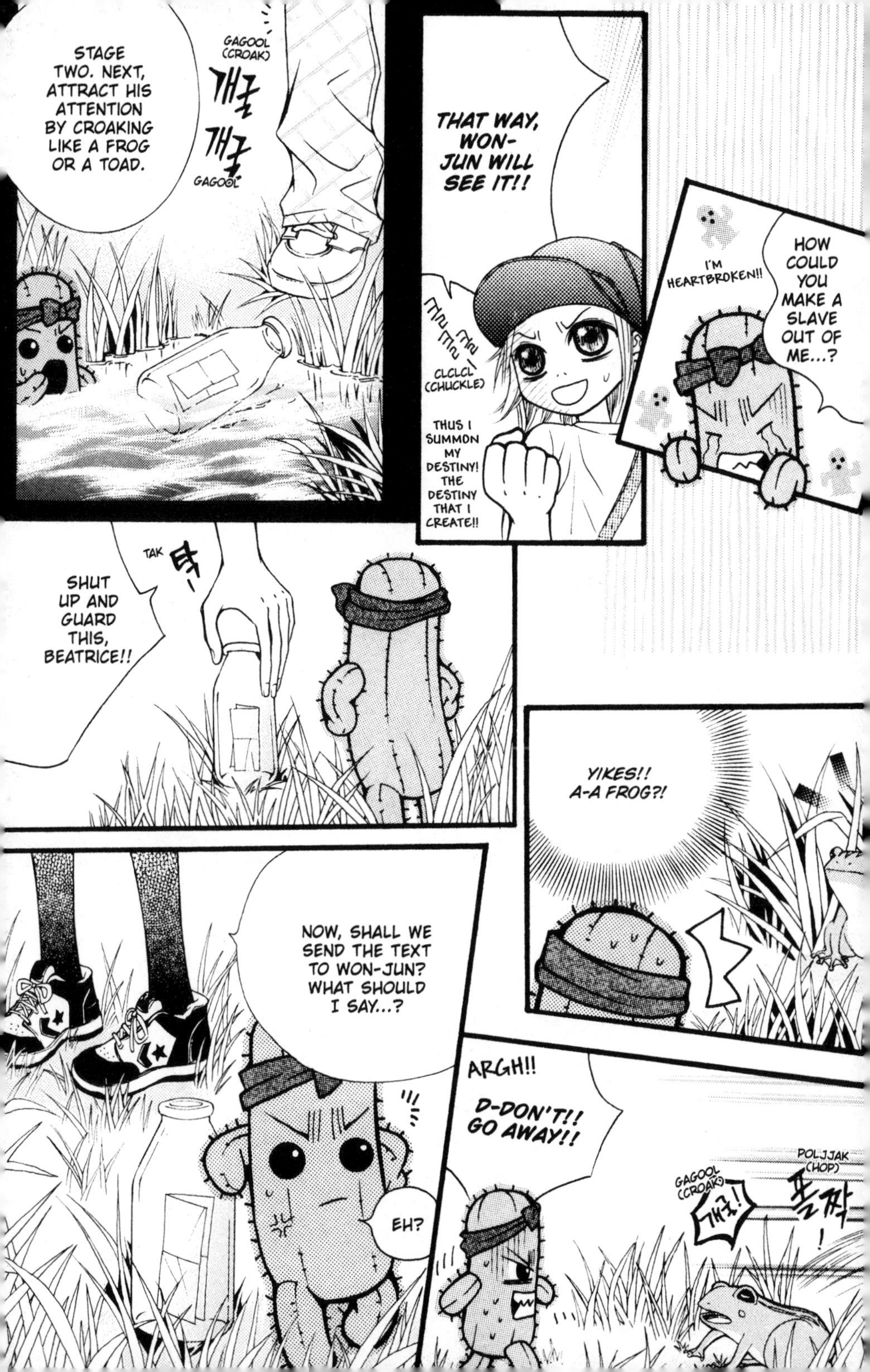
STAGE TWO. NEXT, ATTRACT HIS ATTENTION BY CROAKING LIKE A FROG OR A TOAD.
GAGOOL (CROAK)
개굴
개굴
GAGOOL
THAT WAY, WON-JUN WILL SEE IT!!
CLCLCL (CHUCKLE)
THUS I SUMMON MY DESTINY! THE DESTINY THAT I CREATE!!
I'M HEARTBROKEN!!
HOW COULD YOU MAKE A SLAVE OUT OF ME...?
TAK
탁
SHUT UP AND GUARD THIS, BEATRICE!!
NOW, SHALL WE SEND THE TEXT TO WON-JUN? WHAT SHOULD I SAY...?
EH?
YIKES!! A-A FROG?!
ARGH!!
D-DON'T!! GO AWAY!!
GAGOOL (CROAK)
개굴!
POLJJAK (HOP)
폴짝

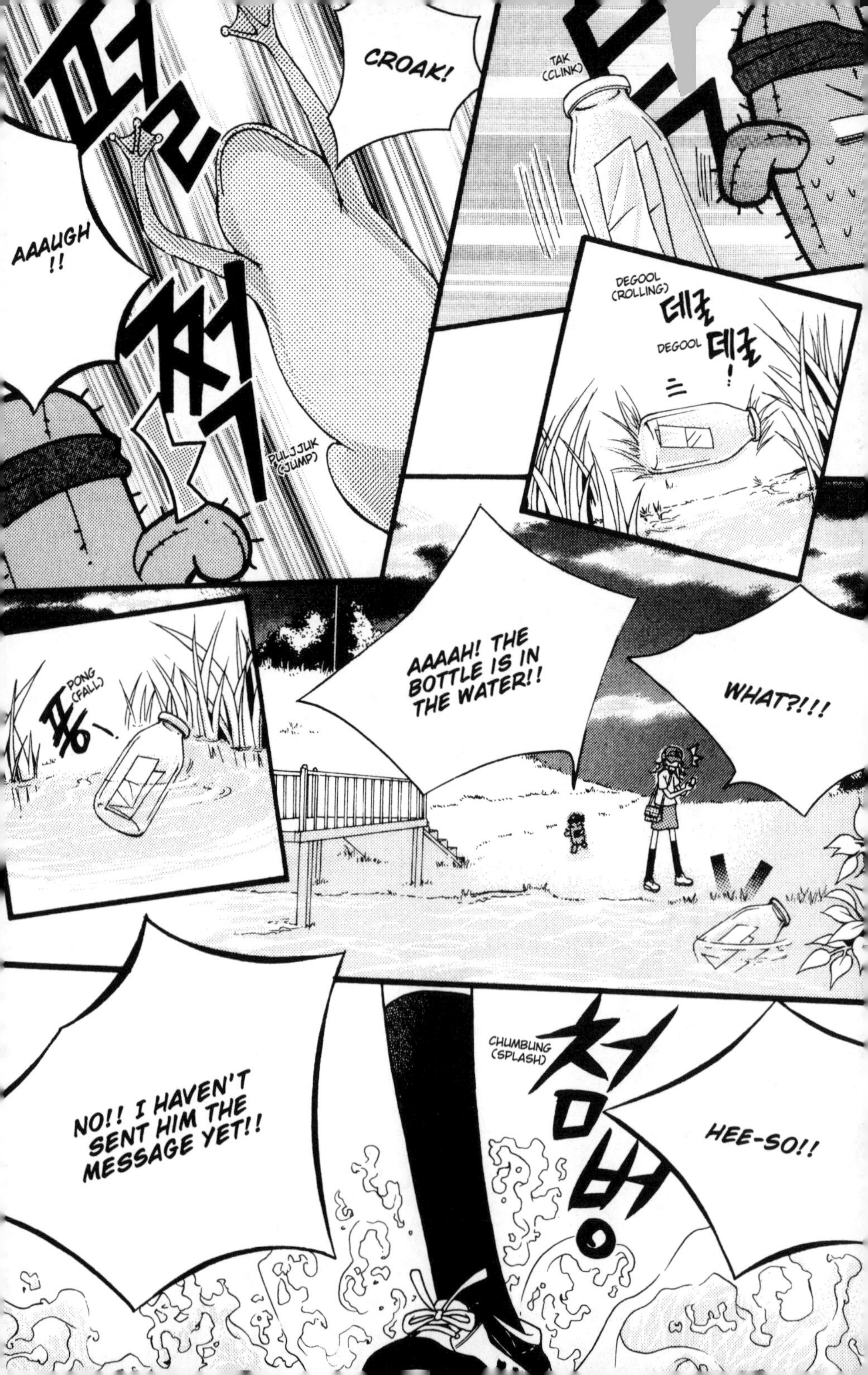
AAAUGH !!
CROAK!
PULJJUK (JUMP)
TAK (CLINK)
DEGOOL (ROLLING)
데굴
DEGOOL
데굴
PONG (FALL)
퐁
AAAAH! THE BOTTLE IS IN THE WATER!!
WHAT?!!!
NO!! I HAVEN'T SENT HIM THE MESSAGE YET!!
CHUMBLING (SPLASH)
HEE-SO!!

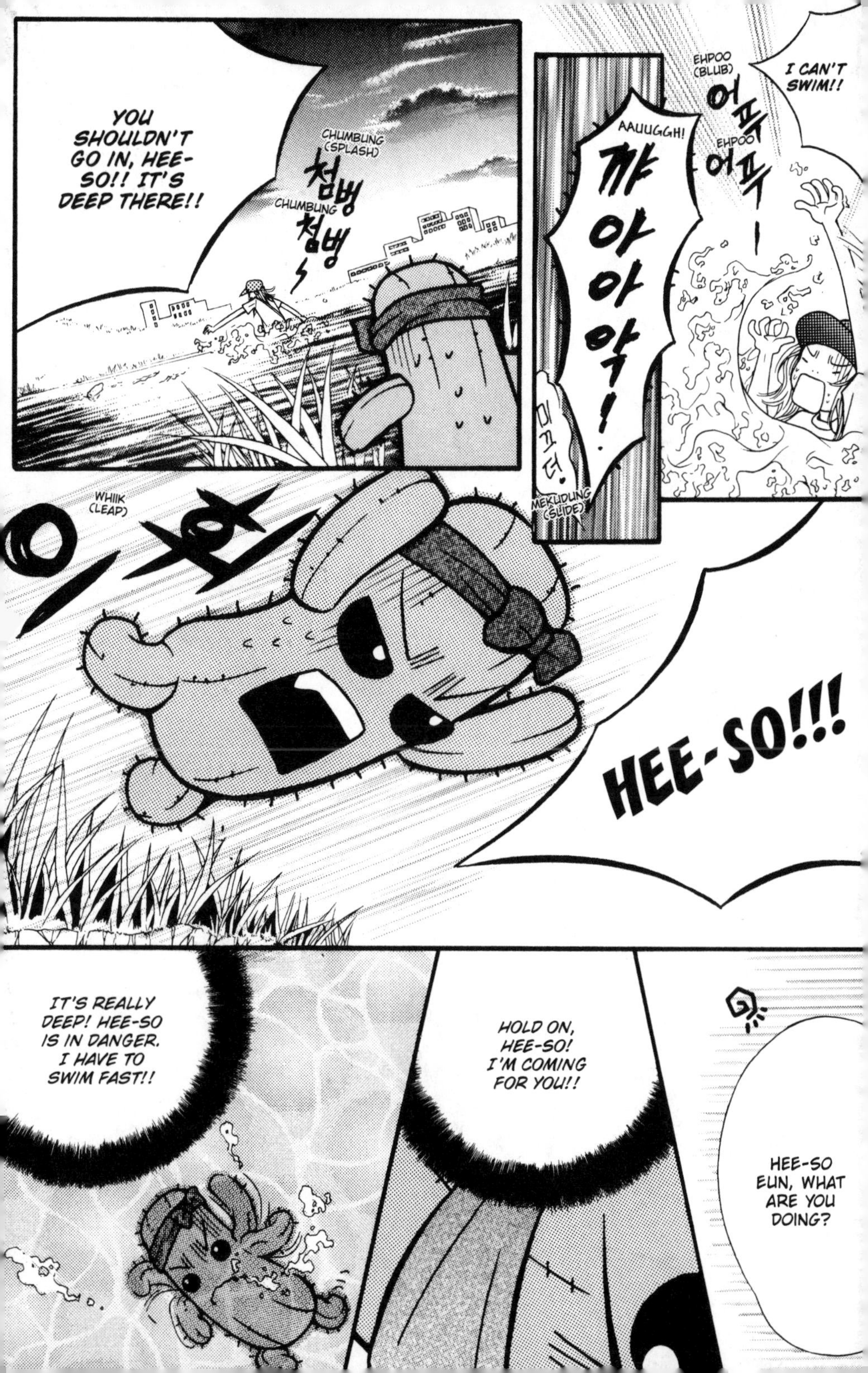
YOU SHOULDN'T GO IN, HEE-SO!! IT'S DEEP THERE!!
CHUMBUNG (SPLASH)
첨벙
CHUMBUNG
첨벙
AAUUGGH!
꺄아아악!!
미끄덩!
MEKUDUNG (SLIDE)
EHPOO (BLUB)
어푸
EHPOO
어푸
I CAN'T SWIM!!
WHIIK (LEAP)
HEE-SO!!!
IT'S REALLY DEEP! HEE-SO IS IN DANGER. I HAVE TO SWIM FAST!!
HOLD ON, HEE-SO! I'M COMING FOR YOU!!
HEE-SO EUN, WHAT ARE YOU DOING?

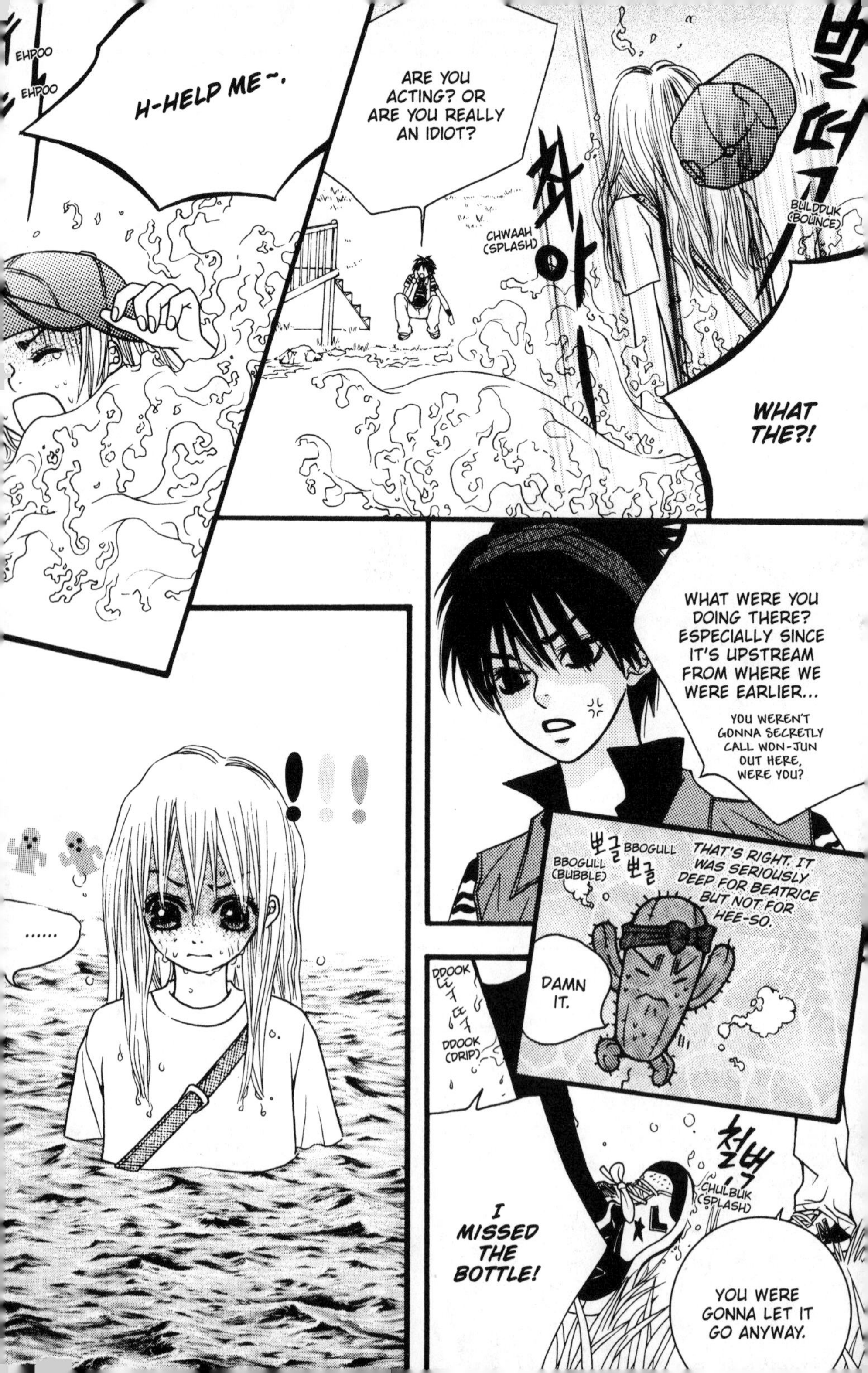

EHPOO
EHPOO
H-HELP ME~.
ARE YOU ACTING? OR ARE YOU REALLY AN IDIOT?
CHWAAH (SPLASH)
BULDDUK (BOUNCE)
WHAT THE?!
......
WHAT WERE YOU DOING THERE? ESPECIALLY SINCE IT'S UPSTREAM FROM WHERE WE WERE EARLIER...
YOU WEREN'T GONNA SECRETLY CALL WON-JUN OUT HERE, WERE YOU?
뽀글 BBOGULL
BBOGULL (BUBBLE) 뽀글
THAT'S RIGHT. IT WAS SERIOUSLY DEEP FOR BEATRICE BUT NOT FOR HEE-SO.
DAMN IT.
DDOOK
DDOOK (DRIP)
I MISSED THE BOTTLE!
CHULBUK (SPLASH)
YOU WERE GONNA LET IT GO ANYWAY.

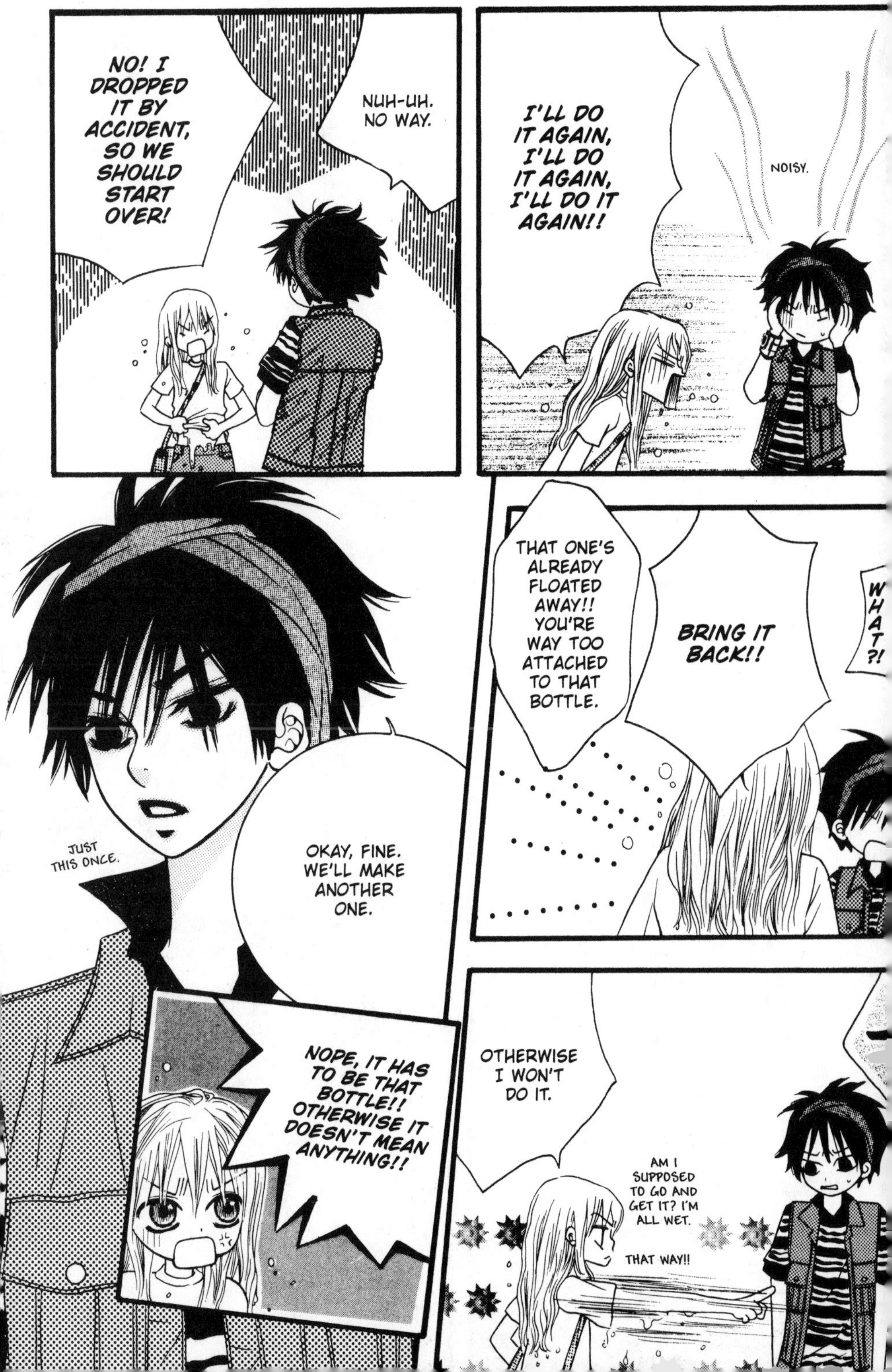
NO! I DROPPED IT BY ACCIDENT, SO WE SHOULD START OVER!
NUH-UH. NO WAY.
I'LL DO IT AGAIN, I'LL DO IT AGAIN, I'LL DO IT AGAIN!!
NOISY.
JUST THIS ONCE.
OKAY, FINE. WE'LL MAKE ANOTHER ONE.
NOPE, IT HAS TO BE THAT BOTTLE!! OTHERWISE IT DOESN'T MEAN ANYTHING!!
THAT ONE'S ALREADY FLOATED AWAY!! YOU'RE WAY TOO ATTACHED TO THAT BOTTLE.
BRING IT BACK!!
WHAT?!
OTHERWISE I WON'T DO IT.
AM I SUPPOSED TO GO AND GET IT? I'M ALL WET.
THAT WAY!!

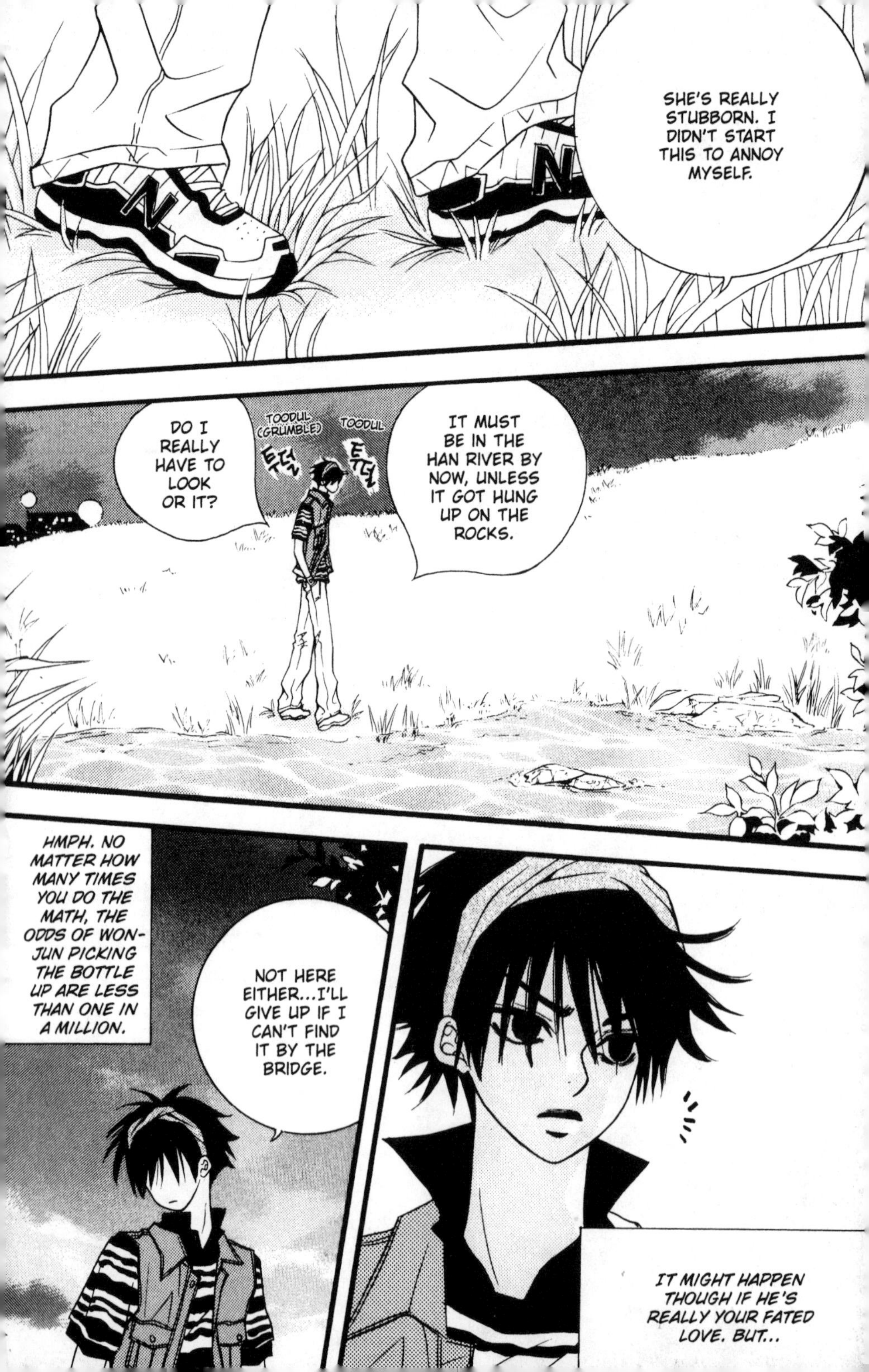
SHE'S REALLY STUBBORN. I DIDN'T START THIS TO ANNOY MYSELF.
DO I REALLY HAVE TO LOOK OR IT?
TOODUL (GRUMBLE)
TOODUL
IT MUST BE IN THE HAN RIVER BY NOW, UNLESS IT GOT HUNG UP ON THE ROCKS.
HMPH. NO MATTER HOW MANY TIMES YOU DO THE MATH, THE ODDS OF WON-JUN PICKING THE BOTTLE UP ARE LESS THAN ONE IN A MILLION.
NOT HERE EITHER...I'LL GIVE UP IF I CAN'T FIND IT BY THE BRIDGE.
IT MIGHT HAPPEN THOUGH IF HE'S REALLY YOUR FATED LOVE. BUT...

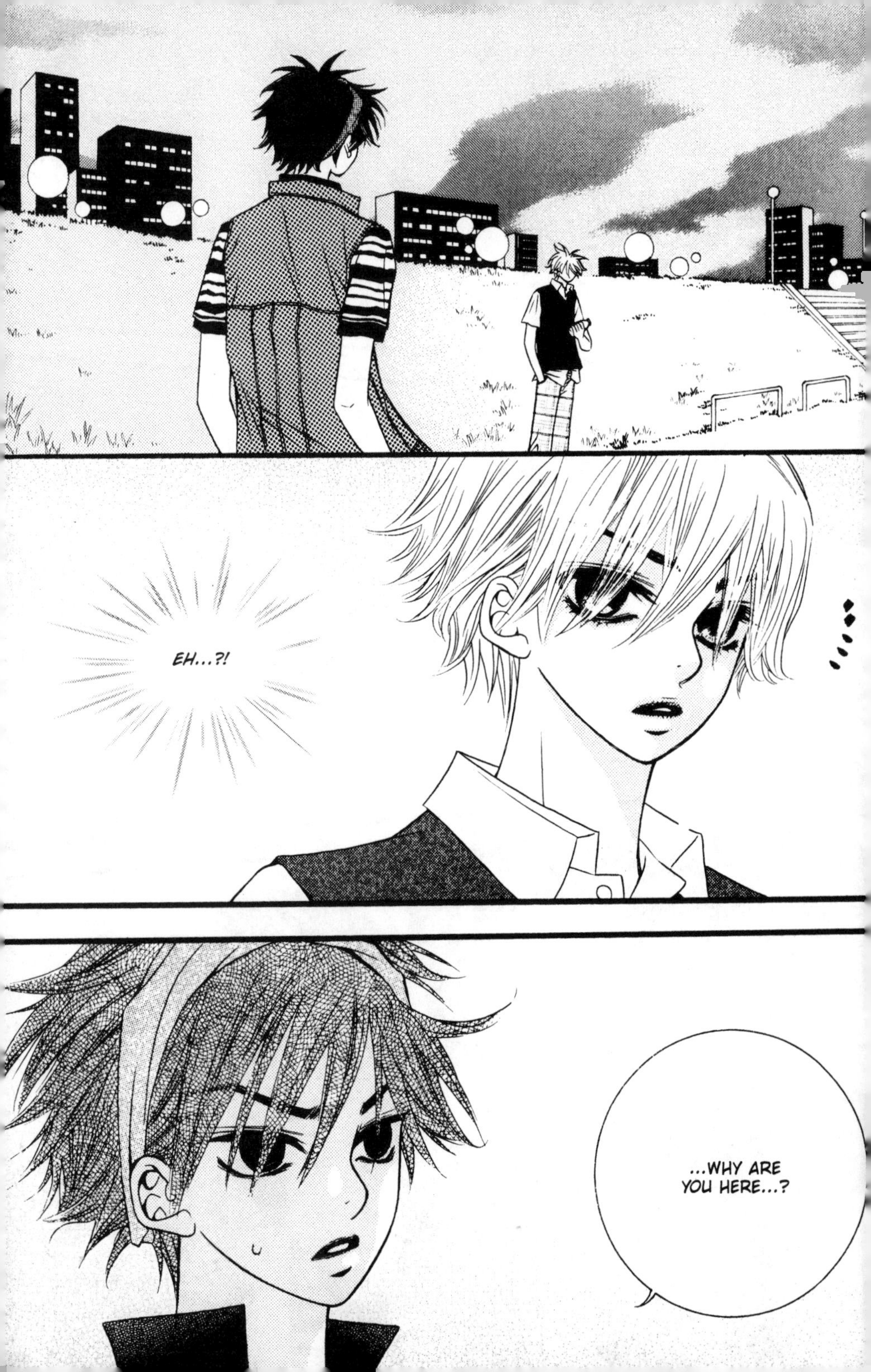
EH...?!
...WHY ARE YOU HERE...?

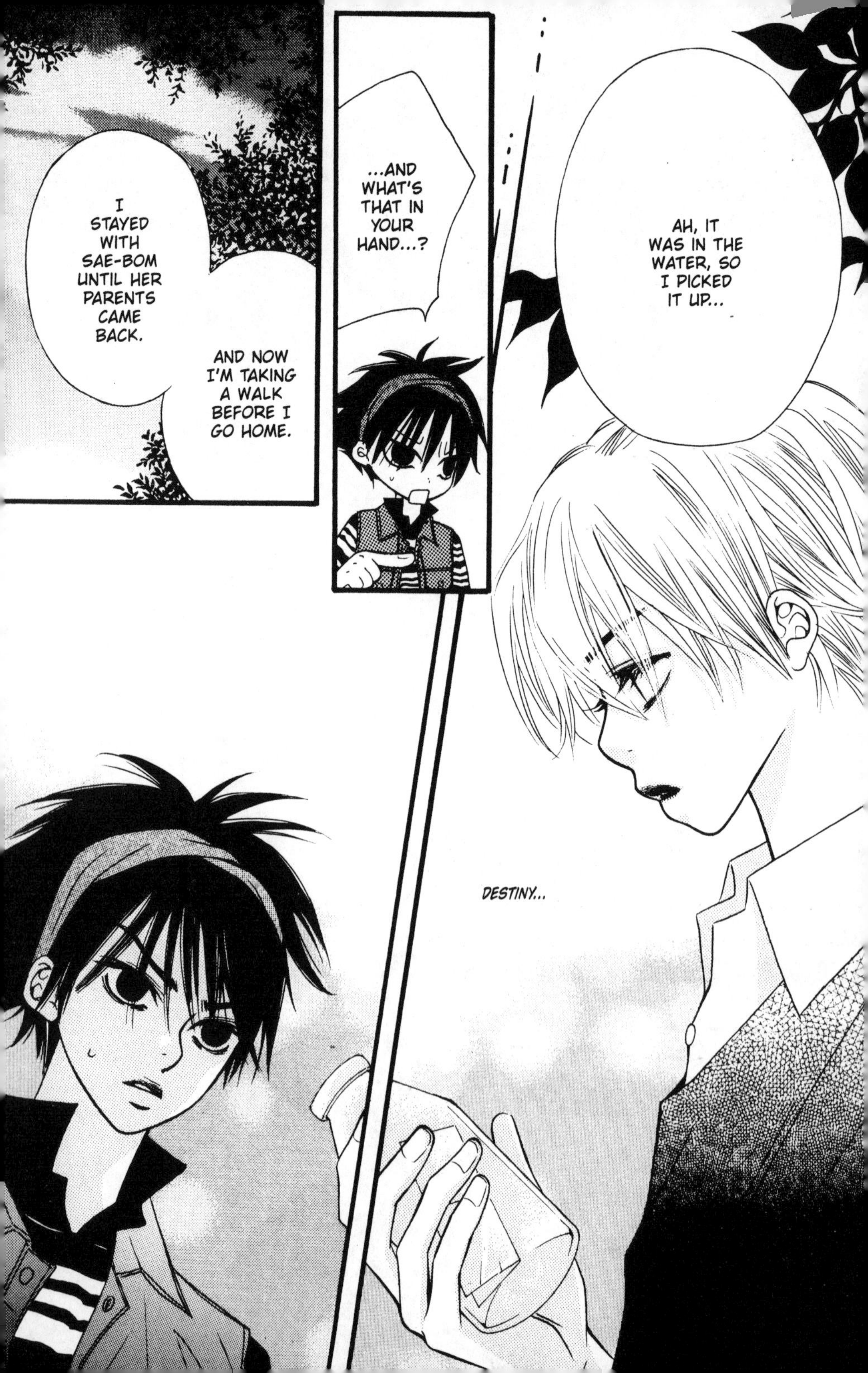
I STAYED WITH SAE-BOM UNTIL HER PARENTS CAME BACK.
AND NOW I'M TAKING A WALK BEFORE I GO HOME.
...AND WHAT'S THAT IN YOUR HAND...?
AH, IT WAS IN THE WATER, SO I PICKED IT UP...
DESTINY...

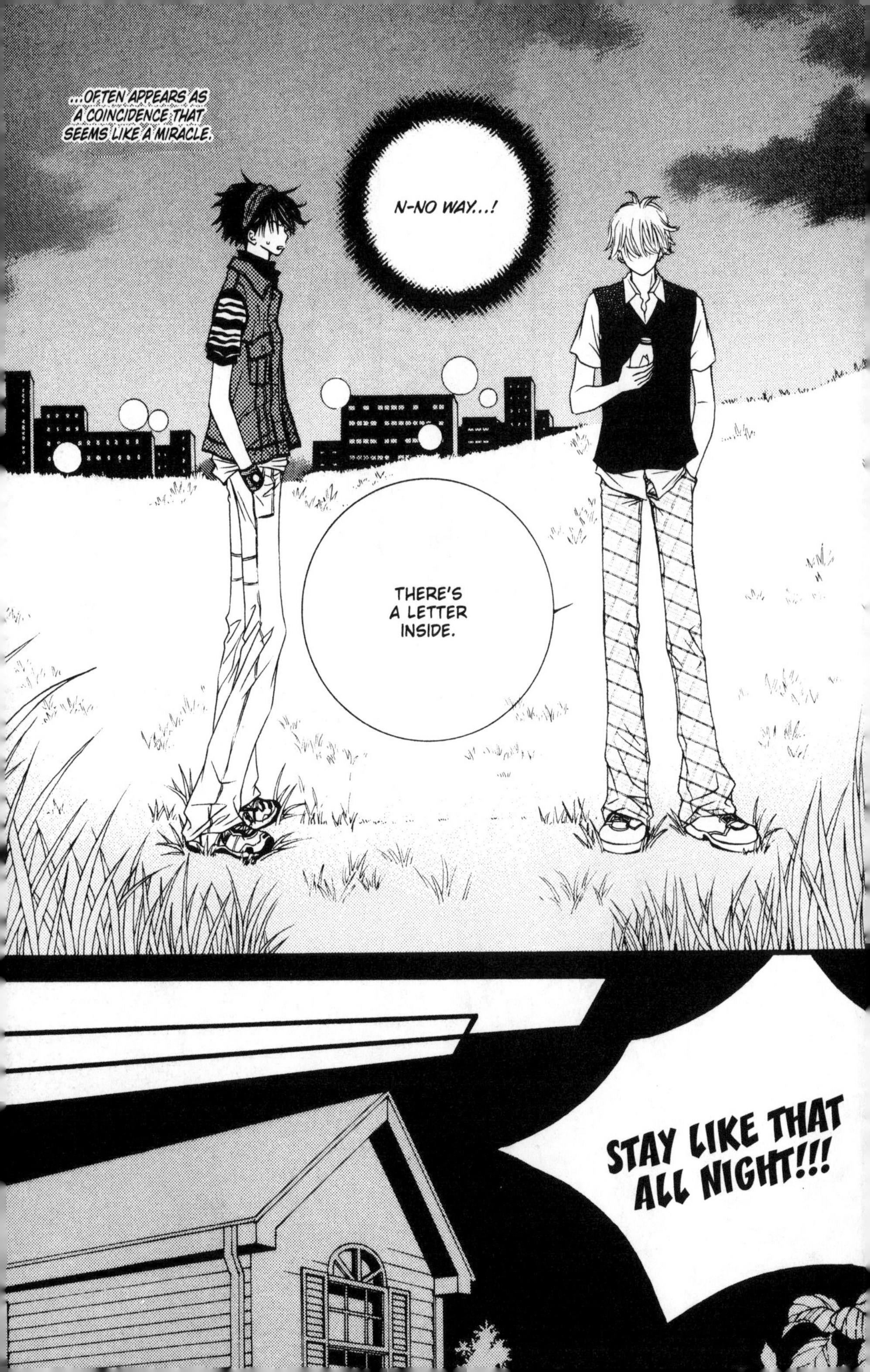
...OFTEN APPEARS AS A COINCIDENCE THAT SEEMS LIKE A MIRACLE.
N-NO WAY...!
THERE'S A LETTER INSIDE.
STAY LIKE THAT ALL NIGHT!!!

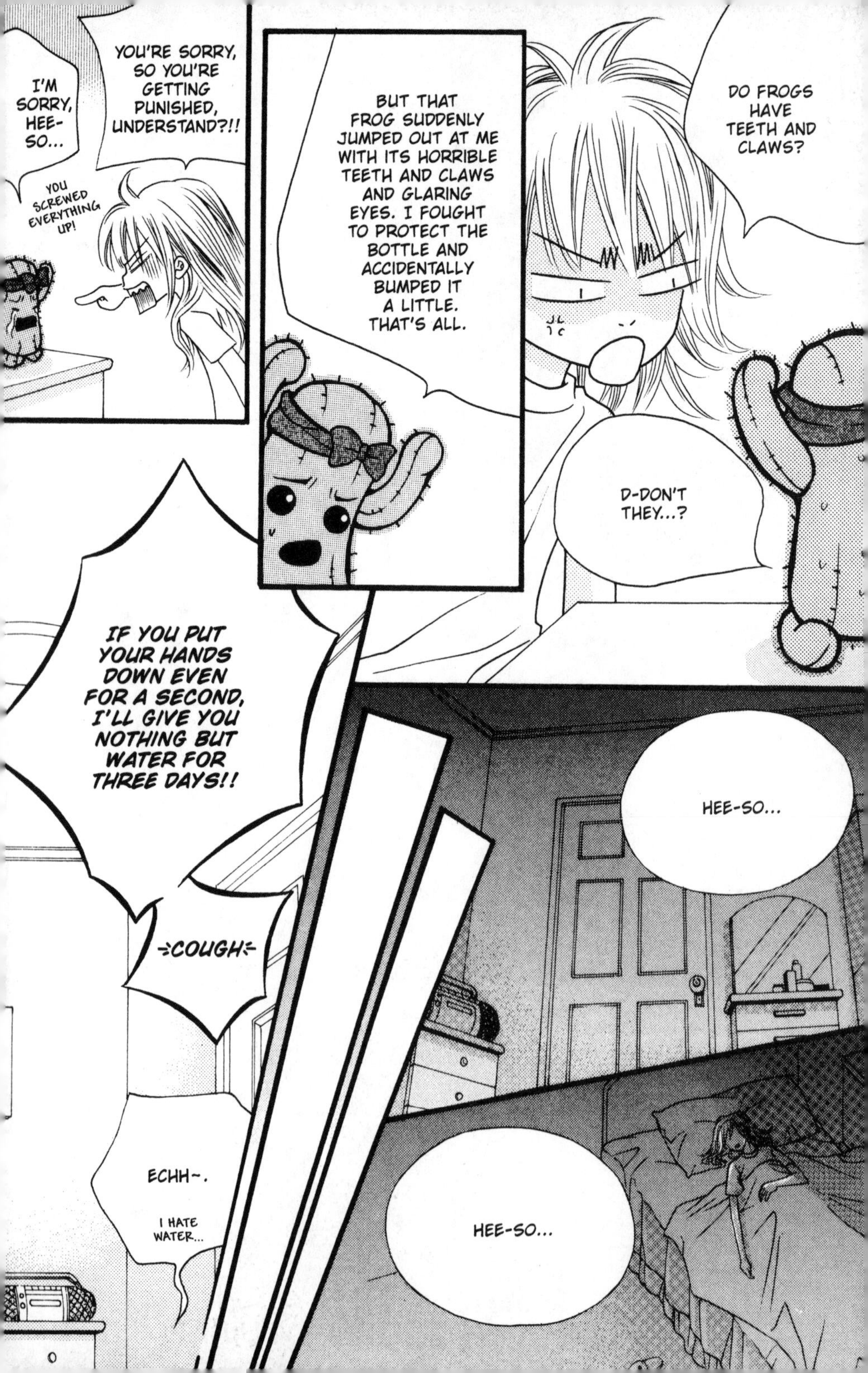
I'M SORRY, HEE-SO...
YOU'RE SORRY, SO YOU'RE GETTING PUNISHED, UNDERSTAND?!!
YOU SCREWED EVERYTHING UP!
BUT THAT FROG SUDDENLY JUMPED OUT AT ME WITH ITS HORRIBLE TEETH AND CLAWS AND GLARING EYES. I FOUGHT TO PROTECT THE BOTTLE AND ACCIDENTALLY BUMPED IT A LITTLE. THAT'S ALL.
DO FROGS HAVE TEETH AND CLAWS?
D-DON'T THEY...?
IF YOU PUT YOUR HANDS DOWN EVEN FOR A SECOND, I'LL GIVE YOU NOTHING BUT WATER FOR THREE DAYS!!
COUGH
ECHH~.
I HATE WATER...
HEE-SO...
HEE-SO...

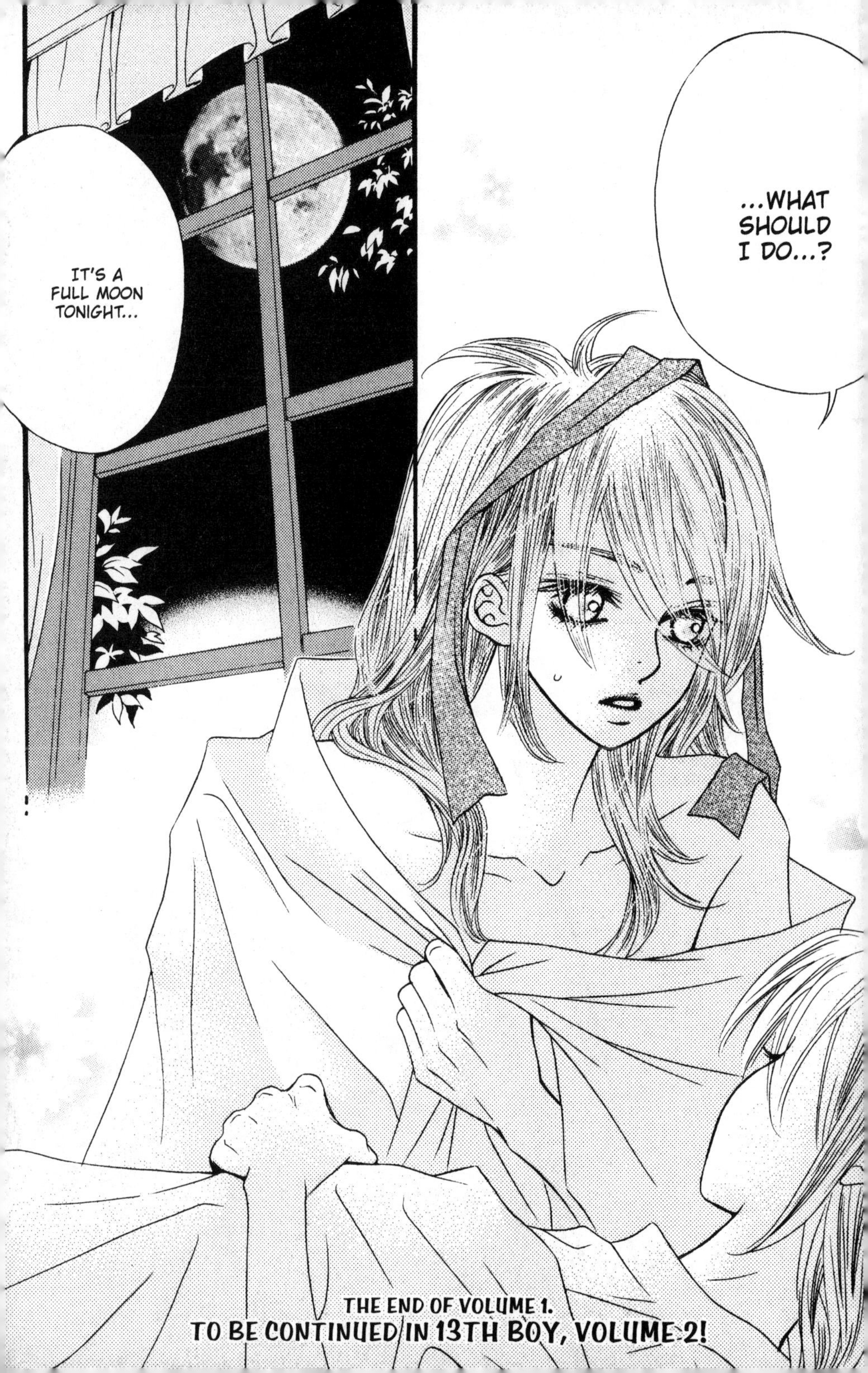
IT'S A FULL MOON TONIGHT...
...WHAT SHOULD I DO...?
THE END OF VOLUME 1.
TO BE CONTINUED IN 13TH BOY, VOLUME 2!

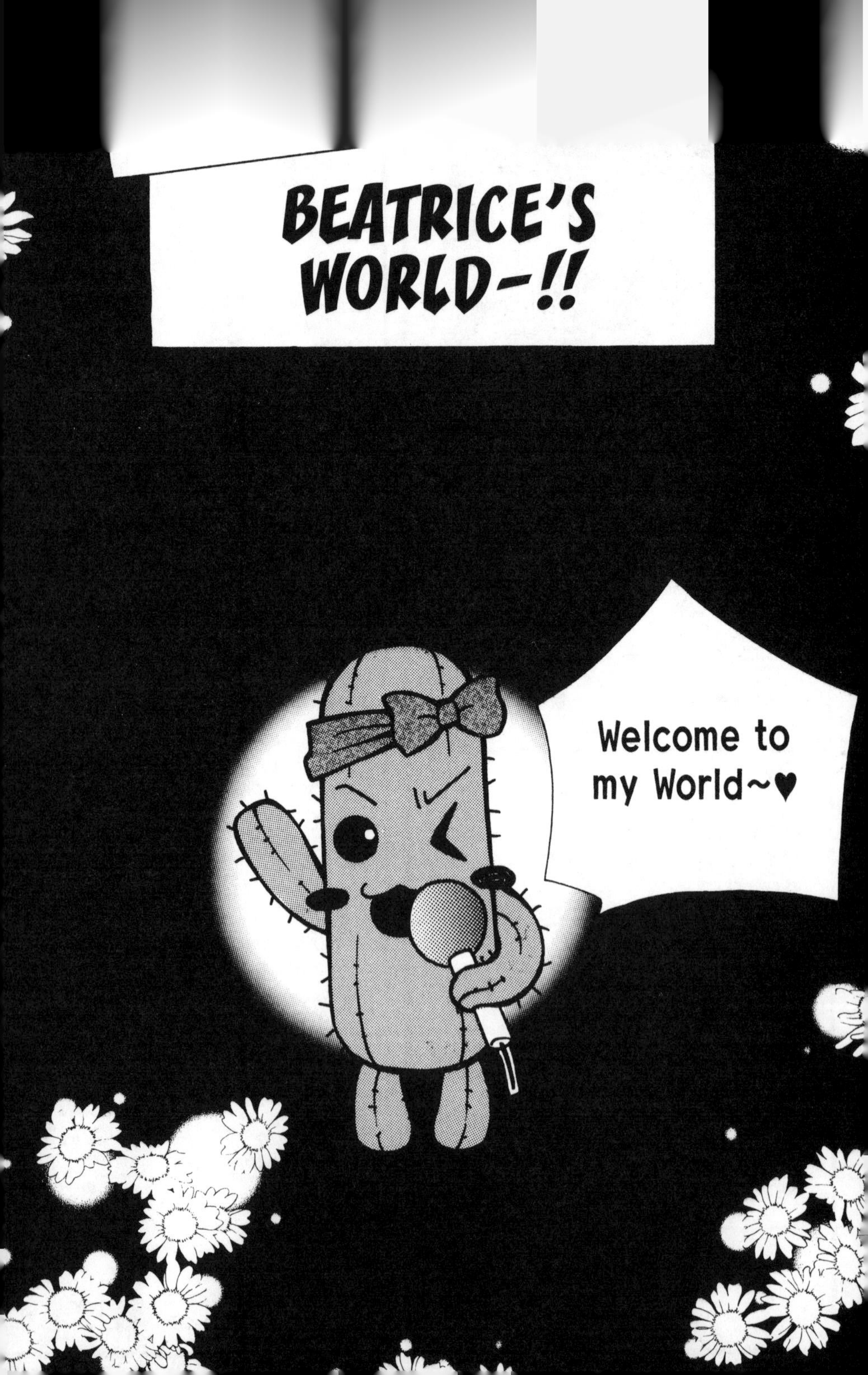
BEATRICE'S WORLD-!!
Welcome to my World~♥

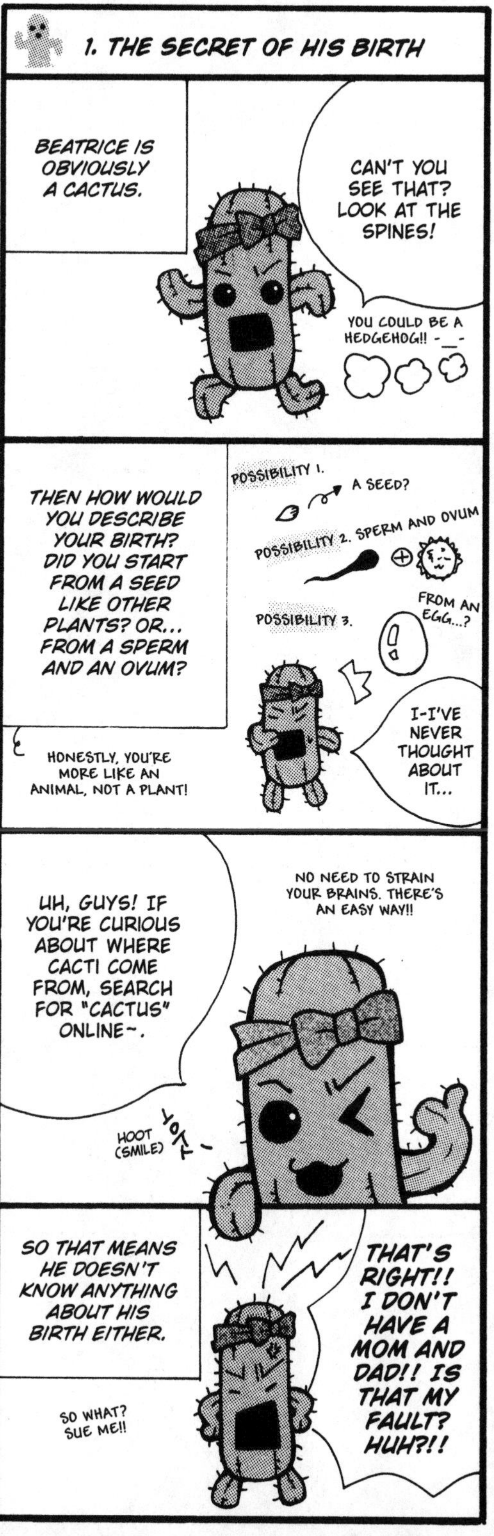
1. THE SECRET OF HIS BIRTH
BEATRICE IS OBVIOUSLY A CACTUS.
CAN'T YOU SEE THAT? LOOK AT THE SPINES!
YOU COULD BE A HEDGEHOG!! -_-
THEN HOW WOULD YOU DESCRIBE YOUR BIRTH? DID YOU START FROM A SEED LIKE OTHER PLANTS? OR... FROM A SPERM AND AN OVUM?
POSSIBILITY 1.
A SEED?
POSSIBILITY 2. SPERM AND OVUM
POSSIBILITY 3.
FROM AN EGG...?
I-I'VE NEVER THOUGHT ABOUT IT...
HONESTLY, YOU'RE MORE LIKE AN ANIMAL, NOT A PLANT!
UH, GUYS! IF YOU'RE CURIOUS ABOUT WHERE CACTI COME FROM, SEARCH FOR "CACTUS" ONLINE~.
NO NEED TO STRAIN YOUR BRAINS. THERE'S AN EASY WAY!!
HOOT (SMILE)
SO THAT MEANS HE DOESN'T KNOW ANYTHING ABOUT HIS BIRTH EITHER.
THAT'S RIGHT!! I DON'T HAVE A MOM AND DAD!! IS THAT MY FAULT? HUH?!!
SO WHAT? SUE ME!!
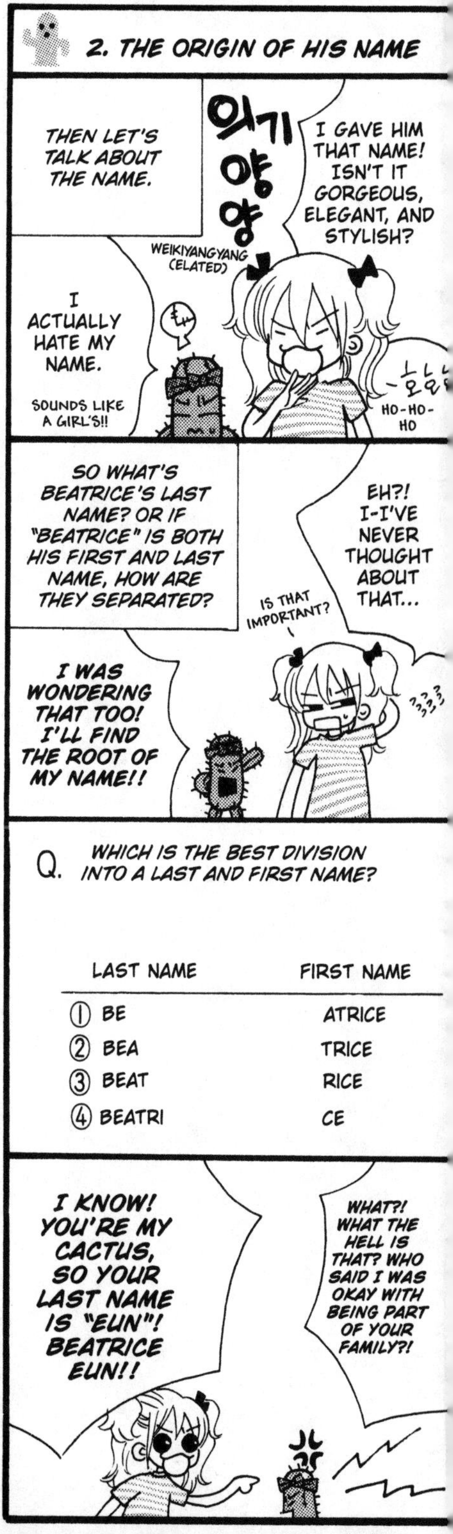
2. THE ORIGIN OF HIS NAME
THEN LET'S TALK ABOUT THE NAME.
의기양양
WEIKIYANGYANG (ELATED)
I GAVE HIM THAT NAME! ISN'T IT GORGEOUS, ELEGANT, AND STYLISH?
I ACTUALLY HATE MY NAME.
SOUNDS LIKE A GIRL'S!!
HO-HO-HO
SO WHAT'S BEATRICE'S LAST NAME? OR IF "BEATRICE" IS BOTH HIS FIRST AND LAST NAME, HOW ARE THEY SEPARATED?
EH?! I-I'VE NEVER THOUGHT ABOUT THAT...
IS THAT IMPORTANT?
I WAS WONDERING THAT TOO! I'LL FIND THE ROOT OF MY NAME!!
Q. WHICH IS THE BEST DIVISION INTO A LAST AND FIRST NAME?
LAST NAME FIRST NAME
① BE ATRICE
② BEA TRICE
③ BEAT RICE
④ BEATRI CE
I KNOW! YOU'RE MY CACTUS, SO YOUR LAST NAME IS "EUN"! BEATRICE EUN!!
WHAT?! WHAT THE HELL IS THAT? WHO SAID I WAS OKAY WITH BEING PART OF YOUR FAMILY?!

3. HOME SWEET HOME

DOG IS IN DOGHOUSE

DOGGY

GGOGGODACK (CACKLE)

CHICKEN IS IN COOP

PIG IS IN PIGSTY

THEN WHAT ABOUT BEATRICE?

HERE COMES MY HOUSE~!!

OF COURSE, I'M IN MY WARM BED!!

BEATRICE

FLOWERPOT!!

DOODONG (TA-DA)

THEY INTERIOR DECORATED

OH RIGHT. HE'S A PLANT IN A FLOWER-POT...

WHAT DID YOU EXPECT? I DEFINITELY CAN'T SLEEP WITH HIM IN MY BED.

4. FOOD

THEN WHAT DOES BEATRICE EAT?

선인장 도감...

저자: 장거리

THE BOOK SAYS THAT YOU SHOULD WATER A CACTUS ONCE A WEEK.

BOOK: CACTUS BOOK / AUTHOR LEE

NO WAY! BRINGING OUT THAT OLD LIE THAT A CACTUS JUST NEEDS WATER! THAT KILLS ME TWICE!

I LOVE FRIED CHICKEN! ESPECIALLY BBQ CHICKEN!!

HUH?

A CACTUS EATING FRIED CHICKEN...? THEN DOES THAT MEAN THAT YOU HAVE ORGANS FOR DIGESTION?

DO YOU POOP TOO?

OH YEAH~. I WAS WONDERING ABOUT THAT AS WELL!!

Y-YOU'LL HURT YOURSELF IF YOU TRY TO FIGURE OUT TOO MUCH!

HUK (GASP) 헉!

LET'S DO AN AUTOPSY TO SEE IF YOU HAVE ORGANS!!

HOODADAK (TAK TAK TAK) 호다닥

까아아아 AAUUUGHH!

HEE-SO IS WAY SCARIER THAN KAIST!!

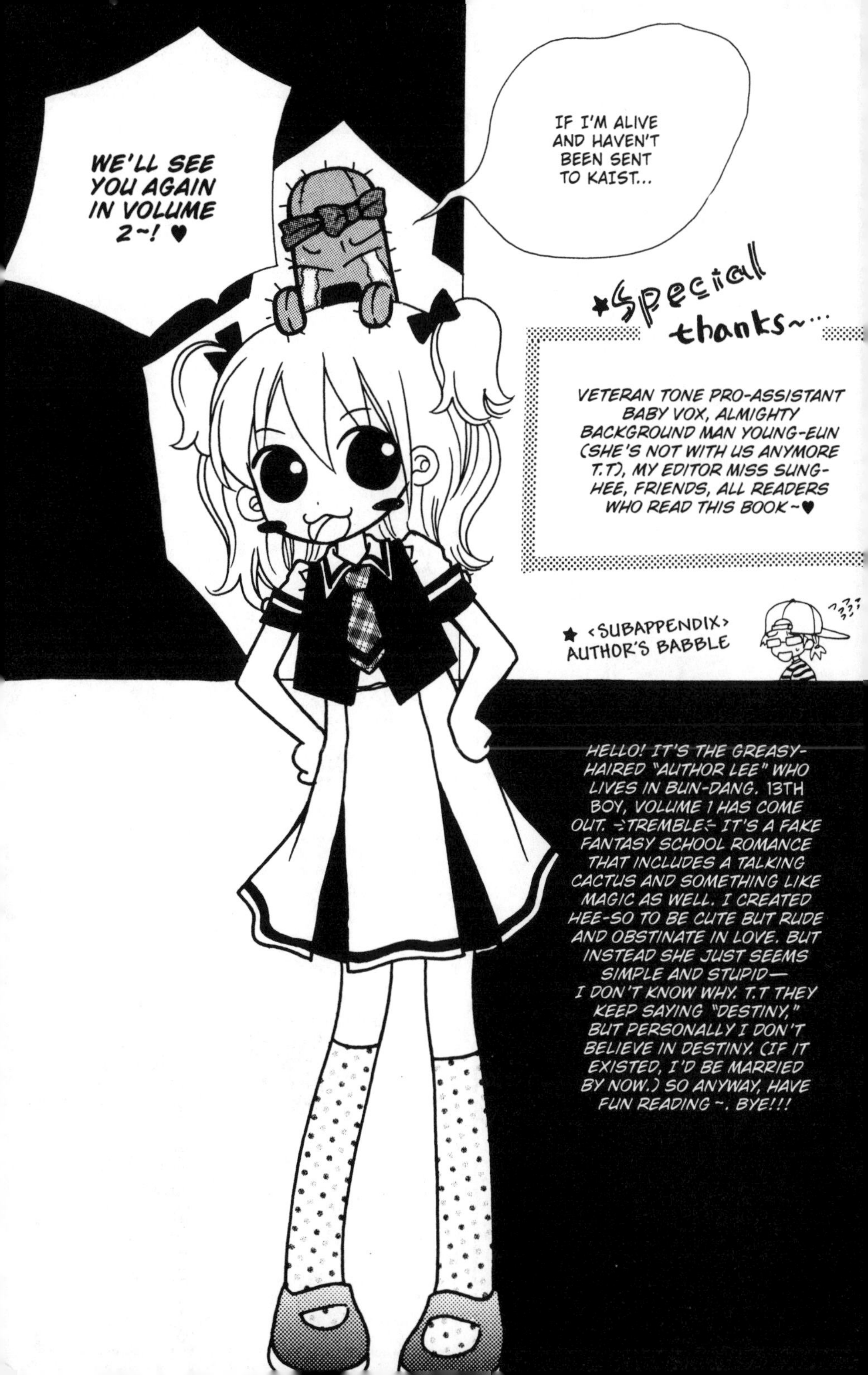
WE'LL SEE YOU AGAIN IN VOLUME 2~! ♥
IF I'M ALIVE AND HAVEN'T BEEN SENT TO KAIST...
★Special thanks~...
VETERAN TONE PRO-ASSISTANT BABY VOX, ALMIGHTY BACKGROUND MAN YOUNG-EUN (SHE'S NOT WITH US ANYMORE T.T), MY EDITOR MISS SUNG-HEE, FRIENDS, ALL READERS WHO READ THIS BOOK~♥
★ <SUBAPPENDIX> AUTHOR'S BABBLE
HELLO! IT'S THE GREASY-HAIRED "AUTHOR LEE" WHO LIVES IN BUN-DANG. 13TH BOY, VOLUME 1 HAS COME OUT. ⇒TREMBLE⇐ IT'S A FAKE FANTASY SCHOOL ROMANCE THAT INCLUDES A TALKING CACTUS AND SOMETHING LIKE MAGIC AS WELL. I CREATED HEE-SO TO BE CUTE BUT RUDE AND OBSTINATE IN LOVE. BUT INSTEAD SHE JUST SEEMS SIMPLE AND STUPID— I DON'T KNOW WHY. T.T THEY KEEP SAYING "DESTINY," BUT PERSONALLY I DON'T BELIEVE IN DESTINY. (IF IT EXISTED, I'D BE MARRIED BY NOW.) SO ANYWAY, HAVE FUN READING ~. BYE!!!